The Competitive Destination

A Sustainable Tourism Perspective

The Competitive Destination

A Sustainable Tourism Perspective

J.R. Brent RITCHIE

World Tourism Education and Research Centre
University of Calgary
Alberta
Canada

and

Geoffrey I. CROUCH

School of Business
La Trobe University
Melbourne
Australia

CABI Publishing

CABI Publishing is a division of CAB International

CABI Publishing
CAB International
Wallingford
Oxon OX10 8DE
UK

CABI Publishing
875 Massachusetts Avenue
7th Floor
Cambridge, MA 02139
USA

Tel: +44 (0)1491 832111
Fax: +44 (0)1491 833508
Email: cabi@cabi.org
Web site: www.cabi-publishing.org

Tel: +1 617 395 4056
Fax: +1 617 354 6875
Email: cabi-nao@cabi.org

A catalogue record for this book is available from the British Library, London, UK

Library of Congress Cataloging-in-Publication Data

Ritchie, J. R. Brent
    The competitive destination : a sustainable tourism perspective / by
J. R. Brent Ritchie and G. I. Crouch
        p.   cm
Includes bibliographical references (p.).
    ISBN 0-85199-664-7
    1.   Ecotourism. I. Crouch, G. I. (Geoffrey I.) 11. Title
G156.5.E26R57 2003
338.4′791—dc21

2003000800

ISBN 0 85199 664 7 (HB)
    978 0 85199 664 6

        1 84593 010 x (PB)
    978 1 84593 010 3

First published (HB) 2003
Reprinted 2005

First paperback edition 2005

Typeset by AMA DataSet Ltd. UK
Printed and bound in the UK by Cromwell Press, Trowbridge

Contents

Preface

_____

Like many published works, this book is the product of a true labour of love. It is an attempt by the authors to capture and convey the essence of what they believe is important to successful tourism.

As the title of the book indicates, the focus of our efforts is the tourism destination itself. While many other paradigms have been the basis of books on tourism, we believe that, from a management perspective, the destination is the fundamental unit on which all the many complex dimensions of tourism are based. Others have, quite appropriately, focused on various aspects of tourism, such as the tourism experience and human behaviour in tourism (Pizam and Mansfeld, 1996). Increasingly, many are examining tourism from an environmental or a sustainable tourism perspective (Swarbrooke, 1999). A great number have chosen to take a more 'micro' perspective by focusing on the operation of the successful hospitality firm (Lefever, 1996). A great many have also focused on marketing in tourism (Morrison, 1989). While all of these different views of tourism are very valuable, we believe that a focus on the destination provides the integrated perspective that a destination must have if we are to comprehend, pull together and manage all the many elements that determine the success of a tourism destination.

We have prepared this integrated approach to destination management on the basis of three main types of input. First, we have benefited enormously from the published works of our many colleagues, who have examined the many facets of tourism in great depth. We trust that we have adequately recognized these contributions, although this is never entirely possible. Second, the book is based on our own research, which has spanned nearly a decade now. This research first sought inputs from managers in various national tourism organizations around the world. More importantly, it has benefited from the insights provided by senior managers from Convention and Visitor Bureaux throughout North America and elsewhere, most of whom are members of the International Association of Convention and Visitor Bureaus. We are especially grateful for their contributions. Further, we have also been the beneficiaries of assistance and critiques from the many graduate students with whom we have worked over the years.

Other than focusing on destination management, what kind of book is this, and for whom has it been written? The book is primarily intended to provide destination managers with an overall understanding of the complex nature of the task they face in their efforts to enhance destination performance, and thus achieve destination success. Due to limitations of space, it cannot and does not seek to provide detailed operational guidance on each of the many dimensions affecting destination performance. Hopefully, however, it does provide a basic understanding of all the many facets of destination management and how they need to be integrated if a destination is to compete successfully on a sustainable basis. In seeking to do so, it strongly stresses the critical and vital role of the destination management organization in providing leadership and coordination for the many destination stakeholders that must contribute and work together if a destination is to succeed.

Despite this primary focus on the destination manager, the book also seeks to serve a second important audience. We define this audience as senior undergraduates and beginning graduate students, whose goal is to understand tourism destination management in both practical and academic terms. While the book (in order not to drive away practising managers) is not heavily biased towards the needs of academics, we have tried to provide a basic understanding of the theoretical foundations of tourism that we feel are essential to our target student population, and that might also be of interest to practising managers who wish to have some insight into the intellectual underpinnings of their daily work.

We are aware that, in attempting to provide this balance between theory and practice, we risk alienating either or both of our intended audiences to some degree. At the same time, we hope they will appreciate the value of the approach we have taken and that, as a consequence, the book may serve peripherally to encourage and strengthen the development of greater understanding between academics and practitioners.

In addition to addressing the academic–practitioner interface, we have also sought to provide a balance across another increasingly important interface in tourism, namely that between those who espouse competitiveness and those who stress sustainability in destination management. We truly believe that both are essential to destination success. We realize that, in setting out to provide this balance, we again risk pleasing neither group. Nevertheless, we are comfortable in walking this fine line because we believe that economic competitiveness is an essential part of true sustainability. At the same time, we also believe that destinations cannot spend their natural capital in order to be economically profitable. To make this point, we place great emphasis on the need to revise the traditional accounting measures of destination performance and success.

In specific terms, how have we attempted to achieve all of the above? To begin, Chapter 1 provides a very brief introduction that simply stresses that the very nature of competition and sustainability has been, and still is, constantly evolving. We stress that destination managers must understand this reality and must take it into account in their efforts to produce the successful destination.

Chapter 2 was written to help all readers (both students and practitioners) to understand the theoretical foundations of the evolving environment in which they work. Towards this end, Part I reviews the general literature on competition with a specific view to relating it to the tourism destination. Part II reviews the literature on sustainability, drawing heavily on the growing body of literature from the past decade on sustainable tourism.

Chapter 3 is the key chapter in the book. It presents and describes our basic model of destination management. Readers who have followed our work over the past decade will be aware that the model itself reflects the evolving nature of destination management. As we have learned, we have slowly revised and adapted the framework to accommodate the many suggestions of managers, students, and the literature. Although this evolution will be ongoing, we felt it was time to pause briefly and to do our best to present what we have learned in book format.

Chapter 4 examines the part of our framework that formally recognizes that many aspects of destination management are beyond the control, and even the influence, of the destination. More particularly, it examines those global forces that generally shape the kind of world we live in, and that specifically have an enormous impact on the nature of tourism and tourism management. In doing so, it constantly stresses that destination managers must use all the judgement they can muster in meeting the challenges these forces present and in seeking to take advantage of the many opportunities they also provide.

After having gained an understanding of the global forces affecting the tourism destination, the reader is brought back in Chapter 5 to the level that will be more familiar on a daily basis: the destination itself, and the various operating components and firms that many people think of as 'the tourism industry'. More specifically, this chapter examines what, in more academic terms, we refer to as the 'tourism system' with a view to providing a basic understanding of the way that destination competitiveness is affected by the way the tourism system functions. In doing so, the chapter recognizes that although it is possible to define or delineate a destination, it does not exist as an entity in the same way that a company is an entity. For this reason, we believe it is important that students and individual industry operators, who traditionally look through the eyes of the firm, should review this chapter with a view to becoming comfortable with the concept of the destination and how firms are perhaps its most essential component in providing visitor experiences – and how it is critical that all firms work together to create a destination that provides truly memorable destination experiences.

Chapter 6 is another pivotal chapter. It examines in detail the core resources and attractors component of our model. In doing so, it provides insights into the fundamental reasons why people visit a destination – that is to say, the factors that are the essence of destination appeal. And since many of these resources and attractions are under the control of the destination, they represent areas where stakeholders and managers can act effectively to enhance the attractiveness of a destination.

Chapter 7 deals with other areas where destination managers can have a substantial degree of control and influence. Although they are not the primary reasons for destination visitation, supporting factors and resources are essential in ensuring that the value of core resources and attractions is not lost, as well as in enhancing their effectiveness in building a competitive destination. These supporting factors and resources are often perceived as less glamorous – because they may be! – but effective management of them can often mean the difference between a mediocre destination and one that is truly successful.

With Chapter 8 we move into what may be viewed as another supporting area, but which we view as a major activity that determines whether much of the effort in destination management is ill-directed, ineffective or largely wasted. The topic of tourism policy, planning and development is regarded by many as the glamorous side of destination management – that is, high-level pontification carried out by those who do not want to get their hands dirty. This said, even the most ardent of front-line staff should appreciate that effective tourism policy can make their lives much easier and greatly enhance their well-being. This chapter provides considerable detail on how destination policy-makers, through effective policy, can provide guidance for tourism planning and development that will create an environment for tourism that enhances the well-being of the community and its residents, and that will contribute to its long-term sustainability. In addition, well-formulated policy can facilitate the growth and profitability of the kind of sustainable tourism that a destination and its stakeholders desire. It is hoped that this chapter will clearly demonstrate how good policy enables a destination to achieve the success it desires, and to do so most effectively.

Chapter 9 returns to what most tourism operators and managers view as the daily realities of the tourism industry. Since there are often overlaps between what constitutes policy and management, this chapter attempts to clarify this distinction throughout, and to identify and explain the nature of the many management tasks that must be carried out effectively on a daily basis if a destination is to attract visitors, and then deliver the kind of memorable experiences it promises and that visitors are expecting.

In Chapter 10 we address an area that might have been dealt with much earlier in the book, but we felt it would be more useful if the contents of the chapters discussed above were already in the mind of the reader. What we have called 'qualifying and amplifying determinants' might also have been called 'conditioners'. In any case, they deal with factors that either moderate, modify, mitigate and filter, or magnify, strengthen and augment the impact of all other determinants. The concern here is that the competitiveness and/or sustainability of a destination may be significantly affected by specific factors that limit or enhance its success in ways that are beyond the control of management. In contrast to the global forces that affect all tourism destinations, the qualifying and amplifying determinants pertain specifically to the destination in question. These conditioners may affect competition and sustainability by subtle and incremental amounts; but, this said, their efforts can also be fundamental, dramatic and dominant, to the point where they can overpower the strength of other categories of determinants of success and turn an otherwise strong or weak destination into a respectively minor or major player.

Our concluding chapter (Chapter 11) is intended to assist managers in translating the concepts and theory of our framework into practice. We also hope that it will provide students with a better understanding of some of the challenges that managers face in their efforts to make a destination work successfully. We entitle this chapter 'The Destination Audit: Putting the Model to Work'. There are three main uses we envisage for the model. The first is as a *communication* tool. In brief, the model establishes a lexicon for understanding, studying, diagnosing, discussing and sharing ideas and thoughts about a destination's competitiveness and sustainability. The second, and perhaps most fundamental, use of the model is as a *framework for management*. In our executive development work, participants have told us that they find that the model provides a useful vehicle for comprehending the magnitude and complexity of the challenges they face on a daily basis as they seek to fulfil their responsibilities. More explicitly, they note that it is much too easy to overlook potentially important factors when faced with the multitude of activities that threaten to overcome them and divert their thinking from what is truly important in determining success.

The final use of our model that is addressed specifically by Chapter 11 is for a *destination audit*. While the term 'audit' is used here in a broader sense than that used traditionally, it still focuses on an official examination of the destination to make sure that everything is in order. Where everything is not in order, the audit seeks to provide recommendations as to what action is necessary, and potentially most effective, in order to move systematically towards greater competitiveness and sustainability.

In concluding, we would like to leave readers with an idea of where we hope to go from here. As we have stressed, the development of the model/framework has been a long-term process – and one that we hope to continue. While our work to date has emphasized the need to gain a qualitative understanding of the factors that contribute to destination success through enhanced competitiveness and ongoing sustainability, it is now entering a phase in which we are seeking to improve the quantitative measurement of the relative importance of each of the various factors that determine the success of a destination. To this end, we are conducting three research projects. The first of these, using a decision-support system, seeks to measure the importance of the model's elements as perceived by destination managers. The second avenue of research is aimed at developing an index of destination competitiveness/success. This index, which is modelled on the index of industrial competitiveness for countries developed by the World Economic Forum (WEF/IMD, 2002), will provide tourism destination managers with a better quantitative insight into the reasons for their success over time. And just as a consumer price index shows which products and services are contributing the most to the overall cost of living, our destination index will identify and measure the relative significance of those performance factors that contribute to a destination's competitiveness and success. While 'competitiveness' and 'success' are clearly distinct concepts, they are nevertheless significantly related.

The final major stage of our destination research programme will seek to model the manner in which destinations change the way they behave and perform when major strategic factors or management practices are changed. The major strategic factors may be either forces from the global (macro)environment that are beyond the control of management (such as the ageing of the population) or those that are implemented strategically by management (such as the creation or hosting of a new mega-event). Substantial changes in management practices might involve overhauling a human resource development approach or finding a new, more effective way to manage visitors. Ultimately, we hope to be able to develop the capability for a model that will assist any given destination and its management to better understand and interpret the likely changes in the behaviour and performance of a destination that will result from any strategic change around or within the destination. While we recognize that this is an ambitious long-term goal that will provide only management guidance rather than definitive answers to specific decisions, we are hopeful that in seeking to achieve it we will help improve destination competitiveness and sustainability.

Finally, we would emphasize that, just as our model has been developed with input from different national tourism offices (which are members of the World Tourism Organization) and large urban centres (or city-states) (members of the International Association of Convention and Visitor Bureaus), our goal is to develop decision support systems, indices of destination success, and destination strategy simulation models for both countries and city-states.

References

Lefever, M. (1996) *Hospitality in Review: a Capstone Text Complete with Senior and Graduate-Level Projects*. Kendall/Hunt Publishing Company, Dubuque, Iowa.

Morrison, A.M. (1989) *Hospitality and Travel Marketing*. Delmar Publishers, New York.

Pizam, A. and Mansfeld, Y. (1996) *Tourism, Crime, and International Security Issues*. John Wiley, New York.

Swarbrooke, J. (1999) *Sustainable Tourism Management*. CAB International, Wallingford, UK.

WEF/IMD (2002) *The World Competitiveness Yearbook*. World Economic Forum and the International Institute for Management Development, Lausanne, Switzerland.

Acknowledgements

_____

The widespread support we have received from both organizations and individuals throughout the preparation of this work has been essential and most gratifying.

From the very beginning, the strong research culture within the Faculty of Management at the University of Calgary (now the Haskayne School of Business) has been the foundation for our efforts. Without the high-quality academic and administrative environment it provided, this project would not have been possible. In this regard, we first thank Dean Michael Maher for his efforts to raise the funds to support the professorship in tourism that allowed JRBR the freedom and the resources to pursue the research on which this book is based. The subsequent efforts of Dean David Saunders to protect and nourish this critical academic foundation, and in particular to enable JRBR to collaborate actively with the World Tourism Organization (WTO), were invaluable and much appreciated.

For GIC, whose work on this book spanned two eras, both the University of Calgary and La Trobe University have provided important support. The support, environment, encouragement and resources provided at the University of Calgary, together with an initial Social Sciences and Humanities Research Council of Canada (SSHRC) grant, were particularly important in the earlier phases of our collaborative efforts. Subsequently, the professorial funding provided to GIC at La Trobe University has enabled us to continue our collaboration from opposite ends of the earth, with regular face-to-face periods along the way.

We extend our most sincere thanks to the SSHRC, whose policy of supporting two successive, related research projects on an evolving topic was especially valuable. This policy permitted us to maintain the time-consuming relationships with members of the WTO and the International Association of Convention and Visitor Bureaus (IACVB) that enabled the research team to gain the confidence and trust of these two leading organizations in the field of tourism. This confidence and trust was a critical factor in the success of our search for information, and allowed us to gain insights that would not have been possible otherwise.

We also wish to extend our thanks to the members of both the WTO and the IACVB. In the case of the WTO, we are particularly grateful to Dr Eduardo Fayos Sola. His moral support and his personal insights into tourism policy (gained from many years as a senior member of the Tourism Department of the Spanish Government) provided us with a unique competitive advantage over other authors who may have an interest in the same topic. In a similar manner, the support of our colleague Mr Donald Anderson, Director of the IACVB Executive Development Program, was also invaluable. The access to senior executives from the leading city-state destinations throughout North America that he facilitated provided us with yet another unique competitive advantage in our efforts to understand how a destination can be made both competitive and successful.

We are also grateful to the many individual members of the WTO and the IACVB who shared with us their experiences and inner thoughts regarding the many complex factors that influence and determine destination competitiveness and sustainability. It is their experiences and thoughts that are the essence of this book. We trust they will find its content to be a fair and accurate distillation of their views, and one that will provide a valuable legacy for future generations of managers and students in the field of destination management.

Speaking of students, we also thank our many graduate students, who have been exposed to various earlier drafts of the thinking in this book and who have provided us with the benefit of initial assessments and suggestions for changes to its contents. In this regard, we are particularly grateful to Mr Stuart Levy, who carried out a personal, in-depth review of a near-final draft of the book. His frank and insightful comments and suggestions have, we believe, provided the reader with a more logical and more coherent expression of our ideas.

Finally, we owe an incalculable debt of thanks to Ms Deb Angus. Her dedication, competence, innovativeness and rigorous attention to detail throughout the long and arduous process of manuscript preparation has more than compensated for our inability to maintain a continuous and consistent authoring schedule in the face of other demands on our time. Without her support, the completion of the manuscript might well have been in doubt. We trust she appreciates the esteem in which she is held by both of us.

As in all our endeavours, we are eternally grateful for the quiet, ever-strong support of our spouses, Rosemary and Linda. Their everyday help makes everything possible – and worthwhile.

J.R. Brent Ritchie and G.I. Crouch

Foreword

_____

The publication of this book has come at a very timely moment in the strategic evolution of the World Tourism Organization (WTO). An understanding of the determinants of the success of a tourism destination has always been of great interest to the traditional country membership of the WTO. However, the recent establishment of a special Task Force on Destination Management within our organization is a direct reflection of the growing importance of this critical theoretical paradigm in the improvement of management performance for our broader membership worldwide.

I am pleased that our Task Force on Destinations is seeking to identify a platform for destination management, one that will provide valid universal guidelines to assist managers in meeting the complex and difficult challenges they face daily in their efforts to develop and manage tourism destinations. To do this, they must develop destinations that have the capability to perform effectively in an increasingly competitive international marketplace – and that will do so in ways that are environmentally, socially and culturally sustainable.

In both its timing and its content, this work, by two internationally recognized tourism scholars, offers great potential for our WTO Task Force as it seeks to fulfil its mandate. Indeed, through good fortune it seems that the stars are aligning themselves as they should. I know that Drs Ritchie and Crouch have been preparing this work for some time now, and it is most propitious that the results of their efforts are being published to coincide with the WTO's focus on destination management as a key priority. We in the WTO are most appreciative of this good fortune and I personally wish to thank the two authors and to endorse both the timing and the quality of their work. I am convinced that the comprehensive and insightful framework on which this book is based represents a 'breakthrough paradigm' – the kind of breakthrough that comes only once in a lifetime – and will provide a widely accepted new model of theory and practice in destination management for many years to come.

Francesco Frangialli
Secretary General, World Tourism Organization

1

The Evolving Nature of Competition and Sustainability

Destination Competitiveness: Its Nature and Its Evolution

The important thing is to try and shape the nature of competition to take control over your own destiny.

(Michael Porter, 1997)

In developing the framework for destination competitiveness, we examine its very nature and how it has evolved from the early beginnings of mass tourism in the mid-20th century to the present day, at the start of the 21st century. The intention is to identify the different components of the 'competitive universe' and to examine how these components define the fundamental nature of the competitive environment in which tourism as a sector must function.

Our examination demonstrates that, just as each of the components of the competitive universe has changed over the five decades in question, the nature of competition itself has evolved substantially. The very essence of competition as we enter the third millennium is quite different from what it was when the first jet aeroplanes took off (Tyson, 1997). It will be useful to understand these changes and their impacts before we develop a model of destination competitiveness for today's world.

Components of the Competitive Universe

An examination of today's competitive universe reveals that changes in its components have radically altered its structure. The implications of this restructuring are that those who are responsible for destination management are operating according to a constantly evolving set of rules that continually redefine the exact nature of competition. Even though the factors that determine the attractiveness of a destination may remain relatively constant, the changing nature of competition requires ongoing reassessment of the ability of a destination to compete.

Competition among tourism destinations is but one manifestation of the broader phenomenon of the new economic competition (Asch and Wolfe, 2001) and, indeed, the even broader phenomenon of human competition in the social, technological, cultural and political spheres. Thus, to achieve a true understanding of destination competitiveness, it is useful to examine briefly the context within which competitive tourism occurs and how this context has evolved to the present time. In effect, we are recognizing that competition among destinations, although it may have distinctive characteristics, reflects the nature of competition in all areas of human activity. The manner in which North American, European and Asian destinations assert their attractiveness and attempt to influence choice behaviour in tourists cannot be divorced from the approaches taken in other industrial sectors. For example, even though tourism may not yet be as important as other economic sectors are to Korea, the aggressive manner in which this country competes in tourism is similar to its approach in the automobile sector. In a different vein, the competitive strategy of the tourism industry of the USA depends heavily on the film and entertainment industry. The ability to sell the American culture worldwide provides the US tourism sector with an enormous competitive advantage. In the same way, the competitive approach of the Indian tourism sector tends to parallel that taken in other areas, such as technology and brand franchising, where indigenous ownership of facilities and investments is considered important.

In the light of the foregoing, it behoves those of us seeking to understand the present nature of destination competitiveness in tourism to review the evolution of the forces affecting competitiveness in general with a view to gaining insights into how tourism has been and will be affected.

The Dimensions of Tourism Competitiveness

The more traditional reviews of competitiveness have focused primarily on the economic dimensions of destination strength and performance. While economic performance is certainly an important dimension of tourism competitiveness, it is only one dimension. Because of the unique nature of tourism, the true ability of a tourism destination to compete also involves its social, cultural, political, technological and environmental strengths. *In summary, what makes a tourism destination truly competitive is its ability to increase tourism expenditure, to increasingly attract visitors while providing them with satisfying, memorable experiences, and to do so in a profitable way, while enhancing the well-being of destination residents and preserving the natural capital of the destination for future generations.*

Given the multidimensional nature of tourism destination strength (Fig. 1.1), it is useful to briefly review how the competitive nature of the world has evolved along each of these dimensions and, more importantly, how this multidimensional evolution has affected the overall competitiveness of destinations.

Economic competitiveness

Michael Porter (1996) has achieved recognition as the guru of the economic competitiveness of nations. As will be seen in the next chapter, we will not hesitate to adopt and/or adapt his approaches or those results of his model of competitiveness that appear pertinent to tourism.

As Porter (1996, p. 166) has reported, the sources of economic competitiveness lie in four broad attributes of a nation (or, in the present context, of a destination), known collectively as the 'Porter diamond':

- *Factor conditions:* the nation's position in the factors of production, such as skilled

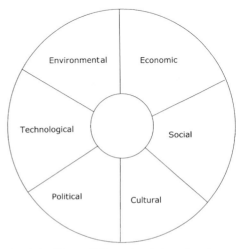

Fig. 1.1. The multidimensional strengths of a tourism destination.

labour or infrastructure, that are necessary for it to be able to compete in a given industry;

- *Demand conditions*: the nature of home-market demand for the industry's product or service;
- *Related and supporting industries*: the presence or absence in the nation of supplier industries and other related industries that are internationally competitive;
- *Firm strategy, structure and rivalry*: the conditions in the nation governing how companies are created, organized and managed, as well as the nature of domestic rivalry.

While the Porter diamond may not be entirely relevant to a tourism destination, it certainly contains a number of insights that should be kept in mind when assessing the economic competitiveness of a tourism destination. In any case, Porter's thinking represents a major benchmark in the evolution of thinking of economic competitiveness over the past decade or more.

Another aspect of the evolution of general economic competitiveness in recent times has been the trend from national to regional competitiveness. One smaller-scale example concerns rural regions where the changing economic base and nature of rural economies have often been addressed by a growing interest in tourism as an area of economic diversification for these communities. At the same time as this has been occurring, however, we have been struck by a counter-trend – the re-emergence of an ancient political and economic structure, the city-state. Because of its significance for tourism we will address it further below. The function of the European Union (EU) probably represents the vanguard of the evolution towards a broad regional emphasis on destination competitiveness. The EU has given rise to the creation of the North American Free Trade Agreement (NAFTA) and to movements to establish similar trade areas in Asia (Asia Pacific Economic Cooperation; APEC) and South America (Mercado Común del Sur; MERCOSUR). Whether this formation of regional trade blocs will lead to true economic globalization remains to be seen.

Political competitiveness

The phenomenon of competition is essentially an effort on the part of groups (large and small) of people to establish a political economic power base that provides them with the ability to control those resources that provide individual and collective well-being. The exact definition of well-being may vary among different groups, but nevertheless sociologists have identified a broad range of indicators that describe the well-being of a society. Typical examples of such indicators of well-being are given in UNDP (2002). These indicators include, in addition to standard measures of economic performance, a wide range of less traditional measures (Table 1.1). The indicators in this table are of great significance in that they provide a foundation, or a primary motivation, for the phenomenon of competition. Since the planet's resources are limited and/or controlled, and since they provide the feedstock for societal indicators, it is not surprising that individuals and groups of individuals attempt to organize themselves so as to enhance their ability to gain control over the resources necessary to ensure their well-being.

Table 1.1. Typical indicators of societal well-being (from UNDP, 2002).

- Gross domestic product (GDP)
- GDP per capita
- Annual change in consumer price index
- Inequality of income distribution
- The structure of trade
- Unemployment
- The extent of the rule of law
- Corruption
- Press freedom
- Measures of collective health (life expectancy, infant mortality rates)
- Measures of intellectual development (public education expenditures, adult and youth literacy rates)
- Measures of technology diffusion and creation (number of telephone lines, number of cellular telephone subscribers, number of Internet hosts)
- Measures of priorities in public spending
- Measures regarding energy and the environment
- Measures concerning general empowerment

While the political competitiveness of destinations is not often considered in many analyses of destination competitiveness, it appears to us that the political strength and stability of a destination is critical to its tourism competitiveness. At the macro level, the global political stability that has followed the Second World War has been an essential underpinning of the growth of tourism since the 1950s. At the micro level, one needs only to examine the extent to which political instability has negatively affected the tourism sector in countries around the world (e.g. Lebanon, Zimbabwe and Israel). Therefore, any framework that seeks to capture the components of destination competitiveness must include a destination's political strength in the macro and micro context.

At a global level, the political restructuring of nation-states has been an ongoing process over the centuries. A look at historic maps over time provides documentation of the manner in which the fixed geographical space of the planet has been allocated and reallocated, in political terms, over the years. While historically this has tended to be a somewhat slow process of transition and change, the past half-century has seen an unusually active period of political restructuring. This restructuring has been driven by three major forces: (i) the decolonization of regions previously held by world powers, such as the UK, France, Spain, Portugal and Italy – a process that has seen the emergence of many new nation-states, particularly in Africa, the former USSR and, to a lesser extent, South America; (ii) the so-called economic hegemony of the USA, a process in which the growing economic power of that country has given it considerable political influence in regions well beyond its formal, legal boundaries; and (iii) the creation of new political entities as a result of shifting political loyalties brought about by increasing global democratization. These changes have been related to diverse factors, such as the outcomes of the Second World War, religion, ethnicity and political ideology.

The implications of this global restructuring for tourism have been substantial. While the physical attractions themselves have not moved or changed significantly, political control by different masters has altered both their attractiveness and their accessibility. International travel has, by definition, grown significantly as new national/international borders have been created, and a trip of 1000 km in a highly fragmented geographical region may result in the crossing of several international borders. In contrast, the same trip in a country like Australia would not be recorded as international travel.

This process of restructuring, which has largely been one of fragmentation rather than synthesis, has also been occurring at the level of the nation-state. By far the most striking example is the former USSR, which has gone from being a huge monolith to one that now includes Russia and a number of independent states. The previous state of Czechoslovakia is now divided into the Czech Republic and Slovakia, and the state of Yugoslavia has fragmented into several distinct nation-states. There has also been some synthesis, however. The merging of East and West Germany, together with the manner in which it occurred, is perhaps the most startling example of synthesis. Also of considerable interest has been the reintegration of Hong Kong back into its motherland, China.

The renaissance of the city-state

In earlier historic times, the most powerful level of political organization was that of the city-state. Cities such as Rome, Athens, Troy and Sparta represented the most powerful and most effective level of competitive advantage. The ability of these concentrations of population to control and exploit the resources of the countryside made them all-powerful in relative terms. In modern terms, we have witnessed the growth and development of a greater, yet still limited number of world cities that are true economic, social and cultural leaders. Not only have they acted as population magnets that attract people both locally and internationally so as to have achieved mega-stature, but in addition many have become cultural and economic centres within whose borders economic power has flourished.

The process of world urbanization is still actively under way and the end results are not yet entirely evident. Nevertheless, it is clear that we are witnessing today a renaissance of the city-state as a centre of economic, political and cultural power. The populations and gross domestic products of many mega-cities around the world (e.g. London, New York, Paris, Tokyo, Mexico City, Beijing and Los Angeles) now rival and outpace those of many nation-states. From a tourism perspective, certain of these mega-cities have become major tourism destinations in themselves. Their ability to manage and market their touristic dimensions in a very controlled and integrated manner has provided a competitive advantage that is not available to larger, more physically dispersed nation-state destinations. This touristic reality is reflected in the power and level of activity in major metropolitan Convention and Visitor Bureaux, whose tourism-related efforts, expenditures and effectiveness frequently surpass those of nations. Indeed, it can be argued that the city-state seriously rivals the country as the primary focus of much strategic thinking when a competitive destination approach is taken to tourism planning and development. The process of urbanization of the world's population has been so powerful that, in addition to the city-states referred to above, we are now witnessing the creation of a great number of second-tier cities having populations of 1 million or more. While not quite city-states, they have developed strong personalities and considerable economic power. Consequently, they can often consider themselves to be true tourism destinations.

Sociocultural competitiveness

When one examines successful tourism destinations around the world, it is easy to conclude that economic and political strength is a genuine asset. It may be easier, however, to conclude that a destination's social and cultural characteristics are more critical for creating a destination that people want to visit. Despite the fact that certain destinations may be economic dwarfs and approach a state of political shambles, they are still places that people want to visit, often in considerable numbers. Why? Simply because they offer a visitation experience that cannot be found anywhere else. For example, Israel, despite its major problems, continues to attract a certain number of visitors

who are sympathetic to its cause. Conversely, other destinations may be economic giants and models of relative political stability, yet still have a modest appeal in many markets as travel destinations. For example, Canada suffers from this deficiency in the eyes of some. In brief, one concludes that the sociocultural appeal of a destination may override all other dimensions in determining its appeal. Were it not for the fact that resident well-being, profitability and environmental sustainability must also be taken into consideration, the sociocultural strengths of a destination might be the dominant determinant of competitiveness.

Technological competitiveness

The technological strength of a destination has only recently entered into the equation determining destination competitiveness. And while technology is only a minor factor in determining the appeal of destinations (minor exceptions are destinations such as Silicon Valley in California and Cape Canaveral in Florida, where the technology of space travel is a growing tourism draw), it has become a major factor in the promotion and distribution of the travel experience for an increasing number of destinations. Perhaps the first most significant step in this process was the airlines' Central Reservation System (CRS). Destinations that were not served by airlines were at a significant competitive disadvantage, and the airlines that controlled the CRS tended to ensure that they were given priority within the system. Consequently, destinations that were served by any of the airlines controlling the CRS had an additional competitive advantage. Public pressure and legislature have generally made airline ownership and control of the CRS much less of a factor. However, suspicions of preference still lurk in the shadows.

The arrival of the Internet represents the latest impact of technology on destination competitiveness. In particular, the traditional use of published material as a source of information to promote destinations has declined substantially. However, published materials and destination call centres with toll-free telephone numbers still remain significant sources of consumer information in certain cases. Another major impact of the Internet is that it has enabled smaller, less powerful destinations to have access to a global market at a cost that is no longer prohibitive. For the visitor, the Internet now offers a power of search and choice that was previously not available.

Technology has also had an impact on the ability of destinations, and firms within them, to enhance the quality of the visitor experience. The growing technical sophistication of interpretive centres has enabled destinations to both inform and educate visitors about the destination they are visiting, as visitors move around and within the destination. Lodging operators increasingly use technology, such as customer databases, to enhance the personalization of the firm–visitor interface and to simplify and accelerate the administrative work associated with visits. In a similar manner, car rental agencies have largely automated sign-in/sign-out procedures. In the extreme, certain properties have virtually eliminated the human interface by allowing clients to make reservations via technology, and then to sign in and sign out without ever interacting with a human. This extreme goes counter to the efforts of many to retain a human touch in dealing with customers. However, achieving the proper balance in high-tech/high-touch is a delicate matter.

Global positioning systems have become another means of assisting travellers. Such systems provide the traveller with detailed information on routing to destinations, at increasing levels of detail. One suspects that once the cost of this technological support is reduced it will become standard, and travel and tourism enterprises are likely to be very attracted to the marketing opportunities this technology presents.

The challenge facing destinations is to know which types of technology are truly desired by visitors, and thus which ones provide a genuine competitive advantage rather than create annoyance or confusion – in some cases adding undesirable or even unnecessary cost. Regardless of the specific answers to this question at a given point in time, it seems inevitable that technological forces will continue to exert their influence. Destinations will need to determine the extent to which technology increases their competitiveness as opposed to reducing their appeal. Research

and judgement will be essential in answering these questions.

Environmental competitiveness

In the past, destinations have used traditional economic accounting when calculating the success of their economic performance, and thus their degree of competitiveness. In recent years, however, environmental economists have increasingly insisted upon full cost accounting when seeking to estimate the true economic liabilities of a destination, as well as its economic assets.

The issue at hand is whether deterioration of the natural environment due to tourism can heavily mask the relative competitiveness of one destination compared with another (Prugh et al., 1995). For example, it has been argued that in earlier days Costa Rica appeared to derive substantial benefits from tourism in traditional economic terms. However, if the 'costs' of the destruction of the country's natural capital are taken into account, it may well be that this high-profile destination, which appeared to be highly competitive, is in reality non-competitive.

Increasingly, in the evaluation of competitiveness it will be necessary to acknowledge the full cost of tourism visitation in practical terms. This may well alter the way in which destinations manage tourism. Destinations that currently practise stewardship of resources should rise in the formal evaluation of their competitiveness, while those that do not will fall.

To summarize, while relatively new on the scene, the environmental dimension of destination performance and competitiveness is slowly but surely growing in importance in both practical and moral terms. In practical terms, visitors are increasingly turned off by destinations that have undergone visual degradation through general overdevelopment or poor resource stewardship. Typical examples might include excessive or improper signage, poor waste control practices and the destruction of wildlife habitats. In moral terms, many segments of the market may simply disagree with certain forms of tourism development in certain kinds of locations.

In response to this growing concern for the environmental integrity of tourism destinations, the phenomenon of ecotourism, while still small in market share, is growing in both stature and importance. Destinations with unique, relatively pristine environments can now build competitiveness by positioning themselves as 'environmental' destinations. While this has in some cases proven to drive visitors away rather than to attract them, it remains a viable strategy for certain destinations.

Despite the risks of specializing in ecotourism, it would appear that maintaining the integrity of a destination's environment will only grow in importance in the coming years and decades. It is not clear whether this can be done in a way that is economically viable in terms of the measures used by most investors today.

Some General Observations on how the Competitive Environment is Evolving

Evolution of the travel experience demanded

The evolution in value systems noted in Chapter 4 has led directly to a major evolution in the fundamental nature of the types of experiences demanded by the market. For example, the focus of the travel experience has shifted away from the family, in which vacation travel tended to emphasize relaxation, with an underlying goal of producing a memorable experience to be shared among all family members. In addition to being shared, these family experiences had as a primary goal the development of bonds among family members. In today's market, the experiences demanded have become more individual in nature. Also, there is greater emphasis on stimulation, social interaction and, more recently, learning. While relaxation has not been completely set aside, the nature of the relaxation experience has changed.

The result of these fundamental changes arising from shifting values is that destination managers are now competing for consumers who have a vastly different mindset and different demographic characteristics.

Demographics are redefining the foundations of competitiveness

In Chapter 4, we note that the changing demographics of the world's population are radically redefining what the great majority of the population finds appealing. Since appeal – or destination attractiveness – is one of the major components of competitiveness, those in tourism (as in all sectors of the economy) must face the reality that a product that is highly successful today may well decline dramatically in competitiveness, even though the physical product is still of high quality. As Foot and Stoffman (2001) argue convincingly, the age structure of a country's population is one of the most powerful tools for understanding the past and forecasting the future. In their 'two-thirds of everything' model, they describe how the collective ageing of a population redefines market demand. They demonstrate the extent of this effect on the real estate market, on the investment market, in retailing, on leisure and recreation, and on transportation systems. Clearly, all of these factors, even if they are not an integral part of tourism, have a strong influence on it.

In a related vein, Foot and Stoffman describe how shifting social values have restructured the composition of the family/household. This change in structure changes behaviour, and this change in behaviour can modify the types of experience sought by travellers and vacationers. If these change, the nature of the competitive destination also changes. In brief, competition in this new millennium may evolve into something that is quite different.

Crisis and renewal are being forced upon destinations as a strategy for competitiveness

Contrary to traditional organizational theory, which emphasizes rationality and control of the management of change, the emerging socioeconomic climate forces destinations to consider redefining competitiveness as the ability to respond effectively to crisis situations. Since the early 1980s, the competitive position of many destinations has been threatened overnight by either a single act of terrorism or a systematic series of acts. These acts have undermined the perceived safety and security of the destination. This has never been truer than in the case of the events of 11 September 2001. The city of New York, a major global tourism destination, has been obliged to deal with a crisis of previously unimaginable proportions. It now appears, however, that the management talent of New Yorkers, with the support of all of the city's residents, has enabled an even stronger tourism destination to emerge.

Lebanon, once a tourism icon of the Middle East, has seen its tourism industry largely obliterated. In North America, growing levels of crime dramatically altered the competitiveness of the city of Miami in the 1990s. Indeed, the problem has become so widespread that Pizam and Mansfeld (1996) were able to assemble an extensive collection of examples of the manner in which terrorism and crime have forced many previously competitive destinations to rethink the nature of their appeal. In each of the foregoing cases, and many others, the constant threat to the security of visitors, or potential visitors, has forced destinations to reassess and redefine their inherent strengths from a competitiveness perspective.

The effect of crime in changing the definition of competitiveness is not due simply to the perceptions and concerns of the visitor. As crime becomes more prevalent within a destination, there is a risk that the most respectable of citizens of that destination change their own behaviour. They often become less friendly as they retreat into a local bubble (Hurst, 1995).

Because of this growing insecurity on the part of both residents and visitors, destination managers need to consider the adoption of a very different style of destination management – one that almost approaches the status of ongoing crisis management. A significant proportion of the resources available for the management of a destination must go into:

• minimizing the possibility of recurrence of criminal or terrorist activity; and
• developing the ability to react immediately and effectively should an outbreak or incident arise.

In any event, a shift in the relative importances of the different factors in the model of destination competitiveness is under way – and the shift may be dramatic. The entire concept of destination competitiveness is redefined.

This chapter has sought to emphasize that the nature of competitiveness and sustainability is in constant evolution, and that as a consequence destination managers must monitor the world around them rigorously to ensure they are anticipating tomorrow rather than reacting to yesterday. In order to do this most effectively, it is essential for them to understand the basic theoretical foundations of the complex concepts of competition and sustainability. In an effort to help both practitioner and student appreciate the essence of these theoretical foundations, we turn in Chapter 2 to a review of the literature on competition (Part I) and on sustainable tourism (Part II).

References

Asch, D. and Wolfe, B. (2001) *New Economy – New Competition: the Rise of the Consumer?* St Martin's Press/Palgrave, New York.

Foot, D.K. and Stoffman, D. (2001) *Boom, Bust and Echo: Profiting from the Demographic Shift in the 21st Century.* Stoddart Publishing, Toronto, Ontario, Canada.

Hurst, D.K. (1995) *Crisis and Renewal: Meeting the Challenge of Organizational Change.* Harvard Business School Press, Boston, Massachusetts.

Pizam, A. and Mansfeld, Y. (1996) *Tourism, Crime, and International Security Issues.* John Wiley & Sons, New York.

Porter, M.E. (1996) *On Competition.* Harvard Business School Press, Boston, Massachusetts.

Porter, M.E. (1997) Creating tomorrow's advantages. In: Gibson, R. (ed.) *Rethinking the Future.* Harvard Business School Press, Boston, Massachusetts.

Prugh, T., Costanza, R., Cumberland, J.H., Daly, H., Goodland, R. and Norgaard, R.B. (1995) *Natural Capital and Human Economic Survival.* ISEE Press (International Society of Ecological Economics), Solomons, Maryland.

Tyson, K.W.M. (1997) *Competition in the 21st Century.* St Lucie Press, Delray Beach, Florida.

UNDP (2002) *Human Development Report.* United Nations Development Programme, New York (available on their website: www.undp.org/hdr2002).

2

Conceptual and Theoretical Perspectives

_____

PART I. THE COMPETITIVE DESTINATION

> Competitiveness without sustainability is illusory.

This chapter consists of two complementary components that are intended to provide the reader with theoretical and managerial interfaces between the two main concepts underlying this book: competitiveness and sustainability. In Part I, we review the theoretical and conceptual foundations of competitiveness. Upon completing this part, the reader should have a basic understanding of what a destination is trying to achieve when it proclaims a goal of enhancing its competitiveness. In Part II, we provide a parallel review of the concept of sustainability. Because the historical roots of this concept are more recent and much shallower than those of competitiveness, there is often no clear consensus regarding what sustainability truly means. Also, the distinction between sustainable tourism and ecotourism is not always clear, as evidenced by Cater and Lowman's pioneering book _Ecotourism: a Sustainable Option_ (1994) and by examination of the chapter _The Sustainability of Ecotourism_, by Burton, in another substantial work by Stabler (1997). A rather different taxonomy is explored by Newsome _et al._ (2002), who include ecotourism as one of four types of natural area tourism (adventure tourism, nature-based tourism, wildlife tourism and ecotourism).

Yet another grey area lies between sustainable tourism and ethical tourism. This issue is examined by Swarbrooke (1999) as he looks to the future of sustainable tourism in a more recent major work on the topic. A further, recent analysis of the relationship between ethics in tourism and sustainability has been provided by Ryan (2002). More specifically, he reviews the _Global Code of Ethics for Tourism_ produced by the World Tourism Organization (WTO) (WTO, 1999, 2000b) and how it will affect the 'equity, management, power sharing and sustainability issues of the New Tourism'. Given the importance of the WTO ethics charter and the long-term impact it will undoubtedly have on the future of tourism – sustainable tourism in particular – an edited version of the charter's main articles is included as Appendix 2.1.

The WTO ethics charter now hangs in many tourism offices around the world, and will slowly but surely pervade the thinking of tourism policy-makers who seek to develop a sustainable, ethical model of tourism within their destinations.

The growth in tourism has spurred significant changes in the way in which destinations are managed. Not so long ago, destinations (whether countries, states, cities or regions) welcomed tourists but did little to intervene in the visitation process, being content to rely on the travel trade to attract and serve visitors.

Destinations no longer take such a passive approach. Competition for a share of the tourism market has intensified as destinations have begun to adopt a marketing orientation. Places are now marketed like any other product to attract industry, investment and residents, as well as tourism. Kotler *et al.* (1993) describe numerous examples of such 'place marketing' and propose a strategic market planning process to attract investment, industry and tourism to cities, states and nations. The use of art, architecture, posters, advertising and images is the focus of a set of readings, edited by Gold and Ward (1994), on the use of publicity and marketing to sell towns and regions.

As a consequence, destinations have created a variety of responses, including setting up national tourist offices, state or regional tourist corporations, Convention and Visitor Bureaux, and economic development agencies. In addition, chambers of commerce, local authorities and industry associations are often now active in the tourism sector. In other situations, interdepartmental committees have been established to integrate and coordinate the activities of basic community infrastructure and service organizations, such as those responsible for transportation, public health and education, in the interest of facilitating a thriving local tourism industry.

Some destinations appear to be coping with this increased competition quite well, whereas others are struggling. In many cases it is the world's traditional destinations that have awakened to the reality that their share of the tourism market is declining. In certain cases, this reality has been cushioned by the fact that tourism is still growing, albeit slower than the international average. This has been the situation, for example, in Western Europe and Canada. In other cases, for example in Malaysia, Hungary and Turkey, there has been an actual decline in the number of visitors and tourism receipts in recent years (WTO, 2000a). At the city level, too, it is evident that some destinations are doing better than others. For example, Atlantic City and Los Angeles appear to have lost some of their gloss over the years, although the declining image of Atlantic City has recovered to some extent in various ways over the last few years. In contrast, some smaller cities, such as San Antonio and Santa

Fe, are often cited as examples of places that have been able to significantly enhance their competitive position.

In response to these changes, many destinations are seeking solutions to the problem of how to become or remain competitive. In doing so, numerous questions often arise. For example, how important are convention facilities? Should the airport be expanded? Would the construction of a landmark help to enhance the image of the destination by providing it with a recognizable icon? Would it be better to concentrate resources on the promotion of the destination? Should a hotel room tax be introduced to fund increased destination marketing? Should there be more municipal government revenues spent on developing or improving visitor-friendly infrastructure/services? Are residents sufficiently visitor-friendly? Would the hosting of a special event like a cultural festival, World Expo or Olympic Games help? Would efforts to reduce crime have much impact, given the media hysteria over isolated events?

Many such questions are being asked but the current state of knowledge provides few answers. Anecdotal evidence alone is not sufficient and, indeed, may seem confusing. For example, some destinations have constructed landmarks or other improvements (e.g. the Gateway Arch in St Louis, the Sydney Opera House, the Riverwalk in San Antonio and the Rock and Roll Hall of Fame in Cleveland) that have enhanced their image. For example, Rubel (1996) describes the City of Cleveland's 'comeback' strategy. Others have ended up with expensive white elephants which have had little impact in attracting tourism. For example, much of Montreal's Mirabel Airport, completed in 1975, remains, in the eyes of many, a cavernous ghost town. Mirabel was opened in 1975 at the cost of $450 million and a bitter expropriation battle. The airport never came close to using its capacity and only covers a fraction of the land taken. Under a transfer proposal involving the transfer of all passenger flights back to the more central Dorval Airport, Mirabel will become an all-cargo and charter airport, an idea welcomed by business groups and airlines (*Travel Week*, 2002). Forcing international flights to use Mirabel, about 60 kilometres north of Montreal, has been cited as a major reason for Montreal's stagnation as an aviation hub when compared with Toronto (*Calgary Herald*, 1997, p. 15).

This chapter begins to examine the concept of competitiveness in terms of its application to tourism destinations. As a concept in business, management and international trade, competitiveness has received widespread interest and attention. Its importance and implications are the subject of some debate, so to begin with we will look at its theoretical underpinnings and managerial consequences. We will try to show how we have arrived at our particular definition of competitiveness and why we believe it is meaningful and managerially useful when applied to tourist destinations. The terms 'comparative advantage' and 'competitive advantage' will be contrasted and we will demonstrate that both forms of advantage are important in understanding the competitiveness and performance of a tourist destination. To shed further light on the topic, we briefly look at the competition among destinations for different market segments. This will help to clarify the relationship between tourism market segmentation, competitiveness, target marketing strategy and the overall performance of the destination. As a destination's ultimate goal is to increase the levels of prosperity of its residents and other stakeholders, it is vital, too, that we consider how prosperity, through tourism development, can be achieved and sustained over the long term. This emphasis on competitiveness implies a deliberate, purposeful effort to manage the destination. Management involves establishing goals, making choices and balancing trade-offs with an overall vision for the destination in mind. So we conclude the first part of this chapter with a few words on the crafting of a destination vision.

Competitiveness: Theoretical and Managerial Dimensions

What is this thing called competitiveness?

Origins

Today, we live in a world of relentless, unceasing competition. The need to compete confronts humans in all endeavours, particularly in sport, employment and, of course, business and international trade. Whereas in the animal kingdom we appreciate the importance of the principle of the survival of the fittest, it seems more appropriate to talk of the survival of the most competitive in the human world.

Critics point to the self-destructive nature of competition and the single-minded focus and reliance on economic growth. Environmentalists, for example, would argue that as the pursuit of economic competition has led us to exceed the capacity of our environment, the phrase 'survival of the most competitive' is an oxymoron.

Nevertheless, today the notion of competitiveness is powerful and pervasive, receiving much of its expression in the business world through the writings of Professor Michael Porter and many others (see, for example, Porter, 1980, 1985, 1990).

The origins of our understanding of contemporary economic theory and the nature of competition begin with Adam Smith who, in 1776, wrote *An Inquiry into the Nature and Causes of the Wealth of Nations*. Smith emphasized the importance of being the lowest-cost producer. He argued that the free market efficiently determined how a country's resources ought to be used in meeting the needs of consumers. However, it was David Ricardo who, when in 1817 he wrote *Principles of Political Economy*, developed the theory of comparative advantage to explain why a country might import a good even when it is the lowest-cost producer. The theory of comparative advantage is based on differences across countries in their endowments of the factors of production (i.e. labour, capital, land and natural resources). Such differences encourage specialization, which in turn creates the need for trade.

A place possessing trading advantages benefits in a number of ways. Industry is attracted to these places, resulting in more employment and higher wages. The increasing concentration of industry results in both infrastructural improvements and an increase in business-to-business alliances and relationships. These changes bring about improvements in living conditions and industrial productivity. If the place is a country, the demand for the country's products boosts demand for, and therefore the value of, its currency. This enables the residents of the country to purchase a greater quantity of imported products. In total, competitiveness means jobs, wealth, improved living conditions, and an environment in which residents can prosper. Therefore, an understanding of what competitiveness is and how it is achieved and maintained is of considerable interest. An excellent reference source that examines a wide variety of perspectives and research traditions on competition can be found in Hunt (2000). Hunt develops a new theory of competition which draws upon these traditions and which he calls the resource-advantage theory of competition.

Definitions

Superficially, competitiveness appears to be a simple concept about which there is little disagreement. According to the *Concise Oxford Dictionary*, to compete is to strive for superiority in a quality. Some athletes compete on the basis of single qualities, such as speed and strength. These athletes, though, would be quick to point out that determination, the will to win, attitude, concentration, stamina, etc. are also very important competitive qualities. Therefore, it is when we try to measure competitiveness that we begin to understand the difficulty in defining it because competitiveness is both a relative concept (superior relative to what?) and is usually multidimensional (what are the salient qualities?). These attributes of competitiveness were emphasized by Scott and Lodge (1985, p. 6), who observed that the 'Evaluation of national competitiveness poses two basic questions: how and in what dimensions do we measure the competitiveness of a national economy, and what standards do we use in determining adequacy? For example, most analyses of competitiveness focus on the trade balance as the key indicator of performance. Is it, however, more important than other factors like market share, real incomes, profitability, and relative changes in productivity? We believe it is the performance pattern measured in several dimensions that is the key, not performance in a single dimension.'

A further complication concerns the unit of analysis and the perspective of the analyst.

Politicians are interested in the competitiveness of the economy (national, regional or local), industry or trade associations confine their interests to their own industry, and business owners and managers worry about the ability of their own firms to compete in specific markets.

It is perhaps helpful to review the definitions of competitiveness employed by others before we try to decide which approach is most suited to an examination of the competitiveness of tourist destinations. Scott and Lodge (1985) viewed national competitiveness as 'a country's ability to create, produce, distribute, and/or service products in international trade while earning rising returns on its resources' (p. 3). They also noted that this ability is 'more and more a matter of strategies, and less and less a product of natural endowments'. As viewed by Newall (1992, p. 94), competitiveness 'is about producing more and better quality goods and services that are marketed successfully to consumers at home and abroad. It leads to well paying jobs and to the generation of resources required to provide an adequate infrastructure of public services and support for the disadvantaged. In other words, competitiveness speaks directly to the issue of whether a nation's economy can provide a high and rising standard of living for our children and grandchildren.' This definition views competitiveness as the key to national prosperity.

'A competitive economy', according to *The Economist* (1994, p. 17) '. . . is one that exports goods and services profitably at world-market prices.' The OECD (WTO, 2000a, p. 47) defines competitiveness in a similar fashion as 'the degree to which a country can, under free and fair market conditions, produce goods and services which meet the test of international markets, while simultaneously maintaining and expanding the real incomes of its people over the long term'. *The World Competitiveness Yearbook*'s definition has varied somewhat over the years. For example, it has defined competitiveness as 'the ability of entrepreneurs to design, produce and market goods and services, the prices and non-price qualities of which form a more attractive package of benefits than those of competitors'. It has also defined world competitiveness as 'the ability of a country or company to, proportionally, generate more wealth than its competitors in world markets' (WTO, 1994, p. 18). Competitiveness is viewed as combining both assets and processes, where assets 'are inherited (e.g. natural resources) or created (e.g. infrastructure)' and processes 'transform assets into economic results (e.g. manufacturing)'. The *World Competitiveness Yearbook* (IMD, 2000, p. 48) examines competitiveness in terms of four fundamental forces that 'are often the result of tradition, history or value systems and are so deeply rooted in the "modus operandi" of a country that, in most cases, they are not clearly stated or defined'. The four dimensions used are attractiveness versus aggressiveness, proximity versus globality, assets versus systems, and individual risk taking versus social cohesiveness.

These definitions attend to the symptoms, results or outcomes of a competitive economy. They help to identify a competitive economy but do little to shed light on the causes of competitiveness.

There seems to be no generally accepted definition of competitiveness. It is perhaps too broad and complex a concept, defying attempts to encapsulate it in universally applicable terms. As noted by Porter (1990, pp. 3–4), 'some see national competitiveness as a macro economic phenomenon . . . Others argue that competitiveness is a function of cheap and abundant labour . . . Another view is that competitiveness depends on possessing bountiful natural resources . . . More recently, many have argued that competitiveness is most strongly influenced by government policy . . . A final popular explanation for national competitiveness is differences in management practices including labour–management relations.' Baker (1987) argues that competitiveness is something more and broader than mere trade statistics. 'Competitiveness – as much a cultural undertaking as an economic or political one – requires changing minds as much as changing policies' (p. 5).

Relative productivity performance too, is often seen as the root of competitiveness (Porter, 1990, p. 6), but Walters (1987, p. 66) warns against placing excessive weight on statistical measures of productivity.

Perhaps the situation is best summed up by Spence and Hazard:

The problem of international competitiveness has been defined in highly diverse ways. These definitions (and the proposed solutions to the problem) are partially inconsistent, and thoroughly confusing to most academics, politicians, policy-makers, and business managers. There is good reason for this confusion. The collection of problems alluded to as 'competitiveness' is genuinely complex. Disagreements frequently occur not only at the level of empirical effects and of policies, but also in the very definition of the problem. Well-intentioned and reasonable people find themselves talking at cross purposes; sometimes it almost seems they are addressing different subjects.

(Spence and Hazard, 1988, p. xvii)

Alternative views

In recent years, governments around the world have embarked on programmes designed to rein in burgeoning national debts, reduce the size of governments, and develop more competitive economies. Critics have questioned whether this all-pervasive, single-minded pursuit of competitiveness has gone too far in the light of the significant social costs. Paul Krugman (1994), for example, in an article titled 'Competitiveness: a dangerous obsession' argued that bad polices have resulted from thinking in terms of competitiveness because competition between nations is fundamentally different from competition between firms. Krugman calculates that 'the growth rate of living standards essentially equals the growth rate of domestic productivity – not productivity relative to competitors, but simply domestic productivity' (p. 34).

In commenting on Krugman's views, *The Economist* (1994), although accepting many of Krugman's central arguments, suggests that competitiveness is too useful a word to prohibit. Relative productivity growth is important as it affects a country's income and well-being. However, in the service sector, of which tourism is a part, productivity has proven to be a difficult concept to measure.

In a later article, Krugman (1996) went on to point out that competitiveness at the level of the enterprise is fundamentally different from the way in which national economies compete. Companies operate as open systems whereas national economies are largely closed systems. As a consequence, although an individual corporation may be quite able to double its market share in a short period, a national economy (i.e. all companies) could not do so because the closed nature of the system would ensure that for gains in one area there will be losses in another. Krugman (1996, p. 48) illustrates this point by noting that, for companies that neither export nor face import competition, one company can increase market share only at the expense of another. 'For companies that do enter world trade any increase in market share creating a trade surplus requires a corresponding export of capital.'

A framework for understanding competition

It is helpful to our understanding of the concept of competitiveness to organize the principal theoretical and managerial dimensions within a coherent framework.

As should be clear from the above, the concept differs as a function of the *level of analysis*. Table 2.1 summarizes these differences.

The structure

The structure of competition between companies within any industry may be viewed as being driven by five forces (Fig. 2.1). Although we readily recognize the competition that occurs as a result of rivalry among existing firms (e.g. in a city, hotel A competes with hotels B, C and D for the business traveller), companies often overlook other important sources of competition. Substitute products or services (e.g. video-conferencing), although often very different in form, compete to serve the same underlying market need (i.e. the need for business persons to communicate). Companies also compete against the threat that newcomers might enter the industry. For example, a hotel with high market share, an efficient operation, competitive prices and strong brand recognition deters new entrants. Competition also occurs for sources of reliable, low-cost supplies (e.g. laundry service) and for

buyers, particularly key corporate accounts (e.g. the corporate travel department in large companies like General Motors).

Porter (1990) conceived of the national 'diamond' to explain the determinants of national advantage in particular industries or industry segments (Fig. 2.2). This perspective might be useful, for example, in understanding the relative competitiveness of the US, Canadian and Australian tourism and hospitality industries. Factor conditions (both inherited and created factors of production) are the inputs to an industry and include human resources, physical resources, knowledge resources, capital resources and infrastructure. National advantage in an industry is influenced by the availability of these factors to that industry, but strengths in other parts of the diamond may overcome disadvantages in factors. Demand conditions, particularly domestic demand and its internationalization to foreign markets, establish the proving grounds for the industry. A high level of domestic demand confers static efficiencies and encourages improvement and innovation. Most national tourism industries depend upon domestic demand for the majority of their business. Foreign demand thrives more readily when domestic tourism is well established. Related and supporting industries that possess their own advantages can stimulate an industry. For example, the leisure and recreation, retailing and entertainment industries share activities that complement the tourism industry. Supplier industries (such as construction, arts and crafts, and food services) that are either unique or cost-efficient confer advantages on the tourism industry. The fourth point on Porter's diamond concerns firm strategy, structure and rivalry. A climate of competition stimulates improvement and discourages stagnation. For example, the deregulation of the airline industry, inter-airline alliances and strong price competition continue to stimulate the demand for air travel.

To the competitive diamond, Porter added two additional variables, chance events and government, which can influence any of the four major determinants. Chance events that suddenly alter the circumstances introduce opportunities for some and threats for others. For example, a terrorist event may direct tourists from one destination to another. Political

Table 2.1. Elements and levels of competition.

Element of competition	Level of competition		
	Companies	National industries	National economies
The structure	Industry competitors Substitutes Potential entrants Suppliers Buyers (see Fig. 2.1)	Factor conditions Demand conditions Related and supporting industries Firm strategy, structure and rivalry Chance Government (see Fig. 2.2)	Science and technology People Government Management Infrastructure Finance Internationalization Domestic economic strength (see Fig. 2.3)
The territory	Target markets	Resources Global markets	Jobs Foreign investment Trade
The stakes	Market share Profitability Survival	Favourable public policies Respect Industrial strength, growth and prosperity International dominance	Economic prosperity Quality of life
The tools	Goods and services Corporate strategy Market research Competitor analysis	Political lobbyists Industry associations Strategic alliances Marketing authorities Industrial policy Cartels Joint promotions	International trade policies and free trade agreements Innovation and entrepreneurship Education and training Productivity improvement Investment Economic policy National culture

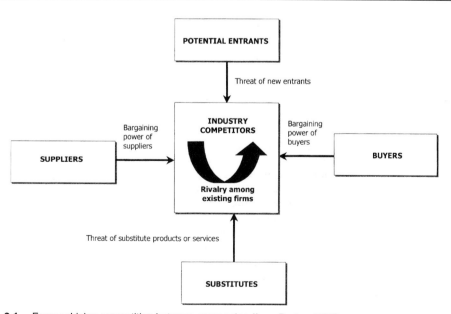

Fig. 2.1. Forces driving competition between companies (from Porter, 1980).

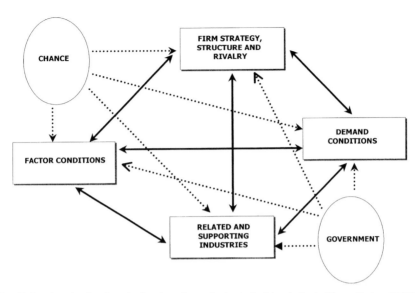

Fig. 2.2. Determinants of national advantage in particular industries (adapted from Porter, 1990).

boycotts or embargoes can suddenly place a tourist destination off-limits. The outbreak of a deadly virus, the collapse of a currency or an environmental catastrophe such as a hurricane or an earthquake can create sudden discontinuities in the pattern of tourist flows. How an industry reacts to these chance events (e.g. the reaction of the tourism industry in Florida during the 1990s to deal with crimes targeting tourists, and floods such as those in Prague, Czech Republic in 2002), either to exploit an opportunity or overcome a threat, can be critically important.

The influence of government can also be significant through its indirect impact on the determinants of national advantage in an industry. In some countries governments may also exert a direct impact on an industry (e.g. government-run national tourist offices and destination promotional campaigns). Governments have tended to become more actively involved in tourism as the stakes have grown. They have both discouraged tourism (e.g. foreign exchange restrictions by France, the UK and Japan in the late 1960s (Bond, 1979; Witt, 1980) and the increase in visa fees for tourists in certain countries), and encouraged foreign travel (e.g. the Japanese government's 'Ten Million Program' to double overseas travel between 1986 and 1991 (Buckley *et al.*, 1989, pp. 381–382)).

The structure of competition between national economies bears some resemblance to the determinants of Porter's diamond because economies are made up of industries. However, by necessity, the determinants are more generic and less industry-specific (Fig. 2.3). The eight factors shown in Fig. 2.3 have been used for a number of years now in measuring the competitiveness of national economies in *The World Competitiveness Yearbook*.

The territory

Just as the structure of competition varies as a function of the unit of analysis, so too does the territory over which competition is fought. Companies compete to attract certain segments of the market that they have targeted in their marketing strategy. For example, the much-troubled British Airways/Air France aircraft Concorde used to compete for very high-yield segments for whom the opportunity cost of time was high or exclusivity in air travel was important. In either case, these segments are willing and able to spend considerable sums of money on air travel. Concorde clearly did not attempt to attract mainstream travellers and indeed deterred them through pricing in order to maintain an exclusive image.

A national industry, on the other hand, competes over global markets against the same

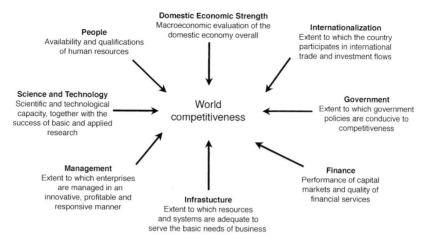

Fig. 2.3. Factors of competitiveness between national economies (from WTO, 1995b).

industry in other nations. The tourism industries in France and Spain broadly covet similar global markets. At the same time, it is important to recognize that the relationships between national tourism industries may not always be competitive. To some extent, for example, the tourism industries in Australia and New Zealand are complementary in terms of attracting long-haul visitors to that region of the world. On a more local level, tourism in the states of Maryland and Delaware in the USA are also quite complementary.

A different type of competitive territory is also relevant at this level of analysis. National industries also compete over national resources against other industries in the same country. Governments seek to allocate resources to growth industries through national strategies (Scott, 1985a). Greater allocative efficiency of the deployment of national resources produces additional national income and wealth (Arndt and Bouton, 1987).

Important resources include land, labour and capital, for example. Favoured industries will find it easier to attract or gain access to these resources. The tourism industry, for example, competes against logging and mining industries for land as these industries involve largely incompatible land uses. The tourism industry must also provide an attractive return on investment if it is to capture a sufficient share of investment capital, and suitable salaries if it is to attract an appropriate mix of labour skills.

When entire national economies represent the unit of analysis, countries compete for a share of the international trade in goods and services. In the current mobile global economy, companies, capital and, to some extent, labour are free to move to locations which possess comparative and competitive advantages. So the competitive territory includes jobs, investment and trade.

The stakes

Whereas the territory represents the ground over which competition is fought, the stakes represent the prize that this territory brings.

For companies, the most obvious prize is profitability. Mere survival in the face of bankruptcy or a hostile takeover attempt is also a reward conferred on competitive companies. In addition to financial stakes, market share bestows legitimacy, authority, power and respect upon companies and their managers because they are recognized as market leaders. As motivation, these social and political rewards may be as significant as those that are purely financial.

By comparison, competitive national industries enjoy a level of international dominance that is shared by all national firms in that industry. Industrial strength, growth and prosperity provide the critical mass and firm foundation for individual companies to pursue global markets. In the tourism industry it would be difficult for a single enterprise (e.g. hotel or attraction) to do well in attracting international visitors if the destination or national tourism industry were not already competitive. Competitive, prosperous industries typically enjoy greater levels of public respect and support from policy makers. As a result, favourable public policies may lead to some continuity in industry success.

The stakes for a nation, economy-wide, are economic prosperity and the quality of the life of its citizens. Nations cannot be competitive in all industries as the factors of production are not shared equally. Every nation must make choices as to which industries provide the best cornerstones for their economy on the basis of factor endowments in which each has a comparative and competitive advantage. Such choices should be based on advantages that are sustainable over the long term, not only economically but also politically, environmentally and socially.

The tools

The tools provide the means by which competitiveness can be managed. Companies use market research, competitor analysis and corporate strategy to establish a competitive position. Ultimately, a company's goods and services embody its competitive capabilities.

Although the competitiveness of an industry depends, in part, on the competitiveness of its individual firms, it is also driven by the collective actions of these firms towards the common good of the industry. For example, strategic alliances, partnerships, joint ventures or promotions, cartels, marketing authorities and industry associations represent organizational behaviours designed to advance the interests and success of the industry. It may be argued that, at times, what companies believe to be in the best interest of the industry may, in fact, sow the seeds of stagnation and decline in the long run. Attempts to protect an industry have often stifled innovation and institutionalized uncompetitive behaviours. Governments seek to influence the competitiveness of national industries through industrial policy, and industries endeavour to shape government policy by employing political lobbyists.

The tools for building and manipulating competitive national economies tend to be rather blunt compared with those available to individual companies. Company tools are more direct in their effect, whereas the effect of national economic tools is more complex, uncertain and gradual. Companies can be managed, but national economies can only be coaxed, cajoled or nudged in a desired direction. Some tools, such as economic policy, international trade policies and free-trade agreements can be modified or tweaked relatively easily. Others, such as national culture, innovation and entrepreneurship, and education and training may take many years to change, if change is possible at all, and it is even longer before the effects on the competitiveness of a nation are felt.

Managing the framework

The levels of competition form a hierarchy in which the nature of competitiveness is addressed at different levels of aggregation. Since competitiveness at each level is interdependent, strategies for competitiveness, in order to be effective, ought to be congruent. Samli and Jacobs (1995) argue that government macrostrategies and corporate microstrategies must be congruent if a country is to develop its competitive advantage fully in the international arena. Companies, national industries and national economies require a shared vision and effective lines of communication if their strategies are to work in concert rather than at cross-purposes. This is unlikely if the different levels do not share the same basic model or understanding of the factors that shape competition. *Consequently, one of the main motivations for writing this book was to propose such a model for the tourism industry as a basis for discussion, debate and research.*

Competitiveness in the service sector

Our understanding of competitiveness is based largely on research in the goods-producing sector. Yet today, in industrialized economies, the service sector dominates. Although most of the service economy is driven by domestic demand, the volume of internationally traded services is increasing rapidly.

It was long believed that there was little scope for international trade in services because it does not involve shipment of a tangible object. However, this has not prevented many industries, such as insurance, banking, education, health services, consulting, transportation, tourism and many others from operating internationally. The modes of international operation fall into three types: (i) the consumer travels to the service (e.g. international tourism); (ii) the service establishes operations in foreign countries (e.g. a business consultant opens a branch office); and (iii) the service is provided remotely using information technology (e.g. mail-order retailing, financial services, distance education, satellite television and e-commerce). Service exports are more significant than most people realize (Mohan, 1990).

Unfortunately, little is known about competitiveness in services (for information on current knowledge of national competitive advantage in services see Sapir, 1982; Palmer, 1985; Siniscalco, 1989; Porter, 1990, p. 239), but international success in service trade is as significant to a nation as international success in traded goods (Porter, 1990, p. 266; Newall, 1992, p. 94; Krugman, 1994, p. 43).

A few researchers have examined the applicability of the theory of international trade to traded services and have generally concluded that there is nothing in the theory which intrinsically makes it less applicable to services. Free trade in services is therefore a good thing for nations. Studies that have examined the validity of the theory of comparative advantage to international trade in services include Deardorff (1985), Feketekuty (1988), Gray (1989), Richardson (1987), Riddle (1986) and Sapir (1982).

Nevertheless, Gray (1989) concludes 'that a single theory of international trade . . . cannot hope to account for all of the kinds of international trade which is undertaken in this world. What is needed, then, is a more flexible body of analysis which will allow studies of specialist sub-categories to be undertaken . . . Instead of a general model of international trade into which international trade in services must be compressed, there is a need for a series of models for separately-identifiable categories of international trade' (p. 99). Tourism, the focus of this book, 'provides an excellent basis for starting work on trade in services for a number of reasons' (Feketekuty, 1988, p. 249).

The Nature of Comparative and Competitive Advantage in Tourism

Understanding the travel trade

To understand something about the trade in tourism services, it is necessary to understand the basic nature of the tourism product and the needs and wants of the tourism market. People travel for a wide variety of reasons. The destination visited may be incidental or central to the reason for travel. For example, a business person may travel in order to visit a supplier and negotiate contracts. In this case, the destination is incidental or subordinate to the firm providing the supplies. If the supplier had been located elsewhere, a different destination would have been involved.

By comparison, the choice of destination is generally central to the pleasure traveller because their travel experience is tied to the destination itself. In this case, the tourism product incorporates the entire destination experience, which is an amalgam of many individual services, such as accommodation, transportation, attractions, entertainment, recreation and food services. Destinations compete to attract this type of traveller by emphasizing the experience they have to offer. This experience, however, is infinitely more difficult to produce and manage compared with most products because it involves so many disparate elements and because the participation or role of the tourist in the experience is so critical. The central role of the destination in this type of situation is the focus of this book.

Richardson (1987, p. 61) notes that the travel and tourism sector is 'fully internationally tradeable in the sense that suppliers from any country could compete in these markets in a fully liberalized institutional environment'. As the tourist is required to travel to a destination in order to receive the destination experience (service), factor conditions are important determinants of attractiveness. Porter (1990, p. 256) notes that 'the role of factor conditions in service competition depends on the form of international competition in the particular service industry. In services where the buyer is attracted to a nation (Type 1), factor conditions are usually important to success. For example, tourism depends heavily on climate and geography, and education and health services depend on the training and skill of local personnel.' We would expect, therefore, that the theory of comparative advantage, which recognizes spatial variations in endowments of the factors of production, would help to explain the competitiveness of tourist destinations. But Porter has argued for a new theory of competitive advantage that goes beyond the limited types of factor-based comparative advantage to incorporate spatial differences in the ability to apply or to make effective use of these factors:

> A new theory must move beyond the comparative advantage to the competitive advantage of a nation. It must explain why a nation's firms gain competitive advantages in all its forms, not only the limited types of factor-based advantage contemplated in the theory of comparative advantage. Most theories of trade look solely at cost, treating quality and differentiated products in a footnote. A new theory must reflect a rich conception of competition that includes segmented markets, differentiated products, technology differences, and economies of scale. Quality, features, and new product innovation are central in advanced industries and segments.
>
> (Porter, 1990, p. 20)

To understand the competitiveness of tourist destinations, therefore, it is both appropriate and essential to consider the basic elements of comparative advantage as well as the more advanced elements that constitute competitive advantage.

Comparative advantage

The distinction between comparative advantage and competitive advantage has not been made completely clear in the literature on competitiveness. The theory of comparative advantage concerns differences in the endowment of the factors of production. And while some, such as the World Economic Forum, have assumed that this covers only natural endowments, the more conventional view is that comparative advantages concern both naturally occurring as well as created resources. The World Economic Forum's *World Competitiveness Report* (IMD,

1994) defines competitiveness as combining assets and processes, where assets are either inherited (e.g. natural resources) or created (e.g. infrastructure), and processes transform assets into economic results. However, the World Economic Forum uses eight factors in measuring competitiveness (Fig. 2.3), omitting recognition of the natural resource assets on the basis of the argument that competitiveness ought to focus only on value added and not on comparative advantage (IMD, 1994, 1995). The created factors of production (i.e. assets) that are included in the World Economic Forum model include human resources (i.e. people) and capital resources (i.e. finance and infrastructure).

Porter (1990, pp. 74–75) groups the factors of production into five broad categories: human resources, physical resources, knowledge resources, capital resources and infrastructure. In a tourism context it seems appropriate to add historical and cultural resources as an additional category, and to expand the infrastructure category to include tourism superstructure.

Human resources

The quantity, quality and cost of human resources available to the tourism industry will shape a destination's competitiveness. The tourism industry employs a diverse range of personnel from bartenders and petrol station attendants to hotel managers, airline pilots, consultants and entrepreneurs. The availability, skills, costs, work ethics and standard working conditions of a destination's tourism managers and employees are critical in an industry that emphasizes customer service.

Physical resources

Physical resources play a fundamental role in attracting tourism to a destination. The diversity, uniqueness, abundance, accessibility and attractiveness of scenic, ecological, recreational and other natural physical features, such as mountains, lakes, deserts and canyons, often represent a primary motivation for travel. A destination's climate, location relative to important markets and geographical size are also important natural endowments. These resources do not necessarily affect a destination's comparative advantages linearly. For example, climates can be too hot as well as too cold, or just unsuitable for certain activities (e.g. skiing). Destinations that enjoy a close proximity to major tourist origins are normally at an advantage, but distant, exotic lands may also be able to benefit from their remote, unspoilt image.

Knowledge resources

Although the tourism industry is not as knowledge-intensive as, for example, the high-technology, education and medical services sectors, knowledge resources are nevertheless important. This is most easily illustrated by comparing the ability, in terms of know-how, of Third World countries to host tourists *vis-à-vis* the industrialized world. Third World destinations often need to import knowledge related to hotel management, engineering, regional planning and marketing when developing the tourism sector. This is reflected in the fact that many of the United Nation's WTO's activities are aimed at assisting developing countries, whereas a number of developed countries have chosen not to be members of the WTO.

Capital resources

The ability of a destination to develop its tourism superstructure and finance its operations depends on the amount and cost of capital available. In turn, the availability of capital depends not only on the overall volume and structure of wealth but also on the extent to which investors believe that the returns from tourism development are commensurate with the risks. In this regard, the financial performance of the tourism industry has been mixed. Notwithstanding the existence of some very large corporations, the predominance of small businesses in the tourism sector means that development often depends on the extent of personal savings and investment as much as it does on capital markets.

Infrastructure and tourism superstructure

The stock of created assets, in combination with the inherited natural assets, supports much economic activity. Infrastructure covers the subordinate facilities, equipment, systems and processes that provide a foundation for a wide range of economic needs and, as a consequence, is often provided by government or public corporations. Examples include roads, water supply, sanitation, health systems, utility services and public services such as fire and police protection, libraries and airports. The tourism superstructure represents the additional created assets which rest upon this infrastructure and which serve visitor-oriented needs and desires. Examples include hotels, restaurants, theme parks, resorts, golf courses and many other facilities.

Historical and cultural resources

These resources may be both tangible (e.g. archaeological artefacts, ruins, monuments, architecture and townscapes, battlefields, art galleries and artwork and museums) and intangible (e.g. music, language, customs and traditions, life styles, values, friendliness and literature). The stock and condition of historical and cultural resources depends upon a nation's appreciation of their value and its ability to care for their condition. Government departments, trusts, arts councils, grants bodies and the degree of public patronage are examples of manifestations of support for cultural activities and the cultural heritage of a destination.

Size of economy

The size of the local economy can also impact a destination's comparative advantage. A larger local population and economy provides several potential advantages. It creates the conditions for greater local tourism demand. It also facilitates the acquisition of needed resources locally. Greater economies of scale lower the cost of these other resources. A larger economy also produces increased competition, leading to a variety of suppliers, product qualities and service. Local entrepreneurial activity in tourism facilitates destination competitiveness in numerous ways (Crouch and Ritchie, 1995).

Resource augmentation and depletion

The resources that make up a destination's factor endowments change over time, altering the comparative advantage of a destination. Naturally occurring resources can be divided into two types: those that are renewable and those that are not. For example, hunting and fishing, provided the stock of wildlife is well above a sustainable level, involves a renewable resource. On the other hand, a sensitive ecological reserve cleared for agriculture or mining is lost for ever despite any reclamation efforts. The stock of created resources, too, changes over time but, because these are created, they are typically more renewable than naturally occurring resources. Nevertheless, certain created resources, particularly those of historical significance (such as an archaeological artefact) or contemporary cultural significance (such as a famous work of art) may not be renewable. This is an example where the distinction between naturally occurring, or inherited, and created or man-made resources becomes moot.

The wise stewardship of resources is critical, therefore, to the long-term competitiveness of a tourism destination. Strategies are required for the education and training of human resources, the protection and care of natural physical resources, the expansion and domestication of knowledge resources, the investment and growth of capital resources, the construction and maintenance of infrastructure and tourism superstructure, and the preservation and fostering of historical and cultural resources.

The World Competitiveness Report (WCR) (WEF/IMD, 1992) makes an important point concerning the role of non-renewable resources in a nation's competitiveness. The report argues that, under the traditional theory of comparative advantage, 'countries are better off if they trade the products or services that give them the greatest advantage, or *least disadvantage*, relative to their possible trading partners' (p. 12). 'A comparative advantage can be based on having an abundance of natural resources in a country, for example oil, whereas competitive advantage can only be based on an entrepreneur's ability to add value to the available resources, by refining the crude oil, say. By merely selling its natural richness, a country does not become better off in the long term – a sale [caused by natural resource degradation] must be written off as a minus on the national balance sheet; selling the value

added resources (and not the resources) creates a surplus that a country can then invest in its economic development' (p. 14). For this reason, the WCR model focuses on value added and ignores inherited factors.

In tourism, however, these arguments concerning the relevance of natural resources to competitiveness do not apply. A country's natural resources are clearly an important source of comparative advantage in tourism. However, in contrast to the sale of resources such as oil or minerals, tourists do not return home with any significant physical elements from the 'exporting' country (other than the odd artefact or photograph). Thus, these resources are not depleted, despite the fact that people have paid for their use. In tourism, the visitor purchases an opportunity to briefly experience such resources as scenery, culture and climate – but this experience does not necessarily create environmental degradation, which would cause a corresponding minus on the national balance sheet. Indeed, the fact that certain visitors have experienced a particular country may enhance its appeal, and therefore its ongoing value, to others.

At the same time, it must be acknowledged that tourism can produce externalities that 'must be written off as a reduction in the domestic value-added since it implies that the quality of the national resources has deteriorated. Countries should not be misled into seeking short-term prosperity at long-term cost. Value added in the long-term is what really constitutes a basis for the prosperity of nations' (IMD, 1995, p. 14). Examples of externalities in tourism that may result in such write-offs include environmental pollution, the despoliation of scenic areas, social fragmentation, the spread of disease, the encroachment into wildlife habitats and the creation of tourist ghettos.

Despite the possibility of the above externalities, it is argued that the tourism phenomenon represents a form of economic exchange that is fundamentally different from the sale of physical resources. With this premise, it can be further argued that, in the context of tourism, inherited, naturally occurring resources are important. A possible counter-argument is that the natural resources of tourism have no economic value in themselves (although many would argue that value cannot be measured in economic terms alone). For example, a scenic valley has no economic value in itself if the only creatures able to experience the scenery are the local fauna. Building a road into the valley, thus providing access for tourists, does, however, provide value. But as value is created only by the building of the road and as the scenery is not sold (resulting in a corresponding depletion of natural resources) it can be asserted that the concept of comparative advantage is relevant or operative in this example. In brief, because value has been added, it may be said to represent a case of competitive rather than comparative advantage.

Despite this counter-argument, there remains a fundamental difference in the sale of an experience related to the use of a resource as opposed to the sale of the resource itself. Indeed, even physical resources require enhancement (or the adding of value) before they can be sold. Oil or minerals in the ground need to be accessed and physically removed from their original location before they become useful commodities. This process is the equivalent of providing access to a beach or a scenic area. However, we argue that the nature of the exchange process is conceptually and fundamentally different.

Competitive advantage

Whereas comparative advantages involve the resources available to a destination, competitive advantages relate to a destination's ability to use these resources effectively over the long term. A destination endowed with a wealth of resources may not be as competitive as a destination that is lacking in resources but that utilizes the little it has much more effectively. By this we mean that a destination which has a tourism vision, shares this vision among all stakeholders, understands its strengths as well as its weaknesses, develops an appropriate marketing strategy and implements it successfully, may be more competitive than one which has never asked what role tourism is to play in its economic and social development.

Earlier we mentioned San Antonio and Cleveland as examples of cities that, although weak in terms of comparative advantages, have been recognized for their ability to improve their competitiveness as destinations. In contrast, Singapore and Russia stand at opposite ends of the comparative/competitive advantage continuum. Russia possesses enormous physical, historical and cultural (i.e. naturally occurring or inherited) resources, yet lacks the human knowledge and capital resources as well as the infrastructure and tourism superstructure (i.e. created resources) required to bring these assets to the market. By comparison, Singapore's natural, historical and cultural resources are inferior, but its endowments in the other factors of production surpass those of Russia. In addition, Singapore seems able to utilize its competitive resources more effectively. Perhaps most notable is Singapore's reputation for service in its hotels and airlines. Singapore is safe, clean and hospitable. Its enterprises are reliable, its prices are competitive in terms of value, and the country functions as a highly tuned nation.

Singapore and Russia have a very different mix of factors (known as factor proportions), but this only partly explains their difference in destination competitiveness. Competitive advantage – the other side of the coin – explains the rest because it introduces the additional effect of differences in the deployment of the resources; that is, where and how a destination chooses to mobilize its comparative advantages. Indeed, Porter (1990, p. 83) contends that offsetting weaknesses is more likely to stimulate businesses to innovate than to capitalize on strengths, and he has noted that nations which are factor-disadvantaged are often stimulated to find innovative ways of overcoming their *comparative* weakness by developing *competitive* strengths.

Modes of deployment

Different destinations have adopted a variety of modes for deploying tourism resources. As noted above, in the past governments played a much less active role in destination management. Today, however, various areas and levels of government are involved in the promotion, regulation, presentation, planning, monitoring, maintenance, coordination, enhancement and organization of tourism resources. The locus of control by government varies from one destination to another. In some countries, the national government may play a dominant role, whereas in others, state or local governments may be more important. For example, in 1996 the US Federal Government ceased operation of the US Travel and Tourism Administration in favour of state-controlled organizations and greater responsibility by industry.

The actions of various industry associations affect the deployment of tourism resources. Paramount bodies, such as the Travel Industry Association of America, the Tourism Industry Association of Canada and the Tourism Council, Australia, and sectoral associations, such as air transport associations, hotel associations and restaurant associations, seek to promote the interests of their membership, and their activities include providing a voice on matters concerning the cost, accessibility, regulation and deployment of tourism resources.

Despite the central role of government and industry associations, the collective actions of the many thousands of individual tourism and related enterprises have the greatest impact on resource deployment. Governments may constrain the way in which resources are used, but, within these constraints, firms decide precisely where and how the resources will be deployed.

Special interest groups such as environmental organizations, community associations, consumer groups, recreational associations and others are often vigilant in expressing their views on tourism development, particularly as it concerns perceptions of adverse ecological, social and cultural impacts.

Tourism resources are likely to be used more effectively when the different modes of deployment share a common view regarding a destination's strategy for tourism development. If this is to occur, stakeholders must agree on a body of research and information which details the state of these resources. Effective and inclusive communication between all stakeholders helps to chart a destination's course. We have a few more words to say about this towards the end of this chapter.

The mobilization or deployment of resources for competitive advantage may be considered to consist of five elements. First, an *audit* or *inventory* of resources is required before they can be deployed appropriately. This involves more than just the cataloguing and listing of resources. It is also important to understand something about the capacity and capability of the resources, including the limitations and consequences of their use. The *maintenance* of resources is the second element. The stock of resources must be maintained in an appropriate way to guard against undue deterioration and to facilitate sustainability. For man-made resources in particular, actions that facilitate the *growth and development* of the stock of these resources are important. Finally, the *efficiency* and *effectiveness* of resource deployment create competitive advantage.

The role of domestic tourism

Globally, domestic tourism receipts amount to about five and a half times international tourism receipts. In most situations, therefore, it is domestic tourism that drives the nature and the structure of a nation's tourism industry. There are, however, a certain number of cases where this is not true (e.g. Bermuda). But generally the supply of the tourism product is driven by domestic or local demand that is typically more stable and reliable and less fickle than demand from distant markets. Hence, solid domestic demand provides a healthy competitive environment and the critical mass of demand necessary to support a thriving tourism and hospitality sector.

Strong domestic demand therefore helps to provide a climate that also encourages inbound tourism and discourages outbound tourism (the import substitution effect). There are obvious limitations to this assertion, however, since domestic travel may not provide a suitable substitute for outbound international travel where specific or unique kinds of travel experiences are involved. None the less, although inbound tourism and outbound tourism are distinct phenomena, strong domestic demand for tourism impacts favourably on both of them by enhancing the attractiveness of the destination to both residents and distant markets.

Destination competitiveness

While destinations compete primarily for economic reasons, with an emphasis on attracting tourist expenditures, other motives may also underlie the development of tourism. For example, international tourism provides an opportunity to showcase a country as a place to live, to do business with, to invest in and to trade with. It may also be used for political reasons to bolster national pride. Increasingly, by means of careful management, attempts are being made through tourism to help preserve ecological resources and cultures. For example, tourism can provide a powerful economic incentive to protect African wildlife in the fight against poaching, or to encourage rural residents to pursue their traditional culture in an effort to stem the flow of people in Third World countries towards overpopulated cities. Tourism also facilitates international understanding and promotes peace (D'Amore, 1988), and may be used as a tool to further the international political goals of a country (Buckley et al., 1989). This multiplicity of goals adds to the difficulty of conceptualizing the destination competitiveness concept.

An additional complication concerns the issue of how resources are allocated across different industries and sectors of the economy. Competitiveness in any sector, including tourism, can be improved by shifting resources away from other sectors. One would hope that governments and the private sector would carry out this resource allocation process with the nation's overall prosperity in mind. There is no guarantee that this will be the case. Some sectors may be more effective than others in lobbying for government support. The agriculture and petroleum sectors, for example, have typically been much more persuasive than tourism in influencing public policy.

Despite these difficulties, it seems reasonable to focus attention on *long-term economic prosperity* as the yardstick by which destinations are to be assessed competitively. A long-term view will help to internalize the broad range of costs and benefits into the *economic picture*.

Poon (1993) calls for greater strategic orientation by tourism destinations if they are to adjust to the competitive realities of 'new' tourism. Mass tourism (or 'old' tourism) involved standardized and rigidly packaged products produced 'along assembly-line principles' (p. 29). New tourism is 'flexible, sustainable

and individual-oriented' (p. 9). 'New tourists are fundamentally different from the old . . . They are more experienced, more "green", more flexible, more independent, more quality conscious and "harder to please" than ever before' (pp. 9–10). She argues that:

Competitive strategies are therefore critically important for tourism destinations to sail a new tourism course. This is so because:

- Comparative advantages are no longer natural.
- Tourism is a volatile, sensitive and fiercely competitive industry.
- The industry is undergoing rapid and radical transformation – the rules of the game are changing for everyone.
- What is at stake is not just tourism but the survival of tourism-dependent economies.
- The future development and viability of tourism-dependent economies will depend not only on tourism, but on the entire service sector.

(Poon, 1993, p. 291)

Poon further suggests four key principles that destinations will need to follow if they are to be competitive: (i) put the environment first; (ii) make tourism a lead sector; (iii) strengthen the distribution channels in the marketplace; and (iv) build a dynamic private sector (p. 24). While these suggestions have merit, one might ask whether there are not other critical competitiveness factors among the many comparative and competitive advantage dimensions that we have only touched upon so far. These four principles are too broad and general to be managerially useful. A deeper, richer understanding of destination competitiveness is required.

The concepts of comparative and competitive advantage provide a theoretically sound basis for the development of a model of destination competitiveness. But no single general trade theory will provide the necessary insight or cover the most appropriate determinants from among the many variables possible.

Gray (1989) notes that 'any general model of international trade must encompass an extraordinarily large number of causal variables . . . a single theory of international trade . . . cannot hope to account satisfactorily for all of the kinds of international trade which is undertaken in this world. What is needed, then, is a more flexible body of analysis that will allow studies of specialist sub-categories' (pp. 98–99).

Richardson (1987) expresses a similar view. No 'single theory is likely to be able to encompass all the characteristics which make trade in services such a complex – and such an exciting – domain' (p. 80).

And Haahti (1986) states that 'The information that should guide the decision maker in dealing with the targeting of competitive [tourism] resources is lacking in this critical area' (p. 13).

A mere listing of comparative and competitive factors, no matter how comprehensive it may be, is not sufficient. It is also necessary to understand the relationship and interplay between factors of competitiveness. That is, a systemic model of destination competitiveness is required. For example, a destination may not possess a dominant position of strength on any particular determinant yet still be highly competitive because its *system* of factors is unique and difficult to replicate. A nation's 'position *vis-à-vis* some determinants may not be unique. However, national advantage arises when the system is unique' (Porter, 1990, p. 147). Porter called his system of national advantage the 'diamond'. In commenting upon the competitive future of the tourism sector, Poon (1993, p. 205) also noted the increasing system-like nature of the industry.

Linking Destination Competitiveness to Performance

Competitiveness is no guarantee of performance. How often can you recall an occasion on which a highly talented sports team, which on paper should have won the game decisively, failed to live up to expectations? If an analysis of competitiveness determined the result, there would be no need to play the game. On a given day a team may fail to perform for a variety of reasons. Perhaps the game plan failed to address the real strengths and weaknesses of the opposition. Perhaps the coach lost a key player through injury, or the execution of specific tactics fell short. Or maybe it was because the opposition simply played above themselves. Whatever the

reason, the result is always in doubt until the game is over.

At any point in time, as we attempt to analyse and assess the competitiveness of a destination we have to rely on the past and what we *think* might occur in the future. But from a managerial perspective it is future performance that we are really interested in. So although the focus of this book is destination competitiveness rather than performance *per se*, a few words on the link between competitiveness and performance are appropriate.

Tourism markets

In order to say that something is competitive, it is necessary to specify the purpose or goal towards which the competitiveness is directed. The same decathlete may be very competitive in some events (e.g. shot-put, discus and hammer-throw, where upper body strength and bulk are important) but weak in others (e.g. the 100-metre sprint, hurdles and high-jump, where speed and agility are critical). Similarly, a destination may possess advantages more closely aligned with the needs of one market segment (e.g. the adventure-seeker) than another (e.g. the culture-seeker).

Some destinations may have a very skewed competitiveness profile, meaning that they have major advantages in some attributes but are severely disadvantaged in others. By comparison, other destinations may be more evenly balanced, offering a broader range of comparative and competitive advantages. The former group of destinations are likely to appeal to a narrower range of tourism market segments (e.g. Hong Kong), whereas the latter group (e.g. the USA) may have the luxury of targeting a wider selection of market segments.

A destination may deliberately decide not to compete for certain market segments, either because it lacks the requisite comparative and competitive advantages or because it has chosen to deploy them towards other, more attractive markets. In these circumstances, is it meaningful to talk of competitiveness with respect to that segment? For example, Mercedes-Benz is generally regarded as highly competitive in the luxury car market. If, however, competitiveness was measured in terms of the company's share of the total automobile market, it would not be considered to be a significant competitor. What are the implications of this viewpoint in tourism? Monaco, for example, does not target the camper segment of the travel market. In fact the principality discourages campers, fearing that their presence in the country may tarnish its image as a destination for the rich and famous – and those aspiring to be rich and famous.

So, as a destination seeks to apply its comparative and competitive advantages, it will look for a match between its competitive strengths and weaknesses, and the opportunities and threats present in each of the segments constituting the global tourism market. The criteria for establishing the degree of match between the destination and the market segment may be grouped according to the following four categories.

- *Nature of demand.* The needs, wants and characteristics of those who constitute the market segment must accord with the comparative and competitive advantage profile of the destination. The fit does not have to be perfect in every respect, but at least in several key elements the destination has to possess a superior ability to deliver the type of tourism experience sought by the segment. As noted in the previous section, however, it is the system, not the simple sum, of competitive elements that matters.
- *Time of demand.* Neither destination competitiveness nor market demand is static. The match between the two must be synchronous. At different times of the year certain resources will be at their peak (e.g. autumn colours, summer festivals, wildlife activity, snow and anniversaries of historical events). Demand will also follow its own set of pressures and constraints, such as the timing of school vacations, quiet periods in industry, or winter 'blues'. The temporal pattern of resources and demand must be harmonious before a match exists.
- *Magnitude of demand.* The capacity of the destination and the size of the market segment must also be compatible. A convention destination like Chicago, for example,

will target larger segments of the meetings and conventions market. Although the city may be able to host smaller conventions, larger conventions offer a more efficient match of resources and markets.

- *Future demand.* How will market segments evolve in the future? Market segments take time to cultivate, therefore a match should be sustainable. Destinations should anticipate the degree of match over the long term.

Target market strategy

Finding a match between a destination's competitiveness profile and the characteristics of certain market segments is only part of the challenge involved in choosing target markets and developing a strategy to pursue them. We also have to consider the response of competitors to these same market segments as well as the goals we have established for our tourism development strategy.

The competition

Other destinations are engaged in the same process of targeting a set of tourism market segments. These destinations may play the role of either enemy or ally. Enemies are destinations whose success occurs at our expense. That is, the choice facing the tourist in the respective segment is either to visit the enemy or to visit us. Allies also covet the same market segment but, for various reasons, complement rather than diminish our efforts to attract these tourists. For example, two (or more) destinations may be allies because their geographical proximity enables packaging of the destinations in the same trip, or their collective marketing efforts may expand the size of the segment to the extent that both destinations experience more demand than they would if either of them was the only competitor in town.

So when choosing market segments to target, the decision should take competitor strategies into account. A small destination may target a segment also chosen by a large ally even though there is a slightly better match with another segment. Or it may choose to target an

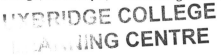

inferior match because its enemies, who have also chosen that segment, are easier to deal with than the competitors, who would have to be faced if it had pursued the segment more closely matched with its competitiveness profile.

The goals

Target markets need not only match a destination's comparative and competitive advantages. A match with a destination's tourism development goals is also important. Our destination may be more competitive in a different segment of the market, but if success in that segment does little to help us achieve our goals we may have gained only a boost to our ego. For example, suppose we had set a goal to expand the economic benefits of tourism beyond a coastal resort region to improve the standard of living of residents in the hinterland. On the basis of our competitiveness profile alone, we may be tempted to target short-stay, big spenders who might never leave the resort itself and whose spending never filters into the surrounding areas, other than perhaps through the fortunate few employed to work at the resort.

But when the decision is goal-driven, a better target market might be backpackers, who stay longer and stray beyond the coast. They may not spend as much as the other segment in total, but the import leakage might be lower because they consume local crafts, food and locally owned accommodation. The competitiveness-profile–segment match may not be quite as good, but what does this matter if the destination's tourism goals are more likely to be achieved as a result. We finish this part of the chapter with a few further thoughts on charting a destination's course.

Destination performance

Although a target market strategy should be goal-driven, the final link between destination competitiveness and performance depends on the implementation of the strategy resulting in a set of actual (not just anticipated or hoped for) achievements that can be compared with the established goals. As noted earlier, the sports team goes into the game with a goal and strategy, but the final result – and therefore the team's performance – rests on the execution of its game plan relative to how well the opposition executes its own game plan.

Goals need to consist of some short-term milestones, but the performance of the destination stemming from its comparative and competitive advantages must ultimately be assessed over the long term. It is easy for a destination to fall into the trap of pursuing short-term apparent gains without any idea of where this will lead in the long term, or whether there may be undesirable consequences that will become apparent only after many years of pursuing a myopic strategy. Scott (1985b, p. 15) made the point that 'competitiveness means earning a rising standard of living, not borrowing it'. Although this was said in connection with the relationship between debt and productivity improvement, one could also apply it to the notion of borrowing from the future to benefit the present. He went on to suggest 'the wisdom of reviewing multiple measures, using a long time horizon, and attempting to relate . . . performance to . . . goals and commitments'.

How does a destination execute its game plan successfully? All the usual rules apply to start with. Words in a strategic document will not leap off the page and into action by themselves, and this is where many strategic plans stall, gather dust and meet their fate. Strategies have to be made to happen by establishing structures for implementation, identifying timelines and assigning responsibilities. The market and the competition need to be monitored continuously so that plans can be adjusted in real time. Performance indicators need to be tracked and contingencies implemented when required.

But a destination faces some additional challenges not normally confronted by a firm trying to implement a strategy. These challenges arise because a destination strives to achieve multiple goals, involves many different stakeholders, often lacks a focal organization that is able to see events from a bird's-eye view, and faces a difficult task in gathering the disparate information required to assess its performance.

Summarizing the steps to destination success

In summary, destination competitiveness and performance are linked by several steps, which are illustrated in Fig. 2.4. Destination competitiveness combines both comparative advantages and competitive advantages; that is, the endowed factors (both naturally occurring and created) and the ability to mobilize and deploy these factors, respectively. The basis of a target market strategy is to find congruence between the competitiveness profile of the destination and: (i) alternative tourism market segments; (ii) the competition (both enemies and allies) and their own strategies; and (iii) the goals which the destination aspires to achieve. The implementation of this strategy results in an outcome that must be judged by comparing it with the destination's goals. To the extent that the strategy achieves these goals, we can say that it has been successful.

In the majority of cases, success tends to be measured by the level of economic prosperity that tourism has provided. However,

a destination may be judged successful if it has achieved other goals that it has set for itself. For example, goals that balance a desired level of economic return with desired levels of preservation or enhancement of environmental and cultural integrity. The challenge facing policy makers is to establish goals that reflect the values and ambitions of destination stakeholders, and then to promote a policy framework that supports the achievement of these goals. Destination managers, tourism operators and all stakeholders must then do their utmost to achieve these goals. In brief, the achievement of destination success is the shared responsibility of everyone.

The Philosophy of Sustainable Competitiveness for Tourism Destination Development

Throughout this chapter we have emphasized that the competitiveness of a tourist destination must be assessed from a long-term

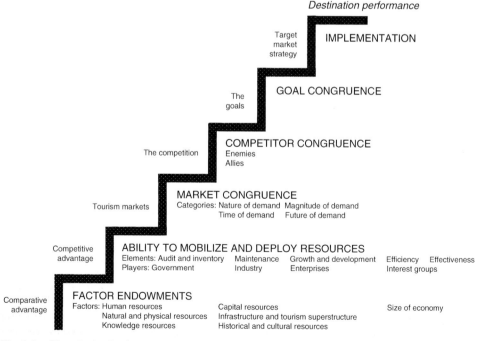

Fig. 2.4. Steps to destination success.

perspective. We have also stressed that the competitiveness of the destination must be linked to the prosperity, standard of living and quality of life of its residents through the vision and goals the destination has set, either explicitly or implicitly. Like companies, destinations face the same risk of developing their tourism sector in a fashion which may have seemed attractive at the time but which proves, over the longer term, to have fallen short of an optimal outcome or, possibly even worse, to have done more harm than good.

For example, suppose that a strategy for environmental protection was so unreasonably extreme as to severely undermine the economic system in the destination, resulting in wide sociocultural and political ramifications. The potential backlash from residents may lead to a situation in which politicians opposed to the environmental protection laws are able to exploit the social and political instability that arises, in order to gain power and defeat these laws.

Consequently, a sustainable solution must strive to achieve a degree of balance among four complementary pillars (economic, social, cultural, political) in such a way that no fatal weaknesses are evident in the system of sustainability. The nature of the inter-dependence between each of the four pillars suggests that the situation is unsustainable in all four pillars if it is unsustainable in any one of them.

The targeting of certain segments of the tourism market has significant implications for the sustainability of the destination's tourism strategy. The behaviour of market segments differs in terms of their ecological, economic, sociocultural and political impacts. Earlier we discussed the need for congruency between the characteristics of target markets and the destination's competitiveness profile, competitor strategies, and the destination's vision and goals. Each of the four pillars of sustainability should enter the search for target markets through the destination's vision and goals. That is, the question of sustainability should be addressed right from the beginning when considering the type of society and community residents wish to create for themselves and for future generations.

Charting the Destination's Sustainable Course: Crafting a Vision and Establishing Goals

As we have emphasized, the competitiveness of a destination derives from a combination of both its resources or assets (naturally occurring or created), which can be deployed to assemble the tourism product, and the ability of the destination to mobilize these resources. Part of this ability to mobilize resources (i.e. competitive advantages) arises from the degree to which the destination has been able to chart a coherent, widely supported course.

The act of *planning* provides no guarantee that a destination will succeed, but it does improve its chances. A tourism development plan can potentially:

- *identify the best courses of action* – a formal planning process requires a more comprehensive and systematic assessment of a destination's strengths and weaknesses, tourism opportunities and threats, and viable alternatives;
- *maximize community and industry support* – planning, if undertaken appropriately, provides an opportunity for all stakeholders to air any concerns and influence the destination's course;
- *mobilize effort towards a shared goal* – a plan acts as a communication tool to ensure that those involved in its implementation have a clear sense of purpose and direction, and an understanding of their role in the process;
- *ensure the efficient use of resources* – as resources are finite, their allocation among alternative, competing uses will result in different outcomes; planning ensures that the resource allocation decision is made explicit.

Tourism planning in the context of overall social and economic development

The development of a destination tourism strategy should occur as a subcomponent of the community's overall social and economic development planning process for two reasons: (i) it will be conducted more efficiently because similar questions will need to be asked and answered in these broader contexts; and (ii) overall goals will not be achieved unless sectoral plans are in harmony.

Kotler *et al.* (1993) highlight the plight facing many cities, regions, states and countries. They ask the question: can places do a better job of forecasting and planning their future? They contend that the four traditional approaches to place development – community development, urban design, urban planning and economic development – each possess flaws that limit their efficiency. In response, they suggest that the *strategic market planning process*, which has been used by business organizations for many years, provides several advantages because: (i) places compete for resources like business; (ii) dynamic, global forces affect their industries; (iii) places compete for tourists, conventions, educated residents, factories, corporate headquarters and start-up firms; (iv) they must be excellent or superior in some special ways; (v) they must be market-conscious and market-driven; (vi) the attributes they develop today will affect their market position tomorrow; and (vii) if they choose the wrong industries they are in the same position as companies that choose the wrong products (Kotler *et al.*, 1993, p. 76).

Kotler and colleagues provide a five-stage strategic market planning process that begins with the completion of the *place audit*. The purpose of the place audit is to understand 'what the community is like and why' (Kotler *et al.*, 1993, p. 81). The audit provides a comprehensive and detailed set of information upon which subsequent planning is based. It should identify the important tangible and intangible characteristics that define the place. That is, its strengths, weaknesses, opportunities and threats. It should also profile the philosophies of its citizens, civic leaders, institutions, businesses and other entities that together constitute the values of the place. Places, like people, possess personalities, and these personalities influence the way in which people wish to live.

On the basis of the place audit, a vision and set of goals must be crafted. This process will be examined in greater detail in Chapter 8, where we present the process of destination policy formulation. In part, this will require the place to make decisions about its desired industrial profile, and it is really only at this point that tourism's role in assisting the place to achieve all of its goals becomes evident. The somewhat separate but integrated process of developing a strategy for tourism begins at this point with the undertaking of an audit of the destination which draws on the place audit but which extends, develops and fleshes it out further in terms of its tourism-related elements. Our final chapter outlines how this might be accomplished.

Places have recognized the growing significance and attractiveness of the tourism industry in their development plans. It has become a major economic sector representing approximately 11% of the world's gross domestic product and a similar percentage of world employment (WTTC, 1995, p. 22). Strategies to develop and market the place as a tourist destination can often proceed symbiotically with other place marketing goals. Place marketing entails developing an attractive image, whether the goal is to attract tourists, residents, investors or business. Indeed, a place that offers an attractive lifestyle and a variety of recreational, cultural and leisure activities serves the needs of both residents and visitors. In general terms, the tourism industry is now firmly established as an economic sector that is as attractive to places, in their plans for economic development, as any other industry. Interestingly, Kotler *et al.* (1993, p. 227) conclude that 'Tourism and the business hospitality market have emerged as viable place development strategies on a footing equal to business retention, business attraction, grow your own businesses, and export-development/reverse investment. In a service-driven economy of aging population, these two businesses are generally expected to grow at rates ahead of the national economy.'

Allocating resources: tourism's share

On several occasions in this chapter we have touched upon the competition between industries for a share of the nation's resources. In particular, we have examined how the theory of comparative advantage provides us (to some extent at least) with a rational basis for resource allocation decisions. But resources are not necessarily allocated rationally. Various influences and dynamics may play a role at least as significant as the rational efficiency approach that underlies the comparative advantage concept.

For example, industries that have been the traditional mainstay of an economy in the past typically exert a significant influence on policy makers. These industries tend to benefit from a lag in the effect of their importance to an economy, such that biased allocation of resources may be perpetuated long after the industry has begun to decline. Indeed, when society finally realizes that these industries are in decline, there is often an attempt, perhaps futile, to maintain or even increase resources to these sectors in an effort to turn around, delay or soften the fall.

Further, these established, traditional industries are often able to more effectively mobilize their constituencies in expressing a consistent, concerted voice towards policy makers. They have, over the years, fine-tuned their message. Over time, too, industries tend to become more like-minded within. Structures and systems evolve, a process that creates a degree of homogeneity in management styles and perspectives. As a result, these industries often exert an influence that exceeds their significance.

The travel, tourism and hospitality sector is, by comparison, often poorly organized. Notwithstanding the fact that humans have been travelling since the origin of civilization, the industrialization of tourism really only began after the Second World War. Despite the enormous size of the industry (WTTC, 1995), it remains highly fragmented in many destinations and consists of many thousands of companies, large and small. In fact, tourism is not an industry in the traditional sense of the word. Industries are traditionally defined from a *product* rather than a *market* perspective. And because tourism is made up of so many diverse products, many people working in the tourism sector still tend to identify more closely with their industry (e.g. lodging, transportation, food services, entertainment and tour operations) than they do with the broader economic sector defined by and derived from tourism demand. While recent efforts led by the WTO (WTO, 2001a) to develop and implement Tourism Satellite Account systems designed to address this complexity are promising, it will take time before these systems are in widespread use. In the meantime, few outside the industry, and perhaps not even all in the industry, recognize the size, scope and significance of tourism. The lag effect we identified above also serves to delay the recognition of emerging industries. The World Travel and Tourism Council was formed several years ago with the express purpose of addressing these challenges, and although governments, social institutions and the public appear to be rapidly altering their perceptions of the industry, these problems still exist to a large extent.

The tourism industry must continue to organize, professionalize, communicate, educate, and conduct and support research if it is to compete effectively for its share of a nation's resources.

PART II. THE SUSTAINABLE DESTINATION

While Part I of this chapter has focused primarily on the theoretical foundations of economic competitiveness, we have continually stressed that destination competitiveness must be viewed from a long-term perspective. This has substantial implications for the way in which a destination is planned, developed and managed.

In the business field, where the concept of competitiveness has received much attention, it has become a tautology to talk of *sustainable competitiveness*. That is, a firm may not be regarded as competitive unless it is able to sustain any advantages it possesses over the long term. Those companies and shareholders who take a much longer-term view of company performance look favourably on investment, research and development, product innovation, employee retention and career planning, etc. By comparison, companies that reward market share, growth and profit performance in the short term, discounting the promise of future profits, tend to encourage cost-cutting, downsizing and the milking of profits. The result is that such a short-term view, while perhaps improving the bottom line for the present reporting period, may encourage actions that harm rather than foster long-term performance. Particularly from a tourism perspective, the concept of competitiveness makes little sense if it borrows from the future in this way, because success and true prosperity are necessarily built over the long term.

A destination which, for short-term profit, permits the rape and pillage of the natural capital on which tourism depends is destined for long-term failure. It is simply a matter of time before the destination's natural capital will be depleted. Some destinations may last longer than others, but in the end the destination's ability to appeal to an ever-demanding, ever-consuming market will decline to an uncompetitive level. It is not only natural capital that must be sustained: all the elements of the core attractors, the supporting factors and the infrastructure must also be maintained and managed in a sustainable manner if market and economic competitiveness is to be maintained.

Because of the fundamental importance of sustainability to the ongoing competitiveness of a destination, it is essential that destination managers understand the concept and how it can be realized. It is with this concern clearly in mind that this chapter seeks to provide readers with the fundamentals they will require in order to meet their managerial responsibilities of stewardship – of caring for their destination in a way that will preserve and enhance its well-being for residents and its appeal for the visitors of tomorrow.

The Birth and Evolution of Sustainable Tourism

Given the relative newness of tourism and tourism management as a field of study, it should not be surprising that the concept of sustainable tourism represents an even newer area of study. This newness, combined with rapid growth, led to the introduction less than a decade ago of a new journal focusing on sustainable tourism as a field of study. In the editors' pioneering introductory article in the *Journal of Sustainable Tourism* (Bramwell and Lane, 1993), they traced the origins of sustainable tourism back to the publication in 1973 of *Ecological Principles for Economic Development* (Dasmann et al., 1973). They further noted that many of the ideas in this work were developed at the International Union for the Conservation of Nature and Natural Resources (IUCN) and referenced in the *World Conservation Strategy* published in 1980 (IUCN, 1980). The subsequent report of the World Commission on Environment and Development (WCED, 1987), frequently referred to as the *Bruntland Report*, is now viewed by many as the next pivotal point in the recognition of sustainable development as a fundamental principle for managing global development. Henry and Jackson (1996) believe that the more general contribution of the holistic analysis arising from 'green' thinking is also responsible, at least in part, for the range of differing perspectives on sustainable tourism – specifically, those of Dobson (1990), Leland (1983), Naess (1990) and O'Riordon

(1981). Henry and Jackson (1996) also point out that 'the key tool of the environmental manager is environmental impact assessment, or project appraisal'. They also emphasize that project appraisal techniques are not limited to environmental impact assessments, but also enable the evaluation of physical, cultural, economic, sociostructural and managerial/employment impacts. This latter point is particularly significant in the context of tourism, since it draws attention to the fact that sustainable tourism involves ensuring sustainability with respect to all the above dimensions, not only the environment. They further point out the need to assess the cumulative impacts of tourism across all projects on an ongoing basis, and provide examples of the approaches of Goodall (1994) and Green and Hunter (1992).

From a destination management standpoint, it is important to appreciate that sustainable tourism does not attempt simply to control development, but that it also seeks to encourage the development and promotion of appropriate forms of tourism – many of which can actually enhance the environmental, social and cultural well-being of a destination in addition to increasing its economic prosperity.

A number of other authors have made significant contributions to our efforts to understand tourism from a sustainability perspective. One of the earlier contributions was made by McKercher (1993), who identified what he terms 'some fundamental truths about tourism' in relation to its social and environmental impacts. These truths are summarized in Table 2.2. McKercher argues that the recognition and understanding of them can play a key role in developing future sustainable tourism policies or, at a minimum, offer valuable insights into the causes and nature of most of the impacts of tourism.

Hunter (1997) offers yet another perspective which merits consideration and understanding by destination managers and policy makers. He asserts that the current paradigm of sustainable tourism development is based on the principles that this kind of development should:

- meet the needs and wants of the local host community in terms of improved living standards and quality of life;
- satisfy the demands of tourists and the tourism industry and continue to attract them in order to meet the first aim; and
- safeguard the environmental resource base for tourism, encompassing natural, built and cultural components, in order to achieve both of the preceding aims.

While Hunter acknowledges that these principles appear to be laudable, he asserts that they are overly tourism-centric and parochial, leading to the creation of tension between the general desire for sustainable development and a more specific search for sustainable tourism development. He further argues that people working in tourism need to re-examine their views on the appropriate scope and scale of tourism, as well as their ability to isolate or contain its impacts. Aside from providing a number of theoretical issues for debate, Hunter notes that, from a practical perspective, the adoption of a less parochial view of sustainable tourism can help ensure that local development policies and objectives for sustainable tourism will rest within broader sustainable development goals at both the regional and the national level.

Table 2.2. Some fundamental truths about tourism (from McKercher, 1993).

- As an individual activity, tourism consumes resources, creates waste and has specific infrastructure needs
- As a consumer of resources, it has the ability to overconsume resources
- Tourism, as a resource-dependent industry, must compete for scarce resources to ensure its survival
- Tourism is a private-sector-dominated industry, with investment decisions being based predominantly on profit maximization
- Tourism is a multifaceted industry, and as such it is almost impossible to control
- Tourists are consumers, not anthropologists
- Tourism is entertainment
- Unlike other industrial activities, tourism generates income by importing clients rather than exporting its product

Sharpley (2000) also questions and examines the true meaning of sustainable tourism and its relationship to its origins in the broader field of sustainable development. He presents a general conceptual model of sustainable development and examines how sustainable tourism satisfies the principles and objectives of this model. While the details of his comparative analysis are too extensive for the present purpose, his basic model (Table 2.3) will be of interest to managers wishing to implement a sustainable tourism philosophy and supporting programmes.

Yet another common issue that arises in efforts to plan and implement sustainable tourism programmes is a blurring of the distinction between sustainable tourism and what Hardy and Beeton (2001) refer to as 'maintainable tourism'. This distinction is much more than semantic, particularly since they assert that maintainable tourism exists when the status quo is being managed simply to deal with concerns related to short-term trends and impacts rather than to address the underlying fundamentals of sustainability. Hardy and Beeton argue that the true nexus between maintainable and sustainable tourism is an understanding of what (destination) stakeholders perceive sustainable tourism to be. They then proceed to pursue their argument logically by asserting the need to formally measure the views of major stakeholder groups (host population, tourist, guest, tourism organizations (operators/regulators) and the natural environment (Cater, 1995)) with a view to achieving balanced tourism. In the realistic situation in which no one element (subjective well-being, environmental health, cultural health or visitor satisfaction) predominates, it will be necessary to make trade-offs among the objectives of each of the stakeholder groups. In short, Hardy and Beeton (2001) are asserting that stakeholder analysis is a logical method for identifying the multiple subjective opinions of those with a stake in tourism, and for planning it in a way that will avoid any costs associated with poor planning and management. They further note the argument of Grimble and Wellard (1997) that a significant advantage of stakeholder analysis is that it provides a way of improving

Table 2.3. A model of sustainable development: principles and objectives (from Sharpley, 2000, referenced from Streeten, 1977; WCED,1987; Pearce *et al.*, 1989; IUCN/UNEP/WWF, 1991).

Fundamental principles	• Holistic approach: development and environmental issues integrated within a global social environment • Futurity: focus on long-term capacity for continuance of the global ecosystem • Equity: development that is fair and equitable and that provides opportunities for access to and use of resources for all members of all societies, both in the present and the future
Development objectives	• Improvement of the quality of life for all people: education, life expectancy, opportunities to fulfil potential • Satisfaction of basic needs; concentration on the nature of what is provided rather than income • Self-reliance: political freedom and local decision making for local needs • Endogenous development
Sustainability objectives	• Sustainable population levels • Minimal depletion of non-renewable natural resources • Sustainable use of renewable resources • Pollution emissions within the assimilative capacity of the environment
Requirements for sustainable development	• Adoption of a new social paradigm relevant to sustainable living • International and national political and economic systems dedicated to equitable development and resource use • Technological systems that can search continuously for new solutions to environmental problems • Global alliance facilitating integrated development policies at local, national and international levels

our understanding of environmental and developmental problems.

Sustainable Tourism: a Comprehensive Examination

Readers wishing a more comprehensive, fully integrated review of the history and content of sustainable tourism are referred to Swarbrooke's excellent treatise on the topic (Swarbrooke, 1999). Some of the highlights of Swarbrooke's review are listed below.

- He gives a very useful examination of different definitions that have been adopted in various settings. A parallel review is provided by Butler (1999) (Table 2.4). After examining all the various definitions, the definition that we like is as follows. Sustainable tourism is tourism that is 'economically viable, but does not destroy the resources on which the future of tourism will depend, notably the physical environment, and the social fabric of the host community' (Swarbrooke, 1999, p. 13). Swarbrooke also provides a useful summary of the relationship between sustainable tourism and other terms (Fig. 2.5).

- He provides an insightful summary of the key issues that are part of the ongoing debate about whether sustainable tourism is a truly practical approach to tourism management in general, and – relevant to our perspective – a viable philosophy of destination management (Fig. 2.6).

- He also provides a very useful summary of the principles behind sustainable tourism management, as originally proposed by Bramwell et al. (1996) (Table 2.5).

Fig. 2.5. The relationship between sustainable tourism and other terms (from Swarbrooke, 1999).

Table 2.4.   Definitions of sustainable tourism (from Butler, 1999).

- Tourism that meets the needs of present tourists and host regions while protecting and enhancing opportunity for the future (World Tourism Organization, 1993)
- Sustainable tourism is tourism and associated infrastructure that: both now and in the future operate within natural capacities for the regeneration and future productivity of natural resources; recognize the contribution that people and communities, customs and lifestyles, make to the tourism experience; accept that these people must have an equitable share in the economic benefits of local people and communities in the host areas (Eber, 1992)
- Tourism that can sustain local economies without damaging the environment on which it depends (Countryside Commission, 1995)
- It must be capable of adding to the array of economic opportunities open to people without adversely affecting the structure of economic activity. Sustainable tourism ought not to interfere with existing forms of social organization. Finally, sustainable tourism must respect the limits imposed by ecological communities (Payne, 1993)
- Sustainable tourism in parks (and other areas) must primarily be defined in terms of sustainable ecosystems (Woodley, 1993)
- Sustainable tourism is tourism which develops as quickly as possible, taking into account current accommodation capacity, the local population and the environment;
  Tourism that respects the environment and as a consequence does not aid its own disappearance. This is especially important in saturated areas; and
  Sustainable tourism is responsible tourism (quoted in Bramwell et al., 1996)

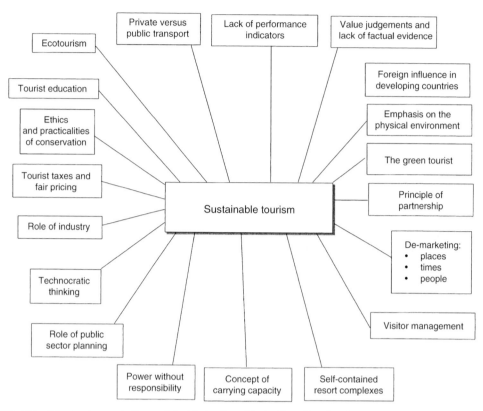

Fig. 2.6. The key issues in the sustainable tourism debate (from Swarbrooke, 1999).

Table 2.5. Principles behind sustainable tourism management (from Bramwell *et al.*, 1996).

- The approach sees policy, planning and management as appropriate and, indeed, essential responses to the problems of natural and human resource misuse in tourism
- The approach is generally not anti-growth, but it emphasizes that there are limitations to growth and that tourism must be managed within these limits
- Long-term rather than short-term thinking is necessary
- The concerns of sustainable tourism management are not just environmental, but are also economic, social, cultural, political and managerial
- The approach emphasizes the importance of satisfying human needs and aspirations, which entails a prominent concern for equity and fairness
- All stakeholders need to be consulted and empowered in tourism decision making, and they also need to be informed about sustainable development issues
- While sustainable development should be a goal for all policies and actions, putting the ideas of sustainable tourism into practice means recognizing that in reality there are often limits to what will be achieved in the short and medium term
- An understanding of how market economies operate, of the cultures and management procedures of private sector businesses and of public and voluntary sector organizations, and of the values and attitudes of the public is necessary in order to turn good intentions into practical measures
- There are frequently conflicts of interest over the use of resources, which means that in practice trade-offs and compromises may be necessary
- The balancing of costs and benefits in decisions on different courses of action must extend to considering how much different individuals and groups will gain or lose

The Parallel Emergence of Ecotourism

Just as the concept and practice of sustainable tourism has taken root and grown over the past two decades, so has the concept of ecotourism. Ashton (1991), however, has questioned the extent to which we have witnessed the growth of a truly new phenomenon or simply the application of a new label to existing forms of tourism. Indeed, Swarbrooke notes that 'some writers use the two terms interchangeably, while others see the terms as diametrically opposed' (1999, p. 318). Readers wishing to examine ecotourism in the same depth as Swarbrooke examines sustainable tourism are referred to an equally excellent treatment by Fennel (1999). Fennel offers insights into the ecotourism phenomenon on the basis of an understanding derived from its roots. He views ecotourism as being based on conservation on three fronts: the maintenance of harmony between humankind and nature, the efficient use of resources and a spirituality that seeks to save resources from use rather than saving them for use. Fennel further stresses that ecotourism relies on smaller, locally oriented developments that are built as part of the environment instead of overwhelming it (p. 135).

There are two other aspects of the Fennel examination of ecotourism that are particularly valuable from a destination manager's viewpoint. First, he highlights Liu's (1994) policy implementation framework for ecotourism (Table 2.6); second, he summarizes Nelson's (1991) conservation management categories (Table 2.7).

Given the ongoing debate, the issue of practically defining and measuring the nature and extent of ecotourism is not easily resolved. However, it has been addressed by Bottril and Pearce (1995). As in the case of tourism in general, the issue arises as to whether ecotourism should be defined from a demand (user/tourist) or supply (resource base/operator) perspective. Clearly, answers must be found to these questions as ecotourism has become a concept that is used widely and daily. Destination managers must decide whether or not this is a market or a market segment, to be pursued or ignored.

The foregoing review of theoretical and conceptual dimensions of sustainable tourism would not be complete without including Butler's (1999) state-of-the-art review of sustainable tourism. While somewhat esoteric in tone, Butler's review does provide some insights and challenges that reflect his thorough understanding of tourism as a social and economic phenomenon. After the obligatory examination of the various definitions of sustainable tourism summarized in Table 2.4, he proceeds to first assert that much of the 'definitional confusion' arises from the imprecise and conflicting definitions of the concept, and particularly the need to distinguish between 'sustainable tourism' and 'the development of tourism based on the principles of sustainable development'. He subsequently argues, giving credit to Craik (1995), for the need to ensure that the concept of sustainable tourism avoids an exclusive focus on the physical environment so as to incorporate a parallel emphasis on the human environment. In making this argument, he emphasizes the position of Bramwell et al. (1996), who identify some seven dimensions of sustainability (environmental, cultural, political, economic, social, managerial and governmental). While all seven of these dimensions may not be of equal significance, the reader should keep in mind the principle of multidimensionality when attempting to understand and implement a sustainable tourism philosophy.

Butler's review contains two additional points that are essential to an understanding of sustainable tourism. First, he stresses the need for policy makers and destination managers to recognize that sustainable tourism includes an implicit obligation to acknowledge that there must be limits to growth in tourism development. While this assertion may not be accepted by everyone, it must at least be refuted in a logical, consistent and justifiable manner.

Secondly, Butler emphasizes that, in a sustainable tourism world, 'a commitment to monitoring is essential'. It is for this reason that our framework for destination management includes a destination policy component that forces destination monitoring and evaluation.

Table 2.6. Policy implementation framework (from Fennel, 1999, as reproduced from Liu, 1994).

Development objectives	Establish economic, ecological and socio-cultural objectives in consultation with local communities; designate specific areas for ecotourism development
Inventories	Survey and analyse the region's ecology, history, culture, economy, resources, land use and tenure; inventory and evaluate existing and potential ecotourist attractions, activities, accommodation, facilities and transportation; construct or consolidate development policies and plans, especially tourism material plans
Infrastructure and facilities	Provide the appropriate infrastructure and facilities, avoiding a reliance on foreign capital; establish means to assist the private sector in developing ecotourism enterprises in line with ecological and cultural standards
Market	Analyse present and future domestic and international ecotourism markets and establish marketing goals; know and understand the market in achieving goals; assist the private sector in its development of marketing strategies
Carrying capacity	Strive to understand the social and ecological limits of use of an area through appropriate management and research; establish social and ecological indicators of use and impact; implement an appropriate pre-formed planning and management framework
Development	Establish a development policy giving consideration to balanced economic, ecological and social factors; form a development plan on the basis of attractions, transportation and ecotourism regions; assist developers to plan and build ecologically
Economic	Consider ways to enhance economic benefits; conduct present and future economic analyses; ensure that profits are made, locals benefit and public revenues are self-sustaining
Environment	Consider ways to enhance the impact of ecotourism on the resource base; link ecotourism with other resource conservation measures (e.g. parks and protected areas)
Culture	Evaluate the socio-cultural impact of ecotourism, prevent negative impacts and reinforce positive outcomes; empower local people to become decision makers; conduct an audit of social impacts
Standards	Apply development and design standards to facilities and accommodation; facilitate the adherence to standards by providing financial or tax incentives and access to specialists
Human resources	Promote job creation and entrepreneurship; establish community awareness programmes; provide adequate education and training for local people
Organization	Establish a working relationship between public, private and not-for-profit organizations
Regulations and monitoring	Establish legislation/regulations to promote ecotourism development, through support for tourism organizations, tour operators, accommodation; establish facility standards
Data system and implementation	Establish an integrated ecotourism data system for continuous operation that provides research and marketing information; identify ecotourism implementation techniques; and collaborate with private industry and educational institutions in implementation

Table 2.7. Categories for conservation management (adapted from Nelson, 1991).

Category I	Scientific Reserve/Strict Nature Reserve
Category II	National Park
Category III	Natural Monument/Natural Landmark
Category IV	Nature Conservation Reserve/ Managed Nature Reserve/Wildlife Sanctuary
Category V	Protected Landscape or Seascape
Category VI	Resource Reserve (Interim Conservation Unit)
Category VII	Natural Biotic Area/Anthropological Reserve
Category VIII	Multiple Use Management Area/ Managed Resource Area
Category IX	Biosphere Reserve
Category X	World Heritage Site
Category XI	Wetlands of International Importance

The World Tourism Organization and Ecotourism

As the moral leader of world tourism, the World Tourism Organization (WTO) has recognized the need to support the principles of sustainable tourism and ecotourism. This leadership has been clearly demonstrated through its sponsorship of the 2002 World Summit on Ecotourism, held in Quebec City, Canada. In addition, the WTO has spearheaded an initial attempt to determine the size and significance of the ecotourism market and has recently commissioned research to provide global estimates of the ecotourism-generating capacity of seven countries: Germany, the USA, the UK, Canada, Spain, France and Italy. A particularly laudable feature of this research was an attempt to coordinate the definition of ecotourism and the research method used by each of the seven experts who conducted the research for the generating countries. Despite this attempt to achieve standardization, the WTO warns readers that the concept of ecotourism was found to vary from one country to another. For this reason, they further caution readers to consider the results as general trends relative to the ecotourism market rather than as absolute reference data. With the above countries clearly in mind, the WTO study *The US Ecotourism Market* (WTO, 2002) was based on the US Department of Commerce's International Trade Administration In-Flight Survey and a survey of US ecotourism operators.

The study of US travellers to overseas countries and Mexico revealed that in 1996 (the first year the category of ecotourism was added), 4.8% of US outbound air passengers reported that they participated in environmental or ecological excursions. By 1999, the percentage had dropped to 4.2% of the total, although preliminary data for 2000 indicate that the percentage has risen back to the 5% range.

An in-flight survey of inbound passengers reveals essentially similar results to those of the outbound survey. In both 1999 and 2000, only 3% of the foreign visitors flying into the USA participated in environmental or ecological excursions.

The authors of the US study note, however, that 'nature tourism', which primarily involves visitors to national parks, is significantly larger than ecotourism. Specifically, some 20% of foreign travellers visited US parks. However, only 8% of outbound American air travellers visited national parks overseas.

The WTO study of US ecotourism provides an interesting practical typology of ecotourism products.

- *By destination* – that is, the countries that appear to be considered as ecotourism destinations. Table 2.8 shows the destination of US ecotourists in comparison with all leisure tourists in 1999. Since the sample of ecotourists responding to this question was relatively small, the percentage of ecotourists must be considered illustrative rather than definitive.
- *By level of service offered* (high-end/ luxury, mid-level, budget-oriented) – the survey of US ecotourism operators indicated that a slight majority of operators targeted the mid-level market. However, only about one-third of ecotourists appear to travel with operators. So an important question remains regarding the level of service being sought by independent travellers.

Table 2.8. Main destination of ecotourists and all leisure travellers. Data are percentages of respondents in each category (from WTO, 2002).

Destination	Ecotourists	All tourists
Western Europe	**16.7**	**36.7**
Germany	2.0	4.6
France	1.9	4.4
United Kingdom	3.9	10.4
Eastern Europe	0.5	1.7
Caribbean	**12.4**	**14.5**
Bahamas	2.3	4.3
Jamaica	5.1	5.1
South America	**12.4**	**6.5**
Argentina	1.2	0.8
Brazil	1.5	1.6
Chile	1.5	0.4
Ecuador	1.5	0.7
Peru	3.9	1.11
Central America	**30.9**	**21.7**
Belize	0.8	0.1
Costa Rica	4.0	1.0
Other (includes Mexico)	25.8	19.4
Africa	**5.2**	**1.4**
Kenya	1.8	0.2
South Africa	7.7	0.4
Middle East	**2.7**	**3.0**
Asia	**9.6**	**3.0**
India	2.3	1.3
Oceania	**10.0**	**2.6**
Australia	5.4	1.6
New Zealand	3.9	0.8

- *By the nature of the ecotourist's travel arrangements* (free and independent travellers and group travellers) – probably account for about two-thirds of the US outbound ecotourism market, so tour operator surveys miss a substantial portion of the market.
- *By ecotourism demographics* (age, income, education, gender) – ecotourists are generally believed to be somewhat older and better educated and to have higher incomes than the average traveller, and appear to contain a slight preponderance of males.

Again, the reader is cautioned that the foregoing data cannot be considered definitive. At best, they are illustrative of US ecotourists.

The WTO study *The German Ecotourism Market* was based on the same definition of ecotourism as that provided by the WTO *Terms of Reference*:

> Ecotourism includes all nature-based forms of tourism in which the main motivation of the tourist is the observation and appreciation of nature.
>
> (WTO, 2001b, p. 4)

An especially interesting aspect of the German study was the impact of language on the interpretation of the definition of sustainable tourism, an impact in which the difference between the terms *Naturtourismus* and *Ökotourismus* is particularly significant and meaningful.

'*Naturtourismus*' refers to a market segment whose distinguishing feature is that it engages in nature-related activities in attractive natural settings, preferably in protected areas. The spectrum ranges from science tourism to wildlife-watching and nature photography, to consumptive activities (fishing and hunting) as well as sports and adventure tourism.

'*Ökotourismus*' refers to forms of *Naturtourismus* that attempt to responsibly minimize negative environmental impacts and socio-cultural changes, help to finance protected areas and create sources of income for the local population.

This German definition is clearly different from the WTO definition. The latter would seem to correspond to the German concept of *Naturtourismus*, although *Naturtourismus* extends beyond nature and wildlife-watching and includes nearly all forms of tourism in natural settings.

The German understanding of *Ökotourismus*, on the other hand, tends to include those aspects of tourism commonly described as sustainable tourism: minimizing negative effects on people and the natural environment while ensuring adequate economic profit.

To put things in perspective, the difference between *Naturtourismus* and *Ökotourismus* can be summed up as follows: *Naturtourismus* refers to a specific tourist market segment and a specific class of package – a form of travel to natural areas in which experiencing nature is the focal point. The environmental impact can be positive or negative, but is of little importance. *Ökotourismus*, on the other hand, claims to minimize or avoid negative effects on the environment (programmatic components) and is, in the end, identifiable as such only by its effects.

As a result of this important distinction, of which the German tour operators interviewed were aware (but not particularly pleased with), the results of the German study on *Ökotourismus* must be interpreted with care. Some of the more interesting of these results are listed below.

- For a good half of Germans, experiencing nature is an important factor for a satisfactory holiday trip. This value is, however, not identical with the interest potential for ecotourism, but merely expresses a general attachment to nature among this clientele.
- Around one-third of German holiday-makers are amenable to ecotourism travel and activities in the narrower sense.
- For 8.0% of those questioned, wildlife watching and enjoyment of nature in an unspoiled landscape were the main reason for choosing their travel destination. For a further 6.4% this was the second most important reason.

It should be noted, however, that marked differences were found according to survey locations. The WTO also emphasizes that their attempts at quantification should on no account be understood as a dependable calculation, but only as a rough approximation that must necessarily be verified by more appropriate representative surveys.

A particularly insightful result emanating from the study of the German ecotourism market was the fundamental knowledge that was obtained about motivation related to the environmental aspects of travel. More specifically, the study classified people into four amenability types with respect to the environmental aspects of holiday travel.

- *Type 1: Uncertain rejecters of environmental aspects on holiday* (26.3% of the German population). Opportunities for nature experience tend not to be important to this type, a built-up landscape does not put them off, and expectations of environmental management by tour operators are slight, as is the willingness to make personal contributions towards the preservation of nature; most important is likely to be an intact environment at the destination. This type is mostly very young, has a low level of education and income, is single and is still in education.

- *Type 2: Those unwilling to pay for environmental protection in the holiday area* (29.0% of the German population). This type shows a very slight willingness to pay for environmental protection measures at the holiday location, but otherwise demonstrates a slightly agreeing response pattern and rather an indifferent attitude to environmental aspects. This type is mostly female, over 60 years old, has a relatively low level of education and income, is mostly in retirement and is childless.

- *Type 3: Socially responsible supporters of environmental aspects on holiday* (14.7% of the German population). Especially important to this type is not only the preservation of nature, but above all respect for the way of life and traditions of the locals. Opportunities for nature experiences, on the other hand, are conspicuously and clearly unimportant to this type. These people are mostly middle-aged and have a high level of education and income.

- *Type 4: Nature-experience-oriented supporters of environmental aspects on holiday* (30.0% of the German population). This type corresponds more or less to those interested in ecotourism packages in the narrower sense, as wildlife-watching and nature experience opportunities are particularly important for them. They additionally have great respect for the culture and traditions of the locals. Unspoiled nature and environment have a strong influence on their travelling satisfaction. More frequently than average, they are middle-aged (30–59 years), have a middle to high level of formal education, have a middle to high net household income, are employed and have small children (up to 14 years).

It was concluded that these four amenability types might provide a useful taxonomy for an international comparison of ecotourism clients. At the same time, it was stressed that the classification represents *attitude* and not *behaviour* types.

The third set of ecotourism study results that were available at the time of writing related to the British ecotourism market. Although all of the WTO ecotourism market studies (as noted above) were given the same terms of reference, the findings of the British study provided some particularly unique perspectives and detailed findings. Those we consider to be most meaningful are outlined below.

As in the German study, the definition of ecotourism in the British report covers two distinct levels.

- The term 'nature-based tourism' is used to mean 'forms of tourism in which the main motivation of the tourist is the observation and appreciation of nature'.
- 'Ecotourism' is used to mean forms of tourism that have the following characteristics:
  - they are all nature-based and the main motivation of the tourists is the observation and appreciation of nature as well as the traditional cultures prevailing in natural areas;
  - they contain educational and interpretation features;
  - they are generally, but not exclusively, organized by specialized tour operators for small groups, and service-provider partners at the destinations tend to be small, locally owned businesses;
  - they minimize negative impacts upon the natural and sociocultural environment;
  - they support the maintenance of natural areas which are used as ecotourism attractions by:
  a) generating economic benefits for host communities, organizations and authorities managing natural areas with conservation purposes;
  b) providing alternative employment and income opportunities for local communities;

c) increasing awareness of the conservation of natural and cultural assets among both local people and tourists.

When the tourism operators responding to the survey on which the study was based were asked to assess the relative importance of different elements of the definition of ecotourism, they responded as shown in Table 2.9.

It is useful to note that the Association of British Travel Agents members were far more sceptical of the concept in that 'Most of the agents present commented negatively on the word and mentioned that when they first saw it on the Agenda and heard it from the researcher, they were not interested. They commented that "eco" makes them think of "eco-warriors" and the extreme end of the UK green movement' (WTO, 2001c, p. 20).

At the Association of Independent Tour Operators (AITO) meeting, ecotourism was felt to be a hangover from the past and to be a meaningless brand name that clients would recognize as having no meaning. Operators felt that, were any AITO member to use the word 'ecotourism' as a marketing device in their literature, it would be more likely to work against them than to attract clients on the basis of any perceived ethical or environmental credentials.

Table 2.9. Relative importance of different elements of the definition of ecotourism.

	Relative ranking of importance
Index value	4
Education/interpretation	3
Specialized tour operators, small groups, destination service providers small and locally owned	2
Provides alternative employment and income opportunities for local communities	1
Minimizes negative impacts on the natural and sociocultural environment	1
Generates economic benefits for host communities, organizations and natural areas with conservation purposes	1
Increases awareness of conservation of natural and cultural assets, among both locals and tourists	1

The 'eco' prefix was considered by many participants to have didactic and self-righteous connotations. It was felt that the word confronts potential clients with responsibilities or demands and is somewhat preachy, especially where clients are buying holidays – and therefore a certain level of escapism.

The foregoing insights into industry perceptions of the term are important in that they demonstrate some of the realities that those responsible for destination management should anticipate and, where necessary, address.

Despite these attitudes of industry operators in a survey of package holidays respondents, 85% of the sample said it was important to them that their holidays did not damage the environment, 68% felt it important that their holiday benefited the people of the destination visited, and 77% said that they wanted their holiday to include visits to experience local culture and foods. In brief, there appears to be a fairly substantial difference between industry operators and vacationers in their attitudes to what we call 'ecotourism'. The British operators saw ecotourism as a small market niche and only some 12% used the term 'ecotourism' in their marketing. At least from a UK perspective, then, ecotourism has a long way to go before being fully accepted.

Some concluding observations

Because the WTO studies represent one of the most comprehensive and intensive examinations of ecotourism, we have attempted to provide an indication of the nature of both their specific results and the richness of their total findings. Despite this, given the limitations imposed by the focus of this book, we have been able to include only a superficial sample of the findings from three of the countries in the total study. We encourage readers who wish to understand the complexity of the topic to review these studies in much greater depth, since we believe they represent an empirical landmark in the field. We feel it only appropriate to conclude this review by presenting (Table 2.10) an excerpt from the British study that cited the 'Code for Travellers' that the publisher of *Rough Guides* will print

as a page in every one of its new guidebooks. While it is not unique, it does provide a summary of what many consider ecotourism to be all about.

Managing Tourism from a Sustainability Perspective

Regardless of how one defines environmentally respectful tourism, it must, like all tourism, be managed effectively. To this end, as our model emphasizes, there is clearly a need for destination managers to develop a framework for monitoring the impacts of tourism (Faulkner and Tidswell, 1997). It is perhaps not surprising that much of the interest in managing tourism from a sustainability perspective focuses on the ecological dimension of sustainability, given the level of concern expressed globally about mankind's pressure on the Earth's environment. However, we contend that there are four primary pillars of sustainable tourism and that appropriate policy and management solutions must be found for each of them if true sustainability is to be achieved. These four primary pillars of sustainability are, in our view, the ecological, economic, sociocultural and political/governance environments.

Ecological sustainability

The ecological or natural environment is a major attraction for many destinations. Often, the experience of a unique natural environment represents the core of a destination's tourism product – the African savannah, the Canadian Rocky Mountains, the Australian outback and coral reefs, the South American rainforests, the Norwegian fjords, the canyonlands of America. For many destinations, these natural phenomena represent the lifeblood of their tourism industries, and any decline in their value will have an adverse effect on the destination.

Residents of these destinations have the most at stake in protection and preservation of their natural environments. But the tourism industry also has an important role to play, not just in terms of ensuring that any tourism

Table 2.10.   Tourism concern (from WTO, 2001c).

Exploring the world

Being sensitive to these ideas means getting more out of your travels – and giving more back to the people you meet and the places you visit

- **Learn about the country you're visiting**
  Start enjoying your travels before you leave by tapping into as many sources of information as you can.
- **The cost of your holiday**
  Think about where your money goes – be fair and realistic about how cheaply you travel. Try and put money into local people's hands – drink local beer or fruit juice rather than imported brands and stay in locally owned accommodation.
  Haggle with humour and not aggressively. Pay what something is worth to you and remember how wealthy you are compared to local people.
- **Culture**
  Open your mind to new cultures and traditions – it will transform your experience.
  Think carefully about what's happening in terms of your clothes and the way you behave. You will earn respect and be more readily welcomed by local people.
  Respect local laws and attitudes towards drugs and alcohol that vary in different countries and communities. Think about the impact you could have. 'The effect on the local community of travellers taking drugs when visiting the hilltribes of Thailand can be devastating. People become trapped into selling drugs to travellers and become addicted themselves, especially young people who want to be like the travellers.' Jaranya Daengnoy, REST.
- **How big is your footprint? – minimize your environmental impact**
  Think about what happens to your rubbish – take biodegradable products and a water filter bottle. Be sensitive to limited resources like water, fuel and electricity.
  Help preserve local wildlife and habitats by respecting rules and regulations, such as sticking to footpaths, not standing on coral and not buying products made from endangered plants or animals.
- **Guidebooks**
  Use your guidebook as a starting point, not the only source of information. Talk to local people, then discover your own adventure!
- **Photography**
  Don't treat people as part of the landscape, they may not want their picture taken. Put yourself in their shoes, ask first and respect their wishes.

The ideas expressed in this code were developed by and for independent travellers. They show what individuals can do to play their part towards Tourism Concern's goal of more ethical and fairly traded tourism. For more information see Tourism Concern's website: www.tourismconcern.org.uk

development minimizes harm to the ecology, but also (and perhaps even more importantly) by providing an economic incentive that encourages preservation and protection.

Some environments are much more unique, fragile, finite and non-renewable than others. Hence there are no universal formulae for managing tourism's negative and positive environmental impacts. Unique solutions are required for unique problems. This implies that each destination must develop its own strategy for sustainable tourism development tuned to its own ecological constraints. In essence, the destination must play the role of steward of the environment in concert with other organizations charged with similar responsibilities.

In pursuing ecological sustainability, the tourism sector should avoid simplistic assumptions about what constitutes environmentally friendly tourism. Ecotourists who visit and experience special, pristine and often remote environments but who minimize their impact by leaving little trace of their visit are to be congratulated. But how are we to judge environmental friendliness? Surely, if one type of tourism (type A) is more environmentally friendly than another (type B), it must mean that as every type B tourist is converted to a type A tourist, the environment will be better off. When viewed in this way, however, who is the more environmentally friendly: the ecotourist in the rain forests of the Amazon or the sun worshipper on the beaches of Rio de Janeiro?

Economic sustainability

As one element of a destination's economy, tourism must help support a viable economic base. A healthy economy enables a country, region or city to pursue initiatives designed to enhance the quality of life of its residents. Maslow's 'hierarchy of needs'[1] tells us that unless physiological needs are satisfied (i.e. food, shelter, basic health-care, etc.) humans are unlikely to concern themselves with higher-order needs. This partly explains why, in Third World countries, environmental protection is low on the list of priorities. We view a healthy economy as critical to a healthy ecology.

So any tourism strategy must be capable of meeting the economic needs and aspirations of residents over the long term. If it is to do so, the following considerations may be influential in determining economic sustainability.

- *Of benefit to many, not just a few.* Costs and benefits should be reasonably evenly spread over the relevant population. Creating an environment in which some individuals benefit handsomely from tourism development while the lives of many deteriorate is untenable. For example, certain forms of tourism development can result in land speculation pushing up the prices for land and increasing rents (both domestic and commercial) and property taxes. Competition for resources may increase prices. Tourists are often prepared or able to pay higher prices for food and other goods.
- *Utilization of local labour.* Residents are more supportive of tourism development and may be prepared to tolerate minor adverse consequences if tourism is an important source of local employment. Returns to local labour filter through much of the local economy. Both direct employment and the indirect employment arising from demand derived from tourism are important. Depending on the availability of local labour and the skills and knowledge resources that are required, the importation of outside labour should not be excessive. Efforts to establish local training programmes will probably be viewed favourably by residents. Tourism development often draws into a region low-skilled people seeking work. Local residents may resent the influx of these newcomers, not just because they take away jobs but, because they also place extra strain on local services.

- *Job security.* Tourism demand can be highly seasonal. Any efforts to enhance job security will improve economic sustainability. For example, employers should explore opportunities to establish a multiskilled, flexible workforce so that employees can be assigned different tasks throughout the year, such as maintenance during the off-season. To the extent that certain firms experience different patterns of demand, there may also be opportunities for employers to collaborate by sharing employees.

- *Wages, salaries and benefits.* Tourism is often perceived to be a low-skilled, low-income sector. While many of the service jobs in tourism and hospitality may be described in this way, the reality is a little different from the common perception. Indeed, recent research suggests that compensation per employee in travel and tourism is similar to that in other sectors, and is often higher (for a regional and national assessment of travel and tourism's compensation levels, see the World Travel and Tourism Council's 1995 Research Edition of *Travel and Tourism: a New Economic Perspective* (WTTC, 1995)). Tourism supports many higher-income jobs, such as hotel managers, skilled construction workers, architects, consultants, researchers, airline pilots, senior government employees, entrepreneurs and numerous others. Some low-skilled employees are able to make a very good living through tips. An economically sustainable tourism strategy will seek to generate a broad range of employment opportunities.

Sociocultural sustainability

The quality of life in a destination depends on more than just economic well-being. The health and vitality of social and cultural systems and institutions helps to create an environment which residents find meaningful in their pursuit of happiness. They may be prepared to trade economic considerations for quality-of-life aspirations.

When tourists travel, the desire to see, experience and learn something of the destination's sociocultural fabric is typically a central element of their motivation. Notwithstanding the fact that the culture tourists experience is often somewhat artificial or inauthentic, the presence and influence of toursists may create impacts on the host society and its culture. These impacts may be temporary or permanent, positive or negative, minor or substantial, and are often greatest when the *cultural distance* between the host and guest cultures is considerable. This might occur, for example, when an American tourist interacts with tribes in Papua New Guinea. In this sort of extreme example, residents of the destination face the dilemma of reconciling their own cultural experience with the actions, values and attitudes of the visitor.

To be sustainable, a tourism development strategy for the destination must address such sociocultural impacts (Craik, 1995). This should be reflected in the destination's vision and goals encapsulating those values, ideals and dreams of the resident community that provide a sense of place. Kotler *et al.* (1993, p. 81) propose a strategic market planning orientation to 'place marketing' that comprises five stages.

1. *Place audit.* What is the community like today? What are the community's major strengths/weaknesses, opportunities/threats, major issues?
2. *Vision and goals.* What do residents want the community to be or become?
3. *Strategy formulation.* What broad strategies will help the community reach its goals?
4. *Action plan.* What specific actions must the community undertake to carry out its strategies?

5. *Implementation and control.* What must the community do to ensure successful implementation?

For some destinations, the significance and role of tourism development in this process, relative to other industrial sectors, may be rather minor (e.g. Chicago), but in places where tourism represents a sizable industry (e.g. Hawaii), tourism issues may be paramount. Solutions that minimize adverse social and cultural impacts (such as crime, prostitution, alienation of certain segments of the population, trivialization of culture and the disintegration of a way of life), while fostering an interest and pride in those things that define a culture or society without placing it in a time warp, present sustainable choices.

Political sustainability

Political sustainability is rarely identified as one of the pillars of sustainability. Yet we feel that it is potentially critical to the acceptability of any solution (Brown and Essex, 1997; Ritchie, 1999). One might argue that if a strategy for tourism destination development is ecologically, economically and socioculturally sustainable, it will probably be acceptable politically. But there is often little consensus or agreement about how one determines sustainability and consequently there is much room for disagreement. It is often a philosophical question, but one that creates much political debate.

In democratic countries, governments tend to reserve their powers to deal with issues at the margins of human behaviour, and because politicians in democracies survive on the basis of widespread support, the political process tends to ensure that political views follow economic, sociocultural and ecological issues and concerns. However, this pattern may not prevail in totalitarian regimes, where the concerns, aspirations and interests of the citizens often seem to collide with the interests and will of the governing elite. In this environment, political acceptability may override all other interests. Yet history has shown that solutions founded on political concerns alone tend not to be truly

Table 2.11. An overall framework for monitoring destination impacts of tourism (from Faulkner and Tidewell, 1997).

Factor 1: Economic and regional development benefits	• The economic benefits of tourism to the region are overrated • Public funding of tourism promotion and facilities is a waste of the ratepayers' money • The use of public funds for tourism promotion and infrastructure development is justified by the benefits this brings to the community • Tourism benefits only a small proportion of the Gold Coast's population • Further tourism development will disadvantage the community and should be discouraged • In general, tourism development brings facilities to the region that improve the quality of life of its residents • Further tourism development is beneficial to the community and should be encouraged • Visitors to the Gold Coast enrich the culture of this area • Overall, tourism reduces the quality of life of Gold Coast residents • I like to see and/or meet visitors to the Gold Coast
Factor 2: Adverse environmental effects	• Increased tourism has caused traffic congestion and made it more difficult to find parking spaces in commercial areas • Tourism has made the Gold Coast a noisier and more congested place in which to live • Tourists are the cause of longer queues and delays in the provision of services in shops and restaurants • Tourism has increased the cost of living on the Gold Coast • Tourism has disrupted the peace and tranquillity of the Gold Coast region • Tourism has resulted in damage to the natural environment of the Gold Coast area • Tourism has resulted in increased litter in our streets and public places
Factor 3: Quality of life and employment opportunities	• Tourism has resulted in Gold Coast residents having a greater range of choice with regard to shopping facilities, restaurants, etc. • Tourism has resulted in a greater range of outdoor and indoor recreational facilities being available to Gold Coast residents • Tourism creates employment opportunities for the Gold Coast region • Tourism brings important economic benefits to the region • Tourism has resulted in a better standard of services being provided by shops, restaurants and other areas of commerce • Tourism has made residents and local public authorities more conscious of the need to maintain and improve the appearance of the area
Factor 4: Improved community environment	• The development of tourism facilities has generally improved the appearance of the area • Tourism has increased the pride of local residents in their city • Tourism has contributed to the conservation of our natural assets • Tourism has made the Gold Coast a more interesting and exciting place in which to live
Factor 5: Cultural erosion	• Servicing visitors from different cultures undermines our own culture • Visitors to the Gold Coast are an intrusion on our lifestyle
Factor 6: Crime	• Tourism has contributed to increased levels of crime and social problems in the Gold Coast region

sustainable. Other public concerns often find a way of expressing themselves in either peaceful, or sometimes violent, ways. The current widespread reaction to the process of globalization is an example where acceptability at higher levels of government does not necessarily meet with similar acceptance by certain segments of the population.

Achieving Sustainable Tourism

The four pillars of sustainability discussed above act as an interdependent system. A particular strategic direction is unlikely to be sustainable if it fails the test of sustainability on any one of the four pillars. Suppose, for example, that the tourism strategy involves exploitation of the ecology at an unsustainable level. The economic structure established to exploit the ecological environment in this way cannot survive because the ecological resources on which it is based will deteriorate over time. A decline in the economic system will, in turn, lead to adverse social and cultural consequences. The resulting political pressures, too, are likely to lead to instability.

Over the last several years, the concept of sustainable development has begun to permeate management practice in the travel and tourism industry. Some destinations have actually introduced codes of practice with the intent of encouraging tourism developers to adopt 'environmentally friendly' practices. One example is provided by the Tourism Industry of Canada (TIAC, 1995). As another example, the Australian Government has developed a National Ecotourism Strategy comprising an accreditation programme and environmental codes of practice (Commonwealth Department of Tourism, 1994). The World Travel and Tourism Council created its Green Globe programme (WTTERC and Hawkins, 1995; WTTC, 1998) to foster improvements in environmental practices and to support an environment research centre. A substantial number of tourism researchers now conduct studies in sustainable tourism, and such research is essential for the successful management of sustainable tourism. The most

fundamental research involves the measuring of the environmental, social, cultural and economic well-being of the destination on an ongoing basis. Faulkner and Tideswell (1997) have reported a framework for monitoring sustainable tourism from an overall destination perspective (Table 2.11). Since the measurement of environmental impact has been a driving force behind the growth of sustainable tourism, the WTO (1995) has developed a special set of indicators emphasizing the environmental impacts of tourism, as summarized by Dymond (1997) and given in Table 2.12.

Creating and Managing a Sustainable Ecotourism Destination

Destination managers who believe that ecotourism is an attractive and competitive option for their destination must clearly understand that, as shown in Fig. 2.7, ecotourists are but one segment of the total market and that ecotourism is just another type of travel experience (Wood, 2002). Nevertheless, the development and management of a competitive destination does involve some specialized approaches that go beyond basic sustainability (UNEP, 2001; UNEP and Wood, 2002). Local participation is especially important, and requires some very basic principles in order to succeed (Table 2.13).

Conclusion

Although much of the traditional concern for sustainability, as related to tourism, has focused on environmentally sensitive areas such as national parks (Butler and Boyd, 2000), we argue that every destination must examine its ability to maintain all dimensions of sustainability (environmental, economic, social, cultural and political) if it is to develop and preserve true competitiveness. We feel that it is appropriate to conclude by repeating the statement we made at the head of this chapter.

Competitiveness without sustainability is illusory.

Table 2.12. Core indicators of sustainable tourism (from Dymond, 1997, sourced and adapted from WTO, 1995).

Core indicator	Specific measures	Generic indicator groupings
Site protection	Category of site protection according to the International Union for the Conservation of Nature and Natural Resources (IUCN) index	Ecological
Stress	Tourist numbers visiting site (per annum/peak month)	Ecological
Use intensity	Intensity of use in peak period (persons/hectare)	Ecological
Social impact	Ratio of tourists to locals (peak period and over time)	Social
Development control	Existence of environmental review procedure or formal controls over development of site and use densities	Planning
Waste management	Percentage of sewage from site receiving treatment (additional indicators may include structural limits of other infrastructural capacity on site, such as water supply)	Ecological
Planning process	Existence of organized regional plan for tourist destination region (including tourism component)	Planning
Critical ecosystems	Number of rare/endangered species	Ecological
Consumer satisfaction	Level of satisfaction by visitors (questionnaire-based)	Economic
Local satisfaction	Level of satisfaction by locals (questionnaire-based)	Social
Tourism contribution to local economy	Proportion of total economic activity generated by tourism only	Economic

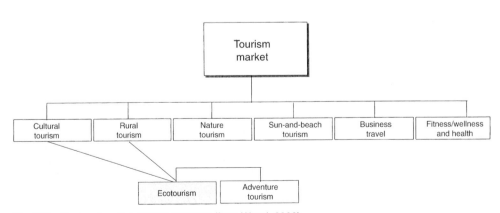

Fig. 2.7. Ecotourism as a market segment (from Wood, 2002).

Table 2.13. Basic steps to encourage community participation (from UNEP, 2001).

Understand the community's role	Communities should exercise control over their growth and development. They will in many cases need technical assistance to make appropriate decisions and should be given adequate information and training in advance. Allocate time, funds, and experienced personnel to work with communities well in advance. Avoid allowing communities to feel they are powerless to influence patterns of development.
Empower communities	Participation is a process that is more than just making communities the beneficiaries of an ecotourism project. Jobs are an important benefit, but they do not replace empowerment. Communities must genuinely participate in the decision-making process. This involves more than just consultation. Processes must be initiated to ensure that communities can manage their own growth and resources wisely.
Urge local project participation	Project managers must identify local leaders, local organizations, key priorities of the community, and ideas, expectations, and concerns local people already have. Information can be gathered for and by the community. The opinions gathered should be disseminated and discussed with the community along with other relevant information such as government market statistics or regional development plans. Training opportunities must be formulated at this phase to help community members gain planning skills, and also the entrepreneurial skills required to run small businesses.
Create stakeholders	Participation can be encouraged at two levels – for individuals and for local organizations. Investment in project development areas should be encouraged, either in cash, labour, or in-kind resources. Developing lodging by local entrepreneurs, and setting standards for local services by local organizations are two good examples.
Link benefits to conservation	The links between ecotourism benefits and conservation objectives need to be direct and significant. Income, employment, and other benefits must promote conservation.
Distribute benefits	Ensure that both the community and individuals benefit from projects.
Identify community leaders	Identify opinion leaders and involve them in the planning and execution of projects. Identify leaders that represent different constituents to ensure that a cross-section of society is involved (including both men and women). Be sure the project has good information on the local social structure. Strategize on the effects of the projects on different social groups and never assume that all parts of society will cooperate or agree. Be strategic and gain appropriate allies early.
Bring about change	Use existing organizations already working in the community to improve its social well-being through economic development. Development associations or local cooperatives are good prospects. Groups involved in organizing recreation can also be good allies. Community participation through institutions is more likely to bring about effective and sustained change.
Understand site-specific conditions	Be aware that authority structures vary greatly in each region. Consensus is not always possible, nor is the full participation of all sectors of society (women are often excluded).
Monitor and evaluate progress	Establish indicators in advance to track tourism's impacts – both positive and negative. Goals such as employment and income levels are only one type of indicator. The project should track negative impacts such as evidence of rapidly escalating prices for local goods, inflation in land prices, antagonism towards visitors, frequency of arrests, change in youth activities, and evidence of drugs, prostitution, and other illicit activities. Ideally, the more the local community is fully involved in ecotourism development, the less these problems should develop. Another important indicator of local involvement is evidence of initiatives within the community to respond to the negative influences of tourism.

(Brandon, 1993)

Note

[1]   Maslow's theory is that human needs are structured as a hierarchy. Higher-order needs become important only when lower-order needs are satisfied. The hierarchy progresses from (lower to higher orders) physiological needs, through security, social and esteem needs to self-actualization needs.

References

Arndt, S.W. and Bouton, L. (1987) *Competitiveness: the United States in World Trade*. American Enterprise Institute for Public Policy Research, Washington, DC.

Ashton, R. (1991) Trends and problems in ecotourism. In: *Proceedings of the 1991 World Congress on Adventure Travel and Eco-Tourism*. Adventure Society, Englewood, Colorado, pp. 22–31.

Baker, J.A. III (1987) Renewing America's competitiveness. In: Barfield, C.E. and Makin, J.H. (eds) *Trade Policy and US Competitiveness*. American Enterprise Institute for Public Policy Research, Washington, DC, pp. 3–10.

Bond, M.E. (1979) The world trade model: invisibles. *International Monetary Fund Staff Papers*, No. 26, pp. 257–333.

Bottril, C.G. and Pearce, D.G. (1995) Ecotourism: towards a key elements approach to operationalising the concept. *Journal of Sustainable Tourism* 3, 45–54.

Bramwell, B. and Lane, B. (1993) Sustainable tourism: an evolving global approach. *Journal of Sustainable Tourism* 1, 1–5.

Bramwell, B., Henry, I., Jackson, G., Prat, A.G., Richards, G. and van der Straaten, J. (eds) (1996) *Sustainable Tourism Management: Principles and Practice*. Tilburg University Press, Tilburg, The Netherlands.

Brown, G. and Essex, S. (1997) Sustainable tourism management: lessons from the edge of Australia. *Journal of Sustainable Development* 5, 294–305.

Buckley, P.J., Mirza, H. and Witt, S.F. (1989) Japan's international tourism in the context of its international economic relations. *Services Industries Journal* 9, 357–382.

Butler, R.W. (1999) Sustainable tourism: a state-of-the-art review. *Tourism Geographies* 1, 7–25.

Butler, R.W. and Boyd, S.W. (2000) *Tourism and National Parks: Issues and Implications*. John Wiley, New York.

Calgary Herald (1997) Airline transfer delay called blow to Montreal. 13 February, p. 15.

Cater, E. (1995) Environmental contradictions in sustainable tourism. *Geographical Journal* 161, 21–28.

Cater, E. and Lowman, G. (1994) *Ecotourism: a Sustainable Option?* John Wiley, New York.

Commonwealth Department of Tourism (1994) *National Ecotourism Strategy*. Commonwealth Department of Tourism, Canberra, Australia.

Craik, J. (1995) Are there cultural limits to tourism? *Journal of Sustainable Tourism* 3, 87–98.

Crouch, G.I. and Ritchie, J.R.B. (1995) Destination competitiveness and the role of the tourism enterprise. *Proceedings of the Fourth Annual World Business Congress*, 13–16 July, Istanbul, Turkey, pp. 43–48.

D'Amore, L.J. (1988) Tourism – the world's peace industry. *Business Quarterly* 52 (3), 78–81.

Dasmann, R.F., Milton, J.D. and Freeman, P.H. (1973) *Ecological Principles for Economic Development*. John Wiley & Sons, London.

Deardorff, A.V. (1985) Comparative advantage and international trade and investment in services. In: Stern, R.M. (ed.) *Trade and Investment in Services: Canada/US Perspectives*. Ontario Economic Council, Toronto, Ontario, Canada, pp. 39–82.

Dobson, A. (1990) *Green Political Thought*. Unwin Hyman, London.

Dymond, S.J. (1997) Indicators of sustainable tourism in New Zealand: a local government perspective. *Journal of Sustainable Tourism* 5, 279–293.

Faulkner, B. and Tideswell, C. (1997) A framework for monitoring community impacts of tourism. *Journal of Sustainable Tourism* 5, 3–28.

Feketekuty, G. (1988) *International Trade in Services: an Overview and Blueprint for Negotiations*. American Enterprise Institute for Public Policy Research, Ballinger Publishing Company, Cambridge, Massachusetts.

Fennel, D. (1999) *Ecotourism: an Introduction*. Routledge, London.

Gold, J.R. and Ward, S.V. (eds) (1994) *Place Promotion: the Use of Publicity and Marketing to Sell Towns and Regions*. John Wiley & Sons, Chichester, UK.

Goodall, B. (1994) Environmental auditing: current best practice. In: Seaton, A.V., Jenkins, C.L., Wood, R.C., Dieke, P., Bennet, M., MacLellan, L.R. and Smith, R. (eds) *Tourism: the State of the Art*. John Wiley & Sons, Chichester, UK.

Gray, H.P. (1989) Services and comparative advantage theory. In: Giersch, H. (ed.) *Services in World Economic Growth*. Institut für Weltwirtschaft an der Universität Kiel, Kiel, Germany, pp. 65–103.

Green, H. and Hunter, C. (1992) The environmental impact assessment of tourism development. In: Johnson, P. and Thomas, B. (eds) *Perspective on Tourism Policy*. Mansell, London, pp. 29–48.

Grimble, R. and Wellard, K. (1997) Stakeholder methodologies in natural resource management: a review of principles, contexts, experiences and opportunities. *Agricultural Systems* 55, 173–193.

Haahti, A.J. (1986) Finland's competitive position as a destination. *Annals of Tourism Research* 13, 11–33.

Hardy, A.L. and Beeton, R.J.S. (2001) Sustainable tourism or maintainable tourism: managing resources for more than average outcomes. *Journal of Sustainable Tourism* 9, 168–192.

Henry, I.P. and Jackson, G.A.M. (1996) Sustainability of management processes and tourism products and contexts. *Journal of Sustainable Tourism* 4, 17–28.

Hunt, S.D. (2000) *A General Theory of Competition*. Sage Publications, Thousand Oaks, California.

Hunter, C. (1997) Sustainable tourism as an adaptive paradigm. *Annals of Tourism Research* 24, 850–867.

IMD (1992) *The World Competitiveness Report*. World Economic Forum and IMD International, Lausanne, Switzerland.

IMD (1994) *The World Competitiveness Report*. World Economic Forum and IMD International, Lausanne, Switzerland.

IMD (1995) *The World Competitiveness Report*. World Economic Forum and IMD International, Lausanne, Switzerland.

IMD (2000) *The World Competitiveness Yearbook: Executive Summary*. International Institute for Management Development, Lausanne, Switzerland.

IUCN (1980) *World Conservation Strategy*. International Union for the Conservation of Nature, Geneva.

IUCN/UNEP/WWF (1991) *Caring for the Earth: a Strategy for Sustainable Living*. International Union for the Conservation of Nature and Natural Resources (IUCN), United Nations Environment Program (UNEP), World Wide Fund for Nature (WWF) World Conservation Union, Gland, Switzerland.

Kotler, P., Haider, D.H. and Rein, I. (1993) *Marketing Places: Attracting Investment, Industry, and Tourism to Cities, States, and Nations*. Free Press, New York.

Krugman, P. (1994) Competitiveness: a dangerous obsession. *Foreign Affairs* 73 (2), 28–42.

Krugman, P. (1996) A country is not a company. *Harvard Business Review* 74 (1), 40–51.

Leland, S. (1983) Feminism and ecology: theoretical connections. In: Caldecott, L. and Leland, S. (eds) *Reclaim the Earth*. Women's Press, London.

Liu, J.C. (1994) *Pacific Island Ecotourism: a Public Policy and Planning Guide*. Office of Territorial and International Affairs, Honolulu, Hawaii.

McKercher, B. (1993) Some fundamental truths about tourism: understanding tourism's social and environmental impacts. *Journal of Sustainable Tourism* 1, 6–16.

Mohan, N.C. (1990) Service exports: better than you think. *Fortune* 4 June, 287–288.

Naess, A. (1990) *Ecology, Community and Lifestyle*. Cambridge University Press, Cambridge.

Nelson, J.G. (1991) Sustainable development, conservation strategies, and heritage. In: Mitchell, B. (ed.) *Resource Management and Development*. Oxford University Press, Oxford, pp. 246–267.

Newall, J.E. (1992) The challenge of competitiveness. *Business Quarterly* 56 (4), 94–100.

Newsome, D., Moore, S.A. and Dowling, R.K. (2002) *Natural Area Tourism: Ecology, Impacts and Management*. Channel View Publications, Clevedon, UK.

O'Riordon, T. (1981) *Environmentalism*. Pion, London.

Palmer, J.D. (1985) Consumer service industry exports: new attitudes and concepts needed for a neglected sector. *Columbia Journal of World Business* 20 (Spring), 69–74.

Pearce, D., Markandya, A. and Barbier, E.B. (1989) *Blueprint for a Green Economy*. Earthscan Publications, London.

Poon, A. (1993) *Tourism, Technology and Competitive Strategy*. CAB International, Wallingford, UK.

Porter, ME. (1985) *Competitive Advantage: Creating and Sustaining Superior Performance*. Free Press, New York.

Porter, M.E. (1990) *The Competitive Advantage of Nations*. Free Press, New York.

Porter, M.E. (1997) Creating tomorrow's advantages. In: Gibson, R. (ed.) *Rethinking the Future*. Free Press, New York.

Porter, M. (1980) *Competitive Strategy: Techniques for Analysing Industries and Competitors*. Free Press, New York.

Richardson, J.B. (1987) A sub-sectoral approach to services' trade theory. In: Orio, G. (ed.) *The Emerging Service Economy*. Pergamon Press, Oxford, pp. 59–82.

Riddle, D.I. (1986) *Service-Led Growth: the Role of the Service Sector in World Development.* Praeger, New York.

Ritchie, J.R.B. (1999) Policy formulation at the tourism/environment interface: insights and recommendations from the Banff-Bow Valley study. *Journal of Tourism Research* 38, 100–110.

Rubel, C. (1996) No mistake about it, Cleveland on a rebound. *Marketing News* (American Marketing Association, Chicago) 1 January, pp. 1, 8.

Ryan, C. (2002) Equity, management, power sharing and sustainability – issues of the 'new tourism'. *Tourism Management* 23, 17–26.

Samli, A.C. and Jacobs, L. (1995) Achieving congruence between macro and micro generic strategies: a framework to create international competitive advantage. *Journal of Macromarketing* 15, 23–32.

Sapir, A. (1982) Trade in services: policy issues for the eighties. *Columbia Journal of World Business* 17 (Fall), 77–83.

Scott, B.R. (1985a) National strategies: key to international competition. In: Scott, B.R. and Lodge, G.C. (eds) *US Competitiveness in the World Economy.* Harvard Business School Press, Boston, Massachusetts, pp. 71–143.

Scott, B.R. (1985b) US competitiveness: concepts, performance, and implications. In: Scott, B.R. and Lodge, G.C. (eds) *US Competitiveness in the World Economy.* Harvard Business School Press, Boston, Massachusetts, pp. 13–70.

Scott, B.R. and Lodge, G.C. (eds) (1985) *US Competitiveness in the World Economy.* Harvard Business School Press, Boston, Massachusetts.

Sharpley, R. (2000) Tourism and sustainable development: exploring the theoretical divide. *Journal of Sustainable Tourism* 8, 1–19.

Siniscalco, D. (1989) Defining and measuring output and productivity in the service sector. In: Giersch, H. (ed.) *Services in World Economic Growth.* Institut für Weltwirtschaft an der Universität Kiel, Kiel, Germany, pp. 38–58.

Spence, A.M. and Hazard, H.A. (eds) (1988) *International Competitiveness.* Ballinger Publishing Company, Cambridge, Massachusetts.

Stabler, M.J. (1997) *Tourism and Sustainability: Principles to Practice.* CAB International, Wallingford, UK.

Streeten, P. (1977) The basic features of a basic needs approach to development. *International Development Review* 3, 8–16.

Swarbrooke, J. (1999) *Sustainable Tourism Management.* CAB International, Wallingford, UK.

The Economist (1994) The economics of meaning. 30 April, pp. 17–18.

TIAC (1995) *Greening the Canadian Tourism Industry.* Tourism Industry Association of Canada, Ottawa, Canada.

Travel Week (Toronto, Canada) (2002) Mirabel will switch to an all-cargo facility within a year. 16 May, p. 8.

UNEP (2001) *Industry and Environment: Ecotourism and Sustainability.* United Nations Environment Programme Division of Technology, Industry and Economics (UNEP DTIE), Paris.

UNEP and Wood, M.E. (2002) *Ecotourism: Principles, Practices and Policies for Sustainability.* United Nations Environment Programme, Paris.

Walters, D.A. (1987) Competitiveness and trade policy: a view for the administration. In: Barfield, C.E. and Makin, J.H. (eds) *Trade Policy and US Competitiveness.* American Enterprise Institute for Public Policy Research, Washington, DC, pp. 65–69.

WCED (1987) *Our Common Future: the World Commission on Environment and Development (The Brundtland Report).* Oxford University Press, Oxford.

WEF/IMD (1992) *The World Competitiveness Report.* World Economic Forum and International Institute for Management Development, Lausanne, Switzerland.

Witt, S.F. (1980) An abstract mode-abstract (destination) node model of foreign holiday demand. *Applied Economics* 12, 163–180.

Wood, M.E. (2002) *Ecotourism: Principles, Practices and Policies for Sustainability.* United Nations Environment Programme, Paris.

WTO (1995) *What Tourism Managers Need to Know: a Practical Guide to the Development and Use of Indicators of Sustainable Tourism.* Consulting and Audit Canada, Ottawa, Ontario, Canada.

WTO (1999) *Approval of the Global Code of Ethics for Tourism* (Resolution adopted by the General Assembly at its Thirteenth Session, Santiago, Chile, 27 September–1 October 1999). World Tourism Organization, Madrid, Spain.

WTO (2000a) *Compendium of Tourism Statistics – 2000 edition* (1994-1998). World Tourism Organization, Madrid, Spain.

WTO (2000b) *Global Code of Ethics for Tourism.* Web address: www.world-tourism.org/projects/ethics/principles.html

WTO (2001a) *Tourism Satellite Account (TSA): Implementation Project – the Tourism Satellite Account as an Ongoing Process:*

Past, Present and Future Developments. World Tourism Organization, Madrid, Spain.

WTO (2001b) *The German Ecotourism Market.* World Tourism Organization, Madrid, Spain.

WTO (2001c) *The British Ecotourism Market.* World Tourism Organization, Madrid, Spain.

WTO (2002) *The US Ecotourism Market – Special Report.* World Tourism Organization, Madrid, Spain.

WTTC (1995) *Travel and Tourism: a New Economic Perspective.* World Travel and Tourism Council. Elsevier Science, Oxford.

WTTC (1998) *GREEN GLOBE Annual Review.* World Travel and Tourism Council, Oxford.

WTTERC and Hawkins, R. (1995) *The Green Globe Programme: Developing a Greener Future for Travel and Tourism.* World Travel and Tourism Environment Research Centre, Oxford.

Appendix 2.1.   World Tourism Organization Global Codes of Ethics for Tourism (from WTO, 2000b).

[Article 1] Tourism's contribution to mutual understanding and respect between peoples and societies

1. The understanding and promotion of the ethical values common to humanity, with an attitude of tolerance and respect for the diversity of religious, philosophical and moral beliefs, are both the foundation and the consequence of responsible tourism; stakeholders in tourism development and tourists themselves should observe the social and cultural traditions and practices of all peoples, including those of minorities and indigenous peoples and to recognize their worth;
2. Tourism activities should be conducted in harmony with the attributes and traditions of the host regions and countries and in respect for their laws, practices and customs;
3. The host communities, on the one hand, and local professionals, on the other, should acquaint themselves with and respect the tourists who visit them and find out about their lifestyles, tastes and expectations; the education and training imparted to professionals contribute to a hospitable welcome;
4. It is the task of the public authorities to provide protection for tourists and visitors and their belongings; they must pay particular attention to the safety of foreign tourists owing to the particular vulnerability they may have; they should facilitate the introduction of specific means of information, prevention, security, insurance and assistance consistent with their needs; any attacks, assaults, kidnappings or threats against tourists or workers in the tourism industry, as well as the willful destruction of tourism facilities or of elements of cultural or natural heritage should be severely condemned and punished in accordance with their respective national laws;
5. When traveling, tourists and visitors should not commit any criminal act or any act considered criminal by the laws of the country visited and abstain from any conduct felt to be offensive or injurious by the local populations, or likely to damage the local environment; they should refrain from all trafficking in illicit drugs, arms, antiques, protected species and products and substances that are dangerous or prohibited by national regulations;
6. Tourists and visitors have the responsibility to acquaint themselves, even before their departure, with the characteristics of the countries they are preparing to visit; they must be aware of the health and security risks inherent in any travel outside their usual environment and behave in such a way as to minimize those risks;

[Article 2] Tourism as a vehicle for individual and collective fulfillment

1. Tourism, the activity most frequently associated with rest and relaxation, sport and access to culture and nature, should be planned and practiced as a privileged means of individual and collective fulfillment; when practiced with a sufficiently open mind, it is an irreplaceable factor of self-education, mutual tolerance and for learning about the legitimate differences between peoples and cultures and their diversity;
2. Tourism activities should respect the equality of men and women; they should promote human rights and, more particularly, the individual rights of the most vulnerable groups, notably children, the elderly, the handicapped, ethnic minorities and indigenous peoples;
3. The exploitation of human beings in any form, particularly sexual, especially when applied to children, conflicts with the fundamental aims of tourism and is the negation of tourism; as such, in accordance with international law, it should be energetically combated with the cooperation of all the States concerned and penalized without concession by the national legislation of both the countries visited and the countries of the perpetrators of these acts, even when they are carried out abroad;
4. Travel for purposes of religion, health, education and cultural or linguistic exchanges is a particularly beneficial form of tourism, which deserves encouragement;
5. The introduction into curricula of education about the value of tourist exchanges, their economic, social and cultural benefits, and also their risks, should be encouraged;

[Article 3] Tourism, a factor of sustainable development

1. All the stakeholders in tourism development should safeguard the natural environment with a view to achieving sound, continuous and sustainable economic growth geared to satisfying equitably the needs and aspirations of present and future generations;
2. All forms of tourism development that are conducive to saving rare and precious resources, in particular water and energy, as well as avoiding so far as possible waste production, should be given priority and encouraged by national, regional and local public authorities;

Appendix 2.1. *Continued.*

3. The staggering in time and space of tourist and visitor flows, particularly those resulting from paid leave and school holidays, and a more even distribution of holidays should be sought so as to reduce the pressure of tourism activity on the environment and enhance its beneficial impact on the tourism industry and the local economy;

4. Tourism infrastructure should be designed and tourism activities programmed in such a way as to protect the natural heritage composed of ecosystems and biodiversity and to preserve endangered species of wildlife; the stakeholders in tourism development, and especially professionals, should agree to the imposition of limitations or constraints on their activities when these are exercised in particularly sensitive areas: desert, polar or high mountain regions, coastal areas, tropical forests or wetlands, propitious to the creation of nature reserves or protected areas;

5. Nature tourism and ecotourism are recognized as being particularly conducive to enriching and enhancing the standing of tourism, provided they respect the natural heritage and local populations and are in keeping with the carrying capacity of the sites;

[Article 4] Tourism, a user of the cultural heritage of mankind and contributor to its enhancement

1. Tourism resources belong to the common heritage of mankind; the communities in whose territories they are situated have particular rights and obligations to them;

2. Tourism policies and activities should be conducted with respect for the artistic, archaeological and cultural heritage, which they should protect and pass on to future generations; particular care should be devoted to preserving and upgrading monuments, shrines and museums as well as archaeological and historic sites which must be widely open to tourist visits; encouragement should be given to public access to privately-owned cultural property and monuments, with respect for the rights of their owners, as well as to religious buildings, without prejudice to normal needs of worship;

3. Financial resources derived from visits to cultural sites and monuments should, at least in part, be used for the upkeep, safeguard, development and embellishment of this heritage;

4. Tourism activity should be planned in such a way as to allow traditional cultural products, crafts and folklore to survive and flourish, rather than causing them to degenerate and become standardized;

[Article 5] Tourism, a beneficial activity for host countries and communities

1. Local populations should be associated with tourism activities and share equitably in the economic, social and cultural benefits they generate, and particularly in the creation of direct and indirect jobs resulting from them;

2. Tourism policies should be applied in such a way as to help to raise the standard of living of the populations of the regions visited and meet their needs; the planning and architectural approach to and operation of tourism resorts and accommodation should aim to integrate them, to the extent possible, in the local economic and social fabric; where skills are equal, priority should be given to local manpower;

3. Special attention should be paid to the specific problems of coastal areas and island territories and to vulnerable rural or mountain regions, for which tourism often represents a rare opportunity for development in the face of the decline of traditional economic activities;

4. Tourism professionals, particularly investors, governed by the regulations laid down by the public authorities, should carry out studies of the impact of their development projects on the environment and natural surroundings; they should also deliver, with the greatest transparency and objectivity, information on their future programmes and their foreseeable repercussions and foster dialogue on their contents with the populations concerned;

[Article 6] Obligations of stakeholders in tourism development

1. Tourism professionals have an obligation to provide tourists with objective and honest information on their places of destination and on the conditions of travel, hospitality and stays; they should ensure that the contractual clauses proposed to their customers are readily understandable as to the nature, price and quality of the services they commit themselves to providing and the financial compensation payable by them in the event of a unilateral breach of contract on their part;

continued

Appendix 2.1. *Continued.*

2. Tourism professionals, insofar as it depends on them, should show concern, in cooperation with the public authorities, for the security and safety, accident prevention, health protection and food safety of those who seek their services; likewise, they should ensure the existence of suitable systems of insurance and assistance; they should accept the reporting obligations prescribed by national regulations and pay fair compensation in the event of failure to observe their contractual obligations;

3. Tourism professionals, so far as this depends on them, should contribute to the cultural and spiritual fulfillment of tourists and allow them, during their travels, to practice their religions;

4. The public authorities of the generating States and the host countries, in cooperation with the professionals concerned and their associations, should ensure that the necessary mechanisms are in place for the repatriation of tourists in the event of the bankruptcy of the enterprise that organized their travel;

5. Governments have the right – and the duty – especially in a crisis, to inform their nationals of the difficult circumstances, or even the dangers they may encounter during their travels abroad; it is their responsibility however to issue such information without prejudicing in an unjustified or exaggerated manner the tourism industry of the host countries and the interests of their own operators; the contents of travel advisories should therefore be discussed beforehand with the authorities of the host countries and the professionals concerned; recommendations formulated should be strictly proportionate to the gravity of the situations encountered and confined to the geographical areas where the insecurity has arisen; such advisories should be qualified or cancelled as soon as a return to normality permits;

6. The press, and particularly the specialized travel press and the other media, including modern means of electronic communication, should issue honest and balanced information on events and situations that could influence the flow of tourists; they should also provide accurate and reliable information to the consumers of tourism services; the new communication and electronic commerce technologies should also be developed and used for this purpose; as is the case for the media, they should not in any way promote sex tourism;

[Article 7] Right to tourism

1. The prospect of direct and personal access to the discovery and enjoyment of the planet's resources constitutes a right equally open to all the world's inhabitants; the increasingly extensive participation in national and international tourism should be regarded as one of the best possible expressions of the sustained growth of free time, and obstacles should not be placed in its way;

2. The universal right to tourism must be regarded as the corollary of the right to rest and leisure, including reasonable limitation of working hours and periodic holidays with pay, guaranteed by Article 24 of the Universal Declaration of Human Rights and Article 7.d of the International Covenant on Economic, Social and Cultural Rights;

3. Social tourism, and in particular associative tourism, which facilitates widespread access to leisure, travel and holidays, should be developed with the support of the public authorities;

4. Family, youth, student and senior tourism and tourism for people with disabilities, should be encouraged and facilitated;

[Article 8] Liberty of tourist movements

1. Tourists and visitors should benefit, in compliance with international law and national legislation, from the liberty to move within their countries and from one State to another, in accordance with Article 13 of the Universal Declaration of Human Rights; they should have access to places of transit and stay and to tourism and cultural sites without being subject to excessive formalities or discrimination;

2. Tourists and visitors should have access to all available forms of communication, internal or external; they should benefit from prompt and easy access to local administrative, legal and health services; they should be free to contact the consular representatives of their countries of origin in compliance with the diplomatic conventions in force;

3. Tourists and visitors should benefit from the same rights as the citizens of the country visited concerning the confidentiality of the personal data and information concerning them, especially when these are stored electronically;

Appendix 2.1. *Continued.*

4. Administrative procedures relating to border crossings whether they fall within the competence of States or result from international agreements, such as visas or health and customs formalities, should be adapted, so far as possible, so as to facilitate to the maximum freedom of travel and widespread access to international tourism; agreements between groups of countries to harmonize and simplify these procedures should be encouraged; specific taxes and levies penalizing the tourism industry and undermining its competitiveness should be gradually phased out or corrected;

5. So far as the economic situation of the countries from which they come permits, travelers should have access to allowances of convertible currencies needed for their travels;

[Article 9] Rights of the workers and entrepreneurs in the tourism industry

1. The fundamental rights of salaried and self-employed workers in the tourism industry and related activities, should be guaranteed under the supervision of the national and local administrations, both of their States of origin and of the host countries, with particular care, given the specific constraints linked in particular to the seasonality of their activity, the global dimension of their industry and the flexibility often required of them by the nature of their work;

2. Salaried and self-employed workers in the tourism industry and related activities have the right and the duty to acquire appropriate initial and continuous training; they should be given adequate social protection; job insecurity should be limited so far as possible; and a specific status, with particular regard to their social welfare, should be offered to seasonal workers in the sector;

3. Any natural or legal person, provided he, she or it has the necessary abilities and skills, should be entitled to develop a professional activity in the field of tourism under existing national laws; entrepreneurs and investors – especially in the area of small and medium-sized enterprises – should be entitled to free access to the tourism sector with a minimum of legal or administrative restrictions;

4. Exchanges of experience offered to executives and workers, whether salaried or not, from different countries, contributes to foster the development of the world tourism industry; these movements should be facilitated so far as possible in compliance with the applicable national laws and international conventions;

5. As an irreplaceable factor of solidarity in the development and dynamic growth of international exchanges, multinational enterprises of the tourism industry should not exploit the dominant positions they sometimes occupy; they should avoid becoming the vehicles of cultural and social models artificially imposed on the host communities; in exchange for their freedom to invest and trade which should be fully recognized, they should involve themselves in local development, avoiding, by the excessive repatriation of their profits or their induced imports, a reduction of their contribution to the economies in which they are established;

6. Partnership and the establishment of balanced relations between enterprises of generating and receiving countries contribute to the sustainable development of tourism and an equitable distribution of the benefits of its growth;

[Article 10] Implementation of the principles of the Global Code of Ethics for Tourism

1. The public and private stakeholders in tourism development should cooperate in the implementation of these principles and monitor their effective application;

2. The stakeholders in tourism development should recognize the role of international institutions, among which the World Tourism Organization ranks first, and non-governmental organizations with competence in the field of tourism promotion and development, the protection of human rights, the environment or health, with due respect for the general principles of international law;

3. The same stakeholders should demonstrate their intention to refer any disputes concerning the application or interpretation of the Global Code of Ethics for Tourism for conciliation to an impartial third body known as the World Committee on Tourism Ethics.

3

A Model of Destination Competitiveness

While Chapter 2 laid the groundwork, in this chapter we present the development of a tourism-specific conceptual model of destination competitiveness. A knowledge of the nature of both comparative and competitive advantage is certainly useful, but if we are to be able to begin to find answers to the types of strategic question facing destination managers today, our conceptual model needs to go beyond such generic concepts to reveal, in greater depth, just what these concepts mean in the context of a tourist destination. That is, to be managerially useful we need to examine further the categories that constitute resource endowments and resource deployments (described briefly in Chapter 2) in order to understand how these constructs are best operationalized to determine destination competitiveness.

What is a conceptual model and what does it do? A conceptual model is a device that provides a useful way of thinking about a complex issue. Most conceptual models depict the believed structure of interrelationships between separate constructs or factors which help to explain a higher-order concept, and they do this by the use of a graphical device such as a diagram, figure, flow chart or some other type of two- or three-dimensional tool. Concepts are the building blocks of theory and consist of two components: a *symbol* (usually a word or term) and a *definition*. Neuman (1994, Chapter 3), provides a very clear explanation of the importance and use of concepts and conceptual models in theory-building. A conceptual model is a collection of concepts that together form a 'web of meaning' (Neuman, 1994, p. 37) and thereby help to clarify our understanding of (in this case) the factors which affect the competitiveness of a tourist destination; it is a model in that it is a simplified description of a phenomenon that is always more complex than a model suggests. A good model has *parsimony*. A parsimonious model is one that seeks to balance the need to maximize explanation with minimal complexity.

A conceptual model can be used for a variety of purposes. It can be used as a basis for research to further test the reliability and validity of the model, or parts of the model, in explaining the actual phenomenon. It can also be used by decision makers to guide the generation of ideas, the analysis of these ideas, recommendations and implementation. In this regard, it is important to recognize that models are not perfect and therefore should not be used in a cookbook fashion. It is always important to check that the basic assumptions and limitations of the model are not violated. Models should not be used to *make* a decision; they assist decision making but should not perform the role of the decision maker.

The conceptual model of destination competitiveness presented in this chapter is not a predictive or causal model. Rather, its primary purpose at this stage of our research is to explain. Neuman (1994, p. 43) distinguishes between *theoretical explanation* and *ordinary explanation*. He notes that a theoretical explanation is 'a logical argument that tells why something occurs. It refers to a general rule or principle. These are a researcher's theoretical arguments or connections among concepts. The second type of explanation, *ordinary explanation*, makes something clear or describes something in a way that illustrates it and makes it intelligible . . . The two types of explanation can blend together.'

We see our model fitting primarily the definition of an ordinary explanation at this stage of our research. The model is relatively abstract in its present form in that it does not lay out specific empirical generalizations. It is best described, in the words of Neuman's typology (Neuman, 1994, p. 51) as a 'theory on a topic', the topic in this case being destination competitiveness. (Neuman's typology, from least abstract to most abstract, includes the following four classes of theory: an *empirical generalization*, which is a specific hypothesis; a *middle-range theory*, which is used principally to guide empirical enquiry; a *theory on a topic*, which uses a range of more abstract concepts and relationships; and a *theoretical framework*, which is often called a theoretical system or paradigm.)

We begin by explaining how we developed the model and where we obtained the information that forms the basis of its structure. Then, in the remaining part of this chapter, we provide a brief overview of the model and its parts in order to provide a wider perspective of the model and its usefulness. In subsequent chapters we examine each of the main components of the model in greater detail.

The Origins of a Conceptual Model

The model that follows arose out of the coalescence of several research activities and ideas. The evolution of the model progressed inductively, beginning with some unrelated research, experiences and *ad hoc* insights that accumulated through other consulting, research, and industry service and experience. In 1992 we began to pool these experiences and related them more systematically to the larger issue of destination competitiveness. Over a period of about 8 years, the concepts and propositions behind the model emerged from the ground up, maturing in its present form. In summary,

our *grounded-research* approach (Glaser and Strauss, 1967) progressed as follows:

1. Before 1992, separate research, consulting and industry service by the authors, particularly in the areas of the determinants of international tourism demand and destination promotion (e.g. Crouch, 1992a,b, 1994, 1996; Crouch *et al.*, 1992) and tourism policy, planning, destination image and mega-events (e.g. Ritchie and Smith, 1991; Echtner and Ritchie, 1993; Ritchie, 1993).
2. The joint preparation of a keynote paper (Basic Report) for the 43rd Congress of the Association Internationale d'Experts Scientifique du Tourism (AIEST), which had as its general title *Competitiveness of Long-Haul Tourist Destinations* (Ritchie and Crouch, 1993).
3. A focus-group discussion on the topic of destination competitiveness with a class of participants attending the University of Calgary's Executive Program in Destination Management (EPDM) in 1992. Participants in this programme work for Convention and Visitor Bureaux (CVBs) across North America. Graduates of the programme are certified as Destination Management Executives by the International Association of Convention and Visitor Bureaus.
4. A series of telephone conference-call interviews on destination competitiveness with a number of presidents and chief executive officers of some of the largest destination management organizations in North America.
5. A special session at the 1993 AIEST Congress using transportable computer hardware and data-entry keypads with Option Finder software (Option Technologies, Fleet, UK), to gather opinions on the topic of destination competitiveness from a group of attendees at the conference.
6. Computer-facilitated focus groups using the University of Calgary's Group Decision Support System Laboratory to expand and formalize the collection of views and opinions on the topic from further classes in the EPDM programme.
7. Feedback, debate and introspection stemming from papers on the topic of destination competitiveness presented at several conferences held between 1994 and 2001.[1]

8. Use of the model in our own teaching with undergraduate and postgraduate students and short-course industry participants.

The qualitative research involving the interviews described in (4) above represented a significant phase in the evolution of the model. The following set of questions guided these open-ended interviews.

- In your view, what are the factors that determine the success or competitiveness of a major tourism destination? Is it possible to prioritize these factors? How would you do it?
- What criteria are you using to assess success or competitiveness?
- Are success or competitiveness factors different for the international and domestic markets? If so, how?
- What do you consider are the greatest competitive strengths of your destination?
- Could you identify several destinations that you consider to be highly competitive in the domestic and/or the international marketplace? Why are they particularly competitive?
- What do you consider to be the main determinants of the 'cost' of a destination? How important is productivity in determining the cost of destination tourist services and, in turn, destination competitiveness?
- How does someone responsible for the success of a destination improve its competitive position? In the short term? In the long term?

No one element of the work outlined above resulted in the development of the model, but each contributed important insights to its formulation. In fact it was apparent that, in all the discussions and interviews that took place, the opinions that were expressed tended to focus on a subset of competitiveness factors. The big picture emerged only by synthesizing and integrating perspectives across all of the inputs to the process. A major reason for this may have been that the topic of destination competitiveness is so broad that there simply was not time during each element of the research to cover all the important dimensions and perspectives. We also found that, particularly during individual

interviews, where the focus tended to be on the more acute competitiveness issues confronting the destination in question, one or two issues often took precedence over all others.

While the model incorporates several categories of factors and sub-factors, it was clear that the relative importance of each factor and the interactions among the factors depend very much on the unique circumstances facing each destination in question. It was also clear that each set of circumstances is dynamic, that is, changes over time in the global (macro)environment and competitive (micro)environment result in changing fortunes and challenges. For this reason, we believe that a general model of destination competitiveness can play an important role in guiding destination managers as they seek to diagnose their competitive problems and develop sustainable solutions.

Figure 3.1 illustrates our conceptual model of destination competitiveness in its present form. It is likely to undergo further refinement and adaptation as our research continues. The level of interest in the model has encouraged us, and the feedback we have received to date has certainly helped us to improve our framework. We hope that the model and ideas presented in this book will help us continue this process.

An Overview of the Model

The global (macro)environment

The tourism system is an open system. That is, it is subject to many influences and pressures that arise outside the system itself. This is the global environment or macroenvironment. It consists of a vast array of phenomena which broadly affect all human activities and which are therefore not specific to the travel and tourism industry in their effect. By comparison, the competitive environment or microenvironment is part of the tourism system because it concerns the actions and activities of entities in the tourism system that directly affect the goals of each member of the system, whether they be individual companies or a collection of organizations constituting a destination.

The macroenvironment is global in its scope. Events in one part of the world today can

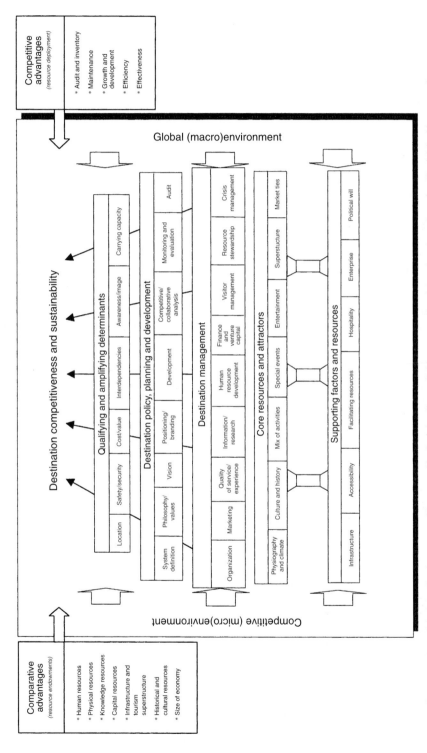

Fig. 3.1. Conceptual model of destination competitiveness. Further details available at: www.business.latrobe.edu.au/staffhp/gichp/destcomp.htm

have consequences for tourist destinations in entirely different regions. Among the many effects of global forces are changes in a destination's attractiveness to tourists, shifts in the pattern of wealth to create new emerging origin markets, changes in the relative costs of travel to different destinations, and the disruption of relations between cultures and nations. These forces present a given destination with a number of special concerns, problems or issues that it must either adapt to or overcome if it is to remain competitive. At the same time, these forces provide destinations with a whole new spectrum of opportunities for innovation and market exploitation.

These global forces can result in events that are profound in their implications for tourism. Yet often it seems that businesses and managers find it difficult or impossible to notice the significance of these developments, either because they often occur gradually over the long term and do not produce significant incremental changes on a day-to-day basis, or because their effect is often indirect, so that the root cause of a problem may be obscure.

The global (macro)environment is in a constant state of change and evolution. Destination managers need to monitor the environment regularly if they are to understand the big picture and anticipate and pre-empt changes that alter the tourism landscape. Marketers will recognize this as the need to avoid marketing myopia.

Macroenvironmental factors are often categorized into six principal groups related to the *economy, technology, ecology, political and legal developments, sociocultural issues* and the changing *demographic environment*. We will discuss macroenvironmental trends and their ramifications for tourist destinations in greater detail in the next chapter. For the moment, however, we provide a brief introduction to the scope of these categories of factors.

Real improvements in wealth have enabled millions of people worldwide to engage in travel and tourism in the modern era. For much of the 20th century, North America and Western Europe produced the greatest share of travellers. This was driven largely by wealth creation in these countries. More recently, economic growth in Asia and the Pacific Rim has opened new markets in these regions and fuelled infrastructural developments that have been the basis for establishing new tourism destinations in these regions also. Economic recessions in the early 1980s and early 1990s and the Asian economic crisis in the late 1990s had measurable effects on global tourism. The *economic environment* profoundly affects global tourism and changes the fortunes of destinations.

Technology, too, has produced sweeping changes, the most significant of which involves transportation technology. The speed, capacity, fuel efficiency, safety and productivity of the technology used by airlines today, both in their aircraft and in their systems and processes, have been behind the real decline in the cost of air travel per seat-mile. Long-haul destinations have particularly benefited from these developments. We emphasize that it is not just *hard* technology that matters here. *Soft* technologies (i.e. changes in systems or processes, or the way in which things are done) have resulted in changes of equal significance, often in combination with hard technology. Information systems (e.g. for computer reservations and global distribution, and the Internet for electronic commerce), financial systems (e.g. credit cards, automatic teller machines, electronic funds transfer), accommodation systems (e.g. computer check-in/check-out, all-inclusive resorts, franchising) and food services (e.g. branding and franchising, operations systems), to name just a few of these soft technologies, have revolutionized practices in tourism and hospitality. Tourism is often inaccurately labelled a low-wage service industry, yet it is clear that many highly skilled jobs are a part of the tourism scene today.

Turning now to the *ecological environment*, it is easy to identify several issues that potentially have enormous consequences for tourism and destinations. To the extent that global warming is a reality, destinations everywhere, from coastal resorts to mountain skiing destinations, may experience significant climatic shifts over the long term and, if some of the predictions are correct, these changes may be enough to virtually destroy tourism in some locations. The depletion of the ozone layer in the atmosphere and better education about the health risks of exposure to the sun have radically altered attitudes towards sun-worship. Air pollution has accelerated the degradation of some of tourism's most famous icons, such as the Taj Mahal and the Parthenon. In addition, the green movement acts as a vigilant watchdog over tourism's potential adverse environmental impacts, ranging from overcrowding (e.g. Yosemite National Park in the USA) to effects on everything from wildlife, flora, reefs, rainforests and sensitive ecosystems. Conversely, hopes are held out for tourism as a saviour of the Earth's ecological heritage through the placing of economic value on the preservation of scenic regions, national parks, wildlife species, etc., so that they may compete with or guard against other means of exploitation and degradation. Economic, in addition to philanthropic, motives may be enough to tip the balance in many cases, particularly in developing regions.

In the *political and legal* arena, the scope of implications of many events for tourism is similarly momentous. As noted by Naisbitt (1994, p. 120), a 'confluence of cosmic events is fuelling growth in tourism'. Naisbitt provides a catalogue of geopolitical events (these include a reduction in the arms race and its effect on resource allocation; an increase in international communications, trade, investment and travel; free trade agreements; a reduction in hostilities between a number of traditional rivals; a reduction in the number of authoritarian regimes; a move to market economies; and the spread of democracy) and their consequences in support of this statement. International travel and tourism is leading the field in the growing international trade in services and has played a central role in the General Agreement on Trade in Services (GATS) and now the World Trade Organization. International air transport agreements are complex and largely bilateral, and the process of reaching agreement shows signs of becoming, albeit slowly, more market-oriented. Migration and the flow of refugees continue apace, often fuelling agonized debates over the levels of immigration in many industrialized countries – debates that are often tainted with accusations of racism. Even concerns over the spread of disease (e.g. AIDS, Ebola, mad cow disease (bovine spongiform encephalopathy) and foot-and-mouth disease), facilitated by international air travel and open borders, has rung alarm bells in political circles. Governments have passed laws ranging from measures designed to punish citizens who engage in sex tourism involving under-age males and females in Thailand and the Philippines, through the Helmes–Burton Law in the USA (which targets corporations and individuals trading with Cuba) to embargoes against rogue states such as Serbia and North Korea. These are just a few of the many political and legal trends shaping tourism and the competitiveness of destinations.

Some of the major *sociocultural trends* shaping tourism are: (i) the back-to-nature movement, with its emphasis on experiential as opposed to material rewards; (ii) the backlash against cultural imperialism; (iii) a heightened sense that aboriginal cultures possess features of great value, in which aboriginals of the younger generation are developing a greater sense of pride; (iv) greater reverence for the enriching qualities which other cultures contribute to the global community; (v) the impact of global communication and its demonstration effect on residents in Third World countries who, as a result, develop a new set of social and economic aspirations; and (vi) tourism's potential for social dislocation. Here too, however, opportunities exist for destinations to use tourism in a way that improves the quality of life of its residents through the judicial development, marketing and operation of its local tourism system. In *Global Paradox*, Naisbitt notes that:

> The biggest industry is driven as no other by individuals' decisions. The smallest players decide. This situation also reflects the paradox of the more universal we become, the more tribal we act. The bigger and more competitive travel becomes, the more authentically distinctive to tourists we will make our cultures.
> (1994, p. 103)

The final macroenvironmental category concerns *demographics*. Foot (1996) claims that an understanding of demographic changes today holds the key to success in business. According to Foot (p. 2), 'Demography, the study of human populations, is the most powerful – and most under-utilized – tool we have to understand the past and to foretell the future . . . Demographics explain about two-thirds of everything.' Whether or not one quite agrees with this claim, it is certainly true that the demographic environment presents some very significant opportunities and threats for tourism over the long term. Those that are most talked and written about, and most readily recognized, concern the ageing profile of the population, at least in developed, industrialized countries. Tourism generally has been quick to realize the implications of this trend. But other changes should not be ignored. For example, the well-established trend towards two-income households has been evident for some time. This has affected tourism by increasing household income but a consequence has been less time for leisure activities. The result is vacations that are more frequent but shorter. More recently, there have been signs of a reverse trend. Increasingly, individuals and couples are questioning the benefits of their work ethic and lifestyle.

The increasing level of education in recent years is a trend that also has important implications for tourism. University degrees, even post-graduate degrees, are no longer the rare commodity they once were. Education has stimulated the desire for travel to experience other peoples, places and ways of life.

We have only touched upon some of the major global forces shaping the tourism industry and the competition occurring between tourist destinations. We explore these trends in greater depth in Chapter 4.

The competitive (micro)environment

As noted above, a destination's competitive (micro)environment is made up of organizations, influences and forces that lie within the destination's immediate arena of tourism activities and competition. These close-in elements of the environment tend to have a more direct and immediate impact than do elements of the global (macro)environment as a general rule, although the opposite is often true. Nevertheless, the microenvironment, because of its proximity and greater sense of immediacy, often occupies the attention of managers because of its implications for the destination's ability to serve visitors and remain competitive.

Apart from the destination itself, the competitive (micro)environment includes other entities that together form the so-called travel trade, in addition to the various tourism markets, competing destinations and a destination's publics or stakeholders. As components of the *tourism system*, they shape the immediate environment within which a destination must adapt in order to compete.

Suppliers provide the basic elements that together form the overall visitor experience. There are many resources or factors that are required by tourism and hospitality enterprises, as outlined in Chapter 2. As the tourism industry is a service industry, a great deal of the product is formed through the actions of individual employees of the many service firms that form the tourism industry. Labour is therefore a key supply factor. Other supply factors include food and beverage producers, the oil and gas industry, local crafts and shopping goods, and the manufacturers of equipment such as amusement park rides, camping equipment and forms of transportation (e.g. aircraft, automobiles, ferries), together with many other goods and services the demand for which is derived from the needs of travellers and tourists. The number, policies and practices of these suppliers drive prices, service levels, visitor choice and product innovation. Their competitive and cooperative actions fundamentally shape the competitive (micro)environment.

Suppliers are connected to tourists through tourism marketing channels consisting of *intermediaries* and *facilitators*. These include *tour packagers*, who assemble tourism products or experiences from among the vast number of alternatives supplied; *retail travel agents*, who provide information, reservation convenience and expertise to tourism markets; *speciality channellers*, such as incentive travel firms, corporate travel offices, meeting and convention planners, who provide specialized forms of travel planning and organization; and *facilitators*, who assist in the efficient and effective functioning of the tourism system by improving the flow of information, money, knowledge, services and people. This last group includes credit card and financial organizations, advertising agencies, market research consultants, embassies and consulates, information technology suppliers, and investors. Without intermediaries and facilitators, the tourism system would gridlock. New forms of marketing channels, such as the Internet, continue to influence the structure and functioning of the tourism system.

Customers – travellers and tourists – are, or at least should be, the focus and source of the driving force in the competitive (micro)environment. Competition to serve customer needs and wants is what ultimately governs the actions of the travel trade. Customers are not just a homogeneous bunch of individual travellers. The desires and tastes of travellers today are more heterogeneous and sophisticated than ever before. Thus, the variety of travel motivations and tourism market segments has exploded in recent years. While many tourists today still seek warm and sunny climates for rest and relaxation, or experiences in traditional destinations like Paris, London, Rome and New York, we now also see travel to distant, exotic destinations, or for eccentric or esoteric purposes. Examples include participation by tourists in archaeological digs, bicycle rides literally around the world, and attendance at international scientific conferences.

Another element of the competitive environment consists of the *competitors* themselves; that is, other destinations, organizations or firms with which an entity competes because they offer broadly similar products to essentially the same group of customers, at least in part. Traditionally, these competitors have been regarded as adversaries. However, in these days of down-sizing, partnerships and virtual corporations, a new word, 'coopetition',[2] is being added to the lexicon of the business world to reflect the fact that other organizations or entities can present both cooperative as well as competitive challenges. Porter (1980, 1990) recognized the complementary and supportive roles of other players. The terms he used to reflect this are 'strategic groups' and 'industry clusters'.

In tourism, these paradoxical, competitive and complementary relationships between tourist destinations have attracted the interest of some researchers. For example, neighbouring destinations often compete for short-haul markets but cooperate in attracting long-haul markets because they recognize the synergistic effect of a cooperative marketing strategy. Nevertheless, destinations do compete with many other destinations in the choice processes used by travellers and tourists. Developing a strong image, differentiating that image from other destinations, and positioning the destination in the minds of potential visitors is very much a task at the heart of destination competitiveness.

A destination's *internal environment* is also an element of the microenvironment or competitive environment that affects its competitiveness. To be competitive, a destination must function as a real entity. That is, it must have a sense of itself; it should have a purpose and be managed in a way that promotes the pursuit of that purpose. This assumes either that some system of governance is in place for a destination or that there exists a shared sense of purpose across the organizations, companies, government departments, networks and individuals that together constitute the destination. Individual tourism organizations do not operate in a vacuum. Hotels work with convention centres, tour operators and attractions depend on one another for their business, airlines and car rental companies coordinate services, destination marketing organizations feature individual operators in their promotions, economic development agencies and financial institutions bring investors and tourism developers together, and so on. How all of these relationships and interactions combine over space and time determines the course taken by a destination. Whether this course is chaotic and uncertain or planned and deliberate depends on the degree to which all these events are congruent.

The final element of a destination's competitive (micro)environment is made up of the many *publics* with which a destination must contend and which it must satisfy. These include the media, government departments, the general public, local residents, financial institutions, citizen action groups (e.g. environmental pressure groups, aboriginal communities, taxpayer associations, consumer groups) and organized labour. The distinction between a destination's internal environment and its publics is rather blurred, as in this instance most publics are internal to the destination. This is not always the case, however. Take, for example, the international reaction to France over nuclear testing in the Pacific Ocean, or the ostracizing of Arizona and the subsequent boycotts affecting the state because of its initial failure to declare a public holiday in honour of Martin Luther King, Jr.

As publics can facilitate or impede a destination's ability to pursue and realize its tourism development goals, it is vital that a destination should develop a good relationship with key publics. This is why destinations have often instituted promotional campaigns within their own precincts to sell the virtues of tourism development.

Chapter 5 delves more deeply into the way in which the competitive (micro)environment shapes the playing field for tourist destinations.

Core resources and attractors

This component of the model describes the primary elements of destination appeal. It is these factors that are the key motivators for visitation to a destination. While other components are essential for success and profitability, it is the core resources and attractors that are the fundamental reasons why prospective visitors choose one destination over another. These factors fall into seven categories: physiography and climate, culture and history, market ties, mix of activities, special events, entertainment and the tourism superstructure.

Because so much of the tourism experience is associated with the physical resources of a destination, the *physiography and climate* of a destination together constitute a factor that can be so important that it dominates other factors of competitiveness. As it includes the overall nature of the landscape and the climate of the destination, it defines the nature of the environmental framework within which the visitor exists and enjoys the destination. It also defines much of the aesthetics and visual appeal of the destination – and because it is a factor over which destination managers have little or no control, much of the built tourism environment is constrained by its characteristics. Thus, to a great extent, a destination's physiography and climate constitute the one parameter of core attractiveness around which other factors must be creatively developed.

Similarly, the *culture and history* of a destination can also be an enormously important factor. Although this factor may be viewed as somewhat more malleable than physiography and climate from a management perspective, the culture and history of a destination are also determined well outside the scope of tourism.

Indeed, it can be argued with great justification that little or no attempt should be made to alter or, especially, to prostitute local culture and history for the purpose of tourism development.

Once this constraint is accepted, however, a destination's culture and history furnish a basic and powerful attracting force for the prospective visitor. This force appears to be growing in significance for many segments of the travel market, particularly in today's world of homogenized tourism, where one destination often seems to resemble another. Thus, if a destination can provide visitors with a unique setting within which to experience lifestyles outside their day-to-day routine, it has a clear competitive advantage. If this lifestyle is complemented by historical environments that contrast with those found in the home situation, the destination has a clear competitive advantage in efforts to create a memorable experience.

The *market ties* component of destination attractiveness is also outside the direct control of tourism destination managers. Nevertheless, it is one that evolves over time and one that can be influenced to varying degrees by those responsible for managing a tourism destination.

The term 'market ties' includes several dimensions along which a destination establishes and builds linkages with the residents of tourism-originating regions. Ethnic ties resulting from immigration patterns that have evolved over time – often long periods of time – provide the strongest and perhaps most enduring linkages for building systematic and predictable travel flows to a destination. The 'visiting friends and relatives' segment of the travel market, while not necessarily the most profitable segment, provides a firm foundation for building tourism within a destination. Even more importantly, it often leads to the establishment of business ties that can generate both a steady flow of visitors and create other forms of economic development. Other ties include religion, sports, trade and culture.

The range or *mix of activities* within a destination represents one of the most critical aspects of destination appeal, and it is one over which destination managers do have extensive influence and control. While the activities within a destination may be defined to a large extent by physiography and culture, there is nevertheless considerable scope for creativity and initiative.

The activities dimension of destination attractiveness appears to be growing in importance as the traveller increasingly seeks experiences that go beyond the more passive visitation practices of the past. In *The Experience Economy: Work Is Theatre and Every Business a Stage*, Pine and Gilmore (1999) argue that customer experience rather than customer service is a hallmark of new economic growth: 'Experiences are a fourth economic offering [the others being commodity, good or service] as distinct from services as services are from goods' (p. 2). The challenge facing the tourism destination manager is to develop those activities that take advantage of the natural physiography of the destination while remaining consistent with the local culture and its value. For example, a nature-based destination should take the opportunity to strengthen its appeal by developing activities that build on this strength; a historical/cultural destination should creatively identify and develop activities that reinforce this foundation of its appeal.

The attractor defined as *special events* represents a distinctive extension to that of the activities mix. It is of particular managerial interest since it is a factor over which destination managers have a great degree of control. The term 'special events' refers to a wide range of happenings that can create high levels of interest and involvement on the part of both visitors and residents. The spectrum of possible special events ranges from modest community festivals to large-scale international 'mega-events', such as the Olympic Games, world expositions and global sporting championships. Special events throughout the spectrum have an important role to play. Local festivals provide the opportunity to involve residents in events of particular relevance to their daily lives, and may also draw visitors from nearby regions. Mega-events (Ritchie, 1984) demand a much higher level of commitment, but provide a much greater opportunity to establish a destination's tourism credentials at the international level. While mega-events are generally more commercial and professional in nature, the decision to host a particular type of mega-event should not ignore the interests and potential for involvement of members of the local community.

Entertainment is another category of destination core resource or attractor. The entertainment industry is a major supplier to travel and tourism. Apart from gambling, the Las Vegas experience is based on entertainment. Many visitors to New York or London include a live show in their travel itinerary. Entertainment can even attract tourists internationally. New Zealand is an important market for theatre productions in Melbourne and Sydney that are too expensive to stage in the smaller New Zealand market. The theatre, concerts, comedy festivals, operas and circuses, such as the *Cirque du Soleil*, are examples of the contribution that the entertainment sector can make to a destination's competitiveness.

The final core dimension of destination attractiveness, *tourism superstructure*, is another factor over whose development destination managers can exert a considerable amount of control. In fact, it is the tourism superstructure, consisting primarily of accommodation facilities, food services, transportation facilities and major attractions, that many people view as the tourism industry.

There are elements of the tourism superstructure that may be categorized by some as supporting factors of destination appeal in that visitors do not, for example, normally choose a destination just to eat and sleep. They visit a destination largely because of the appeal of its attractions. Despite the possible legitimacy of the view that excludes accommodation and food services, it can also be argued with considerable force that the quality of these factors can represent in itself a significant percentage of the overall appeal of a destination. For this reason, the present model defines them as components of core attractiveness.

Chapter 6 expands on the influence of each of these dimensions of core resources and attractors.

Supporting factors and resources

Whereas the core resources and attractors of a destination constitute the primary motivations for inbound tourism, the *supporting factors and resources*, as the term implies, provide a foundation upon which a successful tourism industry can be established. A destination with an abundance of core resources and attractors but a dearth of supporting factors and resources may find it very difficult to develop its tourism industry, at least in the short term, until some attention is paid to those things that are lacking. This may not be easy in a location or region which is poor, undeveloped or under-populated. The question then becomes that of how the destination can begin to use, albeit in a modest way, its abundant attractions to build gradually a tourism industry which will create the wealth, taxes, employment and investment necessary for the provision of the missing supporting elements.

In a region that already enjoys a broad economic base, this question may not arise. Even so, the quality, range and volume of supporting factors and resources are still likely to be significant in shaping the realization of the potential for tourism. Where the question does arise, however, particularly careful planning and management are required to ensure a proper balance between the growth of tourism and the development of infrastructure and other facilitating resources. Without such a balance, economic, social, ecological and perhaps even political systems might be placed at risk.

One of the most important supporting factors is the condition and extent of a destination's general *infrastructure*. Some elements of infrastructure have a very direct influence on destination competitiveness. For example, transportation services and facilities are vital to travellers. Highways, railways, bus services, airports, ferries, etc. convey travellers to and from desired points of interest. The quality of the infrastructure of transportation is as important as its mere existence. A destination is more competitive when transportation systems are reliable, efficient, clean, safe, frequent and able to take travellers to the locations and attractions of greatest interest. In fact, infrastructure elements important to all economic and social activity, such as sanitation systems, communication systems, public facilities, legal systems and a reliable supply of potable water, also provide the basis for an effective and efficient tourism industry.

Successful tourism development also depends on a range of other *facilitating resources* and services, such as the availability and quality of local human, knowledge and capital resources, education and research institutions, financial institutions and various areas of the public service. The labour market, in terms of the skills available, work ethics, wage rates, union demands and government regulations, is particularly important in a sector of the economy where customer service is critical. The availability of capital resources will depend on the extent of local wealth and savings for investment, competition for capital from other industries, government constraints on foreign investment, and the return investors expect from investment in tourism development. The lack of such resources may severely limit a destination's competitive potential.

The vitality, sense of *enterprise*, entrepreneurship and initiatives that play a part in developing new ventures in a destination contribute to its competitiveness in a number of ways. These include competition, cooperation, specialization, innovation, facilitation, investment, growth, income distribution and equity, risk-taking, productivity, gap-filling, product diversification, seasonality management and disequilibria (Crouch and Ritchie, 1995). We discuss these in some detail in Chapter 7. The tourism industry is replete with many small to medium-sized enterprises. The extent to which tourism development advances economic prosperity and the quality of life of residents depends significantly upon the actions and success of these firms. Porter (1990, p. 125) notes that 'invention and entrepreneurship are at the heart of national advantage'. He argues that the role of chance does not mean that industry success is unpredictable, because entrepreneurship is not a random phenomenon.

The *accessibility* of the destination, too, is a supporting factor since it is governed by a wide variety of influences, many of which depend on broad economic, social or political concerns. For example, the accessibility of a destination is affected, in more complex ways than its mere physical location might suggest, by the regulation of the airline industry; entry visas and permits; route connections, airport hubs and landing slots; airport capacities and curfews; and competition among carriers, etc. Within a destination, the accessibility of tourism resources is also a competitive issue. Although the accessibility of resources such as beaches, mountains, national parks, unusual land formations, scenic regions, and lakes and rivers will undoubtedly be influenced by the needs of the tourism industry, other economic, social and sometimes political needs often govern the location of roads and railway lines, for example. A destination's resources are hardly relevant to the issue of competitiveness unless they are accessible to potential tourists and tourism operators alike.

The operating sectors of tourism are responsible for delivering high-quality, memorable experiences. Care must be taken, however, to wrap these experiences in a warm spirit of *hospitality*. Quite simply, it is not enough to deliver all the attributes of an experience in a cold and detached manner. Each individual visitor must feel that they are more than a source of cold cash revenue for the business or destination. Rather, visitors have a natural human desire for warm acceptance as they seek to enjoy the range of experiences the destination has to offer. The challenge facing destinations is to deliver their experiences in a way that enables the visitors to believe they are welcome – that they are truly guests.

A further factor that can support or hinder destination competitiveness is the degree of *political will*. Many destination executives we have spoken to have noted how their efforts to develop their destination have been either assisted by an abundance of political will or frustrated by the lack of it. The saying 'where there's a will there's a way' captures the important role of political support in facilitating efforts by the tourism industry to create a competitive destination. Political will is not a function of the attitudes and opinions of politicians alone. All community leaders shape political attitudes to the contribution that tourism might make to economic and social development and the resulting quality of life in the destination.

In Chapter 7, which focuses on the critical role of supporting factors and resources, we discuss in some depth the need to pay attention to this area as a foundation of successful tourism development.

Destination policy, planning and development

A strategic or policy-driven framework for the planning and development of the destination with particular economic, social and other societal goals as the intended outcome can provide a guiding hand to the direction, form and structure of tourism development. Such a framework can help to ensure that the tourism development that does occur promotes a competitive and sustainable destination while meeting the quality-of-life aspirations of those who reside in the destination.

In order to formulate a strategic framework, it is first necessary to decide or agree on the framework's subject: that is, precisely what it is that the framework is meant to govern. This requires an explicit recognition and common understanding among the stakeholders who are involved in the process concerning the *system definition* of the tourism destination in question. Before different parties can agree or come to a consensus on what needs to be done, they must first agree on the entity for which the strategy is to be developed.

In the process of developing a policy-driven framework for destination development, various philosophical perspectives are likely to emerge among the stakeholders concerned. For example, some destination communities may feel that major resort development is quite compatible with the social and environmental nature of the destination and will provide the best opportunity for creating economic growth and jobs for younger people. In different circumstances, another community might hold the view that a different sort of approach to tourism development is called for. So a community's *philosophy* on the best way to address economic, social, environmental and political goals through tourism development will shape the policy framework. This philosophy needs to fit the circumstances, but there also needs to be some emergent view among stakeholders about the right philosophy, or at least about the prevailing philosophy.

A *vision* is a statement or understanding of what such a philosophy logically suggests makes most sense for the destination. The same general philosophy might suggest different visions in different circumstances. Whereas a philosophy is a way of looking at a problem, a vision is more a view of what one sees when adopting a particular philosophical perspective.

A tourism development policy, if grounded in reality, ought to be based upon an *audit* of the destination and its attributes, its strengths and weaknesses, problems and challenges, past and current strategies, etc. Without some fundamental data on the significant attractions and resources, historical performance, current visitors and other vital information, the formulation of a policy framework for developing the destination remains an abstract exercise. An audit of the destination helps to communicate information and issues to all parties engaged in policy formulation and is a key input to any effort to create and maintain a competitive destination. We view the destination audit as the linchpin in the whole process of managing destination competitiveness. For this reason, we end this book with a chapter that overviews the destination audit process.

Similarly, *competitive/collaborative analysis* is an evaluation of how the destination relates and compares to other destinations and the international tourism system. Because competitiveness is a relative concept, decisions about the most appropriate policy or strategy for developing a destination must be made in the context of what other destinations are doing and how they are performing. A management consultancy recently advertised its services in newspapers by showing two views of a sprinter in an athletics event. In the first frame the sprinter is shown in full flight, apparently in the lead with a couple of other athletes close on her heels. In the next frame the view widens to show a gap in front of the athlete, revealing other sprinters clearly ahead of the pack. It is an effective illustration of how a narrow view can hide a competitor's true position.

A similar issue involves the marketing concept of *positioning*. An athletic sprint event is a one-dimensional race from a starting point to a finishing line. But destination competitiveness is not one-dimensional, and positioning is all about where, in cognitive rather than physical space, a destination is positioned *vis-à-vis* its competitors. Positioning is all to do with how unique a destination is perceived to be in ways that tourism markets value or regard as desirable or important. Destination positioning entails knowing how different market segments currently perceive the destination against competing destinations, which market segments it makes most sense to covet, and therefore target, and how the destination might be effectively and feasibly repositioned with respect to these segments.

Destination policies for tourism *development* should be formulated as an integrative system of mechanisms designed to work in concert, such that overall competitiveness and sustainability goals can be achieved. Development policies should address the full range of important issues that govern destination competitiveness, including both demand- and supply-oriented concerns. On the supply side, policies should address the development and maintenance of resources, such as the destination's physical features; the quality and supply of human capital; the availability and cost of financial capital and the investment attractiveness of the tourism industry; the necessary data and information required for sound business and investment decisions to grow the industry; and the programmes and activities required to put these resources into action for the creation of tourism products and experiences. To the extent that governments assist tourism development and therefore expect a broader socio-economic benefit from this investment, demand policies seek to ensure that the right tourism markets are pursued in the most effective manner with regard not just to the needs of the tourism industry but also to the wider community.

The final element of destination policy, planning and development, concerns the need for and importance of the *monitoring and evaluation* of policies and their outcome. The effectiveness and impact of policies in a complex system can be neither forecast nor predicted with a high degree of confidence when they are first formulated. Also, the eventual outcome is as much a function of how well the policies are implemented as a function of the policies themselves. Hence, the task of policy formulation, planning and development must continue to include research into how well such policies are performing, whether improvements in implementation are needed or, indeed, whether circumstances have changed so as to render the policies no longer relevant or effectual.

The sub-elements of the model discussed above are further explained and developed in Chapter 8, *Destination Policy, Planning and Development*.

Destination management

The *destination management* component of the model focuses on those activities which implement the policy and planning framework established in the previous section of this chapter, enhance the appeal of the *core resources and attractors*, strengthen the quality and effectiveness of the *supporting factors and resources*, and adapt best to the constraints or opportunities imposed or presented by the *qualifying and amplifying determinants*. These activities represent the greatest scope for *managing* a destination's competitiveness as they include programmes, structures, systems and processes that are highly actionable and manageable by individuals and organizations and through collective action.

Perhaps the most traditional of these activities is the function of *marketing* the destination. In practice, destination marketing has tended to focus on the task of promoting and selling the destination. That is, the concept of marketing has been applied to the destination in very limited ways. As a result, there is much scope for the application of a true marketing philosophy.[3] Beyond promotion and selling, marketing responsibilities and activities are manifold. For example, the competitiveness of the destination also depends on product development, packaging and innovation to serve the changing needs of travellers, appropriate pricing policies and practices, the development of effective marketing channels to facilitate the connection between the destination and the potential consumer, and the strategic selection of target markets which might be attracted to the destination, while providing the yield levels and creating the sorts of impacts which will sustain the destination.

The importance of the *service experience* dimension of destination management has also been recognized for some time. Tourists are buying *experiences*, and experiences are made up of all of the interactions, behaviours and emotions which each tourist permits their five senses to perceive and experience. The choice of hotels, restaurants, attractions, tours, etc. is incidental to the choice of the destination. Efforts to enhance the quality of service provided to visitors have recently been complemented by recognition of the need to take a total quality-of-experience approach to visitor satisfaction (Otto and Ritchie, 1995). This approach emphasizes the need to examine the total travel experience of visitors. Essentially, providing individual high-quality service transactions is not enough. As far as possible, destination managers must attempt to ensure a seamless, hassle-free interface among all elements of the total travel experience. In practical terms, this means paying close attention to such aspects as the convenience of transfers between modes of transport or travel packages and the responsibility of travel agents for each component of the travel packages they sell. In brief, on-site and transaction-specific visitor service is not enough.

The *information/research* component of destination management pertains to the development and effective use of information systems that provide managers with the information required for understanding visitor needs and for effective product development. This also involves the regular monitoring of visitor satisfaction and the tracking of industry performance. This monitoring function must be complemented by special research projects designed to provide specialized information for particular decisions. Finally, each destination management organization (DMO) also has the responsibility to disseminate key market and performance information to its members in a timely way. Such information is essential in order to ensure destination productivity and effectiveness.

The concept of the DMO, where the 'M' emphasizes total management rather than simply marketing, is a somewhat recent conceptualization of the *organization* function for destination management. Within this refocused philosophy, a broader view is taken of the destination's organizational structure, which, in the opinion of Nadler and Tushman (1997),[4] may be one of the last remaining sources of truly sustainable competitive advantage. This broader view sees management as responsible for the well-being of all aspects of the destination. It emphasizes the provision of a form of leadership in destination development that makes extensive use of teamwork in all DMO-led initiatives. Destination promotion is no longer the sole purpose of the DMO. While this modified role presents many new challenges, it also provides a much broader range of opportunities for ensuring destination competitiveness.

While financial institutions, financial markets and investors will normally fund most private-sector tourism development (see this chapter, *Supporting factors and resources*; and Chapter 7), some public sector support or programmes can assist the availability of *finance and venture capital* to tourism developers. For example, guided by public policy, governments or DMOs can institute programmes to provide investors with seed funding, grants, loan guarantees, depreciation allowances, capital gains exclusions, taxation concessions and other such incentives in order to stimulate private investment for tourism development. Such programmes should clearly be designed to promote the realization of a destination vision that has been formulated previously.

Similarly, destination management can play a key role in *human resource development* by further encouraging and stimulating education and training programmes designed to meet the specific needs of the tourism and hospitality industries. Although quality education systems are a fundamental element of the facilitating resources (see this chapter, *Supporting factors and resources*), education programmes are required which specifically address the skills required by employers in tourism and hospitality, just as other industries and economic sectors have cooperated with educational institutions to develop graduates' skills in other fields. Australia is an example where educational institutions have responded to the needs of the industry at both secondary and tertiary levels and in terms of both vocational and professional education and training.

As the travel and tourism industry continues to grow rapidly, concerns have been expressed in various destinations that are subject to large numbers of visitors that policies and systems are required for *visitor management* in order to exert some influence over visitor impacts. Calls for visitor management have come from a range of places, including national parks (such as Banff National Park in Canada) and cities (such as Venice). It is in the interests of the local tourism industries to cooperate in order to develop an appropriate approach to visitor management. In the absence of such cooperation, governments and other regulatory authorities may be forced to act if problems are left unattended. DMOs can play an important role in coordinating efforts to institute such industry-regulated arrangements.

An increasingly important challenge for destination managers involves *crisis management*. Destinations have always, from time to time, had to deal with crises affecting visitors – not only the direct effects at the time of the crisis but also the consequences of a tarnished destination image. Anecdotally, in recent years it seems that crises have become more problematic for destinations. The impact of the terrorism of 11 September 2001 in New York and Washington, DC, is an extreme example, in which some visitors to New York and all passengers on board the hijacked planes lost their lives. Not only has the New York Convention and Visitor Bureau had to contend with the significant aftermath of that crisis ever since, but these events have also affected the entire US tourism industry. It is easy to think of numerous other acts of terrorism that destinations have had to contend with over the years. But crises may arise from many different causes, including disease (such as the foot-and-mouth disease outbreak in the UK, Ebola in Africa and mad cow disease (bovine spongiform encephalopathy) in Europe), accidents (such as the canyoning tragedy in Switzerland), crime (which we discuss in some detail in Chapter 10), natural disasters (such as the floods in Europe and fires in the western USA in 2002), political and social problems (such as the violence in Zimbabwe over land laws and the conduct of elections, and cultural and religious violence in parts of Indonesia) and union strikes (such as those by airline staff and other key groups of employees). When such crises occur, destinations need to be able to respond in an effective way to deal with the immediate impact of the event as well as its longer-term consequences. Destinations which respond to such eventualities more effectively or, better still, act to prevent or minimize them as far as this is possible, enhance their competitive position. Proactive crisis management or disaster planning is therefore becoming an additional challenge and responsibility for forward-thinking destinations.

The final component of destination management in our model of destination competitiveness is a new but increasingly significant one. *Resource stewardship* is a concept that stresses how important it is – indeed, that it is obligatory – for destination managers to adopt a caring attitude to the resources that make up the destination. This involves the effective maintenance of these resources and the careful nurturing of those that are particularly vulnerable to any damage that may be caused by tourism. All in all, the stewardship philosophy implies ensuring the effective yet sensitive deployment of all the resources within the destination. The model is then not one of simple economic competitiveness, but one of long-term sustainable competitiveness, which acknowledges the stewardship of ecological, social and cultural resources.

As noted above, because elements that constitute *destination management* are among the most actionable and manageable of those concerned in the quest to develop and maintain a destination's competitiveness, a substantial part of this book (Chapter 9) discusses these activities in greater depth.

Qualifying and amplifying determinants

The potential competitiveness of a destination is conditioned or limited by a number of factors which fall outside the scope of the preceding four groups of determinants (core resources and attractors; supporting factors and resources; destination policy, planning and development; and destination management). This group of factors, which we have called *qualifying and amplifying determinants*, might alternatively have been labelled *situational conditioners* because their effects on the competitiveness of a tourist destination are to define its scale, limit or potential. These qualifiers and amplifiers moderate or magnify destination competitiveness by *filtering* the

influence of the other three groups of factors. They may be so important as to represent a ceiling to tourism demand and potential, but are largely beyond the control or influence of the tourism sector alone.

For example, clearly a destination's *location* has much to do with its ability to attract visitors. A physically remote destination, one that is far from the world's major origin markets for tourism, is clearly at a distinct disadvantage to begin with. A destination that is perhaps equally attractive to potential travellers but which neighbours the major markets is in a much stronger position to be able to convert latent interest into actual visitation because it has the advantages of familiarity and lower travel cost (in terms of both monetary cost and the opportunity cost of travel time).

Although the physical location of a destination does not change (unless we are willing to wait a few million years for continental drift to have an effect), what can change over time, within the span of a decade or two, are the relative locations of important origin markets for tourists. We have seen, for example, in the Asian region the economies of several countries improve markedly over a short space of time. The wealth generated in these countries and the overflow effect in other neighbouring countries have created a huge and growing tourism market in this region. This has led to a shift in the competitiveness of tourism destinations as a result of this one factor – location – alone.

A related but nevertheless different phenomenon is the *interdependencies* that exist between destinations. We touched upon this issue briefly in our discussion of the competitive (micro)environment, where we noted the paradox of competition and cooperation between destinations. The competitiveness of any destination is affected by the competitiveness of other destinations. In part, as we pointed out in Chapter 2, this is because competitiveness is a relative concept. But beyond this there are interdependencies that can significantly affect the fortunes of individual destinations. This can best be illustrated if we consider the situation of stopover destinations for a moment. You can probably think of destinations that depend, at least to some significant extent, on travellers who break their journey to or from more distant destinations. Should the attractiveness of those distant destinations change, either positively or negatively, the stopover destination is sure to experience some consequent effect. Another example concerns the impacts of terrorist events, wars and crime in a neighbouring region. There are many examples of how events such as these have dramatically affected the destination choices of travellers.

This leads us to the specific issue of *safety and security*. Nothing can influence the choices of travellers more powerfully and patently as concerns over safety and security. Of course there will always be the intrepid tourist who disregards travel advisories, warnings or adverse media coverage of events in dangerous destinations. Indeed, some travellers might even seek out dangerous or risky experiences for the excitement and challenge they offer. Most people tolerate a certain degree of uncertainty and risk, but their tolerance levels are normally relatively low. The need for safety, along with the physiological needs of food and shelter, are primary motivational forces behind human behaviour. If potential visitors are gravely concerned about crime, the quality of drinking water, the risk of natural disasters, the standards of medical services, etc., other competitive strengths may amount to very little in the minds of these people. Tourism authorities may launch recovery programmes in response to these problems, and these may help. But problems such as these often dwarf the tourism industry's ability to overcome them.

The *awareness and image* of a destination can also qualify or amplify its competitiveness. The image of a destination can take time to change after the reality at a destination has changed and no longer accords with its previous negative or positive image. A negative image will qualify improvements at a destination and a positive image will cushion the effect of problems such as crime and high living costs. Low awareness will also ensure that destination image changes slowly, but the degree of awareness also affects the likelihood that a potential tourist will even consider visiting a destination. As there are very many destinations today competing for a space in the minds of intending tourists, it is important that tourists are sufficiently aware of a destination if it is to be at least a part of the 'consideration set' of would-be

visitors. The consideration set includes destinations that potential visitors consider when making a choice between alternatives. Destinations that are not considered may be explicitly rejected (the 'inept set') or implicitly ignored (the 'inert set') (Woodside and Lysonski, 1989). More broadly, however, destination awareness and image is the lens through which tourists perceive all characteristics of a destination and therefore effectively all of the other elements of our model.

We have also included *cost/value* as a qualifying and amplifying determinant. At first it may seem strange that we have classified cost in this way when the cost of a destination can be associated with the specific range of goods and services consumed by visitors to the destination and the efficiency with which these products are produced. However, because the cost of a destination to a foreign visitor is driven by such a broad range of local, domestic and global forces, and because cost in itself is so fundamental to the question of competitiveness, it makes more sense to treat cost as a qualifying and amplifying determinant than to incorporate it in any of the other four categories of destination competitiveness factors.

The monetary cost of a destination is governed by three factors: (i) the cost of transportation to and from the destination; (ii) the currency exchange rate (in the case of international travel); and (iii) the local cost of tourism goods and services. Many aspects of the global (macro) environment (e.g. international trade balances, relative interest rates, relative inflation, taxes) and the competitive (micro)environment (e.g. competition, productivity, cost of supplies, labour rates and agreements) will affect costs. Consequently, cost is largely governed by economic structures within the destination and its comparative international position.

Finally, a destination's *carrying capacity* can clearly restrict the further growth or competitiveness of the destination if demand is close to or in excess of its sustainable limit. It can also result in deterioration of conditions at the destination or a decline in its apparent attractiveness. Venice, for example, is clearly an extremely popular destination that is under stress in terms of its carrying capacity. It remains very popular but struggles to cope with visitors at certain times of the year. Indeed, the system of restricted access to Venice effectively imposes a ceiling on visitor numbers during these peak periods.

We discuss the role of qualifying and amplifying determinants in greater detail in Chapter 10.

Notes

[1] These include the 1994 Administrative Sciences Association of Canada Conference in Halifax (Crouch and Ritchie, 1994); an invited presentation in 1994 at the Victoria University of Technology, Australia; the 1994 Quality Management in Urban Tourism conference at the University of Victoria, Canada (Kirker and Crouch, 1994); an invited presentation in 1995 at San Diego State University (Ritchie and Crouch, 1995); the 1995 World Business Congress in Istanbul (Crouch and Ritchie, 1995); an invited presentation in 1996 at La Trobe University, Australia; the 1996 Annual Council on Hotel, Restaurant and Institutional Education Conference (Crouch and Ritchie, 1996); the 1999 Conference of the Council for Australian University Tourism and Hospitality Education (CAUTHE) (Crouch and Ritchie, 1999); the Second Symposium on the Consumer Psychology of Tourism, Hospitality and Leisure (Ritchie et al., 2001); the 31st Annual Travel and Tourism Research Association Conference (Ritchie and Crouch, 2000); and the World Tourism Organization's 2001 Annual General Meeting (Ritchie and Crouch, 2001).

[2] 'Competitive firms in the tourism business have recognized that they must "cooperate" and share in the responsibility for quality tourism growth. This collaboration of "competitors" in the tourism business for a better future in tourism is another expression of what "coopetition" is all about' (Edgell and Haenisch, 1995, p. 2).

[3] The marketing philosophy 'holds that the key to achieving organizational goals consists in determining the needs and wants of target markets and delivering the desired satisfactions more effectively and efficiently than competitors' (Kotler, 1988, p. 17). Promotion and selling represent only a small, albeit important, subset of the range of tasks that constitute marketing. Indeed, the more effective an organization is in marketing, the less effort it needs to make to promote and sell its product (in this case, the destination), because the product will largely promote and sell itself if marketing has succeeded in its aim, so that the product satisfies customers' needs and wants better than competitors' products.

[4] 'In this volatile environment where instability is the norm, we're convinced that the last remaining source of truly sustainable competitive advantage lies in what we've come to describe as "organizational capabilities": – the unique ways in which each organization structures its work and motivates its people to achieve clearly articulated strategic objectives. These capabilities combine an organization's core competencies . . . with the ability to sustain and adapt those competencies in the fulfillment of long-term objectives despite changing competition, altered strategies, and the loss of key employees' (Nadler and Tushman, 1997, p. 5).

References

Crouch, G.I. (1992a) Effect of income and price on international tourism demand. *Annals of Tourism Research* 19, 643–664.

Crouch, G.I. (1992b) *Marketing International Tourism: a Meta-Analytical Study of Demand*. PhD dissertation, Monash University, Australia.

Crouch, G.I. (1994) Demand elasticities for short-haul v. long-haul tourism. *Journal of Travel Research* 33, 2–7.

Crouch, G.I. (1996) Demand elasticities in international marketing: a meta-analytical application to tourism. *Journal of Business Research* 36, 117–136.

Crouch, G.I. and Ritchie, J.R.B. (1994) Destination competitiveness: exploring foundations for a long-term research program. In: *Proceedings of the Administrative Sciences Association of Canada 1994 Annual Conference, 25–28 June, Halifax, Nova Scotia*, pp. 79–88.

Crouch, G.I. and Ritchie, J.R.B. (1995) Destination competitiveness and the role of the tourism enterprise. *Proceedings of the Fourth Annual World Business Congress, 13–16 July, Istanbul, Turkey*, pp. 43–48.

Crouch, G.I., Schultz, L. and Valerio, P. (1992) Marketing international tourism to Australia – a regression analysis. *Tourism Management* 13, 196–208.

Echtner, C.M. and Ritchie, J.R.B. (1993) The measurement of destination image: an empirical assessment. *Journal of Travel Research* 31, 3–13.

Edgell, D.L. Sr and Haenisch, R.T. (1995) *Competition: Global Tourism Beyond the Millennium*. International Policy Publishing, Kansas City, Missouri.

Foot, D.K. (1996) *Boom, Bust and Echo: How to Profit from the Coming Demographic Shift*. Macfarlane Walter and Ross, Toronto, Ontario, Canada.

Glaser, B.G. and Strauss, A.L. (1967) *The Discovery of Grounded Theory.* Aldine, Chicago, Illinois.

Kirker, W.S. and Crouch, G.I. (1994). Competing urban destinations: is productivity a relevant concept? In: *Proceedings of the Quality Management in Urban Tourism Conference, 10–12 November, University of Victoria, British Columbia,* pp. 466–476.

Kotler, P. (1988) *Marketing Management: Analysis, Planning, Implementation, and Control,* 6th edn. Prentice-Hall International, Englewood Cliffs, New Jersey.

Nadler, D.A. and Tushman, M.L. (1997) *Competing by Design: the Power of Organizational Architecture.* Oxford University Press, New York.

Naisbitt, J. (1994) *Global Paradox.* William Morrow, New York.

Neuman, W.L. (1994) *Social Research Methods: Qualitative and Quantitative Approaches,* 2nd edn. Allyn and Bacon, Needham Heights, Massachusetts.

Otto, J.E. and Ritchie, J.R.B. (1995) Exploring the quality of service experience: a theoretical and empirical analysis. *Advances in Services Marketing and Management* 5, 37–61.

Pine, J.B. II and Gilmore, J.H. (1999) *The Experience Economy: Work is Theatre and Every Business a Stage.* Harvard Business School Press, Boston, Massachusetts.

Porter, M.E. (1980) *Competitive Strategy: Techniques for Analysing Industry and Competitors.* Free Press, New York.

Porter, M.E. (1990) *The Competitive Advantage of Nations.* Free Press, New York.

Ritchie, J.R.B. (1984) Assessing the impact of hallmark events – conceptual and research issues. *Journal of Travel Research* 23, 2–11.

Ritchie, J.R.B. (1993) Crafting a destination vision: putting the concept of resident-responsive tourism into practice. *Tourism Management* 14, 379–381.

Ritchie, J.R.B. and Crouch, G.I. (1993) Competitiveness in international tourism: a framework for understanding and analysis. *Proceedings of the 43rd Congress of the International Association of Scientific Experts in Tourism, 17–23 October, San Carlos de Bariloche, Argentina,* pp. 23–71.

Ritchie, J.R.B. and Crouch, G.I. (1995) Developing a successful Canadian/US/Mexican travel destination: a model of competitive and cooperative advantage. *USIA Trilateral Affiliation Program, San Diego State University, San Diego, California, and Colegio del Frontera Norte, Tijuana, Mexico, April 1995.*

Ritchie, J.R.B. and Crouch, G.I. (2000) Are destination stars born or made: must a competitive destination have star genes? In: Nickerson, N.P., Moisey, N. and Andereck, K.L. (eds) *Proceedings of the 31st Annual Travel and Tourism Research Association Conference, 11–14 June, Burbank, California,* pp. 306–315.

Ritchie, J.R.B. and Crouch, G.I. (2001) Achieving destination competitiveness and sustainability: an integrated policy and management framework. Keynote presentation, *2001 World Tourism Organization General Assembly, Seoul, Korea and Osaka, Japan, September 2001.*

Ritchie, J.R.B. and Smith, B.H. (1991) The impact of a mega-event on host region awareness: a longitudinal study. *Journal of Travel Research* 30, 30–10.

Ritchie, J.R.B., Crouch, G.I. and Hudson, S. (2001) Developing operational measures for the components of a destination competitiveness/ sustainability model: consumer versus managerial perspectives. In: Mazanec, J.A., Crouch, G.I., Ritchie, J.R.B. and Woodside, A.G. (eds) *Consumer Psychology of Tourism, Hospitality and Leisure,* Vol. 2. CAB International, Wallingford, UK, pp. 1–17.

Woodside, A.G. and Lysonski, S. (1989) A general model of traveler destination choice. *Journal of Travel Research* 27, 8–14.

4

The Macroenvironment: Global Forces Shaping World Tourism

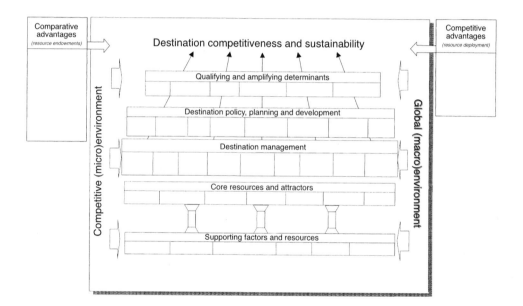

In Chapter 1, we reviewed the evolution of competition from the early days of global socio-economic activity to the present. In that review, it was seen that the nature of competition on a particular day is shaped by the context of the day. It follows that, as the factors defining context change over time, they set in motion a parallel evolution of competitiveness itself.

An examination of the factors defining the context of competitiveness confirms their global nature. In speaking of the 'global nature' of these factors, we mean not only that they affect competitiveness in all parts of the world

but also that they are beyond the influence of any one individual group or organization.

In the same way, just as certain global factors define the nature of competition, others exert a major influence on the ability of a given destination to compete successfully in the marketplace. The goal of this chapter is to identify these global forces and to examine the manner in which they affect each of the components of our model of destination competitiveness (Chapter 3).

While this book focuses primarily on the factors and processes within a destination that

©CAB International 2003. *The Competitive Destination: a Sustainable Tourism Perspective* (J.R. Brent Ritchie and Geoffrey I. Crouch)

determine its competitiveness and sustainability, the analytical framework which we have described in Chapter 3 also stresses that destination performance and success can also be influenced significantly by a broad range of global forces. These forces are so pervasive that their influence extends well beyond tourism into all aspects of the economy and society. Since tourism is, of course, part of the global totality, it must attempt to adapt to or take advantage of those forces which it cannot control or even influence.

Global Forces: an Onionskin Taxonomy

This chapter first seeks to identify and categorize these global forces, and subsequently to provide readers with a basic understanding of the challenges and opportunities they create for the tourism destination in its effort to succeed. There are undoubtedly a variety of ways in which these forces might be categorized. The framework we have found appealing is that given graphically in Fig. 4.1. As shown, the totality of global forces affecting destination competitiveness/sustainability is captured within what we term an 'onionskin taxonomy'. By this we mean that the global forces may be viewed as consisting of different layers surrounding the destination (represented by the globe in the centre). The innermost layer, or layer 1, of the 'onion' consists of three types of forces that tend to affect changes in the performance and well-being of the destination most directly, in that they normally fluctuate widely and rapidly within short periods of time. These forces can usually be categorized as economic, political and technological. The next layer of the onion, layer 2, contains forces that

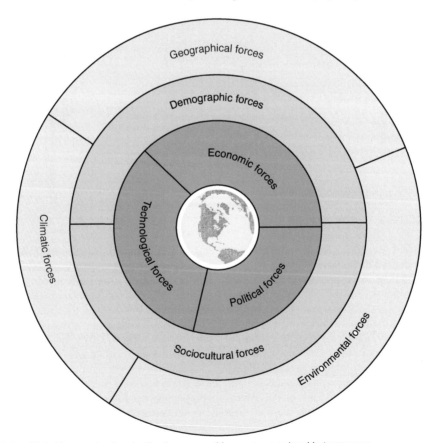

Fig. 4.1. Global forces shaping destination competitiveness: an onionskin taxonomy.

tend to be somewhat more stable, and therefore a bit easier to predict. We have placed demographic and sociocultural forces in layer 2. Finally, there are forces that, in normal times, are quite stable and that can be anticipated with a fairly high degree of reliability. In this layer (layer 3) we have placed climatic forces, geographical forces and environmental forces.

In presenting this taxonomy, we stress that it reflects the stability of the global forces but not necessarily their importance. Consequently, at any given point in time, any particular force within any of the layers can be having the greatest impact on destination competitiveness/sustainability/success. For example, climate may be the greatest determinant of competitiveness for particular destinations. At the same time it is one that is normally the most predictable within a broad range. In contrast, while political stability may overwhelm climatic desirability at a given point in time as a factor affecting a destination's competitiveness or sustainability, this is usually not the case for most destinations.

In other situations, the rapidly evolving culture of a destination (such as the changes occurring in the USA resulting from the influx of immigrants and the rapidity with which technological and social innovations are introduced) may be one of its main competitive strengths in both industry and tourism. By comparison, highly stable environmental forces within the USA contribute relatively little to the competitive abilities of the country, and thus its ability to attract visitors profitably. Should a significant environmental concern suddenly emerge, it could become a major deterrent to visitation in the short term.

To summarize, when examining the global forces that may create challenges and opportunities for a tourism destination, it is essential to examine both their importance and their stability/predictability. Unimportant forces (i.e. forces that have little effect on a destination's competitiveness) that are unstable may be ignored. Important but stable forces must be addressed, but they offer a destination time to prepare for their consequences. It is the important forces that become unstable that pose the greatest challenge, but they often present the greatest opportunities for managers of a tourism destination.

Table 4.1 attempts to capture visually the above discussion by comparing the varying combinations of stability and importance of impact of the different global forces that affect destination competitiveness and sustainability.

The outer layer

The forces we are dealing with here are in many ways so fundamental that true change is

Table 4.1. Global forces and their significance for destination management: stability versus importance of impact.

	Low impact	Medium impact	High impact
Very stable	Require minimal amount of DMO attention (hotel capacity)	Specific managers should review these factors to understand changes of particular relevance to their area of responsibility (destination infrastructure)	Require high attention on a periodic basis to detect 'surprises' (climate)
Modestly stable/ unstable	Require some monitoring by lower level management to detect (visa policies)	Require some monitoring by middle management (airline prices)	Require systematic attention by middle-level management to identify unusual changes (price levels)
Very unstable	Require ongoing monitoring by a mechanical system and lower-level DMO managers (short term exchange rate fluctuations)	Require sophisticated monitoring to detect specific types of shifts of particular significance (Internet marketing)	Require constant attention by top-level DMO managers (political situation)

too slow to allow any meaningful measurement from the standpoint of managerial action.

Climatic forces

An examination of the data regarding the climate of any given destination (Pearce and Smith, 1990) shows that the temperature, the amount of precipitation and the number of hours of sunshine are relatively predictable on a seasonal basis. Because of this, the nature of destinations is usually quite stable over time. Consequently, tourism operators, investors and tourists themselves can plan with a reasonable degree of confidence the development of a destination and the choice of a destination for a vacation.

While we know that not every visitor likes the same kind of climate in their destination, we also know that certain types of destinations do tend to be preferred over others. For example, warm, sunny destinations are generally preferred to cold, dreary ones. Despite this reality, it is important that those market segments that do prefer unusual climes can count on their expectations being met – and vice versa.

It is interesting to note that, given the current concern about climate change, certain colder destinations might be the beneficiaries of global warming, while traditional, sunnier places could be net losers. This is of course no reason to encourage climate change, but it does demonstrate that not all tourism destinations will necessarily be affected negatively.

Environmental forces

While the environment and the climate tend to be interlinked in this Kyoto era, they are distinct and do present some very different types of challenges. While it may be simplistic, it may be helpful from the standpoint of destination management to view climatic challenges as those that are 'above ground' while environmental challenges involve issues 'on or below' the ground. Examples of these issues include species diversity and protection, wildlife habitat preservation, the maintenance of water quality and aquatic biodiversity, the destruction of farming-quality land, the use of pesticides and the quality of the food system, hazardous waste, and the protection of vegetation.

Every destination manager is increasingly faced with the questions of how far tourism is contributing to environmental degradation, and whether and to what extent any such degradation affects the appeal of the destination and the quality of the visitor experience. The challenge is to know the extent to which any environmental damage that tourism causes can be minimized, and how this can be achieved. At the same time, some opportunities present themselves as a result of environmental interest and concern. These include the strong and growing (although still small) ecotourism market, the development of interpretive centres and guiding, increased interest in wildlife viewing (including marine life), and travel for environmental education.

In summary, in many ways concern for the environment has now taken centre stage in tourism. This reality is a reflection of a broad societal realization that protection of the world's natural environment is imperative. It is increasingly clear that 'spaceship earth' has a limited capacity to sustain life as we know it. Consequently, tourism policy makers in particular need to examine carefully what the tourism industry's relationship with responsibility for the environment should look like – and how to proceed with realizing this vision.

While scientific debate still rages with respect to the above questions, it is becoming increasingly clear that the majority of governments in the world believe that global warming is serious, and that it has been exacerbated, if not caused, by excessive carbon emissions into the atmosphere. As a result, most nations appear to be moving towards ratification of the Kyoto agreement, an agreement that commits all signatories to reducing overall emissions by at least 5% below 1990 levels during the commitment period 2008–2012 (United Nations, 1997, p. 9).

Should the Kyoto agreement be ratified and implemented by the majority of the world's nations, it could have serious consequences for travel and tourism, at least as we know it today. The use of fossil fuels for transportation and their polluting effect are obvious problems in this respect, and the continued economic growth of the tourism sector might be severely affected unless alternative, non-polluting energy sources become available at competitive prices for consumers.

From a destination management perspective, it appears that climatic forces – in particular global warming – should generally be viewed as an important challenge for tourism. Although the climate would historically have been classified as a highly stable and relatively benign global force in terms of the challenge it presents, such may not be the case in the future.

Geographical forces

In geographical terms, destinations have traditionally been viewed as very stable. The land on which they are located is fixed. The world has watched as colonies (the geographical extensions of powerful countries) have become independent, as large countries have split into many smaller ones (most notably the Soviet Union) and, in some cases, as new countries have been formed from two or more older nations. With the stroke of a pen, the measured amount of international travel has both increased and decreased as the number of nations has shifted both upwards and downwards. As a result, in the eyes of many travellers destinations have been both created and eliminated. While all this has been happening, technology (more specifically, the jet aircraft) has effectively shrunk the tourism globe. From a traveller's perspective, in about 1950 the geography of the world was suddenly squeezed. It then stabilized again for some 50 years. But now, with space tourism entering the equation, the traditional geography of destinations has potentially been destabilized again.

In the more immediate future, it is the ongoing, sometimes subtle process of globalization that poses a more serious challenge. Although this process clearly brings with it challenges that appear to be changing the geography of the world, the changes brought about by globalization are in reality less geographical than economic and cultural, and so they will be addressed later.

The intermediate layer

While there are no clear dividing lines between the inner, intermediate and outer layers of our onionskin taxonomy of global forces, it is nevertheless important to distinguish among these layers. As shown in Fig. 4.1, the intermediate layer is judged to contain two major categories of forces: demographic and sociocultural. The forces contained in this layer are not necessarily any more or less important than the inner layer forces. However, they are much more stable and predictable.

Demographic forces

In their treatise *Boom, Bust and Echo*, Foot and Stoffman (2001) put forth extensive argumentation concerning the profound impact of population demographics in determining what is important to people and the way they make decisions in a broad range of areas. Leisure and travel constitute one of these areas. Indeed, Foot and Stoffman devote an entire chapter to discussing how the nature of leisure will change as populations age, and they emphasize that both government policy and private investment can avoid costly errors by understanding the nature of these changes. Specifically, Foot and Stoffman note that, as might be expected, older people do not play active sports as much as younger ones do – hence the decline in the popularity of tennis and downhill skiing. Perhaps surprisingly, they also predict that the era of growth in professional spectator sports might be coming to an end. They note that half of those aged 18–24 years attend sports events, but that only 30% of those aged 45–64 do so. In brief, they observe that a nation of young people is a society of hockey and tennis players but that a nation of older people is a society of gardeners and walkers, and conclude that the data on the effect of ageing on leisure pursuits is remarkably stable over time and that these facts have important implications for public policy.

As for the travel market itself, Foot and Stoffman note that the travel business recruits many of its customers from affluent individuals in their late 40s and older, and that as the number of people in this group expands in the years to come the travel industry will reap benefits. They further predict that ecotourism, the cruise industry and gambling and casinos are destined for growth as the number of over-50s increases dramatically.

Sociocultural forces

There is fairly clear recognition that our world, after centuries of relative stability, is currently undergoing a number of fundamental shifts in the social and cultural foundations that we have taken for granted. Several of these shifts, while massive, are so subtle that it is difficult to know if they are truly substantial or merely transitory. Also, there are certain cultural characteristics of destinations that are by their nature unchangeable. The history of a destination is the most obvious (and perhaps the only) characteristic that is truly unchangeable.

Those global forces that are highly stable but appear to be undergoing shifts of significance to tourism include, most obviously, areas such as value systems, the way we work, the language used to communicate within a society, and food preparation and delivery systems.

It is the pervasive spread of Western values that may be the most fundamental value shift that has been important in the creation and expansion of the phenomenon we call tourism. While we can legitimately question whether all the changes that Western values are bringing about are positive, it is hard to assess their impact, their desirability and, indeed, their long-term stability.

The way that cultures function, or generally work, to ensure their survivability and well-being is another cultural characteristic that, despite its stability, has been changing and affecting tourism. Although the recent breakdown of the communal (or communist) system is viewed by many as an economic change, it is more fundamentally a change in the values underlying the way we work and share the results of our efforts. A review of the way tourism functioned in communist bloc countries shows vividly how much the shift to the capitalist model of work has changed tourism. While most would argue that this shift has provided positive results in terms of competitiveness and sustainability, it remains to others to furnish a comprehensive evaluation of the benefits across the entire sector.

Another fundamental component of culture, the nature of the language that societies use to communicate, has also, after many years of stability, been undergoing widespread change. Traditionally, there has been an extensive number of local languages used by relatively small groups, tribes, clans and countries. Now we are witnessing a diminution in the number of languages being employed by increasingly large language groups, which are defined not only by nations but by much larger economic and cultural regions. As one stands back and assesses the situation, it might be argued that the world is moving towards a global community in which we may have a very limited number of working languages, such as English, Spanish and Chinese. Indeed, as technology moves towards the ability to instantly translate an individual's speech, we could reach a situation of only one universal language of communication that makes the original language spoken irrelevant. Because the tourism industry has always been very sensitive to the language problem, not only do all these changes have profound practical implications, but – and this is equally important – they also have profound implications for the understanding of host cultures.

Since food is the essence of human survival, it is not surprising that it plays a part in the culture of a destination, and thus it has traditionally become an important dimension of the appeal of many destinations. Although this will remain true for many years, food and the food delivery system have not escaped the forces of change that tourism destination managers must consider, in both strategic and operational terms. Perhaps the most powerful force has been the pervasive growth of the fast-food system (Schlosser, 2001). It can be argued strongly that fast food reduces the quality of food in terms of its richness, the variety of food types, the nuances of taste and the ability to reflect cultural traditions. Conversely, its worldwide success is not without reason. The fast-food preparation and delivery system reflects a universal ability to manage costs, to control and meet taste expectations, and to provide well-defined nutritional content. While the nutritional content of fast-food systems can clearly be criticized, this is not the fault of the concept but rather of the desire to please consumer palates in the search for greater market share and profitability.

The growth of branded fast-food systems has had enormous implications for the travel market, particularly for those market segments that are seeking reliability, quick service and familiar tastes rather than innovation and the excitement of the new flavours that can be provided by cultural dishes and their exotic taste experiences.

The inner layer

The inner layer of our onionskin model contains three major types of global forces that, because of their high rate of change within relatively short periods of time, must be monitored constantly, particularly if they are judged to have a great impact on destination success.

Economic forces

While a number of economic forces within a destination can be controlled or influenced by destination managers, there are many others that cannot – hence their classification as global forces. Factors such as the shift to a market economy, international exchange rates, interest rates, the buoyancy of the world economy, the existence and structure of world trading blocs, and the amount of savings consumers have in the bank all create special challenges (or realities) that must be recognized and adapted to by a destination if it is to remain relatively competitive in the world marketplace. Conversely, these same forces also present a range of new opportunities that, if appropriately prepared for, can enhance destination competitiveness.

An important consideration to keep in mind is that, by definition, these global forces and the realities and opportunities they present apply equally to all destinations. It is the ability of each destination to adapt to these realities and to seize the opportunities that will eventually determine if the destination will emerge as competitive or become more competitive.

Technological forces

'Technology' is a very imprecise term that can mean many different things. The definition may be very narrow, focusing on specific areas such as microelectronics, computers and biotechnology. On the other hand, it can also be defined very broadly to include the technology

of management; for example, how you organize a destination management organization (DMO) or how you control large-scale production in logistical systems (Porter, 1997). This distinction is sometimes referred to as hard versus soft technology.

However defined, technology has had and continues to have dramatic impacts on the ability of destinations to compete. The introduction of the jet engine defined the arrival of long-haul mass tourism, particularly enhancing the competitiveness of more remote destinations. Computer reservation systems have totally restructured information management and flows, and have enabled multinational chains to dominate key sectors of the accommodation market. The Internet continues to dramatically change the way large numbers of consumers access information before and during travel, and how they make travel purchases. The result has been a major shift in marketing practices and in the power structure within tourism-related marketing systems.

The emergence of the Convention and Visitor Bureau (CVB) as the primary form of DMO has almost single-handedly redesigned the power structure of planning and decision making at the municipal level. It can be argued that the CVB organizational approach provides a range of operating strengths and efficiencies that enhance the ability of destinations to gain competitive advantages over destinations that use other organizational approaches, or none at all.

Because technology evolves so rapidly, a major challenge facing DMO managers is to ensure that they are up to date from both a hardware and software perspective. Otherwise, a hard-earned competitive advantage can vanish quite quickly.

Political forces

The world of politics represents another type of rapidly shifting global force that can substantially alter the ability of a destination to compete. A change in government at the local, regional or national level often brings with it a change in political ideology. Such ideological shifts can result in major modifications of fiscal, environmental and immigration policies, for example, and any of these can either enhance or detract from the appeal of a destination and the efficiency of its tourism operators.

It should be understood that senior DMO managers must be capable of effectively interfacing with government officials at every level, since these officials have control over policies and programmes that can alter the ability of the destination to compete. At the municipal level, a DMO faces the major challenge of attempting to educate local politicians concerning the benefits that tourism already provides to their constituents. Lack of sophistication and general unawareness on the part of politicians concerning the nature of tourism and the extent of its contributions are widespread and common. This, combined with the constantly shifting composition of municipal councils, means the job is never done.

At more senior levels of government, the increasing sophistication of politicians and the longer terms of office they seek can make the task of interfacing with policy makers somewhat less frustrating. Conversely, the fact that senior-level politicians have greater resources available to them means that it is much more costly, in terms of the amount of information needed and the degree of preparation required, to make arguments to support positions when dealing with governments at high levels. The best example is undoubtedly in the area of the environment, where rigorous standards may give rise to extensive environmental screening of tourism development proposals. Aside from cost considerations, the politically sensitive nature of many initiatives leaves little room for poorly prepared documentation or incompetent presentations.

The Interdependence of Global Forces

While we need to study each of the global forces affecting tourism in considerable depth, great care must be taken to avoid examining them in isolation. Despite their individual significance, it must be recognized that these forces are highly interdependent; that is, the impact of each is dependent on the impact of all factors as a whole. In contrast to the emergence and growing importance of the city-state

destination, the apparent gelling of Europe as an economic, political, social and possibly cultural entity, combined with the emergence of Asian and North/South American trade blocs, provides a foundation for examples of what might be termed the 'superdestination'. Whether these entities possess substantial meaning from a tourism destination perspective remains to be seen. As opposed to the city-state, which does appear to provide an ideal management unit as a tourism destination, the superdestination may well prove unappealing or unmanageable for tourism purposes. In either case, those responsible for destination management need to be vigilant and prepared to adapt as soon as either outcome appears inevitable.

Analysing and Understanding Global Forces

So far in this book, we have expended considerable effort in order to identify and categorize from a macro perspective the global forces that affect or may affect the competitiveness and sustainability of a tourism destination. In order to make this effort more conceptually and practically useful, we now attempt to provide greater insight for both academics and managers.

The first way in which greater meaning can be extracted from the global forces is to identify the challenges that must be overcome in dealing with them. A second is to identify the opportunities they present to enhance destination competitiveness. Because of limited space in the present treatise, we will examine only a small number of global forces in order to demonstrate the essence of the analysis we are suggesting. In doing so, we will use a tabular format (Table 4.2). A particular merit of the tabular format in which the analysis is summarized is that it lends itself to ongoing updating and/or expansion. It may also be adapted to the needs of individual scholars and practitioners in order to reflect their particular situation.

To keep the framework current for a given destination, it is important that management maintains a monitoring system to identify and analyse the global forces it believes are relevant to their needs. Periodic working group sessions

Table 4.2.   Challenges and opportunities presented by global forces: examples for a selected subset of forces.

Challenges	Opportunities
Economic forces	
Shifts to the market economy	
• Many high-quality public facilities and attractions that have traditionally been supported and/or subsidized by governments will come under serious funding pressures	• Market competition will prove a powerful force in keeping the costs of travel under control, thus keeping tourism accessible to a large percentage of the population
• It will become more difficult to justify and publicly finance large scale 'mega-projects' or 'mega-monuments', some of which become major symbolic tourist attractions. Also, supporting infrastructure, such as roads and airports, will be more difficult to finance	• There will be new opportunities for innovative financing for mega-projects and mega-developments that enjoy the support of the residents of a destination (e.g. community boards)
Formation of regional trading blocs	
• New trading blocs will force changes in traditional patterns of business, conferences and meeting travel	• The same trade blocs will encourage new vacation travel patterns due to the 'travel follows trade' phenomenon, and the natural formation of new personal relationships
Accelerating influence of the global/transnational firm	
• The marketing power of the transnational firm and its greater access to lower-cost capital will weaken the competitiveness of local firms within a destination	• Certain smaller destinations may be able to broaden their global appeal beyond previous times when they were ignored by global firms
The steadily growing role of China as an economic force	
• The steady economic growth of China presents a global force that all countries/destinations must increasingly accommodate in all their assessments of future competition. An 'open' China will have great appeal as a tourism destination	• While China will be a strong future competitor, this threat will be more than offset by the enormous potential number of visitors that the world's largest country will shortly be providing
The copy-cat economy	
• Any innovations introduced are copied so rapidly that it is difficult to recoup profits quickly enough to justify the investments that were made to develop and market the innovations	• Certain innovations introduced by competitors may fit your destination very well – and if copied quickly enough may provide competitive/profit opportunities without having to make the investments that would normally be required
The new mistrust of the capitalist system	
• The new and growing mistrust of the capitalist system that has been introduced by corporate failures (primarily in North America) has meant that the quantity and quality of information supplied to investors and the marketplace has introduced substantial new costs to destination management, and may slow down the decision-making process	• Those destinations and firms that have a clear record of integrity will have a significant competitive advantage
• The new fear that has been introduced into corporate management, in efforts to ensure visible honesty, risks creating, at the extreme, excessive risk aversion by both investors and managers	• Traditional, high-quality destinations should see less threat from new competitors, thus providing the opportunity to build up their cash flows from earlier investments
	• High-integrity destinations that have nothing to fear from the revealing of dishonest practices should not hesitate to proceed with aggressive developments that they believe in

continued

Table 4.2.   *Continued.*

Challenges	Opportunities
• There is a real possibility that traditional amounts of venture capital will dry up as a reflection of investor fears. This could threaten not only innovations, but sustainability as well	• Those destinations that have adopted a transparent, community-based, consensus-oriented approach to destination planning and development can (and should) emphasize this strength, not only in tourism but also in other industry sectors
Small can be profitable	
• Tourism in the developing nations needs to avoid the high-cost, high-tech model of the Western world and to involve local populations in a meaningful way that is to their benefit • Tourism in the developing world should focus on opportunities involving basic projects that encourage active involvement of the local population	• Rather than being forced into the industrialized world's rat race based on high-tech mega-projects, tourism in developing nations should be built around traditional lifestyles using appropriate technologies. This assertion is not simply idealistic. Indeed, firms such as Philips and Motorola have shown that this approach can be profitable • Developing destinations can develop without incurring extremely high investments in facilities and personnel
The mid-life crisis in marketing	
• The approaches that worked so successfully over decades for the 'boomer generation' just don't seem to work for younger consumers, the up-and-coming travel market • Advertising specifically needs to be substantially revised if it is to have an impact on the under-30 market in particular. The whole concept of 'cool' is radically different for the younger and the older market segments	• There are greater opportunities for destination repositioning, but in-depth research is required in order to get it right
Technological forces	
The knowledge-based society	
• Modern technology is increasingly attempting to provide alternatives to physical travel. Teleconferencing is finally gaining wider acceptance; virtual-interface technology purports to provide the travel experience without travel • Knowledge-based employees tend to work in sanitized, controlled environments. With this conditioning, they may shun travel experiences that are physically challenging, moderately uncomfortable, or culturally threatening	• Travellers will increasingly want to truly experience and understand a destination. As a result, they will be interested in spending more time in a region and interfacing with residents in more meaningful ways • Travellers of the future will be increasingly receptive to technologies and services that facilitate travel while reducing costs and minimizing the need for menial and/or demeaning labour
The technology–human-resource dilemma	
• The human-resource base of the tourism industry is ill-equipped for and thus ill-disposed towards the widespread adoption of technology. At least passive resistance can be expected at all levels • Introducing technology without losing the warmth of the human experience is difficult. Choosing the appropriate balance of high-tech/high-touch requires insight and good judgement	• Because of the present low level of penetration of technology in tourism, there is great potential for significant gains in performance and productivity in both facility design and service delivery • Education and training levels will have to increase if managers and staff are to select and implement technology-based improvements in an effective manner

Table 4.2. *Continued.*

Vaunted technologies that don't measure up

- Many technological advances that promise to reduce costs, improve managerial performance, or to help destinations enhance the quality of the visitor experience simply don't deliver on the promises they make. Trying to decide which technologies to adopt is a frustrating and often costly experience, both in the short term and over the longer term

- By hiring and retaining high-quality, committed employees who have the 'tourism virus' (i.e. individuals who truly believe in tourism as a career), a destination is more likely to remain competitive on a sustainable basis. Fortunately, tourism is one industry where salary is not the only or even the primary factor that attracts employees

Electronification of the global monetary system

- Because tourism involves many small firms, the cost of introducing a mandatory and cashless society would impose a disproportionate cost on the tourism sector (just as a services tax would) relative to other sectors of the economy
- Because a high percentage of tourism employees rely on tips as a significant part of their income (which in traditional terms tend to be unreported or under-reported), electronification could affect income and cause hiring difficulties
- The introduction of the euro has reduced somewhat the exotic nature of foreign travel in Europe. The creation of a world currency would further homogenize the world, thus continuing to detract from the excitement of travel

- The eventual creation of a single global economy could reduce costs and increase profitability in the tourism sector
- Destinations that successfully learn to differentiate themselves in meaningful yet hassle-free ways will gain an increased competitive edge.

Technology is changing the social contract of the workplace

- Members of society are increasingly finding that there is no haven from e-mail and the telephone – and no excuse not to produce at any hour of the day, or to turn the kitchen table into a workstation
- How will we strike the proper balance of work and life?

- Tourism thinkers need to help redefine the concepts of work and leisure and attempt to accommodate them in the experiences they offer
- Tourism should stress that, relative to other sectors, it has always attempted to provide career opportunities that provide employees with a better balance between leisure and work in their lives

Sociocultural forces

Shifting value systems

- Leisure/vacation travel could be viewed as frivolous, wasteful and harmful in a world where economies are stagnant, renewable resources are declining and toxic emissions threaten the health of the planet
- The developing mood to look inward may lead to greater economic protectionism (at the macro-level) and more home/family-oriented uses of leisure time (at the micro-level). Both developments would reduce the demand for travel

- Increased emphasis on special interest tourism – such as cultural, educational and professional-development travel – may greatly strengthen and enrich the meaning of the travel experience
- Increased emphasis on human relationships may encourage new forms of tourism in which contact between hosts and guests is less superficial and leads to more intense and enduring relationships

continued

Table 4.2.   *Continued.*

The spread of democratic values

- The tourism planning and development process will be increasingly constrained and slowed by the need for meaningful public involvement and input
- It will be more difficult for individual operators to proceed with non-conforming developments
- Innovations will sometimes risk inhibition

- Implementation of approved development plans will be easier as surprises are minimized and broader agreement results from public involvement
- The formulation of 'resident responsive visions' of local/regional tourism will create more commitment to tourism and greater coherency in the tourism product/experience provided by a destination

Increasing cultural diversity in a homogeneous world

- The power and success of franchises and enterprises with globally recognized brand names will increasingly put pressure on small, independent travel and tourism operators
- The integrity of truly unique and interesting cultural events and attractions will be threatened as they attempt to respond to visitor demands for more access and greater frequency

- Traditional cultural events and activities that are no longer economically viable may be preserved through tourism
- Increasing acceptance of the value of other cultures will greatly broaden the range of facilities, events and attractions of potential interest to tourists

Quest for stability and security

- Increasing levels of crime in tourist destinations are a major deterrent to both leisure and conference travel
- Ageing populations, under-funded medical systems and the growth of AIDS have heightened concerns about the cost, availability and safety of health-care services for travellers

- Organized travel and/or receptive visitor services that shelter and protect the traveller from crime will be welcomed; destinations that eliminate or control crime will be preferred
- Firms offering specialized products and services that protect the health of the travellers and/or facilitate access to reliable and reassuring medical services in foreign environments will have a strong competitive edge

Political forces

Rise of the city-state

- Large countries will find it less desirable and less productive to undertake general awareness-type promotions; budgets for such promotions will decline
- Smaller destinations having no particularly unique characteristics will find it even more difficult to compete with more high-profile centres

- Highly focused destinations with high visibility, good access, an attractive product and the will to develop a distinctive image will dominate the market
- Strategic alliances and reciprocal agreements between city-states that complement one another will grow in importance

Addressing the north–south gap

- The tourism infrastructure in developing countries (in both quantitative and qualitative terms) is in many cases totally inadequate at the present time
- The disparity between the wealth and well-being of developing-world residents and developed-world tourists frequently creates unhealthy tensions between hosts and guests, as well as distortions of local lifestyles

- Many developing countries have extremely rich cultures and histories that have not been experienced by many segments of the traditional tourism markets
- The relatively low level of visitation to many developing countries provides alternatives that could take the pressure off heavily visited sites in traditional tourism destinations

Table 4.2. *Continued.*

Pressures for population migration

- Nations/economic communities may become much more demanding in terms of visitor entry requirements as they perceive that tourists risk transforming themselves into refugees or *de facto* immigrants
- Destination residents may become increasingly less tolerant of visibly or linguistically different visitors, who they see as posing a threat as potential immigrants

- Diverse multicultural societies created through immigration will create increased demand for travel as individuals exchange visits with families and friends
- Ethnic groups in tourism-generating countries will have the opportunity to develop educational/cultural travel experiences for their compatriots. Such experiences could involve both pre-travel and travel experiences

Demographic forces

Demographic shifts are occurring which will dramatically influence the level and nature of tourism

- The ageing of travellers from traditional tourism-generating countries will cause demands for new experiences and new facilities. As a consequence, existing tourism plants may become economically obsolete
- Increasingly diverse lifestyles will make market segmentation increasingly important. However, the tailoring of designer vacations will make it harder to standardize the tourism product and thus to control costs
- Patterns of travel are being changed by increasingly diverse lifestyles. The changes are rendering much of the current tourism product obsolete

- For the next 20 years the residents of developed nations aged 45–65 will increase substantially. These individuals will have the time, the discretionary income and the desire to travel
- Firms that can read, anticipate and respond to the specific needs/desires of high-quality niche or special interest markets in innovative ways will have great opportunities for success
- Astute analysis of ongoing lifestyle changes will provide considerable insight into opportunities for innovative products, and even for new destination development
- The ageing of travellers will increase their sensitivity to health concerns and the need to build the supply of medical facilities into the tourism product
- Increasing concern for health will strengthen the appeal of traditional health spas and open up opportunities for a broad range of new health businesses, physical well-being destinations/resorts

The coming battle for immigrants

- The ability to absorb foreigners could determine whether nations in the industrialized world will grow or stagnate
- Unless destinations are able to attract the kind of immigrants that have an interest and capability in tourism, they will see their competitiveness decline

- Many destinations that set up systems and processes that will attract and integrate substantial numbers of immigrants into their economies – (the service sectors in particular) will find that they have an advantage over those that do not
- Destinations that can attract immigrants having an interest and skills in tourism will enhance their competitiveness

continued

Table 4.2. *Continued.*

Environmental forces

The environment in the Kyoto era
- There is a recognition that there are finite limitations to tourism development, in terms of both physical and social carrying capacity of destinations
- Virtually all future tourism development will be constrained by the need for environmental impact assessments
- The non-economic costs of tourism will need to be factored into development decisions. The costs of development, using non-traditional accounting frameworks, will increase, thus forcing higher prices on the travel experience

- Conservation, preservation and restoration present new themes for the design of tourism experiences. Regions that are presently undeveloped or in a natural state have a unique opportunity to provide an attractive experience to visitors
- Emphasis on the quality of the tourism experience will reduce growth in the number of travellers, but enhance net financial and non-financial impacts on tourism destinations

Recognition of the value of non-capital assets
- Intangibles such as brands and intellectual property process (organizational capital) and the environment need to be recognized as major items on the balance sheet of destinations
- Traditional accounting principles can greatly understate the true value of a destination or a tourism firm

- By getting investors to recognize the value added by visitor bureau organizations and a quality environment, the value of tourism to a local, regional or national economy could be substantially increased

to review the results of the monitoring process and to integrate them into management thinking and strategic planning can be very useful. While the use of external consultants can be helpful in enhancing this process, it is not necessary.

Global forces and tourism demand

It is important to understand the manner and the extent to which global forces can affect the various dimensions of tourism demand. The most obvious aspect of these effects is that of demographic forces, such as the current ageing of the population of many of the tourism-generating countries. This factor is affecting such aspects of demand as the characteristics of travellers, the nature of travel undertaken, the price sensitivity of demand, the timing of their travel, and the spatial distribution of demand (i.e. where they travel). Most importantly, the total economic value of travel is affected. Similarly, many of the global forces, such as technology, politics and environmental forces, also affect virtually all the dimensions of tourism demand.

Global forces and tourism supply

Just as destination managers need to understand the detailed effect of global forces on demand, they must also be able to comprehend the systematic effect of these forces on the various dimensions of tourism supply within their destination. Figure 4.2 provides an overview of how this analysis might be undertaken. In brief, managers must carefully examine the most significant and current global forces and how they might affect most of the important core resources and attractions. They must also study their impact on the destination's supporting factors and resources, its superstructure, its activities, its events, its culture, and even its climate and physiography.

Assessing the impact of global forces on destination performance

An important first step in global performance analysis, as the previous section argues, is to understand global forces from a macro perspective. From a destination management perspective, it is important to comprehend

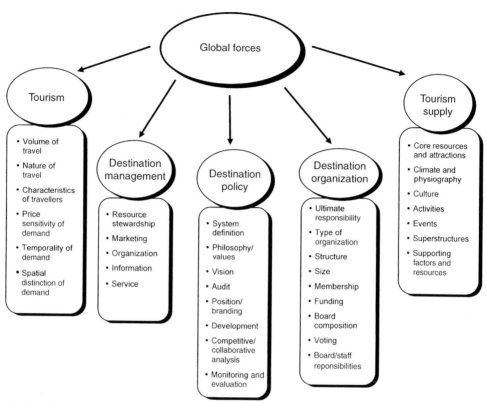

Fig. 4.2. Global forces: an analytical framework for assessing their impacts.

how a given global force might affect more generally the preference for a particular destination. For example, as people age, they tend to seek less adventurous destination experiences. In addition, as global concern about terrorism grows, the destination manager needs to know how this might affect perceptions about the safety of various destinations. Figure 4.2 provides a framework that may be helpful in this regard. In summary, this framework attempts to stress that global forces can affect both the attractiveness of various components of the destination and the effectiveness of the different policy and managerial processes that determine management performance within the destination, and thus its ultimate success.

Global forces and destination policy

Since global forces are by nature major and long-term, it is not surprising that their effects on policy may be substantial. For example, changes in political forces may substantially alter the system of philosophy and values on which tourism within a destination is developed. Broad changes in consumer reaction to advertising may force quite meaningful alterations in the positioning and branding policy for a destination. Similarly, all aspects of a destination's tourism policy need to be examined in relation to each and every global force of significance.

Global forces and destination management

While many, if not most, destination managers tend to consider global forces as being rather irrelevant to their responsibilities (i.e. they belong to policy makers!), they must nevertheless keep in mind that these forces do – sometimes more than they realize – affect the daily functioning of the destination. For example, recent criticisms regarding the lack of integrity of information provided to investors are very relevant and will be of much greater relevance in the future. And while destination positioning may be primarily a policy responsibility, the development of positioning programmes must be done through promotion and advertising that will convince visitors that the destination will deliver the experience that is communicated by its positioning. Consequently, the global force related to the generation gap in advertising effectiveness cannot be ignored. Similarly, although many concerns related to destination organization and resource stewardship may indeed be of the greatest relevance to policy makers, they cannot be ignored by those making daily operational decisions in these areas.

Global forces and destination organization

Here again, we are dealing with the fine distinction that often occurs between organizational policy decisions and those related to daily operational decisions concerning the organization. While the major decisions related to the nature of the destination organization, such as the type of organization, its structure and size, board composition and voting procedures, are policy decisions that are often not affected by global forces, a plethora of other operational decisions can be significantly affected by these forces. Perhaps the most notable of these is the growing change that is occurring at the interface between the nature of work and the quality of life. This is one force that all employees must deal with.

References

Foot, D.K. and Stoffman, D. (2001) *Boom, Bust and Echo: Profiting from the Demographic Shift in the 21st Century.* Stoddart Publishing, Toronto, Ontario, Canada.

Pearce, E.A. and Smith, G. (1990) *World Weather Guide.* Random House, New York.

Porter, M.E. (1997) Creating tomorrow's advantages. In: Gibson, R. (ed.) *Rethinking the Future.* Free Press, New York.

Schlosser, E. (2001) *Fast Food Nation: the Dark Side of the All-American Meal.* Houghton Mifflin, Boston, Massachusetts.

UN (1997) Kyoto Protocol. United Nations Framework Convention on Climate Change, 1–11 December. Available at: unfccc.int/resource/docs/cop3/07a01.pdf

5

The Competitive (Micro)environment: the Destination and the Tourism System

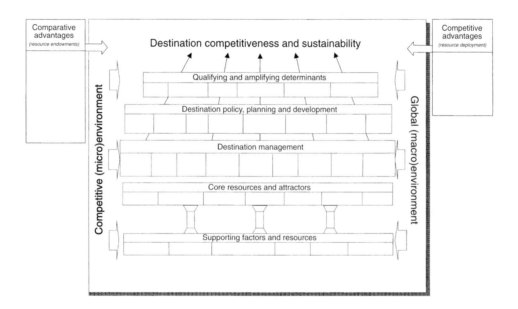

©CAB International 2003. *The Competitive Destination: a Sustainable Tourism Perspective* (J.R. Brent Ritchie and Geoffrey I. Crouch)

Having discussed some of the global forces and trends shaping today's tourism and hospitality industry in the preceding chapter, we now turn to the industry – or perhaps more correctly, the *tourism system* – itself, to see how destination competitiveness is affected by the way in which the tourism system functions. We introduced some of the principal elements of the competitive (micro) environment in Chapter 3, but it is now time to take a closer look at how these elements are structured in the context of a tourism destination.

Normally, when the competitive (micro) environment is considered, the perspective taken is that of an individual enterprise or organization. Under these conditions (i.e. when the unit of analysis is a company), the competitive (micro)environment is usually depicted as illustrated in Fig. 5.1 (see for example Kotler et al., 1996, pp. 102–105). In this situation, the main groups of players are the company itself (i.e. its internal environment), its competitors, suppliers, customers and publics, and the marketing intermediaries and facilitators that help connect the company to its customers.

However, the subject of this book is the destination, not the individual tourism enterprise. Although it is possible to define or delineate a destination, this does not exist as an entity, at least in the way that a company is an entity. A company is well defined by law. Its actions, policies, control of resources and organizational structure are manifest. A destination, on the other hand, is a geographical rather than a legal or business entity. Although a destination management organization (DMO) may have been constituted to spearhead or facilitate tourism development and management, its ability to do so for the destination as a whole does not compare to the power of a company to govern its own internal environment. Whereas a company governs, directs and controls, a DMO merely influences, facilitates and coordinates. The DMO is not the destination.

Figure 5.2 is an adaptation of Fig. 5.1 that reflects the relationship between one destination, the principal elements of the tourism system and other tourism destinations. The competitive (micro)environment for the destination in question includes both local and foreign enterprises and organizations. Local tourism and hospitality enterprises provide a destination with the goods and services that constitute the tourism experience provided by the destination. A destination's suppliers and supporting

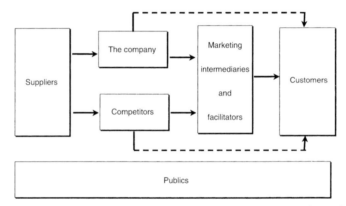

Fig. 5.1.   A company's competitive (micro)environment (adapted from Kotler *et al.*, 1996).

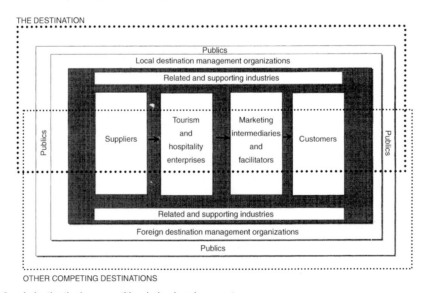

Fig. 5.2.   A destination's competitive (micro)environment

industries, marketing intermediaries and facilitators, publics and customers may be both local and foreign. The situation is similar for alternative destinations.

Figure 5.2 illustrates an intersection between destinations. This intersecting region identifies players within each element of the competitive environment that are connected with more than one destination. For example, many of a destination's customers are also likely to be potential or existing customers of other destinations. The majority of marketing intermediaries and facilitators (e.g. travel agents, tour packagers, financial institutions) serve the tourism and hospitality industries in numerous destinations. Suppliers too, such as souvenir manufacturers, food and beverage suppliers and the oil industry, often serve multiple destinations, but many small suppliers may only provide for the needs of the local destination and tourism industry. Similarly, small local tourism and hospitality enterprises, such as hotels, restaurants and attractions, may only serve their local destination, but increasingly, as the globalization of the tourism industry progresses, multinational tourism enterprises (such as airlines, hotel chains, restaurants and theme parks) operate in many different destinations.

The destination, then, is really a loose collection of enterprises, organizations and groups which work together in a semi-organized, partly cooperative fashion, but which are ultimately driven largely by their own self-interest. These organizations may perceive that a large part of their own self-interest rests with the interests of the destination itself. In these situations, one would expect to see a great deal of interaction, communication and cooperation, as well as a shared sense of vision about where the destination is trying to go. A DMO, if one exists, is likely to play a focal role in these instances. The opposite situation – that is, disorganization, alienation and dysfunction – is also a possibility where tourism organizations perceive that the costs of cooperating as a destination outweigh the benefits.

The opposing forces of *competition* and *cooperation* among organizations centred around the destination shape the actions, styles and *modus operandi* of the destination as a whole. Both of these forces are vital to a competitive destination. Cooperation strengthens the destination because it increases the extent to which relevant organizations are trying to move towards the same goal. Competition, on the other hand, creates an environment in the destination that encourages innovation, quality, efficiency and effectiveness. While both competition and cooperation can enhance the competitiveness of the destination, some forms of both can be destructive when they are incongruent with the overall direction and goal of the destination.

In this chapter we look at the individual elements of the competitive (micro)environment in greater detail. We begin by examining the basic elements of the microenvironment in turn: suppliers and supporting industries, tourism and hospitality enterprises, marketing intermediaries and facilitators, customers, and the DMO and other publics. We finish the chapter with three further sections that integrate the impacts of these elements in terms of their overall effect on the destination in question, the effect of competing destinations, and the tourism system as a whole.

Suppliers

The first component of the competitive (micro)environment that shapes the determinants and structure of destination competitiveness is suppliers. The USA is a strong tourist destination in part because of the low cost of energy and the low cost and high quality of food production. Labour productivity rates are also comparatively high in the USA. Natural, cultural and historical resource endowments are also important factors in tourism production. Although not consumed by the tourism industry in the same way as energy, food or construction materials, these resources are also a form of supply or factor inputs. Competitive advantages in home-based supplier industries such as these confer potential advantages on a destination, particularly when they produce inputs that are important for overall industry innovation and performance.

For the purposes of this discussion we define suppliers as those firms or organizations that supply the tourism industry with basic factor inputs, such as labour, materials, equipment and facilities. Related or supporting industries, on the other hand, although playing a somewhat similar role to that of suppliers, are those which share activities in common with tourism but whose demand is not principally derived from travellers or tourists. For example, cultural industries provide products and services that are complementary to those of the tourism industry, but tourists usually represent a minor share of the market for these products. In contrast, airlines and hotels, for example, derive the great majority of their demand from the travel and tourism industry, so we classify these as tourism and hospitality enterprises in Fig. 5.2 rather than as related or supporting industries. We discuss the role of related and supporting industries later in this chapter. (For a discussion of the impact of related and supporting industries on national advantage in a particular industry, see also Porter, 1990, pp. 100–107.) The services of financial institutions, advertising agencies and marketing research consultants, etc. facilitate tourism marketing and are also discussed separately later in this chapter (in the section *Marketing Intermediaries and Facilitators: the Industry's Lubricants*).

Suppliers that provide the inputs to the 'downstream' tourism industry are many and varied because tourism consumption is a close microcosm of consumption in general (studies have found that changes in the cost of tourism goods and services follow approximately changes in the general consumer price index). Some of the more important supplies and suppliers, however, include the following: labour (including education and training), energy, construction equipment and materials, land/real estate, primary produce and its wholesalers, recreational vehicle producers (such as manufacturers of automobiles, mobile camping homes, snowmobiles and water craft), manufacturers of entertainment and recreational equipment and technology (e.g. theme park rides and attractions, camping goods and fishing and hunting suppliers) and aircraft manufacturers. Many of the resources used in the tourism industry are 'free', such as beaches, scenery and national parks.

How important are the suppliers of these resources to the competitiveness of tourism destinations? In Chapter 2 we emphasized the importance of both resource endowments (comparative advantages) and the ability of a destination to deploy its resources appropriately (competitive advantages). Clearly then, supplies (endowments) and suppliers (deployment) are a cornerstone of competitive tourism development. Interestingly, in the case of tourism, many of the most important resources (e.g. national parks, other public lands, public facilities, infrastructure) are in public hands and are thus controlled by governments, who are therefore a type of supplier to the tourism industry. However, a government's role in this regard, unlike that of most other suppliers, should and must take the form of stewardship rather than commercial exploitation, to maximize benefits to society as a whole over the long term. The tourism industry must compete against other industries for the opportunity for access to a share of these resources.

Suppliers are also important because their productivity determines the cost of inputs, and cost is a major determinant of competitive advantage. In addition, supplies may be an important source of innovation, new technology, new materials and new ideas and processes. For example, the US tourism industry enjoys an advantage arising from its leadership in various entertainment technologies. The USA also benefits from the many excellent tourism and hospitality schools situated within respected universities. US energy costs are also low, and service quality standards are generally high. French cuisine and the training of chefs confer a distinct advantage on the French tourism industry. The low cost and high quality of food and wine produced in Australia are advantages for that country as a tourist destination.

Strong, home-based suppliers are able to lower input costs, raise input quality and assist downstream users to utilize inputs more effectively. As Porter (1990) notes, their proximity to downstream customers reduces transaction costs and encourages preferential, rapid and efficient resource utilization. National pride also ties home-based suppliers more closely to their domestic customers, and cultural bonds enhance communication and cooperation.

Although we have emphasized the competitive strengths conferred by the presence of strong home-based suppliers, foreign alternatives might also enhance a destination's competitiveness. This is particularly the case for developing countries or regions that lack options domestically. However, some care may be required by destinations in these circumstances to ensure that the dependent relationship on foreign suppliers is managed in the best long-term interests of the destination and its residents. The transfer of technology may, for example, be part of such a relationship.

Tourism and Hospitality Enterprises

A destination's tourism and hospitality enterprises provide the backbone of its product. It is these firms that actively produce the core commercial services that tourists consume once they are at the destination. They are distinguished from other commercial enterprises involved in the competitive (micro)environment (i.e. suppliers, related and supporting industries, and marketing intermediaries and facilitators) in that: (i) the products and services they produce are targeted principally at tourist markets; (ii) they produce *core* services and products for tourists; and (iii) they have a high level of interaction with tourists.

Collectively, however, these enterprises do not produce and deliver all of what a tourist consumes while visiting a destination because the tourism and hospitality industry's product is no less than the gestalt of all experiences, commercial and otherwise, arising from the destination as a whole. And as we discussed earlier, much of the quality of the visitor experience stems from non-commercial activity, such as enjoying the climate and scenery, mixing socially with local inhabitants, using free public services and infrastructure, and strolling along a beach.

Thus, the competitiveness of a destination is significantly dependent on the competitiveness of its local tourism and hospitality enterprises, both individually and collectively. What is it that creates a situation in which some destinations enjoy a strong, vibrant tourism industry with numerous active, innovative and competitive firms whereas other destinations lack these characteristics? There appear to be two principal explanations. First, the tourism industry may be driven by an abundance of comparative advantages that favour tourism development. For example, climate, scenery and historical or cultural resources may act as a catalyst for tourism development and entrepreneurial behaviour. But as we have discussed earlier, effective resource deployment (competitive advantage) is not guaranteed by resource abundance (comparative advantage) (recall the comparison between Russia and Singapore in Chapter 2, Part I).

The second principal explanation is that a variety of social, cultural, political and economic factors may create a more fertile environment in which enterprises are able to develop, grow, flourish and sustain competitive advantage in tourism. We explore this matter in greater detail towards the end of this chapter and again in Chapter 8. For the moment it is important to note that these factors differ across destinations, and that the nature and mix of these factors may be conducive or detrimental to the creation of a competitive, thriving cluster of tourism and hospitality enterprises.

Porter (1990, p. 117), who has examined this situation extensively, notes that 'Among the strongest empirical findings from our research is the association between vigorous domestic rivalry and the creation and persistence of competitive advantage in an industry'. Therefore, an environment that encourages vigorous rivalry is more likely to result in innovative, adaptable and customer-responsive tourism enterprises ready to exploit new market opportunities and technological advancement. Rivalry also places emphasis on the efficiency of operations and opportunities for productivity improvements.

The tourism industry covers a large number of enterprises that vary greatly in size and in the nature of their products. There are some very large enterprises, such as the airlines, hotel corporations and some food service firms. As tourism continues to grow, many of these companies have become major multinational operations. There are also a vast number of small to medium-sized enterprises spread throughout the industry. Many of these are very small firms representing the grass roots of the industry, but increasingly, through the expansion of franchising and management contracts, the tourism and hospitality industry is undergoing something of a revolution in the concentration, consolidation and cross-ownership of many of these small companies. Small businesses, though, are likely to remain a feature of the tourism and hospitality industry.

As in any industry, industry associations may play a critical role in creating the sort of environment that affects the health and vitality of tourism enterprises in a destination over the long term. Positive outcomes, for example, might stem from concerted efforts, coordinated through these associations, to maintain, improve and foster factor creation. Many strong industries have found that the establishment and funding of university research centres can help an industry and its enterprises to better address long-term development issues. In tourism, there is a need for more interdisciplinary research, which commercial research is often unable or unwilling to address. While commercial research tends to focus on the needs of individual enterprises, interdisciplinary research can attend more to the needs of the industry and destination as a whole. Issues concerning the social and environmental effects of tourism, sustainable tourism development and the broad questions of destination competitiveness are examples of research needs that specialized university centres would be able to address. Australia's Cooperative Research Centre for Sustainable Tourism Pty Ltd, in which government, industry and 15 universities participate, is an excellent example of the sort of arrangement that can foster interdisciplinary and strategic industry research.

Industry associations may also take a lead role in developing industry standards, improving training and professional standards, and demonstrating the need for specialized infrastructure or tourism superstructure.

There is also the risk, however, that some collective industry actions, although superficially appearing to be in the best interests of the industry as a whole, may work over the long term to decrease industry competitiveness. For example, 'It is often argued that domestic competition is wasteful, because it leads to duplication of effort and prevents firms from gaining economies of scale. The right solution is seen as nurturing one or two firms who become "national champions", with the scale and strength to compete against foreign rivals or, alternatively, to promote inter-firm cooperation' (Porter, 1990, p. 117). Porter found this view not to be supported by overwhelming evidence. The net effects of inter-firm rivalry work to promote rather than hinder industry competitiveness over the long term.

The perceived profitability or returns on investment, together with the perceived risks of investing in tourism enterprises in a destination, will influence the interests of investors and entrepreneurs in the tourism and hospitality industry. Differences between destinations in these perceptions and in attitudes towards short- and long-term profitability and risk will substantially govern the extent of private sector interest in tourism development and the competitive attributes of destinations that depend upon this interest.

Finally, where pride and prestige are at stake, greater importance may be placed on a nation or destination doing well in an industry. Where tourism is seen to be an important tool for economic development and prosperity, tourism and hospitality enterprises are more likely to attract promising graduates into the industry, as well as entrepreneurs and capital resources. Increasingly, many cities and nations take great pride in showcasing their home to the world.

Marketing Intermediaries and Facilitators: the Industry's Lubricants

Tourism and hospitality enterprises are connected to customers through tourism marketing channels consisting of intermediaries and facilitators. This system of contacts, interconnection and accessibility between operators and customers enables destinations and their enterprises to reach the market with their products and services. The same system provides a convenient and efficient network that allows customers to access tourism products and services from around the world. Thus, the competitiveness of a destination is in part dependent upon the efficacy with which the destination utilizes marketing intermediaries and facilitators.

Intermediaries and facilitators streamline the tourism system by performing several worthwhile functions that confer advantages on operators and customers. Middleton (1994, pp. 205–206) identified ten of these functions.

1. Points of sale and convenient customer access, either for immediate purchase or for booking in advance.

2. Distribution of product information, such as brochures and leaflets, to provide choice for customers.

3. Display and merchandising opportunities.

4. Advice and purchase assistance, such as itinerary planning and helpful product knowledge.

5. Arranging transfer of title to a product through ticketing and travel documentation.

6. Receiving and transmitting sales revenue to principals.

7. Possible provision of ancillary services, such as insurance, advice on inoculations, visa applications, passports and travel advisories.

8. Possible sources of marketing intelligence for principals.

9. Supplementing the principal's promotional activities.

10. Receiving and assisting with complaints from customers.

In addition to these ten functions, intermediaries and facilitators perform several other valuable roles, including the following.

11. Buying in bulk and sorting and assembling tourism services into packaged tourism products.

12. Sharing risks with regard to demand fluctuations and uncertainties.

13. Financing part of the transfer of services to customers by purchasing services and reservations in advance.

14. Branding to enhance awareness and customer assurance.

15. Accreditation systems and providing a pool of funds in the industry to protect customers against bankruptcy and fraud.

16. Providing a network that more effectively reaches into the market.

17. Providing ancillary services that support all of the above functions.

The distinction between intermediaries and facilitators rests with the degree to which the function performed is associated directly with the delivery of the tourism service by the operator to the customer. Travel agents, tour packagers and wholesalers, travel shows or exhibitions (both consumer and trade shows) and speciality channels, such as incentive travel houses, corporate travel departments, meeting and convention planners, automobile clubs, discount travel clubs, tourist information centres, information kiosks and global distribution systems or computer reservation systems, play a direct role in the transfer of information and reservations between operator and customer, and are therefore performing roles as marketing intermediaries. Conversely, facilitators such as financial institutions (credit cards, travellers cheques, currency exchange, etc.), insurance companies, advertising agencies, market research consultants, embassies and consulates, information technology providers and the Internet perform indirect functions which assist or facilitate the activities of the travel trade.

Some players in the tourism system may perform roles that could be classified, from the perspective of a destination, either as a tourism and hospitality enterprise or as a marketing intermediary. For example, an airline may transport customers to a destination as well as performing a role as a tour packager/wholesaler through its vacations department. It may then transport tourists within the destination after arrival.

A destination's use of marketing intermediaries and facilitators is clearly going to affect its overall competitiveness. What is less clear is just *how* competitiveness is shaped by these alternatives. A large, dominant destination, such as the USA, will seek to use marketing intermediaries and facilitators intensively. Indeed, it has the positioning and power in the market to command the attention, interest and compliance of the travel trade. By contrast, a small, developing destination will need to be much more selective in its choice of channel options and strategies. For such a destination, it may make much more sense to focus marketing resources so that it is able to achieve a critical mass in its use of channel options. It might, for example, enter arrangements with only one retail travel chain to act as a specialist agent.

A further strategic issue for a destination and its use of intermediaries and facilitators concerns the relative emphasis on 'push marketing' versus 'pull marketing'. A destination emphasizing push marketing seeks to gain the cooperation of the travel trade through commissions, other financial incentives and promotional programmes and assistance directed to players in the marketing channel itself. A pull marketing strategy, on the other hand, focuses on the generation of strong consumer demand through consumer promotions that, in turn, elicits the cooperation of the travel trade. In this case, customer demand *pulls* tourism services and products through the marketing channel.

Opportunities for more direct marketing that bypasses intermediaries and facilitators are increasing. The Internet, toll-free telephone numbers and ticketless travel are allowing destinations and their enterprises to expand their direct communication with customers and achieve higher profitability by minimizing commissions to intermediaries. This is particularly relevant in the airline industry. On the other hand, some operators that have tried to rely solely on direct marketing are struggling to survive on this basis alone. For example, Greyhound Airlines in Canada found that it had to switch to using travel agencies to provide the one-stop-shopping convenience that travellers were seeking.

A destination which possesses strong home-based players in international tourism marketing channels has an advantage over destinations that lack the loyalty, pride and cultural ties which local intermediaries and facilitators are likely to display towards their own local destination.

The interest of foreign-based marketing intermediaries and facilitators in a destination will depend on the intrinsic touristic qualities and potential of the destination. In addition, however, as with any foray into foreign markets by multinational enterprises, all factors likely to affect the returns and risks of operating in such destinations will weigh heavily on any such decision. Government policies, social norms and general business practices within a destination can affect the attractiveness of a destination for foreign-based intermediaries and facilitators. We explore some of these issues further in the last three sections of this chapter.

Customers: the Ultimate Driving Force

Although the competitive (micro)environment is subject to numerous forces and motives,

customers and their needs stand as the ultimate driving force behind competition and competitiveness. Competitive actions derive from customer demand. If we are to understand the competitive (micro)environment and its impact on destination competitiveness, we surely need to understand how customers affect destinations.

In Chapter 2, we briefly discussed the significance of domestic tourism, noting that, with few exceptions, destinations derive the majority of their customers domestically. Domestic tourism significantly exceeds the volume of international tourism, so that for most national destinations it is domestic tourism demand that has shaped the nature and competitiveness of the nation's tourism industry.

As we move from an international to a regional or local perspective, however, the proportion of customers of tourism services originating from outside the borders of the destination increases. Nevertheless, domestic, local or home-based demand has a particularly critical impact on the actions of competing firms and the functioning of the destination tourism system as a whole.

Destinations that enjoy a sizeable local demand (which is the case in most industrially developed countries or regions) have a reliable, comparatively stable demand base upon which tourism can be planned and developed. While foreign inbound tourism may experience ups and downs, local demand remains somewhat insulated from foreign disturbances.

Strong local demand creates an environment that fosters the development of a rich variety and range of tourism amenities, facilities, attractions and services. Indeed, without substantial local demand, many of these facilities and services, particularly those provided by governments and funded through taxation, would not exist to the same extent. Governments provide public services which the private sector cannot or will not provide. While foreign tourists may be able to enjoy the benefits of these public services and facilities, where they exist, it is domestic demand that provides the real basis for their need and funding.

The economies of scale that the tourism industry enjoys are therefore largely driven by the size of local demand. But more important than these static efficiencies are the dynamic impacts of local demand (Porter, 1990, p. 86). For example, in competing for local customers, tourism and hospitality enterprises are more likely to engage in more competitive behaviour in general. Foreign visitors may only visit and use the commercial services of a destination once, whereas local people remain the cornerstone of each tourism firm's customer base. Local customers are also much more knowledgeable about the range of choices available to them in their own backyard. So domestic demand provides very significant stimulation for local competition.

Local or domestic demand for the touristic services of a destination also shapes the nature and character of the industry. For example, the French penchant for fine cuisine and social discourse has resulted in a tourism and hospitality industry that is characterized, in part, by wonderful restaurants and street-side cafés. American tourists display a propensity for big entertainment, so it is not surprising to find that theme parks, gambling and cruises are characteristic of the US tourist industry. Australians have a very outdoor lifestyle and hence the tourism industry is strong in outdoor recreation and experiences, particularly in coastal environments.

Local demand is also an important influence on the improvements and innovations that govern competition. Take the hospitality sector as an example. In crowded Japan, the cubicle hotel room was born. In contrast, the US demand for service, variety and choice has created an enormous range of hotel styles and classes.

Where local customers are more demanding and sophisticated, competing firms are accustomed to providing higher levels of service. Americans, for example, complain more readily about substandard service than most other cultures. A destination with a more experienced and demanding home market must develop knowledge, skills and services which meet new emerging and advanced customer needs and tastes. Being further along the learning curve, these destinations are then in a stronger competitive position to provide these experiences to foreign markets as these emerging travel trends and fashions spread to other countries.

Domestic tourism preferences (and associated local competitive strengths in the tourism industry) may spread out to foreign markets. A variety of factors may contribute to this diffusion of customer tastes and demand. For example, residents of a destination themselves travel to other destinations, taking their experiences and tastes with them. The media, movies, fashion, food, music and other forms of cultural communication and ties between destinations facilitate the demonstration effect of fashions in travel and tourism experiences. In addition to cultural ties and influences, several other forms of interdestination relationships may also contribute to the diffusion of customer preferences and demand, including migration, history, sport and politics. For example, consider how tastes in food have spread around the world.

We emphasized above the important effect of home demand on the competitive behaviour of firms in a destination, and noted how local customers are more knowledgeable about local tourism products and services and are often more price-sensitive towards them. In addition, there may be a certain pride associated with a firm's competitiveness in its own local market. Notwithstanding these points, foreign customers also represent a strategically important market that drives the egos of managers of local tourism enterprises. There may be a certain prestige associated with success in servicing foreign markets. Destinations also display a strong interest in foreign markets because they represent new money. And whereas local markets are, to some extent, captive markets, foreign markets are freer to choose alternative destinations. In this sense, destinations today must be internationally competitive if they are to attract foreign customers.

A destination experienced in the ways of other cultures is also likely to develop competitive strengths in its ability to serve and satisfy foreign customers. A multicultural destination, or one that has had a history of serving foreign visitors on business or education, for example, is more likely to have acquired and diffused the knowledge of other cultures into its tourism and hospitality firms.

A final impact of customers on the competitive (micro)environment concerns the degree of congruency between targeted customer segments. As customers must be present in the destination to experience its tourism product directly, interaction among customer segments is inevitable. The choice and mix of targeted segments determines how customer behaviour affects local residents as well as other tourists. A destination that has carefully considered which customer segments represent an appropriate and congruent match with its tourism development goals, tourism resources, resident attitudes and opinions, and other customer segments is augmenting its competitive strengths. Discordant selection of markets will weaken its competitive position.

Related and Supporting Industries

The effect of related and supporting industries on destination competitiveness operates in a similar fashion to that of suppliers. Instead of factor inputs, however, we are now dealing with parallel, complementary products and services that reinforce and strengthen a destination's tourism industry by their presence in the destination. Earlier we mentioned various cultural industries as an example. The arts are part of the activities of many tourists, particularly in urban regions. Theatre, music, literature, film, live entertainment, art galleries, festivals, etc. are key elements in the competitiveness of many successful urban destinations, such as New York, Paris and London. While these cultural events and activities are normally patronized and attended by local residents in the majority, they may be so significant as to attract large foreign audiences, which is the case for Broadway in New York and the West End of London. There is also a significant flow of New Zealand tourists to Australia to take in some of the major theatre productions in Melbourne and Sydney, which can be too expensive to stage in New Zealand, given the size of the market there.

Sport, leisure and recreation industries, too, can enhance the competitiveness of tourism destinations where local strengths exist in these areas. Major events, such as the Summer and Winter Olympics, the World Cup in soccer, world athletics championships, golf tournaments and American-football championships are coveted by many urban destinations. Although many of these events are often held only once in a particular location, their impact on tourism can be substantial. Some cities, however, have a longstanding reputation for their enthusiasm for sport and prowess in regularly hosting major sporting events. In sports-crazed Australia, for example, Melbourne's reputation for attracting, hosting and attending national and international sporting events, such as the Formula One Grand Prix, the World Motorcycle Championship, the Australian Open Tennis Championship (the first leg of the Grand Slam circuit) and football, cricket and golf tournaments, has made Melbourne something of a Mecca for sports enthusiasts.

A strong retail industry offering a wide range of competitively priced, high-quality goods may also complement the destination's tourism industry. Shopping can be a major tourism activity, accounting for a substantial share of tourist expenditure. The Japanese, in particular, are known for their propensity to return home with many purchases for themselves and their friends and family. Some city destinations are also known for the excellent variety and quality of their restaurants. Although retailers and restaurants rarely gain more than a small share of their customers as tourists, competitive strengths in these related industries nevertheless advantage their location as a tourist destination.

As we noted above, a destination endowed with strong, thriving and competitive related or supporting industries is of benefit to the tourism industry, but what is at least as important is the degree of cooperation and coordination that occurs between them. Indeed, many of these other industries have recognized that the tourism industry represents a significant opportunity for their ongoing success and even survival. The arts community, for example, has begun to realize the importance of the tourism market and, in many places, is now working enthusiastically with tourism enterprises, organizations, joint ventures and alliances to obtain a greater share of the market.

Destination Management Organizations

The role of DMOs has strengthened and spread as destinations have attempted to play a more proactive role in fostering and managing the benefits of tourism development. Increasing competition for tourism dollars has prompted responses at all levels of destination development and management. At the international level, organizations such as the Pacific Asia Travel Association, the Baltic Sea Tourism Commission, the Caribbean Tourism Organization and the Tourism Council of the South Pacific seek to advance tourism development across cooperating nations.

National destinations have established national tourist offices. At the next level, states, provinces and territories have also created similar organizations. Many cities today have their own Convention and Visitor Bureaux, and smaller municipalities or rural regions have, in many cases, set up regional tourism bureaux or offices.

Some cooperation between the different levels of DMO is evident, but at this point in time the extent of cooperation seems generally to be rather limited. If the real objective of DMOs is to advance the overall interests of the area, residents and industry it represents, greater cooperation would appear to be called for.

Although we have chosen to use the word 'management' in labelling these organizations, many of the organizations who label themselves as DMOs see the word 'marketing' in this initialism. However, for many such organizations 'marketing' is an exaggeration of the extent of their role. Marketing is a much broader function than promotion, yet some of these organizations seem to believe that any activity that is not directly promoting the destination is a waste of effort and funds. This view is certainly counter to the modern view of marketing, which regards promotion as only one of a number of complementary tools available to a marketer.

Where a DMO adopts a role limited primarily to promotion, the role of the DMO is little different from that of other marketing intermediaries and facilitators. There are, however, some DMOs that have begun to adopt an expanded perspective of their role beyond promotion and even marketing alone. And because we believe that the trend will continue in this direction as competition between destinations intensifies and the interest in tourism's broader economic, sociocultural and ecological impacts

increases, we believe it is time to let the 'M' in 'DMO' stand for 'management'. For this reason, we illustrate in Fig. 5.2 the role of the DMO, stretching from the upstream (i.e. suppliers) to the downstream (i.e. customers) reaches of the competitive (micro)environment.

The DMO is not the only player involved in the broad task of destination management. All entities of the competitive (micro)environment have a potential role in this task. Industry associations typically represent individual enterprises. Several different government departments (dealing with transportation, the environment, education and training, economic development, etc.) have an interest and responsibility in this area. Numerous publics, which we will examine in the next section, also strive to express views on the matter of how a destination is developed and managed over the long term.

In Chapter 9 we examine destination management, including the role of the DMO, in some detail. For the moment, however, it is sufficient to note that the DMO plays a potentially critical role in managing the competitiveness of the destination it represents. Notwithstanding the more restricted range of tasks that many DMOs currently pursue, the DMO is often either the only or the most pivotal organization with the broadest mandate for destination competitiveness.

Publics: Stakeholders and Watchdogs

The competitive (micro)environment is bordered by a number of institutions, organizations, groups and individuals that, although not directly part of what we might call 'the industry', nevertheless exert an influence – possibly a very considerable influence – on the behaviour and practices of those within the industry. Publics are all of the groups and individuals who are affected by a destination's tourism development, either materially or psychologically. In this sense, then, they are the destination's stakeholders or watchdogs.

The general public is one such stakeholder. Citizens, in general, take an interest in tourism development and its impacts on their quality of life. In the past we might have defined the general public in terms of its geographical proximity to the destination (e.g. residents of a city, state or nation). Today, however, many individuals take an interest in issues on a global scale because circumstances in one part of the world (e.g. pollution, the economy, social problems) can affect other regions. The phrase 'the global village' encapsulates these public attitudes. For this reason, tourism's general public may indeed be global. The exploitation of aboriginal peoples, the destruction of the environment and the desecration of a cultural heritage of global significance are examples of tourism development issues that might arouse worldwide attention.

The local residents of the destination – those members of the general public most immediately affected – are another important public. These are likely to be among the most vocal of the groups demanding a say in how tourism is developed in their own community. Citizen-action groups may be formed to represent certain opinions and viewpoints on issues related, for example, to the environment, aboriginal rights, taxation, development and growth, and social problems.

Another important public is labour, particularly organized labour. Tourism today is a sophisticated industry and, as such, it must compete against other industries to attract the necessary mix of skills, talents and workplace attitudes. Additionally, as the tourism industry operates around the clock and relies heavily on standards of customer service, labour publics can play a critical role in the competitiveness of tourist destinations. We explore this in greater detail in the next section.

Other important publics include financial institutions and investors, the media, the various government departments and authorities (particularly in transportation, the environment, economic development, planning, education and industrial policy), and a number of consumer groups (such as the International Airline Passengers Association, the Rail Users Consultative Committee in the UK, the Association of Business Travellers and the Professional Convention Management Association).

The role of publics in a destination's competitive (micro)environment is a critical one. With the right communication, and interaction between the industry and these publics, a mutually supportive relationship can exist which ensures that, over the long term, a destination can develop its tourism industry in a way that benefits all stakeholders. On the other hand, if the tourism industry views publics merely as impediments to growth and development to be defeated or overcome, an environment of mistrust, suspicion and opposition can emerge, and this is likely to hinder destination competitiveness and prosperity in the long run.

A destination's tourism industry must compete for the opinion of the general public as well as of all other publics if it is to be competitive. This is more likely to occur in cases where democratic principles are prevalent, there is a tradition and culture of tolerance for the views and opinions of others, communication and consultation are normal practices, and society has set up mechanisms (such as town hall meetings, review boards and task forces) which facilitate and encourage the contribution of public opinion to the process of visioning, planning and development. As discussed in Chapter 2, the will of a society to envision its future and plan for tourism's role in this future is the cornerstone for the successful management of the role of publics in a destination's competitive (micro)environment.

The Destination: Internal Environment and *Modus Operandi*

Figure 5.2 illustrates the relationship between all of the elements of a destination's competitive (micro)environment discussed so far in this chapter, namely suppliers, tourism and hospitality enterprises, marketing intermediaries and facilitators, customers, related and supporting industries, DMOs and publics. Some portion of the players in each of these categories will be associated with any particular destination. For example, certain suppliers will provide a destination with inputs and resources to the tourism and hospitality industry, and that destination will serve some portion of global tourist market segments (i.e. customers).

The bold dotted line in the figure delimits the subset of players in the competitive (micro) environment associated with a particular destination. This is the destination's internal environment. By 'internal environment' we do not necessarily mean only organizations or individuals that are located within the boundaries of the destination. Rather, the internal environment is to be interpreted as consisting of all entities which are involved in the operation and delivery of the destination's tourism product or experience. Customers are also part of this environment because they, too, participate in the production of the product. Similarly, the light dotted line identifies the subset of players associated with other competing destinations. The intersection between these two subsets includes those firms, organizations, groups or individuals that are associated with more than one competing destination. For example, many multinational enterprises or organizations would belong in this intersecting region.

So far in this chapter we have examined the individual effect of each group in the microenvironment on destination competitiveness. In this and the next two sections we briefly consider effects across groups.

The internal environment of the destination and its *modus operandi* – that is, the characteristic way in which the destination goes about the business of organizing and developing its tourism industry, attracting visitors and operating itself to serve tourists – are shaped by the practices, traditions and values that distinguish one destination from another. Porter (1990, pp. 107–124), who studied the competitive advantage of national industries, examined firm strategy, structure and rivalry within a national industry as a manifestation of these attributes. He noted that the goals, strategies and ways of organizing firms within industries vary among nations. One would expect to find variation among destinations in the *modus operandi* of their own tourism industries. The greatest variation is likely to exist among destinations defined at the national or supranational/continental level. But some variation could also be expected among cities, regions or states within a particular nation or culture as, even at this level, we can observe different regional 'personalities'.

In what areas might variations exist which could significantly affect the competitiveness of a destination? One such area concerns government policy. Policies that encourage sustainable forms of tourism development, attract investors and provide appropriate infrastructure, support facilities and a competitive environment will improve the competitiveness of the destination.

Another area is the attitudes and styles of managers of tourism and hospitality enterprises in the destination. Are they consistent with the principles of stewardship of the destination's resources? Are they willing to compete globally for tourist markets? What are their attitudes to matters such as customer service, innovation and different languages and cultures?

Social differences, too, are likely to be important. For example, resident attitudes to visitors shape a destination's reputation for friendliness and hospitality. Attitudes to work, wealth, risk-taking, skill development, authority and customer service are each important. For example, in some countries servile positions (e.g. that of a waiter in a restaurant) are regarded more highly than in others. Talented people are attracted to industries that carry a degree of national prestige and priority.

The degree of traditional rivalry among a destination's tourism and hospitality enterprises is a catalyst for innovation, productivity and improvements, and a focus on customer satisfaction. On the other hand, appropriate forms of cooperation among enterprises are also important. For example, the willingness of firms to cooperate in the marketing of the destination and in packaging complementary services would be expected to enhance destination competitiveness. Inappropriate forms of cooperation, that is, cooperation designed to reduce competition among firms rather than to improve the product and service delivered to customers, impedes the development of a competitive destination.[1]

Vertical cooperation among different levels of the tourism marketing channel can lead to efficiencies and product improvement as long as such cooperation does not stifle competition by precluding other enterprises.

Outside of the cruise and all-inclusive resort markets, individual enterprises produce only one element of the product purchased by the tourist (i.e. the destination experience). As a result, there is considerable scope for productivity improvement through inter-firm cooperation. And as long as the focus is on better serving customers rather than on blocking competitors, the competitiveness of the destination should improve as a result.

Other Competing Destinations

Likewise, other competing destinations possess their own unique internal environment and *modus operandi*. No two destinations share the same competitive profile because each destination has its own characteristic mix of traditions, values, goals and styles. Hence, as we noted in Chapter 2, destination competitiveness is not something that can be measured along a single dimension. A destination may be very competitive in meeting the needs of one tourist market segment, but quite uncompetitive in a distinctly different segment where a very different competitive profile is called for. For this reason, it makes no sense to observe that destination A is a competitor to destination B without reference to a market segment context.

But there is a further issue that governs the relationship between destinations, and it concerns the relative geographical proximity of the destinations concerned, and of the market as well. For example, the province of British Columbia in Canada and the state of Washington in the USA largely compete against one another to attract tourists from the Pacific Northwest region (i.e. Alberta, British Columbia, Washington, Idaho, Montana and Oregon). But this same province and state are complements for markets outside the Pacific Northwest. That is, a potential visitor from the east coast of North America would be likely to regard British Columbia and Washington as part of the same destination. In other words, the destination is no longer defined by provincial or state boundaries but by the Pacific Northwest region as a whole. Strengths in one part of this larger region add to or complement, rather than compete against, strengths in other parts of the region as a whole.

So nearby or neighbouring areas generally become complements rather than substitutes the more distant the market. Anastasopoulos (1984) did find, however, some research data to suggest that pairs of countries may not be mutually competitive or complementary as tourist destinations. He inferred from his research that Italy and Yugoslavia are mutually competitive; however, Italy seemed to be Greece's competitor, but Greece seemed to complement Italy. Yannopoulos (1987) also noted that non-symmetrical complementary relationships appear to exist.

All of this points to the necessity of determining the significant competitive and complementary relationships between destinations for each targeted market segment, so that a destination has a clear understanding of the competitors it should benchmark itself against, the complements it should partner with, and the competitive profile required for each market segment.

The Tourism System: Integrative Impacts

One of the most dramatic transformations to occur in the tourism and hospitality industry since the early 1980s has been its globalization. Over time, the business of tourism has shifted from a regional or national clustering of activity to operate on an increasingly global scale. And although small enterprises remain the lifeblood of the industry and continue to vastly outnumber large tourism and hospitality corporations, big businesses and multinational enterprises (MNEs) in particular are profoundly changing the way the tourism system functions, worldwide.

These large corporations are bringing economies of scale, branding and improved management practices to the industry that are beyond the ability of many smaller firms. However, at the same time as these changes are occurring, tourist markets are becoming increasingly sophisticated, demanding and diverse in their needs. As a consequence, changes in the business of global tourism have not been allowed to ignore these equally significant changes in the market. The globalization of tourism, then, has seen great change in terms of both supply and demand.[2]

The global scale of the tourism system today and the accompanying globalization of the business of tourism have significant ramifications for destinations. Multinational tourism and hospitality enterprises are prevalent now in most sectors of the industry, but particularly in hotels and resorts (ITT Sheraton, Marriott, Club Med), airlines (One World and Star alliances), food services (McDonald's, Hard Rock Cafe, Planet Hollywood), retail travel agents (Thomas Cook, Thompson's, American Express), entertainment (Disney, *Cirque du Soleil*) and tour wholesalers/operators (Gray Line Worldwide, Insight Vacations, Trafalgar Tours). Enterprise growth, mergers, and acquisitions, partnerships and alliances, management contracts and franchising, business networks and virtual corporations, etc. have resulted in tourism and hospitality MNEs that may have operations in a large number of destinations. Each enterprise views its business as a portfolio of operations in different destinations. The success and profitability of the MNE is therefore a function of its ability to manage this portfolio of destinations by allocating resources among operations in each location, and adding destinations to and deleting them from its portfolio.

The competitiveness of a destination in each market segment will be a major factor in the portfolio management decisions of MNEs in tourism. Any increase or decrease in the inherent competitiveness of a destination will be magnified by the strategic decisions multinationals make either to increase/expand or decrease/withdraw from a destination.

Notes

[1]   Porter (1990, p. 667) notes that direct competitor-to-competitor cooperation usually undermines the competitive advantages of industries in the long run. 'Indirect cooperation, where joint efforts involving competitors take place through independent entities, can be beneficial in some circumstances', such as cooperative research and development, or trade association programmes for the purpose of factor creation. 'The best structure is one in which cooperative activities are managed independently and have precise charters, so that participants face no mixed motives in being involved. At the same time, companies must compete vigorously on product development, pricing, and other aspects of strategy.'

[2]   Poon (1993) discusses in detail the juxtaposition of these interdependent changes in demand and supply, describing the global transformation as a change from 'old tourism' to 'new tourism'. Chapter 4 of Poon's book examines the emergence of new tourism in terms of the attributes of new consumers, new technologies, new production practices, new management techniques and new frame (i.e. environmental) conditions.

References

Anastasopoulos, P.G.E. (1984) Interdependencies in international travel: the role of relative prices. A case study of the Mediterranean region. PhD thesis, New School for Social Research, New York.

Kotler, P., Bowen, J. and Makens, J. (1996) *Marketing for Hospitality and Tourism*. Prentice Hall, Upper Saddle River, New Jersey.

Middleton, V.T.C. (1994) *Marketing in Travel and Tourism*, 2nd edn. Butterworth-Heinemann, Oxford.

Poon, A. (1993) *Tourism, Technology and Competitive Strategies*. CAB International, Wallingford, UK.

Porter, M.E. (1990) *The Competitive Advantage of Nations*. Free Press, New York.

Yannopoulos, G.N. (1987) Intra-regional shifts in tourism growth in the Mediterranean area. *Travel and Tourism Analyst* 1987 (November), 15–24.

6

Core Resources and Attractors: the Essence of Destination Appeal

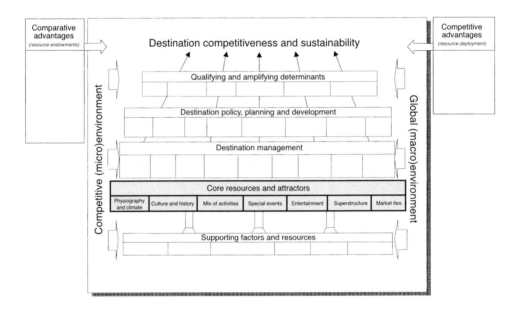

One of the great challenges facing tourism managers is to clearly understand the factors that motivate individuals to choose one particular destination over the myriad other possibilities. When all the complexities of destination choice are stripped away, it is essentially the core resources and attractors that underlie the basic desire to travel to a given destination. These also provide the foundation for an exciting and memorable destination experience. As shown in Fig. 6.1, the core resources and attractors are of seven major types.

1. The *physiography* of the destination, most particularly the landscape, scenery and climate. In effect, it is the visual and sensual pleasure derived from these elements that provides some of the most fundamental physical enjoyments of tourism.

2. The *culture and history* of the destination in turn furnish much of the intellectual satisfaction from visitations.

3. The range and mix of *activities* available at a destination provide the primary foundation of both the physical and emotional stimulation that excites and challenges the visitor.

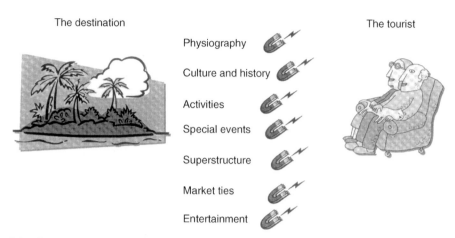

The destination   The tourist

Physiography

Culture and history

Activities

Special events

Superstructure

Market ties

Entertainment

Fig. 6.1. Core resources and attractors: the factors that motivate travel and draw visitors to a destination.

4. The various *special events* offered by a destination create much of the dynamics and the uniqueness that make a destination memorable.

5. The different components of the destination's *superstructure*, while often highly varied in nature, tend to provide a substantial percentage of what is perceived as the fundamental tourism character of a destination.

6. The types of *entertainment* found at a destination are frequently designed to complement the different activities and events that a destination offers. Conversely, for other destinations the strength of the entertainment may itself be the primary appeal of the destination.

7. The strength of *market ties* frequently serves as a major catalyst for destination visitation that involves human relationships.

Destination Physiography and Climate: the Natural Edge

From a tourism management perspective, it is somewhat ironic that natural physiography and climate – among the most important determinants of destination competitiveness – are largely beyond the control and even the influence of destination managers. The extent to which the natural climate and terrain are hospitable to humans provides a set of natural parameters (Fig. 6.2) that either endow a destination with competitive appeal or create barriers that must constantly be adapted to, overcome or managed around. A comfortable, constant climate immediately provides a baseline of attractiveness for the great majority of visitors. While niche markets may seek unique and demanding climates, these are generally the exception. Market segments wishing to visit extremes of hot and cold, such as deserts, jungles and arctic regions, represent a relatively small percentage of the total travel market. While these market segments may be lucrative in the right circumstances, they do not represent the mainstream of tourism.

Those destinations that are blessed with a 'natural edge' are becoming increasingly attractive in today's world of overpopulation and pollution. Indeed, this dimension of destination appeal has become so significant that it has recently resulted in the creation of 'natural area tourism' (Newsome *et al.*, 2002). Newsome *et al.*, in turn, identify four subcategories that they define as adventure tourism, nature-based tourism, wildlife tourism and ecotourism. Regardless of the semantics, their book provides an excellent overview for those destination managers who wish to develop and focus on the natural edge as the strategic philosophy for a destination.

The majority of destinations that have a favourable climate tend to build their competitive position around this natural advantage. Spain, for example, has developed a symbol

- Climate (absolute, relative, variability, consistency)
- Topography
- Size
- Water (lakes, rivers, oceans)
- Forest
- Desert
- Rural and urban areas
- Air quality
- Scenery
- Flora, fauna
- Wildlife

Fig. 6.2. Destination physiography and climate: elements of the natural edge.

based on the sun that has almost become its national flag. The many island destinations that enjoy favourable climates in attractive locations have given rise to the well known three 'S's' in tourism: sun, sand and sea. Aggressive marketers have sometimes added a fourth 'S'. As is well known in marketing, sex sells!

Closely tied to climate is the actual physical character of the destination. The degree to which the physiography of a destination is hospitable to human activity again provides very fundamental advantages and disadvantages. Relatively smooth, vegetation-covered terrain that has convenient access to fresh water and high-quality recreation areas provides humans (and animals) with a physical environment that most easily accommodates their physiology. While variations in topography, as well as in vegetation and wildlife, add novelty and variety, the human body prefers to avoid extremes.

Other destinations may not possess entirely favourable climates but are blessed with magnificent scenery. Regions that contain rugged mountain ranges provide some of the world's most spectacular scenery. The Alps of Europe, Asia's Himalayas, South America's Andes and the jagged Rockies of North

America all compete to attract travellers who seek eye-popping mountain views, the thrill of traversing high mountain passes and, for some, the challenge of mountaineering in the world's most elevated peaks.

An excellent example of a destination that thrives on the appeal of its majestic vistas is Canada's Banff National Park. In this instance, the destination is so successful that we are faced with the need for both marketing and 'demarketing'. The goal of tourism marketing is to attract visitors who are interested in high-quality nature but to limit total visitation to a level that is not injurious to the environmental health of the region.

As we embark on a new century, Banff National Park currently welcomes over 5 million visitors annually. The park is so successful that this level of visitation risks incurring ecological damage so severe that it could eventually destroy much of the park's appeal. The ecological damage that experts allege is taking place relates both to the level of visitation (the number of people) and the type of visitation (what people do while in the park). Because of the park's success, the environmental marketing goal is to ensure that visitors who are attracted will respect the environmental integrity of the region.

From a destination marketing perspective, the challenge in such situations is twofold. First, the overall level of demand needs to be be kept at a point that can be comfortably accommodated by the existing infrastructure. This seeks to make optimal economic use of existing investments without creating the need for new facility developments that could contribute to environmental degradation in the area. Second, within existing levels of visitation, attempts must be made to attract those visitors whose behaviour while in the Park is most environmentally sensitive. Such visitors will have minimum impact on the ecological integrity of the Park.

Marketing efforts that pursue the above goal have two characteristics. First, they should be such as to appeal to environmentally conscious individuals. Second, they must be placed within media most commonly read/viewed by environmentally conscious citizens. Regardless of how it is done, all marketing related to the natural edge of a destination's physiography and climate must constantly keep in mind that this competitive edge is a gift that is only sustainable if it is carefully managed.

Those destinations that possess neither a particularly favourable climate nor outstanding scenery are left to improvise in their efforts to compete in the very competitive tourism marketplace. For many, this amounts to an often futile effort to attract visitors to a destination that most would prefer either to leave or to bypass. The spark of genius is especially required in such situations. Branson, Missouri (a very 'ordinary' destination) has become the number one bus tour destination of the USA through the development of a very special and limited product that appeals to a very specific segment of the population – it is claimed to have more live entertainment than anywhere else in the USA. Las Vegas, USA, emerges as a destination that demonstrates how an arid desert region can be transformed into a tourism Mecca through ingenious policy changes combined with managerial imagination and entrepreneurship. Before lavishing too much praise on Las Vegas, however, one must keep in mind the importance of location. Its proximity to the large markets of California provides a comparative advantage that greatly strengthens its competitive position. In contrast, other destinations that must live with more limited markets and an unfavourable (or at best mediocre) physiography or climate must initiate strategies to counter, minimize or even take advantage of their impacts on the destination's ability to compete. Some of these strategies will now be discussed.

- *The building of artificial environments that negate the environmental inhospitality of a region.* By far the most common way of managing around adversity is evident in the thousands of air-conditioned convention centres and hotels that attract and accommodate visitors to destinations all over the world, whose climates many consider unbearably hot and humid during certain times (or even all) of the year. By creating comfortable artificial worlds within well-known destinations during their off season, some destinations have managed to remain relatively competitive, thereby keeping a large investment in facilities and employees operating and acceptably profitable.

- *Using a unique attraction to effectively take physiography and climate out of the picture as a competitive factor.* For example, the city of Xian, China, a quite average destination, attracts large numbers of visitors by promoting the recently discovered terracotta soldiers. This site is a world-class archaeological find whose uniqueness and quality enable this modest urban destination to build a thriving tourism industry.

- *The development and promotion of a special event that takes advantage of and even highlights physiographical and/or climatic adversity.* As an example, Quebec City, Canada, tackled the adversity of the coldest climatic period of the year by creating the Quebec Winter Carnival, in effect a celebration of winter. Part of the celebration involves the construction of ice sculptures as part of an international ice-sculpting contest, and the hosting of a canoe race across the broad, ice-filled St Lawrence River attracts the international media, which in turn multiplies the reputation of the destination. The event has become so successful from a tourism perspective that it has led to the building of an 'Ice Hotel', where occupancy during the 10 days of the event economically justifies its construction and operation. Imagine attracting visitors who are happy to pay relatively high rates to sleep in a hotel whose walls are made of ice!

- *The enhancement of overall destination awareness through media attention drawn by some unpleasant aspect of the destination that is of little interest to most tourists.* Hiroshima, Japan, the now-famous 'Bridge on the River Kwai' in Myanmar (formerly Burma) and the Little Big Horn area in Montana, USA are located in areas that might normally not attract visitors, but because each of these locations gained notoriety as a result of a military event they do tend to attract a certain category of tourist. As a further example, the country of Nepal in the Himalayan mountains, despite its spectacular scenery, has had to counter the negative realities of its inhospitable location by basing much of its tourism promotion on the fact it is located near the base of one of the world's highest and most well-known challenges for many of the world's mountaineers. The *Marathon des Sables* in Morocco in northern Africa draws world-wide attention to one of the hottest, most inhospitable areas of the word. While the location of the race is not itself a major tourism destination, the event attracts considerable media attention to Morocco, thus helping the country build world awareness and enhancing the competitiveness of other aspects of the destination.

- *The use of mega-events to build the global reputation of a destination and to leave behind visible legacies that may in time become destination icons.* Perhaps the most audacious of all efforts to enhance the reputation of the competitiveness of an often rather ordinary destination is through the hosting of what are termed 'mega-events'. Relatively unknown cities have attained international prominence by hosting the Olympic Games (both Summer and Winter). Cities such as Innsbruck (Austria), Calgary (Canada), Sapporo (Japan) and Salt Lake City (USA) are now modestly famous worldwide as a legacy derived from the hosting of the Olympic Games. Even much smaller centres, such as Lake Placid (USA), Lillehammer (Norway) and Albertville (France), have had a brief moment of fame through their involvement with the Olympic movement. International Expositions and World Fairs are another type of well-established form of mega-event that can build the present and future competitiveness of a destination. The 1937 Paris International Exposition in France not only attracted visitors but also left behind the Eiffel Tower, arguably the world's single most recognizable tourism icon. Expo '67 in Montreal represented the worldwide coming of age of Canada as it reached its 100th birthday as a country, and truly placed it in the world of international tourism. Expo '86 in Vancouver, Canada served as the stimulus for imaginative development that has moved Vancouver closer towards being regarded as one of the great cities of the world, a service that the 2000 Summer Olympics also rendered to Sydney, Australia. Perhaps more significantly, Expo '86 in Vancouver served as the catalyst for making tourism the number one industry in the entire province of British Columbia. Even much smaller cities, such as Spokane (Washington, USA), Knoxville (Tennessee, USA), Brisbane (Australia), Seville (Spain) and Hanover (Germany) have seen their more modest stature substantially enhanced through their hosting of smaller, yet highly significant international expositions in 1974, 1982, 1988, 1992 and 2000, respectively.

- *The establishment of niche (specialized) attractions in very unattractive or mundane regions of a destination.* While Disney World is now globally successful, it must not be forgotten that it was originally built on a large, unattractive swamp area of central Florida, USA, and is based on the original concept of Disneyland for

California, USA. In brief, Disney World is an example of how a worthless swamp area has been transformed into a travel Mecca. In the process, the success of Disney World has driven the growth of Orlando, a city which now has some 105,782 hotel rooms and which provides, through tourism, employment for 211,000 persons. More importantly, it has provided and continues to provide memorable vacation experiences for both young and old visitors from around the world. The establishment of the Baseball Hall of Fame in Cooperstown, New York, USA, has put the name of this small destination on the lips of many Americans and made it a Mecca for baseball fans.

The overall conclusion that must be faced, from a destination management standpoint, is that certain destinations may possess distinct natural advantages for a large percentage of many market segments. Destinations that lack these natural advantages face two main alternatives.

- They may make efforts to adapt to their geographical reality by minimizing the negative consequences of their climate and topography. The examples above show how this has been done.
- They may restrict their marketing efforts to, or focus them on, those market segments for which the negative dimensions of a destination's topography or climate are of less concern, or even of special appeal. Two examples follow.
  - Tours to the Antarctic, which appeal to a very limited percentage of the travel market. However, those who do wish to travel to this remote area, to see the penguins and rare ice formations, are willing to pay on the order of $10,000 per person to experience this very unique destination.
  - Tours to the jungles of the Amazon, which seek to attract those who desire a unique travel experience. While safety is not inconsequential, tourists to the Amazon are prepared to accept food and accommodation

that do not appeal to a large percentage of the travel market.

No one destination can hope to attract or host all types of visitation, even though it may dream of attracting each and every traveller at least once! Given this reality, it behoves any particular destination, once it has clearly defined its appeals and benefits, to develop marketing programmes targeted at those most likely to value these appeals and benefits. This approach is not only logical – it is financially realistic.

The challenge inherent in implementing the above approach is to identify the individuals in the market segments of probable interest – or to at least identify the media by which they are most likely to be reached.

Destination Culture: the Lure of Human Distinctiveness

Culture, broadly defined, is a second very powerful dimension of destination attractiveness. As one classic study has demonstrated (Table 6.1), the cultural and social characteristics of a region are second only to physiography (natural beauty and climate) in determining the attractiveness of a tourism destination (Ritchie and Zins, 1978). While this study is somewhat dated and relates directly to only one specific destination, it is one of the few that provides some indication of the relative significance of a destination's culture as a factor in determining its market appeal.

The elements of culture

The study by Ritchie and Zins (1978) identified some 12 sub-components or elements of culture that were important in influencing the tourism attractiveness of a region. As seen in Fig. 6.3, these elements are:

- the *handicrafts* of the region;
- the *language* spoken by residents;
- the *traditions* that characterize the region;
- the *gastronomy* or style of food preparation particular to the region;

Table 6.1.   Relative importance of general factors influencing the attractiveness of a tourism region (from Ritchie and Zins, 1978).

Factor	Ordinal rank in importance	Average importance on interval scale	Interval order of importance	Overall order of importance: two methods
Natural beauty and climate	1	9.24	1	1
Cultural and social characteristics	2	8.64	2	2
Accessibility of the region	3	7.77	4	3
Attitudes towards tourists	4	8.23	3	3
Infrastructure of the region	5	7.76	5	5
Price levels	6	7.03	6	6
Sport, recreation and educational facilities	7	6.97	7	7
Shopping and commercial facilities	8	4.97	8	8

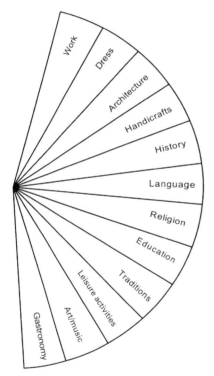

Fig. 6.3.   The role of culture in determining the attractiveness of a tourism region.

- the *art and music* identified with the region, including paintings, sculpture and concerts;
- the *history* of the region, including its visual reminders;
- the methods of *work* or technology particular to a region (such as a space centre, fishing and farming);

- *architecture*, both exterior and interior, which lends a distinctive appearance to a region;
- the *religion* that is of particular significance to a region (including its visible manifestations);
- the *education* system that is characteristic of a region;
- styles of *dress* that are characteristic of a region; and
- *leisure activities* reflecting the distinctive lifestyles of a region.

What is culture?

There have been a number of attempts to define culture. One basic dictionary definition of culture is as follows:

> The totality of socially transmitted behavior patterns, arts, beliefs, institutions and all other products of human work and thought characteristic of a community or population.
> (Adapted from *American Heritage Dictionary*, 1985, p. 348)

Another definition of particular interest is this:

> A historically created system of explicit and implicit designs for living, which tend to be shared by all, or specifically designated members of a group at a specified point in time.
> (Kluckhohn and Kelly, 1945)

The emphasis here is on the explicit components of culture that are readily visible to the traveller.

As might be expected, all the elements of culture are not equally effective as 'sub-attractors' to a destination. Furthermore, it is important that the destination manager realizes that the different elements of culture appear somewhat differently to non-resident visitors to a region and to those who live in or near the destination. The extent to which non-residents and residents agree or disagree on which cultural events attract them to a destination and the relative importances of these elements in attracting them are summarized in Table 6.2. While there are certainly similarities in the importance of each of the elements between the two market segments, it can be seen that traditions and history and the appearance given to a destination by architecture tend to have greater drawing power for visitors from outside the destination. Destination managers will also want to note the high degree of importance accorded by both residents and non-residents to the gastronomy of the region. It would appear that high-quality, distinctive meals are a powerful element in the cultural dimension of a destination's attractiveness. In general, it appears that residents often underestimate the extent to which visitors are interested in things that they themselves regard as commonplace. For example, in Melbourne, Australia, a proportion of homes are sold by auction. Tourists have often been known to turn up at these house auctions not to purchase but simply to observe them as an element of the local culture.

Similarly, Ritchie and Zins (1978) found that the factors of education, dress and religion were accorded little importance by both residents and non-residents. The most notable difference between the evaluations for these two groups involved the relative importance of the leisure activities element. The point to be made is that the different elements of culture may have different levels of appeal to resident and non-resident tourists. So destination managers should seek to determine how best to utilize culture as a core attractor for each market segment of interest.

Major dimensions of cultural attractiveness

As Ritchie and Zins (1978) noted, although great care had been taken in specifying the 12 elements of culture, it was possible that certain aspects of tourism attractiveness regarding culture were present more than once within the framework of those variables retained for study; that is, it was possible in the extreme case that two or more of the items employed in a given case were really different measures of the same underlying dimension of attractiveness of a tourism region. Accordingly, each of the scales was further analysed to discover whether a more restricted set of dimensions might underlie the scales measuring the general and cultural attractiveness of a tourism region.

From this analysis four major dimensions of cultural attractiveness were identified. Based on these findings, destination managers need to recognize that visitors may typically focus on the following main aspects of a destination from a sociocultural perspective:

- the basic elements of *daily life*, that is, how people go about their daily living;
- the more sophisticated elements of the *good life* of residents, such as art, museums and food;
- the elements of *work* in the society; and
- cultural *remnants of the past*, with emphasis on museums, architecture and religion.

Table 6.2. Relative importance of sociocultural elements influencing the cultural attractiveness of a tourism region: non-residents compared with residents (from Ritchie and Zins, 1978).

Elements	Overall order of importance: non-residents	Overall order of importance: residents
Traditions	1	3
Gastronomy	2	2
History	3	5
Architecture	4	7
Handicrafts	4	3
Leisure activities	6	1
Art and music	7	5
Language	8	9
Work	9	8
Dress	10	11
Education	11	10
Religion	12	11

Forms of culture

From a tourism perspective, culture may also usefully be viewed as possessing different forms as well as different elements. In the study of Ritchie and Zins (1978), three distinct forms of culture were defined: *animated* forms, *inanimate* forms and *daily life* forms. Respondents were asked to judge the relative value of each of these forms in determining the cultural attractiveness of a tourism region for both residents and non-residents.

For both residents and non-residents, animated forms of culture were consistently rated the most essential elements from a tourism standpoint. Inanimate forms were also rated highly from the point of view of non-residents; they were considered least important from the perspective of residents of the region. Finally, daily life forms were generally viewed as less important, although they were rated slightly higher than inanimate forms in the case of residents.

The implication of these categories is that visitors perceive the culture of destinations in terms of three forms. The daily life form relates very directly to the underlying dimensions of the daily life and good life dimensions noted earlier. At the same time, visitors view culture as being either animate or inanimate. The animated dimension relates to the 'humanness' or 'degree of liveliness' that one finds in certain cultures compared with others. The inanimate dimension relates to all the markers of the past and present – the buildings and structure of cities.

Culture and consumption

While the foregoing discussion identifies those cultural aspects of a destination that attract visitors, it is also important to keep in mind that travel is but one form of consumption and that, as McCracken (1988) has argued, 'culture is the lens through which all phenomena are seen'. Ironically, while destination culture is a major attraction, the way in which a visitor experiences or 'consumes' a given culture depends heavily on the visitor's own cultural background. Destination managers need to keep this reality in mind when providing travel products, services and experiences to a visitor. In summary, from the traveller's perspective it is highly likely that the destination manager does not always (or even frequently) convey the thoughts or provide the experiences intended. While this is a very basic psychological concept, destination managers need to keep it constantly in mind.

Activities: the Nike 'Just Do It' Mentality of Travellers

Despite the importance that members of the tourism industry ascribe to the comfort of accommodation, the efficiency of transportation and the quality of service provided, we must never forget that these functions are generally taken for granted by the visitor. The real reason for visiting a destination is to *do* things – to actively *participate* in activities that stimulate for the moment, and then to leave as a participant who has vibrant memories of what he or she has done. In seeking to make a destination attractive and competitive, it is essential to ensure that it offers a broad range of activities, of memorable things to do.

From a destination perspective, activities may be categorized in many ways. One form of classification is given in Fig. 6.4. The actual classification system used is not necessarily important. What is important is that destination managers attempt to provide a broad mix of activities. This mix, however, should observe the following principles:

- it should be consistent with the nature and topography of the destination so as to appeal to the kind of visitors that tend to come to the destination;
- it should be consistent with the values of the local population, or at least not be flagrantly opposed to their values;
- it should observe local regulations and legislation;
- it should provide activities that are complementary, so as to provide opportunities for a wider range of visitors;
- it should offer activities that are uniquely appropriate to the particular nature of the destination;

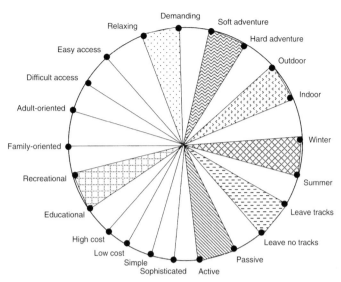

Fig. 6.4. The activity characteristics classification wheel.

- it should provide activities across all seasons found at the destination; and
- it should provide activities that are economically viable yet, where appropriate, suited to a range of incomes.

Special Events: In Search of the Stroke of Genius That Creates Destination Uniqueness Through Local Insight and Entrepreneurship

Perhaps the major challenge facing destination managers is to develop a unique or distinctive position among the large number of destinations from which potential visitors can choose. If a destination is blessed by some uniqueness of nature (e.g. the Grand Canyon in Arizona, USA), by some relative uniqueness of its culture (e.g. the province of Quebec, Canada, within North America, the Masai Mara region of Kenya and the Afro-Caribbean-influenced Atlantic coast of Costa Rica), by a long and distinctive history (e.g. Rome, Italy), by a particularly outstanding work of design, engineering or architecture (e.g. Paris, France) or by some other unique dimension, then it has a tremendous competitive advantage. But if, like many destinations, it must rely on innovative insight and/or simply hard work to create for

itself a unique characteristic that makes it stand out in the marketplace, then the development of special events has proved to be one way to achieve visibility and to build a reputation. While mega-events and/or hallmark events (such as a World Fair and the hosting of Olympic Games, the Super Bowl, the World Cup of soccer and G8 gatherings of world leaders) can raise a destination from obscurity to international prominence, there are only so many of these ready-made events to go around. Given this reality, destinations must seek to develop their own mega-event or hallmark event. In this regard, have you ever asked yourself why the Boston Marathon is held in Boston? Or, more generally, how is it that a running race that could be held almost anywhere in the world has become so famous that it stands out among all other marathons? Similarly, we may ask why the Master's Golf Tournament, the Kentucky Derby, the New Orleans Mardi Gras, the Munich Oktoberfest and the Calgary Stampede have achieved such international recognition and acclaim when there are plenty of other golf tournaments, horse races and local celebrations. What is the key factor – the stroke of genius – that elevates what could be ordinary to being renowned? Superficial reflection indicates that it may just be a question of fortunate timing or a stroke of luck. On the other hand, more careful analysis indicates it is often the insights and commit-ment of one individual, combined with hard work, persistence and a lot of community effort, that creates an event that consistently rises above the ordinary and that outperforms all others in terms of the unique experience it is perceived to provide to visitors and residents alike.

The term 'stroke of genius' is particularly relevant to the Masters Golf Tournament. Looking to provide a service to golf by hosting a tournament, world-famous golfer Bob Jones and his colleague Clifford Roberts decided to host an annual event, starting in 1934 (visit www.masters.org for further details). Their devotion to excellence has created not only a world-renowned event, but also a golfing facility in Augusta (Georgia, USA) that is nearly as revered as the birthplace of golf, St Andrews, Scotland.

Many well-known events have their origins tied to religious themes. The New Orleans Mardi Gras started in the 1700s as a pre-Lenten ball (www.nola.com/mardigras). The German Oberammergau Passion Play, which is held every 10 years in the Bavarian region, was originally based on deeply held religious con-victions. While it retains its religious roots, it has increasingly become a tourism event that attracts visitors from all over the world.

The Olympic Games, both Summer and Winter, are the flagship example of a growing number of sports-based events that can contrib-ute in a major way to increasing international awareness of the host destination – even though the event may only be held there only once in several generations. Aside from enhancing the general awareness of the host city, an Olympic Games often tends to create a highly simplified 'one-liner' in the mind of the world population. As an example, the 1972 Munich Games are remembered for the terrorism they engen-dered, the Mexico City Games of 1968 have become the symbol of Black Power, and the 1976 Games in Montreal are remembered for the 'legend of debt' they left behind. The Los Angeles Games of 1984 marked 'the beginning of the commercialization' of the Games. The Moscow Games of 1980 were the 'Games no-one attended'. The Atlanta Games of 1996 are remembered by many as the 'Games of the bomb', while the Sydney Games of 2000 were

just 'a success'. Other international events, such as the soccer World Cup, other world champi-onships (tennis, curling, etc.) and events such as the US Super Bowl that attract high levels of media attention can help to create, build or enhance a destination's awareness and image.

Clearly, there is a difference in the roles of one-time and repeating events. While one-time events may provide a worldwide burst of expo-sure for a destination, the impacts and aware-ness can be fleeting if there are no follow-up activities to consolidate the destination's reputation. The value of ongoing, annual events is that they provide destination managers with the ability to slowly build awareness and reputa-tion. Like the Masters, 'Wimbledon is Wimble-don' because every year it is sure to typify the pinnacle of excellence in tennis. Similarly, the New Orleans Mardi Gras, the Oktoberfest in Munich and the Running of the Bulls in Pamplona (Spain) are celebrations that are rooted in local values and have acquired interna-tional stature in terms of their reputations, their appeal and their ability to draw visitors from all over the world. Through time, they have tended to characterize a destination and to make it a must-see, often whether or not the event is actually occurring at the time of visitation.

While the foregoing provides examples of events that have attained success and that have provided host destinations with visibility and the basis for ongoing tourism and community development, the ability to develop events that will serve as drivers for destination competitive-ness on a sustainable basis requires systematic analysis in order to achieve an understanding of the underlying factors that determine event success, combined with professional management that takes advantage of this understanding.

One of the world's leading experts in the field of event management is Dr Donald Getz. His book, *Event Management and Event Tourism* (Getz, 1997), has become a classic reference. As Getz notes, there are a number of fundamental underlying factors that create or heighten the quality of specialness that is essen-tial for an event if it is to help a destination achieve the stature and level of recognition that turns an event core attractor into a truly competitive advantage for a destination. These factors are summarized in Table 6.3. While

Table 6.3.   Factors that help to make an event a competitive core attractor (from Getz, 1997).

- A multiplicity of goals: specialness is related to the diversity of goals that events successfully pursue
- Festive spirit: specialness increases with the ability of events to create a true festive spirit. The ambience can encourage joyfulness (even revelry), freedom from routine constraints, and inversion of normal roles and functions
- Satisfying basic needs: all the basic human needs and related leisure and travel motivations can be satisfied in part through events. Specialness increases as the number of needs and related motives are better satisfied
- Uniqueness: mega-events rely on a must-see, once-in-a-lifetime uniqueness to attract visitors; all events, to some degree, can manage their product and promotions to create the specialness associated with a unique happening
- Quality: poor quality will destroy any pretence of being special; high-quality events will go beyond customer expectations and generate high levels of satisfaction
- Authenticity: this is related to uniqueness, in that events based on indigenous cultural values and attributes will be inherently unique. To the tourist, specialness will be heightened by a feeling of participation in an authentic community celebration
- Tradition: many events have become traditions, rooted in the community, and attractive to visitors because of the associated mystique. Hallmark events, which are closely associated with the host community, so that event and destination images are mutually reinforcing, are traditional by nature
- Flexibility: events can be developed with minimal infrastructure, can be moved in space and time, and can be adapted to changing markets and organizational needs. This fact makes them special products for organizations and destinations
- Hospitality: the essence of hospitality is to make every event-goer feel like an honoured guest. In destinations, the tourist is provided with community hospitality and the resident is proud to be a host. Some events and communities are recognized for the special welcome they give to visitors
- Tangibility: all elements of the event can be themed to maximize festive spirit, authenticity, tradition, interactions and customer service. Theming adds to the feeling of specialness
- Symbolism: the use of rituals and symbols together adds to the festive atmosphere, and can also give an event special significance above and beyond its immediate purpose and theme
- Affordability: events providing affordable leisure, educational, social and cultural experiences will be special to large segments of the population without the means to pay for alternatives
- Convenience: events can be special opportunities for spontaneous, unplanned leisure and social opportunities. This is of increasing importance in a hectic, work-oriented world, especially in urban environments

every event will not possess all of these characteristics, destination managers should seek to identify those that are most relevant to the kinds of events that seem to fit their destination.

Efforts can then be directed towards activities that enhance the specialness of an event, and that therefore heighten its probability of achieving sustainable success. While none of these factors alone determines success, an event's uniqueness provides the one element that every destination manager wants above all others. This said, it must also be emphasized that it is careful management of all factors that ultimately determines the extent to which a given event will add to the core attractiveness of a tourism destination. This multidimensional view of event success clearly implies that there

is more than one type of event that can be a successful core attractor.

As noted earlier, those events that tend to have the greatest and often the most lasting impact on the reputation and renown of a destination are referred to as 'hallmark events' and 'mega-events'. While there may be an overlap between these two categories, they can be broadly distinguished as follows. Hallmark events are events that, irrespective of their size or economic impact, are so unique and of such a quality that their very mention immediately brings to mind the destination that hosts them. The Boston Marathon (USA), the Wimbledon Lawn Tennis Championships (England), the Oktoberfest (Germany) and the Mardi Gras in New Orleans (USA) are examples of hallmark events.

Table 6.4. A classification of hallmark and mega-events (adapted from Ritchie, 1984).

Classification	Examples and locations
World fairs/expositions	• Expo 1967, Montreal • Knoxville 1982 • New Orleans 1984 • Vancouver 1986 • Brisbane 1988 • Taejon 1993 • Lisbon 1998 • Hanover 2000
Unique carnivals and festivals	• Mardi Gras, New Orleans • Quebec Winter Carnival, Quebec City • Oktoberfest, Munich • Stampede, Calgary
Major sports events	• Summer Olympics, Los Angeles, 1984 • Winter Olympics, Calgary, 1988 • World Cup soccer, Spain, 1982 • Marathons, Boston • Grand Prix racing, Monza • Wimbledon Tennis Championship, London • Master's Golf Tournament, Augusta
Significant cultural and religious events	• Oberammergau, Germany • Papal coronation, Rome • Royal wedding, London
Historical milestones	• Los Angeles Bicentennial • 500th Anniversary of the discovery of America (1492–1992) • Australia Bicentenary, 1988
Classical commercial and religious events	• Wine purchasing, France • Royal Winter Fair, Toronto • Floriade '82, Amsterdam
Major political personage events	• Presidential inaugurations • Funerals of heads of state, e.g. Tito, Yugoslavia; Brezhnev, Russia • Papal visits • Major political leadership conventions • G8 economic summits

A more complete classification is given in Table 6.4. A formal definition of hallmark events is as follows.

> Major one-time or recurring events of limited duration, developed primarily to enhance the awareness, appeal and profitability of a tourism destination in the short and/or long term. Such events rely for their success on uniqueness, status, or timely significance to create interest and attract attention.
>
> (Ritchie, 1984, p. 2)

While mega-events may be or may (and often do) become hallmark events, they are defined primarily by their size and economic impact rather than their status or significance. Regardless of whether a large event is formally classified as a hallmark event or mega-event, it will provide a range of impacts (Table 6.5) that include both positive and negative components. The challenge facing destination managers who seek to incorporate such events into their strategic planning is to try to manage the positive benefits while minimizing the negative ones.

Not all events that are important to a destination's success are large or internationally significant. Getz (1997) has provided a typology

Table 6.5. Types of impacts of hallmark events and mega-events (from Ritchie, 1984).

Impact	Manifestations	
	Positive	Negative
Economic	• Increased expenditures • Creation of employment	• Price increases during event • Real estate speculation
Tourism/ commercial	• Increased awareness of the region as a travel/tourism destination • Increased knowledge concerning the potential for investment and commercial activity in the region	• Acquisition of a poor reputation as a result of inadequate facilities or improper practices • Negative reactions from existing enterprises due to the possibility of new competition for local manpower and government assistance
Physical	• Construction of new facilities • Improvement of local infrastructure	• Environmental damage • Overcrowding
Sociocultural	• Increase in permanent level of local interest and participation in type of activity associated with event • Strengthening of regional traditions and values	• Commercialization of activities which may be of a personal or private nature • Modification of nature of event/activity to accommodate tourism
Psychological	• Increased local pride and community spirit • Increased awareness of non-local perceptions	• Tendency towards defensive attitudes concerning host regions • High possibility of misunderstandings leading to varying degrees of host/visitor hostility
Political	• Enhanced international recognition of region and its values • Propagation of political values held by government and/or population	• Economic exploitation of local population to satisfy ambitions of political elite • Distortion of true nature of event to reflect values of political system of the day

(Table 6.6) that identifies seven categories of planned events that can be found in virtually every culture and community – and that can make a significant contribution to the strength of a destination's competitiveness as a travel destination. While many of the events in Getz's typology are individually relatively small and not as glamorous as most hallmark or mega-events, they collectively furnish a destination with a continuous stream of visitors. Over time, this stream of visitors serves to provide an important foundation for destination sustainability. Also, over time, it is not uncommon for a relatively modest community event to acquire a certain mystique that gradually turns the host city or region into a must-see destination. Indeed, many (if not most) of today's hallmark events and mega-events were once of very modest proportions. This reality should inspire and encourage destination managers to dream creatively, while at the same time making sure that the small things get done well.

Entertainment – the Show Must Go On!

Entertainment – not autos, not steel, not financial services – is fast becoming the driving wheel of the new world economy.
(Wolf, 1999, p. 4)

Just as shoppers have come to expect milk producers to add Vitamin D to their product, consumers are looking for the E-Factor in every product . . . that's E as in Entertainment.
(ibid., p. 27)

These two quotations from Micheal S. Wolf's *The Entertainment Economy: How Mega-Media Forces are Transforming our Lives* are selected examples to illustrate how large and pervasive the entertainment phenomenon has become in recent years. Since tourism is a big and growing part of our lives, it is to be expected that entertainment will be an increasingly important core attractor. And without doubt it is. As has been noted earlier,

Table 6.6. A typology of planned events (from Getz, 1997).

Cultural celebrations	Educational and scientific
• Festivals	• Seminars, workshops, clinics
• Carnivals	
• Religious events	
• Parades	• Congresses
• Heritage commemorations	• Interpretive events
Art and Entertainment	**Recreational**
• Concerts	• Games and sports for fun
• Other performances	
• Exhibits	• Amusement events
• Award ceremonies	
Business and Trade	**Political and state**
• Fairs, markets, sales	• Inaugurations
• Consumer and trade shows	• Investitures
	• VIP visits
• Expositions	• Rallies
• Meetings and conferences	**Private events**
	Personal celebrations
• Publicity events	• Anniversaries
• Fund-raiser events	• Family holidays
Sport Competitions	• Rites of passage
	Social events
• Professional	• Parties, galas
• Amateur	• Reunions

certain destinations – most notably Las Vegas – have become primarily entertainment-driven destinations.

Activities and events have established themselves as traditional components of destination attractiveness for virtually all destinations. Entertainment, however, has tended to be a local characteristic of certain destinations, such as London, New York (in the English-speaking world) and Paris. The theatre in London, the Broadway shows of New York and the nightlife follies of Paris grew up primarily as entertainment for the large metropolitan populations that surrounded them. Because they were well established before television sharply reduced their geographical advantages, they have been able not only to survive, but to become an important reason for much of the visitation to these 'gateway cities'. Las Vegas owed its beginnings to the draw of legalized gambling, but it has slowly but surely transformed itself into an entertainment Mecca. While gambling remains, the entertainment extravaganza that is taking place within an increasingly fantastic mix of fantasyland/hotel complexes is enabling the destination management team to reposition this Xanadu in the desert as a family vacationland.

But Las Vegas should not be given all the attention. For many years, as noted above, the theatre districts of New York and London have been major tourism draws, but these two cities have had so many other attractors that the entertainment dimension of core attractors, while substantial, has not seemed quite so overwhelming as it does in Las Vegas today.

Las Vegas, however, is not alone in the use of entertainment as a key core attractor. While Disneyland, Disney World, Disney Europe and Disneyworld Japan are attractions that include many activities, they have also integrated a broad range of entertainment into a total package that draws and retains visitors. Other, smaller destinations have focused their appeal on some specialized aspect of the entertainment industry. Nashville (Tennessee, USA) has, from a tourism perspective, grown up around the 'Grand Ole Opry', a traditional Mecca for country music for more than 75 years.

But Nashville has not escaped competition. Branson (Missouri, USA) bills itself as the 'Live Music Show Capital of the World', with over 30 theatres playing host to over 60 shows. The success of Dollywood, located in the same country music region of the USA as Nashville, demonstrates how a destination can be built around the reputation and performances of a single entertainer, in this case, Dolly Parton, a well-known, highly identifiable country music singer. Of particular interest with regard to Branson and Dollywood is that in both cases the destination has been developed from a limited resource base, somewhat similar to the situation of Las Vegas' original site. In both cases, however, rather than working as employees of an entertainment complex, many entertainers have sought to keep control of ownership and development.

In Europe, because of its richness in historic and cultural attractors, American-style entertainment destinations have not been seen as either necessary or desirable. Just the same, and despite their lower profile, the many ingrained cultural performances throughout Europe, and indeed many major cities in

Asia and in isolated parts of Africa, are also significant 'cultural tourism' attractors for more limited segments of the travel market. As indicated earlier, the Oberammergau Passion Play, held every 10 years in southern Germany, is a religion-based entertainment spectacle having major tourism implications. In South America, the Inti Raymi Festival is held annually in Cusco, Peru, to render homage to the sun god Inti (see www.condorjourneys.adventures. com/peru for further details).

Developing and managing entertainment tourism

Since there are few destinations that have the established entertainment head-start of London, New York, Las Vegas or Oberammergau, most destination managers who feel they wish to develop entertainment as a core attractor are faced with the challenge of conceptualizing and developing the kind of entertainment package that will provide their destination with a competitive/sustainable advantage. To meet this challenge requires an understanding of how tourism and entertainment are, or can be, linked in a realistic yet imaginative manner.

A useful starting point for achieving this understanding is an overview work by Hughes (2000). He provides some basic definitions that managers may find useful in understanding the arts, entertainment and tourism (Table 6.7).

Tourism Superstructure: 'If You Build it, They Will Come!'

Tourism superstructure is defined as buildings or facilities that primarily serve the needs or interests of tourism/hospitality visitors. While the majority have been built specifically for tourism, others, perhaps built in earlier eras for other reasons, now serve mainly as tourism attractions. The most common examples of this superstructure are hotels, restaurants, visitor information centres and visitor attractions. Unfortunately, 'tourism superstructure' is a term that hides much of the glamour that the reality contains. While 'activities' refers to the general range of things people can do and events that are highly focused on thematic sets of activities, the tourism superstructure provides most of the facilities in which many of the events take place or in which entertainment is provided. Certain tourism superstructures are so unique that they are attractions in themselves (e.g. the Eiffel Tower in France, the Leaning Tower of Pisa in Italy, the Empire State Building and the Statue of Liberty in New York City, the Golden Gate Bridge in San Francisco, the Tower of London and the London Eye in England, Sydney Harbour Bridge and Sydney Opera House in Australia, the statue of Christ the Redeemer in Rio de Janeiro, Brazil, China's Great Wall, the Parthenon in Athens, the Taj Mahal in India, and Ankor Wat in Cambodia).

Certain other examples of tourism superstructures are almost complete destinations in

Table 6.7. Initial definitions (from Hughes, 2000).

- Visitors: non-local residents who are either day visitors or staying visitors (tourists)
- Tourists: people who travel and stay away from home overnight
- Arts: performing arts and entertainment (a more popular form of the performing arts) performed in theatres, concert halls, arenas, etc.
- Arts-related tourism: any tourism that includes a visit to the arts (regardless of initial interest, etc.)
- Arts-core tourists: travel in order to see the arts
- Arts-peripheral tourists: travel for some non-arts purpose, but also see the arts
- Culture-core tourists: travel in order to visit cultural attractions
- Culture-peripheral tourists: travel for some non-cultural purpose, but also visit cultural attractions
- Seaside resort: a coastal town, the prime function of which is as a holiday destination. This is different from the US use of the term 'resort', which refers to a purpose-built holiday complex similar to a large hotel rather than a town
- Tourist board: an organization, usually with government involvement, which has the role of promoting a town, region, state or country as a tourist destination. Also known as a visitor bureau, convention and visitor bureau, tourist authority, tourism commission, etc.

themselves. The most famous of these are Las Vegas, and the Disneyland and Disney World complexes in California and Florida, USA, respectively. Among other so-called theme parks of worldwide fame is LegoLand in Denmark. Often many somewhat lesser attractions are clustered together to create a major composite attraction. Examples include California with Disneyland, Knott's Berry Farm and Universal Studios; Florida with Disney World, Busch Gardens, Wet 'n' Wild and Universal Studios; and the Gold Coast of Australia with Warner Movie World, Dreamworld, Wet 'n' Wild and Sea World.

In addition, there are many built complexes worldwide that, because of the distinctiveness of their architecture, their contents or some other unique aspect, have become must-see attractions for visitors to the destination. Well-known examples include the world-famous museums (such as the Louvre in Paris, the Smithsonian Institution in Washington, DC and the Hermitage in St Petersburg, Russia) and structures such as the Taj Mahal in India, the Royal Temple of the Grand Palace of Ayutthaya in Bangkok, Thailand, the Forbidden City in Beijing, China, the cathedral of La Sagrada Familia in Barcelona, Spain, Westminster Abbey in London, England, St Peter's Basilica in Rome, Italy, the Kennedy Space Center at Cape Canaveral, Florida, and the Air and Space Museum in Washington, DC, USA.

Attractions such as these have become strong magnets for visitors. And each time another photograph showing a visitor at one of these attractions goes into a photograph album

(be it paper-based or electronic), its reputation is further enhanced.

A more structured framework that destination managers may find helpful for analytical and planning purposes is given in Table 6.8. As shown, this framework envisages three main types of tourism superstructure. The functional elements listed in the table are those that have been developed almost exclusively with tourism in mind. While they are not always glamorous, they are essential for the functioning of the tourism system.

Elements of the second type are termed 'enhanced built elements'. This term reflects the fact that although these elements were not, in general, built with tourism in mind, their current and potential appeal as attractors has been well recognized and they have been actively enhanced by the tourism industry to the point where their original purpose has faded into the background, and they have largely been absorbed into the tourism superstructure.

Finally, there is a parallel set of elements that we may term 'enhanced natural or normal elements'. Generally, these attractions were 'just there'. While they have some natural appeal to visitors, they are in many cases isolated, difficult to access or unknown. However, even a natural part of a destination must be managed much as many other components of the destination are managed. This may be done by means of 'industry enhancement' (which may involve the physical upgrading of the natural element and/or physical improvements to facilitate access to the phenomenon or convenience in viewing or experiencing it)

Table 6.8. Tourism superstructure: an analytical framework.

Functional elements	Enhanced built elements	Enhanced natural or normal elements
• Hotels	• Museums	• Churches, cathedrals
• Bed & breakfast facilities	• Zoos	• Natural wonders
• Restaurants	• Unique office buildings/towers	• Historic landmarks
• Visitor centres	• Olympic legacy sites	• Unique industrial sites
• Airports	• Sports stadiums	• Unique architecture
• Theme parks	• Homes of famous people	• Evolving natural conditions
• Cruise ship ports	• Space centres	(e.g. ice-fields)
• Car rental locations	• Unique/well-known commercial	• Universities
• Convention centres	residential districts	• Disaster areas
• Unique sites and interpretation centres		

Those ties that:
- are beyond influence, but can be nourished
- can be created and developed
- can be supported
- are of a long/intermediate/short nature
- are fundamental vs. transitory
- are personal vs. commercial
- are social vs. professional

Fig. 6.5. The ties that bind.

and through advertising and promotion to enhance awareness of the phenomenon or to increase its renown.

Market Ties: the Ties That Bind

Despite the magnificence and attractiveness of many destinations, which make them the choice of millions of tourists, there are many less obvious attractors that stimulate people to visit destinations they would not normally visit. Figure 6.5 provides a graphic overview of what we term 'ties that bind'. These ties can be

viewed as falling into two major categories: personal and professional/organizational. The challenge facing the destination manager is not only to identify the individuals to whom these ties apply but also to determine how the destination can use these bonds to stimulate, facilitate or divert travel to the destination in question.

Personal ties

Probably the strongest and most enduring of personal ties that bind are those of *family*.

Historical patterns of migration, trade and culture have created these family ties. Close behind are those due to *friendship*. Together, these two markets make up what is commonly known as the 'VFR' (visiting friends and relatives) market. Since destination managers can do relatively little to create or influence family or friendship ties, they must do their best to encourage visits to the destination by existing family and friends. This may be done by creating events such as 'Old Home Weeks' and family/graduation reunions, in which residents are encouraged to invite relatives for a visit to celebrate the passing of time. Less directly, destinations may create events that appeal to a broad audience, but also stimulate destination residents to invite family and friends. The history of a mega-event like the Olympic Games provides an excellent opportunity for invitations of this type – invitations which many family and friends are only too pleased to accept.

Another intensely personal type of tie is related to an individual's *religion*. While religious activity is normally localized in nature, religious organizations from time to time organize large, centralized events that stimulate members of the faith to gather together. In certain religions, there is a strong inherent motivation to visit particular religious cities. Mecca (for the Islamic faith), St Peter's Basilica in Rome (for the Catholic faith) and Jerusalem (for the Jewish, Christian and Islamic faiths) all have special meaning and thus serve as motivators for travel to these destinations. In contrast, other religious conferences move from one site to another, thus presenting potential opportunities for a limited number of destinations to compete for their business.

Somewhat related to religion may be destinations that reflect the *ethnic roots* of people now living all over the world. Individuals of African-American ethnicity have returned to visit various African destinations where their ancestors were born and lived. People of Scottish origin not uncommonly wish to visit the Scottish Highlands, or even to play a round of golf at the birthplace of the sport, St Andrews. Similarly, persons of French, Italian, German, Polish, Hungarian (and so on) ethnic origin can often be incited to visit their homeland at least once in their lifetime, preferably with their entire family.

Sports can also be a tie that binds. At the personal level, amateur sport can be the underlying motivation that brings together both individuals and families having common sporting interests. Aside from participating themselves in sporting tournaments that reflect common interests, it is not unusual for entire families to follow the exploits of one family member who is particularly good at a given sport. Hockey and figure-skating come to mind here. Also, various countries share certain sporting heritages that stimulate tourism (e.g. soccer, cricket and rugby).

Finally, a type of personal relationship that has emerged is one that is directly derived from technology. The ability to use Internet chat groups has greatly facilitated communication among individuals having common interests. These technological relationships may, over time, become so strong that they create what have been termed 'cybertribes' – groups of 'cyberfriends' who become emotionally attached. These emotional attachments may eventually lead to direct personal friendships that, in turn, lead to interdestination travel.

Organizational and professional ties

While personal ties are strong, it may well be that organizational ties are more pervasive as motivators of travel, and they may create greater value of travel. In general, they offer the destination manager greater opportunities to stimulate and influence travel-related decisions.

The world of *conventions*, *conferences* and *corporate meetings* is highly dependent on ties that bind. Managers from all levels and areas of a large corporation regularly converge on destinations that provide them with functional meeting facilities, often combined with supporting recreational or vacation opportunities. Similarly, members of a plethora of different *associations* come together annually to get to know one another, to share ideas and to extend their personal and professional networks. These associations may have a common interest that is *professional*, *fraternal* or simply *social*. In any event, they offer the destination manager a unique yet demanding opportunity to influence the choice of destination where the particular convention, conference or meeting will be held, and possibly its timing.

Other ties are often more basic, more associated with daily life – and are thus often overlooked in significance by destination managers, even though their long-term and ongoing impacts on travel may be very substantial. The structures of *economic trade blocs* and *political unions*, once they are consolidated, have tremendous influence on travel flows. For example, the creation of the North American Free Trade Agreement (NAFTA) and its European and Asian equivalents has determined and restructured travel patterns, particularly those concerned with organizations and professionals. While the trading/political bloc decisions are beyond the control of destination managers, they may have influence (sometimes substantial) during the formative stages. Similarly, the existence of *monetary system blocs* (such as the dollar bloc, the Euro bloc and the UK pound bloc) has a similarly subtle but important influence on political and corporate decisions and the travel related to these decisions.

Although *military travel* is formally excluded from World Tourism Organization travel statistics, it is still real, with real economic consequences. Just as trade and political ties influence travel and tourism flows, so do military alliances. The North Atlantic Treaty Organization (NATO) is undoubtedly the most influential of these alliances, and probably the one with the greatest impact on the travel system and travel expenditures (even though they are not formally counted). It is clear that decisions related to military travel are beyond the purview of destination managers. Just the same, an astute destination manager may see – and seize upon – a whole range of travel decisions that are on the periphery of military travel and that take advantage of off-duty travel by military personnel.

Finally, the process of *education* can create ties that bind for a lifetime. Students who study in a foreign country establish links and relationships that frequently underlie travel- and tourism-related behaviours for many years. For example, young students who undertake their studies in the USA and the UK commonly develop ties that influence a whole range of personal and professional decisions for the rest

of their lives. An astute destination manager can encourage the establishment of education linkages between his/her destination and markets where long-term links are seen as desirable. The pay-off is admittedly long term, but the USA and UK have demonstrated that it can be powerful and significant.

To conclude, identifying and/or developing the ties that bind requires astuteness, careful research and innovative marketing. But this process can provide cities, regions and countries with powerful competitive advantages that are definitely sustainable. The key point that must be made when starting is to distinguish between those that are personal and those that are organizational, institutional or professional. While they eventually become intertwined, they require distinct research and marketing approaches.

References

American Heritage Dictionary: Second College Edition (1985) Houghton Mifflin Company, Boston, Massachusetts.

Getz, D. (1997) *Event Management and Event Tourism*. Cognizant Communication Corporation, New York.

Hughes, H. (2000) *Arts, Entertainment and Tourism*. Butterworth-Heinemann, Oxford.

Kluckhohn, C. and Kelly, W.H. (1945) The concept of culture. In: Linton, R. (ed.) *The Science of Man in the World Crisis*. Columbia University Press, New York, pp. 78–107.

McCracken, G. (1988) *Culture and Consumption: New Approaches to the Symbolic Character of Consumer Goods and Activities*. Indiana University Press, Bloomington and Indianapolis, Indiana.

Newsome, D., Moore, S.A. and Dowling, R.K. (2002) *Natural Area Tourism: Ecology, Impacts and Management*. Channel View Publications, Clevedon, UK.

Ritchie, J.R.B. (1984) Assessing the impact of hallmark events: conceptual and research issues. *Journal of Travel Research* 23, 2–11.

Ritchie, J.R.B. and Zins, M. (1978). Culture as determinant of the attractiveness of a tourism region. *Annals of Tourism Research* 5, 252–267.

Wolf, M.J. (1999) *The Entertainment Economy: How Mega-Media Forces are Transforming our Lives*. Random House, New York.

7

Supporting Factors and Resources: Elements that Enhance Destination Appeal

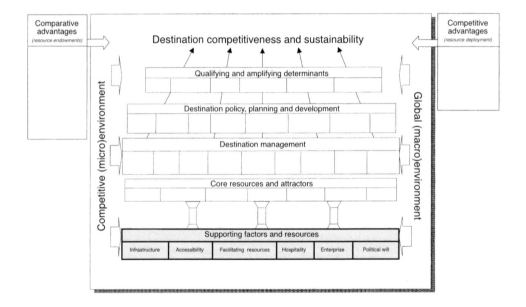

Figure 3.1 positions *supporting factors and resources* as the foundation of a competitive tourism and hospitality industry. The *core resources and attractors* represent the principal 'pulling' force driving the demand for destination tourism, but if these are inaccessible, if the private sector is unable or unwilling to create the necessary business services which bring core resources to the market, if the economic and social infrastructure is insufficient, and if the resources which facilitate tourism development are limited or substandard, abundant core resources and attractors will be significantly constrained in their ability to pull tourists.

Describing supporting factors and resources as the *foundation* of a competitive tourist destination is quite apt. Any structure requires a solid foundation if it is to function effectively. While the superstructure is very visible and serves to house the main functions that a structure performs, the supporting foundation remains mostly buried and hidden, yet it fulfils a vital role. Supporting foundations and resources are the equivalent of the footings and foundations, the basement, boiler, plumbing and electrical systems, etc., without which the rest of the structure cannot perform. The tourism superstructure is akin to the walls and floors, corridors, stairways and open spaces, while the other core resources and attractors represent the tenants and contents of the building; that is, the *sine qua non* for attracting visitors and customers. To take the analogy one final step further, those involved in *destination management* are, one might say, the structure's landlords.

So supporting factors and resources are critical to the competitiveness of a destination, but specifically how is competitiveness affected? When the foundation of a building is weak and insufficient a building might tilt, sink, buckle or crack a little, causing it to perform below expectation. Perhaps even the use of the structure might need to be restricted in order to minimize further undue deterioration. If the foundation is completely inadequate, the structure might fail catastrophically. Likewise, if the supporting factors and resources of a destination are insufficient the result can range from performing a little below visitor expectations to major failure, damaging the longer-term fortunes of the destination.

On the other hand, when the foundations of a building have been overdesigned the result is barely noticeable. The building may have cost more to construct, and this may affect landlords, tenants and guests, but there will be no significant positive impact on the building's ability to perform the job for which it was designed. Similarly, tourist satisfaction and demand and destination competitiveness, although bolstered, will not benefit from over-abundance to the same extent that insufficiency in supporting factors and resources would reduce destination competitiveness.

As is also the case with qualifying and amplifying determinants (Chapter 10), supporting factors and resources cannot be controlled or manipulated by a tourist destination with any significant sensitivity. An industrialized nation is likely to enjoy a general abundance of these elements, whereas a Third World or developing nation is likely to be deficient in these areas, possibly to a considerable extent. While the tourism industry can, no doubt, pursue programmes and influence government policy, which might help to address any weaknesses, it

is unlikely, on its own, to be able to control or reverse a less-than-adequate competitive profile in this area.

Nevertheless, a destination must pay a good deal of attention to this aspect of competitiveness if balanced decisions are to be made and resources allocated in the most effective manner. For example, a poorly developed destination with deteriorating roads, a contaminated water supply system, a poorly educated population that knows little about starting and managing small businesses, and an untrained labour force, might find that until some of these problems are addressed at least to some extent, improvements in any of the other four groups of factors may realize little overall advance in competitiveness. Even worse, residents may object strongly to seeing public funds go towards improving conditions for tourists while residents continue to live in squalor. This must be balanced with the fact that, in such a situation, it is the ailing economy which is failing to provide the tax dollars that could go towards improvements in infrastructure, education and government-backed funding programmes for new ventures, for example. This is where tourism dollars may have a role to play in kick-starting economic growth and fuelling other aspects of economic and social development that, in turn, facilitate continued tourism development. There are no easy answers here: each destination's circumstances are unique, calling for tailored solutions.

Our model of destination competitiveness identifies six groups of supporting factors and resources. The first concerns the state of a destination's general *infrastructure* and its impact on destination competitiveness. Under *accessibility*, the model accounts for the ease or difficulty confronting tourists in travelling to the destination. The chapter then turns to a discussion of the *facilitating resources* of a supporting (rather than core) nature that enable the industry (specifically human, knowledge and financial capital). A further area of support stems from the friendliness and general level of *hospitality* displayed by the destination's host community. We will also look at the ways in which a sense and spirit of *enterprise* and entrepreneurship contribute to competitive destinations. Finally, there is *political will* – we will consider the question of the political standing of the tourism industry and how this may affect government support for tourism development.

Infrastructure: Providing a Foundation for Successful Tourism

Elements of infrastructure can be broadly classified into two groups from a tourism destination perspective. The first group, which might be labelled *general infrastructure*, includes the facilities, systems and services, etc. that one normally tends to think of as infrastructure. This would include a destination's transportation systems (e.g. roads and highways, airports, rail systems and facilities, bus terminals and services, ferries and shipping, taxis, and related services), public safety (police, fire and other emergency services), water resources and supply systems (for both potable and industrial uses), electrical generation and transmission systems (e.g. power stations, high-voltage power lines, domestic and industrial delivery, electrical contractors), sanitation and drainage systems (e.g. sewage systems, treatment plants, storm drainage systems, garbage pickup, flood control works), natural gas services (extraction, processing, distribution and delivery services), telecommunications systems (e.g. telephone, telegraph, satellite services, cellular phone systems, cable companies, broadcast services, fibre optics), mail and freight services (e.g. regular mail, couriers, trucking companies, airlines and rail services), medical systems (hospitals, clinics, laboratories and testing, ambulance and paramedical services, and related services), financial systems (e.g. banks, credit unions, credit card companies, brokers, stock markets), administrative services (e.g. the legal system, government departments), the education system (e.g. schools, universities, vocational colleges, libraries), a system of national defence, and so on.

Beyond these forms of infrastructure are other basic services which tend generally not to be thought of as infrastructure but which provide critical support services to the effective functioning of destinations. Such basic services typically derive only a minor portion of their demand from tourists and visitors, so for this reason ought to be regarded as infrastructure rather than as tourism superstructure. Examples of such *basic services infrastructure* include the broad range of retail and shopping facilities, food stores, garages and vehicle maintenance facilities, gas (petrol) stations, drug stores (chemist shops), bookstores and news kiosks, hairdressers, dry cleaners, launderettes (e.g. laundromats), etc.

The basic services infrastructure is normally delivered by the private sector. In contrast, much of the general infrastructure is provided by governments and funded through the various forms of taxation – at least, this has been the case in the past – on the basis that society as a whole benefits from their provision. However, many of these systems and services have been privatized as governments grapple with deficits, customer service is seen to be superior in the private sector, and methods of charging actual users are developed and instituted. Destination competitiveness is therefore a function of the ability of both the public and private sectors to provide and maintain the sorts of infrastructure that sustain tourism development and the needs of both the travel trade and its customers.

While a philosophical debate about the respective roles of the public and private sectors in providing infrastructure offers no clear answers, what is of real importance is the quality of the infrastructure, regardless of who happens to be responsible for its creation, operation and maintenance. The quality of a destination's infrastructure cannot be assessed with one or two simple measures. In general, however, the quality of a nation's infrastructure is very largely a function of the level of wealth, prosperity and productivity enjoyed by the nation and its citizens. However, across destinations which enjoy similar levels of wealth, we can observe differences in the quality of infrastructure which seem to depend on further factors, such as: (i) attitudes of citizens to the importance of infrastructure in social and economic development and quality-of-life issues; (ii) the competency of policy makers, planners and managers to anticipate, coordinate and develop infrastructure strategies; (iii) the extent to which governments and industries display innovative behaviour (consider, for example, the quality of infrastructure and attitudes to innovation in a place like Singapore); (iv) the incentives available to the private sector to participate in infrastructure operations and development; (v) cultural attitudes and norms; and (vi) population densities.

The quality of infrastructure can also vary spatially within a destination. This difference is usually most evident between urban and rural environments. Urban infrastructures benefit from a larger population, concentration of industries, government patronage and higher incomes and taxes.

A number of salient infrastructure qualities are worth emphasizing *vis-à-vis* destination competitiveness. Visitors and tourists are likely to be particularly concerned with issues affecting reliability, efficiency, safety, cleanliness, design, ease of use, availability, cultural and language sensitivities, way-finding, integrity, etc. Visitors, for example, are often confused or uncertain in an alien environment. They may find it hard to know what to do or where to go because signs are in a foreign language. Tourists often find that large, unfamiliar airports present labyrinthine uncertainties. The purchasing of a train or metro ticket from an automatic vending machine may present a daunting challenge to tourists who find the instructions hard to follow, and they may rely instead on watching how the local people use these machines to obtain their tickets.

Tourists require answers to all sorts of infrastructure-related questions, such as do the trains run on time? is the water safe to drink? where can I find a reliable doctor? how do I make a long-distance telephone call? what is the cheapest way to get from A to B? what voltage is the electrical system? what type of gasoline (petrol) does my rental car require? when are the banks open? and as a disabled traveller, will I be able to cope?

Destinations must make their infrastructure as user-friendly as possible for visitors, yet most destinations do a particularly poor job in this regard. It is easy not to appreciate the considerable difficulties visitors may have, because we take for granted the fact that local residents are familiar with the answers to these questions.

Many problems of this sort can be addressed through good design. Finding your way in an airport, for example, can be aided a great deal by the way in which open spaces,

corridors, doorways and signs, etc. are arranged. A subway system with maps available in all locations, simple-to-use ticket vending machines with a small number of fare options or an unlimited day-use fare, and an attendant who is there to help those in difficulty are essential if unfamiliar users of the system are to be able to cope. Good design addresses much more than just the architectural and physical appeal of an infrastructure facility. Designers should be equally concerned with functional layout, process flow, the suitability of equipment, and the impact of the facility on the ability of service employees to perform their duties. Designers need to be aware of the lessons of environmental psychology.

Infrastructure quality affects destination competitiveness in important ways. First, the quality of a destination's infrastructure may serve to attract or deter tourists. In the process of choosing a destination, the image of infrastructure will play some role. For example, the general image of Russia's infrastructure is one of poorly maintained roads, deteriorating public buildings and unreliable airline and rail services, etc. By comparison, Japanese infrastructure is perceived to be very modern, clean, safe and reliable, but many first-time Western visitors may be concerned about problems arising from linguistic differences. These images and expectations may influence destination choice.

A second major way in which infrastructure may significantly shape destination competitiveness concerns the degree to which the functioning of the tourism system is helped or hindered by infrastructure. Suppliers, tourism and hospitality enterprises, marketing intermediaries and facilitators, related and supporting industries, and destination management organizations depend upon infrastructure in order for the tourism system to function efficiently and effectively. Entrepreneurs may develop strong ideas for creating new tourism ventures but find that they are not feasible because the required utility services are unavailable in the location demanded by the venture, or perhaps transportation services to the site are inadequate. Alternatively, the cost of infrastructure services may be prohibitively expensive.

What can a destination do to improve and maintain the necessary standard in its infrastructure? Again, this is a difficult question because many elements of infrastructure are subject to very broad concerns and influences. However, if the tourism industry is not participating in infrastructure decisions and voicing the needs and concerns of the industry, infrastructure will meet the needs of industry only by chance rather than by design. The destination management organization and industry associations clearly play a pivotal role in this regard. In terms of public infrastructure, the industry must seek to work with relevant government departments, town and regional planning bodies, public officials, political and civic leaders, and utilities, etc. With respect to the infrastructure provided by the private sector, destinations need to undertake studies and market research to help demonstrate a need for the infrastructure services that are lacking, and in this way they can attract investors who see a business opportunity in filling the gap.

Accessibility: Addressing the Curse or Blessing of Location

Destinations can also vary greatly in terms of the ease or difficulty involved in travelling to and entering the region concerned. While accessibility is in part governed by spatial issues, location alone is not enough to explain the extent to which tourists are able to travel to and within a destination. So, as a supporting factor, accessibility concerns a set of issues different from those we will discuss in Chapter 10 in connection with the qualifying and amplifying determinant of *location*.

Until the recent peace accord between Israel and Jordan was signed, these two neighbouring destinations were effectively inaccessible from one another. Within China it has traditionally been difficult for Western tourists to move around freely. The airline hub-and-spoke system can sometimes make the journey to a nearby location quite lengthy and time-consuming. These are just a few examples of ways in which a destination's location alone can belie the degree to which it is accessible to tourists.

Accessibility can be determined by numerous factors. One of these relates to any formalities and barriers involved in obtaining the necessary permission to be allowed entry into the destination. Destinations employ a variety of methods of controlling access to visitors and of prescribing any conditions upon which entry is permitted. These regulations and practices are most evident at the national level but can apply in more subtle ways to regions within nations. For example, the 'product' offered by a destination may be targeted to attract a certain market segment. This targeting may implicitly, and perhaps even explicitly, seek to deter visitors from non-targeted segments. For example, an exclusive coastal resort may wish to attract wealthy individuals or couples but might see families as adversely affecting the quality of the tourism experience provided to the resort's targeted market. Pricing practices, facilities, the number of beds per room, and even the image and message communicated to customers through all forms of promotion, may be designed to deter certain potential customers as much as to attract others.

While these methods of persuasion work in non-exacting ways, visas and other forms of permits are much more direct and specific in terms of the restrictions they place on a visitor. Visas are most often used to restrict access to potential visitors that a nation would find quite unacceptable or undesirable, such as criminals, terrorists and drug-smugglers. Visas, however, are often used to control illegal migration and to govern permissible activities, in particular to provide a mechanism for restricting the rights of employment, payment of taxes, etc.

Visas, however, are used for political as well as legal purposes. They can be used to retaliate against the citizens of a nation when disputes arise over trade, human rights, etc. The US Helms–Burton Act, for example, was introduced to restrict access into the USA of anyone doing business in or trading with Cuba in a way that involves American assets confiscated by Cuba when Fidel Castro came to power. This was a controversial piece of legislation and has particularly irked Canada and a number of European nations that have economic relations with Cuba.

The Spanish government retaliated against Canada in the mid-1990s when a Canadian frigate seized a Spanish trawler operating off the Grand Banks fishing grounds, but in international waters, using an illegal net to catch undersized fish. It did so by stopping the issue of visas to Canadian tourists for a brief period. This created particular hardship for some tour groups already operating in Europe when the restriction was imposed.

In Myanmar, the government required tourists to exchange US$200 for Foreign Exchange Certificates (FECs) upon entry and spend the FECs before departing the country.

In the past, some countries behind the iron curtain required tourists, in order to gain entry, to undertake to bring in and spend a certain sum of money before departing the country.

Some countries display a ready willingness to use various forms of control, restriction or intimidation of tourists for political purposes. Visas are the most obvious of these methods. The requirement to hold an appropriate visa can therefore depend on a range of sometimes complex political, legal, social and economic issues. The need for visas is often, therefore, determined on a bilateral basis between countries and may depend upon the existence of extradition treaties, trade disputes, smuggling, refugee problems, illegal migration, etc.

A further way of controlling access arises from government restrictions over airline landing rights. In the past, many governments have either owned and operated or at least had a major stake in national flag-carrier airlines. Governments believed, and most still do, that the national interest was at stake in seeing and facilitating a strong national airline. Notwithstanding the fact that, in recent years, many governments have privatized national airlines and have reduced their share of ownership, most nations today still see a need to exert their authority in order to ensure that the national airline is able to survive and prosper in an era of cut-throat competition. By and large, this authority is exercised on a bilateral basis by offering landing rights to a foreign airline on a reciprocal basis so that the nation's own flag-carrier has access to other markets. In recent years, government intervention and regulation has been relaxed somewhat. For example the Open Skies agreement between Canada and the USA has further stimulated the demand for air travel. Although airlines welcomed this move, a number of airlines still struggle to make a profit. The Open Skies

agreement did little to save Canadian Airlines from its financial problems and it eventually yielded to Air Canada. An airline with landing rights may still find, however, that it is difficult to operate in a destination. Its access may still be restricted in terms of the availability of a sufficient number of landing slots (i.e. available take-off and landing times and gate facilities). In these days of congested airport facilities and congested skies, the future growth of the airline industry faces continued capacity problems.

As the airline industry continues to privatize, commercialize and rationalize, inter-airline alliances, code-sharing, cross-ownership, etc. are reshaping the way in which the industry operates. The use of airport hubs, too, as briefly discussed earlier, is also helping airlines to operate more efficiently, perhaps, but not necessarily more effectively. This has opened up some opportunities for small regional carriers to exploit routes and markets that are poorly served by the larger airlines. The success of Southwest Airlines in the USA dramatically demonstrates the importance of customer service as an operational strategy.

The tourism industry in many instances often calls upon governments to increase airline access, believing that this will bring many more visitors to the destination. The industry also frequently believes that existing airlines are not doing enough to increase the frequency of inbound flights. Airlines counter-argue that they would be quite prepared to increase flights if the demand called for this, but are reluctant to do so unless and until they are sure that most flights will be able to operate profitably. The tourism industry and airlines are therefore frequently engaged in a circular argument, the industry asserting that more visitors would come if there were more flights and airlines pointing out that there would be more flights if there were more demand.

It is in the interest of airlines to see destinations performing successfully in attracting visitors, as the result can only be more business for airlines. The challenge for destination managers is to find ways in which destinations and airlines can work together to help develop and maintain competitive industries. Boeing, for example, has provided a service to destinations for a number of years, and the World Travel and Tourism Council, representing many of the world's largest travel and tourism enterprises, has worked with several destinations to help them further build their tourism sectors.

Of course, airlines are not the only mode of tourism transportation and access, although they do vastly dominate long-haul travel. Automobiles, buses, trains, ferries and other ships also provide important modes of accessibility for short-haul travel to destinations and for access to sites within destinations. Appropriate forms of transportation infrastructure, as noted in the preceding section, are a prerequisite if a destination hopes to avoid being held back in its tourism development by limited accessibility.

To address the question of accessibility, destinations must fully adopt and practise the marketing philosophy, as we have noted earlier. As marketing deals with everything that is required to satisfy the needs and wants of targeted customers, this philosophy, when practised effectively, ensures that any organization pays attention to any issue which affects the satisfaction of customers' needs and wants. Destinations that equate promotion with marketing are likely to fall into the trap of blindly focusing an undue level of effort on building tourism demand while losing sight of some of the hurdles involved in satisfying that demand.

For a destination to have an impact on decisions that affect its accessibility, it needs to ensure that it is a player in these decisions. And it is not enough for the tourism industry to simply be at the table expressing faith in the idea that better accessibility will result in more visitors. The destination needs to be doing its own unbiased and rigorous research to demonstrate how demand is hindered by existing constraints in access, and what would be different if these constraints were relaxed or removed.

Facilitating Resources: Human, Knowledge and Financial Capital

In Chapter 2 we briefly described the six elements that constitute a destination's comparative advantages. These elements, or resource endowments, were human resources, physical resources, knowledge resources,

capital resources, infrastructure and tourism superstructure, and historical and cultural resources. Physical resources, historical and cultural resources and tourism superstructure were discussed in detail in Chapter 6, where we explored a destination's core resources and attractors. Earlier in this chapter we also examined the important role of infrastructure in supporting the development of a competitive tourism destination. This leaves human, knowledge and financial capital resources that can be deployed and used to support the development of the tourism industry, and these will be discussed below. In Chapter 9, we also examine the role of destination management in developing and fostering the supply of such resources to serve the needs of the tourism industry.

The human resources required to serve the needs of a tourism destination are particularly diverse. Unfortunately, however, the important role of human resources in facilitating tourism development is typically overlooked or underestimated. This attitude to the significance of human resources in tourism and hospitality has much in common with similar attitudes that seem to exist generally towards many other areas of the service economy. There is a general misconception that employment in the service sector requires few skills and that the supply of suitable human resources is not a critical issue for the development of the industry. This general view seems to be held most acutely in the case of jobs in the tourism and hospitality sector. That is, such jobs are seen to entail a preponderance of tasks which demand skills no greater than those of the stereotypical 'hamburger-flipper'.

In Chapter 5, however, we discussed the competitive (micro)environment of the tourism system and emphasized the broad range of firms and organizations that play a role as the engine of tourism development. While tourism and hospitality may require human resources to fulfil lesser-skilled forms of work, such jobs are only the tip of the tourism and hospitality employment iceberg. There are many forms of work in the travel trade that call for specialist skills. We will examine some of these in a moment, when we turn our attention to knowledge resources. The important point is that the supply and quality of human resources to the tourism and hospitality sector are critical for several reasons.

First, a destination's competitiveness is based on its ability to deliver unique, superior, unforgettable and hassle-free *experiences* to visitors. Although the purchase of tangible goods may form a part of tourism consumption, tourism experiences are predominantly delivered through the many intangible services that collectively constitute the destination experience. That is, the tourism product is largely the result of the deeds, acts and performances provided to visitors by a destination through individuals who are employed to interact with and serve the industry's customers. As many service firms have come to realize in recent years, exceptional customer service delivered by employees who have the appropriate skills and attitudes represents both a key to success and also, perhaps, one of the greatest challenges. Given the level of unemployment in many economies today, finding employees is not the problem. But finding people who have the right attitude to their work, particularly where it involves serving customers, is, as many firms attest today, one of the great challenges in human resource management.

Because the cost of a destination is inherently a critical competitiveness issue, a second major factor is the cost of available human resources, given the labour-intensive nature of many types of tourism and hospitality enterprises. Human resource costs depend upon the general level of wages and salaries in a destination's economy, labour productivity, work ethics, labour unions, and typical working conditions and employee benefits. Research by the World Travel and Tourism Council found that the level of wages and salaries in jobs created by tourism is similar to that in the economy generally. The Council has estimated that travel and tourism compensation is approximately 5% higher than the average compensation in other economic sectors among OECD countries (WTTC, 1993).

A third factor is the attitudes to careers in tourism and hospitality, which also vary significantly internationally. In some countries, careers as chefs, waiters and small business entrepreneurs are held in much higher regard than in other countries. The tourism and hospitality sector must recognize that its success depends upon the quality of the people it employs. Like any industry, tourism and hospitality must compete against other industries, professions and careers to attract the brightest, most talented and resourceful people to its ranks.

The skills, knowledge and know-how that turn human resources into productive assets are the final reason for the importance of human resources to the tourism industry. The World Tourism Organization places great emphasis on the dissemination of knowledge and the development of tourism and destination management skills in Third World and developing destinations. Without the necessary knowledge resources, a destination attempting to build, maintain and manage its competitiveness is likely to find that its ability to do so is severely limited.

The diversity of organizations in tourism calls for a diversity of skills and knowledge. Any effort to list the broad range of skills and knowledge required is likely to merely trivialize the matter. Suffice it to say that the knowledge resources required for a competitive destination are as different as, for instance, engineering, the culinary arts, service quality management, marketing, hotel management, environmental management and new venture development.

Educational and research institutions must play a key role in conjunction with the industry to help develop the knowledge and human resources required to lead the industry into a new era of professionalism. Recognizing this need, many governments have established specialist training organizations for the development of the necessary vocational skills in tourism. The government of Canada, for example, through Industry Canada, has established the Canadian Tourism Human Resources Council. The World Travel and Tourism Council sponsors the Pacific Rim Institute of Tourism's activities on human resource management issues in tourism.

There are also a number of other organizations which take a leading role in tourism and hospitality education and training, including the Council for Hotel, Restaurant and Institutional Education and the Travel and Tourism Research Association. Numerous associations have been formed in the last several years to promote and facilitate education and research in many countries, including the Council for Australian University Tourism and Hospitality Education, the Asia-Pacific Tourism Association, the American Marketing Association's Special Interest Group in Tourism, Hospitality, and Leisure Marketing, the Tourism Society in the UK, and the European-based Association Internationale d'Experts Scientifique du Tourisme, to name just a few. Several electronic bulletin boards have been established to facilitate communication among tourism educators and researchers. Some of these are TRINET (Tourism Research Information Network), HOTEL-L, infotec-travel and tourism-request.

Academic institutions and the academic community have recognized and responded to the industry's education and research needs with enthusiasm. For example, in the USA, the UK and Australia, academic programmes in tourism and hospitality have multiplied significantly. The World Tourism Organization has encouraged this growth in education and research by designating an international network of specialist university centres in tourism and hospitality management. The World Tourism Organization has also prepared a list of knowledge and skills (known as the Graduate Tourism Admission Test, or GTAT) that it believes will help the industry and educational institutions determine the education and research needs of students. Paralleling this growth in education, training and research has been an explosion in the publishing of academic journals in the field. The argument could be made that there may now be too many academic institutions offering programmes in tourism and hospitality, spreading the limited qualified faculty too thinly, and that governments might do better by concentrating such resources in fewer institutions.

Despite the rapid expansion taking place in tourism and hospitality education and training, attitudes within the industry to the important role of education and research seem to be changing slowly. Few managers in the industry today graduated from such programmes because there were so few programmes of this type in existence when most of today's industry's leaders went through university. The tourism industry, however, is gradually developing more professional attitudes and traditions with respect to the role of education. The new

breed of educated professionals entering the industry today, it is hoped, will help expedite these changes.

While academic institutions are changing the shape of education in tourism and hospitality, the industry and individual firms and organizations have a responsibility to continue to encourage employee training and development on the job. The industry's future, and that of the destinations it represents, rests with the quality, knowledge and skills of the people it recruits and the careers it fosters.

Tourism development and destination competitiveness also depend on available financial resources. The supply of financial resources to an industry depends principally on the financial performance of that industry. An industry that provides a satisfactory return on investment will attract greater financial resources. Financial performance in the tourism and hospitality industry has been rather mixed over the years. There have been some very poor projects and investments, but there are also a number of large, successful and profitable corporations in the tourism and hospitality field. Every sector of the industry (airlines, hotel corporations, restaurants, tour operators, etc.) has its winners and losers, the quality of management dictating the fate of each individual company. The high proportion of small businesses in tourism, many of which are lifestyle enterprises rather than entrepreneurial ventures, has produced an industry in which managerial talent and financial competence is a scarcity. As an industry, tourism also displays alluring qualities that seem sometimes to attract investors with more money than common sense.

The mixed and sometimes very poor financial performance of many enterprises in the industry has created an investment climate in which financial institutions and investors are now much more wary. Perhaps the industry needs not so much an increase in investment and financial capital, but smarter investment.

Destinations can play a role here to encourage the availability of investment capital by helping to inform, advise and direct investors and investment into appropriate projects and areas of clear market need. Research studies and reports on market trends, tourism products, demand forecasts, etc. will help to provide investors with the sort of information needed for wise and effective decision making. The Tourism Forecasting Council[1] in Australia is an example of one initiative in which the financial community has come together to undertake the sort of research that is necessary if tourism projects are to be based on sound and reliable information. Efforts like this, in conjunction with quality education, training and research programmes, will help to build a better basis upon which investment decisions in tourism and hospitality development can be made. This in turn will foster a financially successful industry that will continue to attract the interests of all forms of investment capital.

Hospitality: Resident Attitudes Towards Tourists and Tourism

It is quite common to observe the claim by many destinations that its people are among the friendliest. While it is possible for all destinations to have friendly residents and employees in the tourism industry, it is by definition impossible for all or even most to be the friendliest. Thus it is likely that only a few exceptional destinations can really differentiate themselves, at least partly, on the basis of being particularly friendly and hospitable. Nevertheless, clearly friendliness and a spirit of hospitality can serve to enhance a destination's competitiveness.

While the hospitality of tourism industry employees is an important part of the overall *service experience* that we discuss in detail in Chapter 9, the hospitality displayed by residents is more a general supporting factor and is governed more by social and cultural values than by tourism industry training. Many destinations, however, do endeavour to promote the economic significance of the tourism industry to residents, with the goal of gaining their support as well as encouraging friendly and hospitable behaviour and a welcoming attitude towards tourists. So destinations must encourage their permanent residents to behave as friendly hosts to visitors who are in unfamiliar surroundings. They should convey a friendly attitude and, when required, offer basic information and a helping hand. These small but important gestures will do much to foster a destination

spirit of hospitality that will, in turn, greatly enhance the perceived value of all other aspects of the visitation experience.

Tourists expect generally to be treated with friendliness and courtesy. So when they experience such behaviour they find it unremarkable, and it is therefore unlikely to significantly affect their overall perception of a destination and their degree of satisfaction. Research has shown that it usually takes the unexpected (i.e. experiences that occur outside some 'zone of tolerance'[2]) for there to be a substantial positive or negative impact on customer satisfaction.

Thus, surprisingly high levels of service, friendliness and hospitality can leave an indelible impression in the mind of a visitor. Unfortunately, it seems anecdotally more common that surprisingly poor hospitality leaves a sour taste for many visitors. Tourists are often very vulnerable. They visit unfamiliar places and may not know from whom or how to seek help when problems occur. Indeed, they may simply not have the time or money to take action if, for example, a paid-in-advance tour fails to be provided or visitors are affected by criminal activity. In such circumstances, when residents come to the aid of a distressed tourist, sometimes this good-samaritan response can have such a powerful impact that the visitor actually ends up feeling good about their experience.

While the hospitality displayed by a destination's residents towards tourists and tourism can play an important role in a destination's competitive profile, hospitality is not a prerequisite for competitiveness. It is possible for a destination to do well in spite of the reputation of residents. France, for example, is not known for a friendly attitude to tourists yet has been able to maintain a position as one of the world's leading tourist destinations. New Yorkers also have a reputation as being tough, bad-mannered and short-tempered, with little time for or interest in assisting visitors. However, New York has long been one of the great tourist cities of the world.

So friendliness and hospitality matter and can make a significant difference, but usually at the margins. Few, if any, destinations have established their competitiveness on the basis of friendliness alone. Indeed, it might be argued that sometimes the poor reputation or behaviour of a destination's residents might even be an attraction in itself. First-time visitors to New

York might expect and actually even want the stereotypical New York taxi experience so they can return home having experienced the real thing.

We are not advocating actions to maintain poor service or inhospitable residents, but merely pointing out that one should always try to understand the views and expectations of the visitor when managing destination competitiveness, and that authenticity, as perceived by visitors, should play a part in these considerations.

Enterprise: the Generation of Human Energy[3]

In capitalistic, free-enterprise systems, it is axiomatic to note the economic importance of business enterprises. Small enterprises particularly are regarded as the engine of free-enterprise economics, typically accounting for the largest portion of employment and output. In a functional sense, Baumbeck and Lawyer (1979) note three particular reasons for the importance of small, independent businesses. First, all business is interdependent. Big businesses and small businesses work hand in hand as both suppliers and buyers, enabling each business to specialize. Second, in addition to these complementary relationships, competition among businesses provides the stimulus for change and improvement. 'It is the best insurance that our economy will remain dynamic and provide a continuous stream of innovations, new ideas, experiments, and pioneering efforts' (p. 13). The third reason is that small business provides the greatest source of new ideas and inventions and a proving-ground for them.

The tourism, hospitality and leisure industries are replete with small to medium-sized enterprises. Quinn et al. (1992) attribute this to the relatively low entry barriers, the small number of restrictions that are imposed and the few skills required. To this list could be added the desire by many to mix pleasure with business by turning a leisure hobby into a living. The attractiveness of these industries often extends beyond economic motivations.

The small enterprise has inherent advantages where: (i) a high degree of flexibility is required because of frequent changes in demand, the demand for small quantities in a wide variety of styles, or rapidly developing techniques of production; (ii) manual labour and personal attention to details by the owner/manager are of dominant importance; (iii) demand is strictly local; and (iv) both raw materials and finished products are perishable. Tourism fits these conditions extremely well, with the exception of condition (iii), as the necessity for travel in tourism negates its significance (Baumbeck and Lawyer, 1979, p. 16).

Therefore, tourism enterprise – the small tourism business in particular – is of fundamental importance to the development of tourism as an industry. However, 'there are very few specific works which address the relationship between tourism and entrepreneurship' (Din, 1992, p. 10). 'This topic remains a relatively neglected research focus in the literature on tourism and economic development, and yet it holds an important key to understanding tourism's impact on local economies' (Shaw and Williams, 1990, p. 68).

Several authors have noted the role of entrepreneurship in the development of a tourism destination. Butler (1980) views entrepreneurial development by local residents as occurring spontaneously in response to growth in tourist demand. Christaller (1964) emphasizes the direction of tourism development from a core outwards to peripheral regions, aided by a ready supply of entrepreneurs. The evolutionary perspective of Butler and the diffusionist perspective of Christaller do not apply, in the view of Din (1992, p. 18), in Third World destinations, where 'the receiving community may not possess the cultural and economic capacity to appreciate the opportunities, let alone exploit them'. Din (1992) and Echtner (1995) therefore emphasize the importance of entrepreneurial training in these situations.

Porter's (1990) model for the determinants of national advantage (covered in Chapter 2) captures the principal link between enterprise and industry competitiveness in two of the four factors which constitute his competitive 'diamond' (see Chapter 1): firm strategy, structure and rivalry, and related and supporting industries. Porter also notes the role of chance driven by entrepreneurship. 'Invention and entrepreneurship are at the heart of national advantage' (Porter, 1990, p. 125). Porter argues that the role of chance does not mean that industry success is unpredictable, as entrepreneurship is not random.

Tourism enterprise, particularly with regard to entrepreneurship, new venture development and small business, contributes to destination development and competitiveness in the following possible ways.

- *Competition*. Clearly, a competitive destination depends in part on a local tourism industry consisting of numerous alternative suppliers who must survive on the basis of services that are either unique or superior in some way or are available at a lower cost. Competition among firms creates an environment for excellence.
- *Cooperation*. The interdependence of business (as discussed above) and mutual self-interest in the success of the destination encourages inter-firm cooperation. Cooperation is evident in the form of marketing alliances, sectoral associations and management structures.
- *Specialization*. The existence and growth of numerous tourism enterprises enables each firm to concentrate on its core competencies and expertise. The diverse nature of the tourism product and the growing sophistication of travel consumers demands more specialized services.
- *Innovation*. A competitive destination is aided by the development of innovative tourism services and experiences. New ventures and small businesses provide an ideal mechanism for the identification and development of new ideas.
- *Facilitation*. Tourism relies on the provision of numerous ancillary services, such as marketing research consultants, food services, laundries, automotive repairs and financial institutions. Destinations function more effectively when these services are abundant.
- *Investment*. The flow of investment capital (both debt and equity) to the tourism industry is possible largely through the efforts and existence of tourism enterprises seeking to exploit profitable opportunities.

- *Growth*. The growth of the destination depends largely on the actions of individual enterprises. Time- and location-dependent services seek multisite, multiservice or multisegment growth strategies. Franchising, management contracts and consortia occur frequently.
- *Income distribution and equity*. Tourism enterprises help to disperse the economic benefits of tourism development throughout the local population. In particular, small, locally owned firms localize the economic benefits. Resident support for tourism development fosters a competitive destination.
- *Risk-taking*. Tourism entrepreneurs encourage innovation and development through their willingness to assume a substantial share of the financial risk. Many ideas might never get off the ground without this contribution.
- *Productivity*. The productivity of the destination tourism system is likely to be improved when entrepreneurs are willing and able to exploit opportunities that benefit the destination.
- *Gap-filling*. A healthy system of enterprise ensures that market gaps and unmet needs remain unrecognized and unfilled for only a short time.
- *Product diversification*. A destination's diversified portfolio of tourism products, services and experiences enhances its attractiveness and therefore its competitiveness.
- *Seasonality*. A destination's seasonal constraints can be partly overcome when tourism enterprises expand the range of seasonal experiences available.
- *Disequilibrium*. Market disequilibria created by, for example, changes in regulations or technology are perceived and adjusted to quickly where enterprise thrives.

Despite these numerous contributions, several problems and challenges are also evident. The existence of so many small businesses in tourism means that many owner-managers lack the skills, expertise or resources to function efficiently and effectively. The alluring qualities of the tourism industry have often led many entrepreneurs to make bad investment decisions. Dreams of an attractive lifestyle may cloud economic judgements.

The relatively low entry barriers, the few skills required and the small number of restrictions or regulations imposed in the tourism industry encourage the proliferation of small firms (Quinn *et al.*, 1992). Many small tourism firms lack business training and do not appreciate its value. They are often very reluctant to invest in staff training when employee turnover is high and employment is seasonal. Owner-managers often have little understanding of how to finance their business and most are so busy ˙or distracted by their own business that they fail to recognize their dependency on the competitiveness of the destination as a whole.

Externalities, particularly environmental, social and cultural ones, are also often significant in tourism. Small tourism enterprises may not recognize or care about the wider and long-term consequences of some of their actions.

Those who have examined the extent of research in tourism enterprise, particularly the role of the small business, have been disappointed to find little effort to date. Shaw and Williams (1990, p. 71) noted that the 'literature is remarkably uninformative on the influence of small or medium-sized business . . . little is known about the economic behavioural characteristics of entrepreneurs within tourism economies or, more importantly, the impact of the entrepreneurs on economic development'. Berrett *et al.* (1993) and Quinn *et al.* (1992) drew the same conclusion. Quinn *et al.* (p. 12) noted a concentration of research effort on larger tourism establishments and recognized the difficulty of carrying out research on small tourism firms because they are typically sceptical of investigation, often operate in the black economy, generally do not wish to be part of 'the system', and are not encouraged by the attitudes of industry trade associations to research.

If we wish to understand tourism's contribution to economic development and the impact of tourism enterprise on a destination and its competitiveness, then 'a major advance . . . can be achieved through research on entrepreneurial activity' (Shaw and Williams,

1990, p. 79). Such research might address the following important needs:

- a typology of tourism ancillary firms and the functions they perform;
- an analysis of the interdependencies between enterprises and their role in the destination tourism system;
- an appraisal of the specific and unique managerial challenges in tourism, particularly of the small firm;
- an assessment of the information needs of small firms and the ways in which government and industry associations could assist; and
- a study of the effective role of industrial policy in stimulating the desired behaviour of entrepreneurs in tourism.

There is much speculation and debate about the employment market. The structure and nature of work seem to be undergoing fundamental changes, at least in developed economies. Firms are not only downsizing but are frequently contracting out for many services. A consensus seems to be emerging that more people will become self-employed in order to create a need for their skills and services, and that future economies will consist of 'virtual corporations' involving a network of smaller enterprises.

Tourism destinations are very much like these virtual corporations. And just as there has been much interest in the competitiveness of traditional business entities, we can expect to see growing interest in the competitiveness of these new types of business structures. In tourism, we already have an opportunity to explore this phenomenon.

Political Will: Is Tourism Part of the Political Landscape?

Although tourism has been an important economic sector for some time in most countries, cities, towns and regions in comparison with other, more traditional economic sectors, the tourism industry has long struggled for recognition by governments. The attitude of government to the industry has largely been one of general indifference. Other industries, employing fewer people and contributing less towards a nation's gross domestic product, have historically attracted more interest and attention by governments. Implicitly, there seemed to be a view that tourism was a frivolous industry creating little wealth and involving low-skilled, low-paying jobs and, although important in terms of quality of life, it was of limited benefit to a society compared with agriculture and high-tech industries, for example.

This view has been changing, and increasing numbers of governments and policy makers are recognizing the valuable economic and social contribution made to societies by the tourism industry. Nevertheless, in many destinations political will and interest in supporting tourism development are not high on the agenda.

One of the important roles of government is to set policies and allocate scarce resources. Tourism development may not receive much support from government because other industries are seen to be more important when viewed from this perspective. When such is the case, provided attitudes are informed by the facts about tourism, there can be little argument. However, often the tourism industry has been ignored more by default and ignorance than by a proper assessment of the facts.

Australia is an example where political will and an interest in the fortunes of the tourism industry has been a particularly important factor behind its competitiveness. In the mid-1980s, a member of the then federal Labour government, John Brown, was particularly effective in convincing his colleagues in government that Australia should devote much greater resources to the promotion of Australia as a tourism destination. A personal friend of Paul Hogan (of *Crocodile Dundee* fame), John Brown recruited the actor's assistance to present an argument to the federal government that the tourism industry of Australia could become a major trade initiative. Subsequently, this relationship led to the series of very successful television commercials promoting Australia as a tourism destination overseas. Although the extent of government support for tourism in Australia has had its ups and downs ever since, John Brown's success has had a major and long-term impact on the high profile enjoyed by the tourism industry in Australia both in the minds of the general public as well as politically.

Although we have so far focused the discussion of political will on government and politicians, it must be emphasized that political will should be viewed more broadly. All elements of an organized society and its systems reflect and are affected by political will. So, for example, the willingness of institutions to work together to enable the development of tourism is also a reflection of the extent of political will in a destination. Where political will creates a supportive environment, tourism entities are more likely to display a progressive and innovative approach towards the development of tourism and the strategic direction it takes. They are more likely to suggest new or innovative solutions in the knowledge that at least these ideas will receive fair consideration and will be judged on merit. The saying, 'where there's a will, there's a way' illustrates this point. The presence of political will helps drive ideas and initiatives forward. The absence of political will stymies good ideas or serves to discourage ideas in the first place.

Notes

[1]   The Tourism Forecasting Council was established and structured by the Australian Minister for Tourism to draw on the experience and expertise 'of the private and public sectors in tourism, construction, property investment and finance . . . to encourage awareness among investors that, like other opportunities, investment in tourism facilities needs to be based on professional business planning, long-term operating viability and an achievable vision of the industry's future' (Commonwealth Department of Tourism, 1994).

[2]   According to Zeithaml and Bitner (1996), a customer's zone of tolerance ranges between their 'desired service level' and the level they consider to represent 'adequate service'.

[3]   This section is based largely on the paper by Crouch and Ritchie (1995).

References

Baumbeck, C.M. and Lawyer, K. (1979) *How to Organize and Operate a Small Business*, 6th edn. Prentice-Hall, Englewood Cliffs, New Jersey.

Berrett, T., Burton, T.L. and Slack, T. (1993) Quality products, quality service: factors leading to entrepreneurial success in the sport and leisure industry. *Leisure Studies* 12, 93–106.

Butler, R.W. (1980) The concept of a tourist area cycle of evolution: implications for management of resources. *Canadian Geographer* 24, 5–12.

Christaller, W. (1964) Some considerations of tourism location in Europe: the peripheral regions – underdeveloped countries – recreation areas. *Papers of the Regional Science Association* 12, 95–105.

Commonwealth Department of Tourism (1994) Forecast: the first report of the Tourism Forecasting Council, Australia. Canberra, Australia, Commonwealth Department of Tourism.

Crouch, G.I. and Ritchie, J.R.B. (1995) Destination competitiveness and the role of the tourism enterprise. *Proceedings of the Fourth Annual World Business Congress, 13–16 July, Istanbul, Turkey*, pp. 43–48.

Din, K.H. (1992) The 'involvement stage' in the evolution of a tourist destination. *Tourism Recreation Research* 17, 10–20.

Echtner, C.M. (1995) Entrepreneurial training in developing countries. *Annals of Tourism Research* 22, 119–134.

Porter, M.E. (1990). *The Competitive Advantage of Nations*. Free Press, New York.

Quinn, U., Larmour, R. and McQuillan, N. (1992) The small firm in the hospitality industry. *International Journal of Contemporary Hospitality Management* 4, 11–14.

Shaw, G. and Williams, A.M. (1990) Tourism, economic development and the role of entrepreneurial activity. *Progress in Tourism, Recreation and Hospitality Management* 2, 67–81.

WTTC (1993) *Travel and Tourism: a Special Report from the World Travel and Tourism Council*. Elsevier Science, Oxford.

Zeithaml, V.A. and Bitner, M.J. (1996) *Services Marketing*. McGraw-Hill, Columbus, Ohio.

8

Destination Policy, Planning and Development

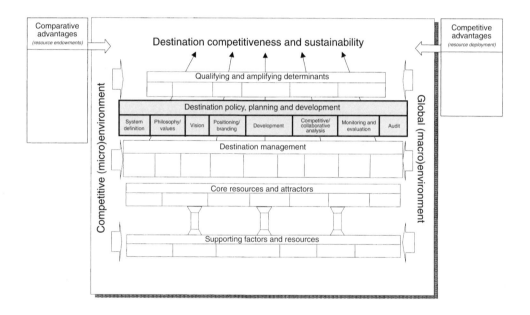

By this point, readers should have an under-standing of the global forces that influence tourism in general and destination competitive-ness and sustainability in particular. They should also have some grasp of the opposing forces of *competition* and *cooperation* among organizations within the destination – and the important role of the destination management organization (DMO) in shaping the mode of operation of the destination as a whole. Indeed, we argue that the DMO plays a particularly critical and vital role in efforts to ensure that the expectations of stakeholders (both internal and external) are satisfied to the greatest extent possible.

Chapter 6 focused on the explicit identifi-cation of those *core resources* and *attractors* that provide the primary motivation for visiting the destination, while Chapter 7 examined the *supporting factors and resources* that make it possible for the tourist to visit the destination easily and comfortably.

An attractive, well-functioning and highly competitive destination does not exist by chance. It requires a well-planned environment within which the appropriate forms of tourism

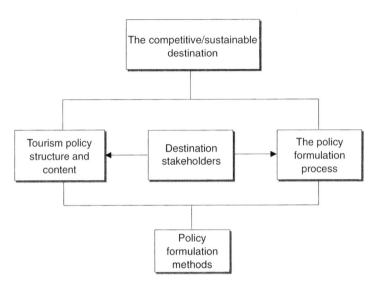

Fig. 8.1.   The responsive competitive/sustainable tourist destination: a managerial framework.

development are encouraged and facilitated. Tourism policy is the key to providing this environment. This chapter explores the nature of tourism policy and describes how effective tourism policy, planning and development should be structured, formulated and implemented.

The use of formal statements of tourism policy is a relatively new dimension of tourism, and it is being increasingly acknowledged for the impact it can have on the long-term success of a tourism destination. The concept of 'master planning' has been around for some time, but the need for high-level strategic planning involving the explicit definition of major policies, reflecting an ongoing consensus among all the stakeholders in a tourism destination, is the outgrowth of ongoing social changes. All citizens are demanding a greater level of participation in the formulation of policies and programmes and development that affect their daily lives. Figure 8.1 emphasizes how policy content and the policy formulation process must reflect these changes. All of these pressures together have led to the overall need to build competitive and sustainable destinations. It must constantly be kept in mind that, as we formulate these policies, we must be sensitive to the views of all destination stakeholders (Table 8.1).

The Nature of Tourism Policy, Planning and Development

Because the importance of tourism policy has not been recognized until recently, it is ill understood by many in the industry. We argue, however, that it is characterized by the following main features.

- It must focus on macro-level policies; that is, it must be concerned with societal views of the direction which tourism development should take at the subnational, national and even transnational levels.
- It must be designed to formulate policies having a long-term perspective.
- It must concentrate on how critical and limited resources can best respond to perceived needs and opportunities in a changing environment.
- It must recognize the intellectual nature of the process of policy formulation, and so must incorporate tacit knowledge and personal experience as important sources of information in addition to more conventional methods of research and study.
- It must encourage and stimulate organized creativity so as to avoid policies based on stereotyped or outmoded perceptions.

Table 8.1. A listing of the many stakeholders that DMO managers feel are relevant to destination success (from Sheehan and Ritchie, 2002).

Hotels/hotel association
City/local government
Regional/county government
Attractions/attraction association
State/provincial tourism department
Board of directors/advisory board
Convention centre/banquet facilities
Members
Community/citizens/residents
Restaurants/restaurant association
University/college
Chamber of commerce
Sponsors
Airlines
Federal government
Hospitality industry
Local economic development authority
Media
Regional convention and visitor bureaux
Visitors/tourists
Advertising agency
Arts/arts association
Destination management company
Meeting planners
Non-tourism industry
Other policy makers in area
Public facilities
Parks department
Recreational
Retail stores/association
Travel companies/association
Volunteers

- It must be constructed to permit and facilitate a continuing dynamic social process requiring inputs from multiple sources.
- It must break down the traditional boundaries between disciplines and industry sectors in tourism.
- It must relate policies of the tourism subsystem to those of the total socioeconomic system of a nation or region of which it is a part.

In summary, tourism policy formulation can be characterized as a dynamic social process within which an intellectual process is imbedded. From a terminology standpoint, the output of this process is commonly referred to as an overall strategy for tourism development. However, because of the lack of rigour commonly associated with the term 'strategy', it is considered advisable to reserve its use to the description of specific major actions or patterns of actions that might be used to attain the objectives of a tourism system. In place of the term 'overall strategy', the more appropriate concept of the 'megapolicy' will be employed.

Distinguishing between destination policy, planning and development and destination management

We also wish to clarify and emphasize the important distinctions between destination policy, planning and development (DPPD) and destination management. This clarification is critical since, at a superficial level, there may appear to be overlap and/or duplication among the terms and concepts used in both.

Although both DPPD and destination management seek to improve the competitiveness and sustainability of the destination, they differ fundamentally in that DPPD is essentially an intellectual process that uses information, judgement and monitoring to make macro-level decisions regarding the kind of destination that is desirable, the degree to which ongoing performance and related changes in the nature of visitation and the physical character of the destination are contributing to the achievement of the kind of destination that stakeholders want.

In contrast, destination management is more of a micro-level activity in which all the many resident and industry stakeholders carry out their individual and organizational responsibilities on a daily basis in efforts to realize the macro-level vision contained in policy, planning and development. Both DPPD and destination management must be done well to achieve destination success. If the policy is ill-conceived and poorly implemented, the efforts of many can be misdirected, ill-supported and ultimately wasted. Conversely, no matter how brilliant a policy and its associated planning and development, it can collapse like the proverbial house of cards if daily management and operational tasks are not performed effectively and efficiently.

In order to make the above distinction between policy and management clearer in operational terms, let us examine the phenomenon of destination positioning/branding, which is relevant and important at both the policy and management levels of our destination competitiveness/sustainability framework (Fig. 3.1).

> We are defined by the experiences and actions of our lifetime. So are brands.
>   (Bedbury and Fenichell, 2002, p. 19)

At the policy level, we are concerned with the overall manner in which the destination is perceived, from a strategic perspective, by the marketplace with respect to the total package of experiences it delivers compared with major competitors. In more everyday parlance, this strategic package of experiences can be referred to as a 'destination brand'.

At the same time, there are many aspects of branding that must also be addressed at the level of destination management. For example, it is important to develop a destination logo that conveys the desired strategic brand image and to regularly monitor destination brand awareness within key market segments. It is these daily support activities related to branding that translate a grand concept into a marketplace reality.

Tourism Policy: a Definition

Tourism policy can be defined as:

> a set of regulations, rules, guidelines, directives and development/promotion objectives and strategies that provide a framework within which the collective and individual decisions directly affecting tourism development and the daily activities within a destination are taken.

The purpose of tourism policy is to create an environment that provides maximum benefit to the stakeholders of the region while minimizing negative impacts. The hosting of visitors by a tourism destination is primarily undertaken to provide its stakeholders (Table 8.1) with a broad range of economic and social benefits – most typically employment and income. This employment and income allows stakeholders to reside in and to enjoy the quality of the region. Tourism policy seeks to ensure that the hosting of visitors is done in a way that

maximizes the benefits to stakeholders while minimizing the effects, costs and impacts associated with ensuring the success of the destination. In effect, tourism policy seeks to provide high-quality visitor experiences that are profitable to destination stakeholders, while ensuring that the destination is not compromised in terms of its environmental, social and cultural integrity. As Table 8.1 demonstrates, DMO managers must appreciate the fact that a destination's stakeholders include a broad spectrum of individuals and organizations. While many are residents of the destination, many are not.

Why is tourism policy important?

Because it is often poorly understood, tourism policy is often overlooked as an important factor in ensuring the success of a tourism destination. Perhaps its most important role is to ensure that a given destination has a clear idea of where it is going or what it is seeking to become in the long term. In parallel, it must strive to create a climate in which collaboration among the many stakeholders in tourism is both supported and facilitated. In more specific terms, tourism policy fulfils the following functions:

- it defines the rules of the game – the terms under which tourism operators must function;
- it sets out activities and behaviours that are acceptable;
- it provides a common direction and guidance for all tourism stakeholders within a destination;
- it facilitates consensus around the specific vision, strategies and objectives for a given destination;
- it provides a framework for public and private discussions on the role of the tourism sector and its contributions to the economy and to society in general; and
- it allows tourism to interface more effectively with other sectors of the economy.

In the light of the foregoing, it is important to keep in mind that tourism policy affects the extent to which all of the day-to-day operational activities – such as marketing, event development, attraction operations and visitor reception programmes – are successful. It is not just a theoretical concept but has very real implications in day-to-day practice.

Areas addressed by tourism policy

In general terms, a formal tourism policy for a given destination will address such areas as (at the national level):

- the roles of tourism within the overall socioeconomic development of the destination region;
- the type of destination that will most effectively fulfil the desired roles;
- types and levels of taxation;
- financing for the tourism sector (sources and terms);
- the nature and direction of product development and maintenance;
- transportation access and infrastructure;
- regulatory practices (e.g. airlines, travel agencies);
- environmental practices and restrictions;
- industry image and credibility;
- community relationships;
- human resources and labour supply;
- union and labour legislation;
- technology;
- marketing practices; and
- foreign travel rules.

A warning: the tourism destination and tourism policy do not exist in a vacuum.

In all of the foregoing discussions, it needs to be kept in mind that tourism policies are but part of the social, economic and political policies which govern and direct the functioning of the overall society within which tourism exists and functions.

In brief, there are a number of more general policies (regulations, rules, directives, objectives, strategies) that are controlled by governments and by other industry sectors and organizations, which may have a significant effect on the success of tourism and tourism destinations. These include:

- taxation – affects costs and therefore profitability;
- interest rate policy – affects costs and therefore profitability;
- bilateral air agreements – determines foreign visitor access;
- environmental policy – limits growth and access to attractive but sensitive areas;
- customs and immigration policy – can facilitate or hinder international visitation;
- communications policy – can restrict the use of certain advertising media;
- minimum wage policy – can affect labour markets;
- welfare policy – can influence the nature and behaviour of the work force;
- education policy – can affect the quality of the workforce;
- cultural policy – can affect the preservation and promotion of national heritage;
- foreign investment policy/regulations – can affect the availability of investment capital;
- local zoning policy/by-laws – can restrict or encourage tourism facility development;
- national/provincial/local policy with respect to funding support for major public facilities (e.g. stadiums, convention centres, museums, parks) – can drastically affect destination attractiveness;
- infrastructure policy – can make destinations safer for visitors;
- currency and exchange rate policies – directly affect destination cost competitiveness and may discourage resident travel to foreign destinations; and
- the legal system – determines consumer/ visitor protection legislation (e.g. liability for failing to deliver advertised facilities, tours or experiences).

To summarize, there is a whole range of social, economic, legal and technological policies that greatly affect the appeal, attractiveness, competitiveness and sustainability of a tourism destination. Some are under the control of the tourism sector (such as visitor satisfaction, guarantee policy, truth in advertising policy), but the great majority are not. Thus, the challenge facing tourism managers is to try to influence global policies where they can and adapt to them as effectively as possible where they cannot.

The many other influences on tourism policy

As we have stressed above, tourism does not exist in a vacuum. It can only function smoothly if it shares, cooperates and dialogues effectively with many other sectors of society and of the economy (Fig. 8.2). Many of these sectors have little understanding of, or explicit interest in, tourism in the region – unless, of course, visitor activity somehow appears to detract from the functioning or well-being of another sector. Conflicts between tourism and other sectors most commonly arise when there is competition for a shared resource (e.g. the extractive industries), where there is a common need for specific individuals or types of individuals (e.g. those engaged in entertainment, technology and education sectors) or where there may exist a divergence of philosophical views (e.g. in the environment, parks and transportation sectors).

Each of these interfaces can pose either a threat or an opportunity for tourism. The environmental sector and the extractive industries have traditionally viewed tourism as a competing force; the technology, entertainment and transportation sectors most often perceive tourism as an ally or a business opportunity. The political and governmental sectors provide a pervasive policy environment that the destination, in collaboration with its many sector partners, must constantly assess and attempt to modify where necessary.

In order to dialogue and to present its case effectively at each interface, the tourism sector must be as capable, as well-trained and as well-prepared as the professionals of any specific sector at any given point in time. Otherwise, tourism risks being undermined and weakened. Consequently, it may miss a critical market opportunity or fail to establish an innovative alliance or partnership. All too often, tourism's lack of sophistication and preparedness has

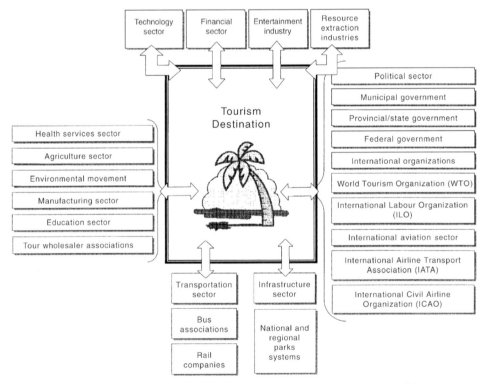

Fig. 8.2. Tourism: some of the multiple interfaces between tourism and other sectors of the economy and society where policy can affect destination competitiveness and sustainability.

resulted in government decisions and policies that significantly weaken its ability to compete – or to compete more profitability. In certain cases, the tourism sector has not even been aware of the extent to which it has been disadvantaged by its naiveté or by its failure to proactively and adequately prepare its case. This can be particularly disastrous in public forums, where both the issue at hand and the industry's long-term credibility can be lost.

The multidisciplinary nature of tourism and tourism policy

As explained earlier in this book, tourism is, by its very nature, a multidisciplinary phenomenon (Fig. 1.3). The tourism experience is influenced by a range of economic, psychological, societal, technological, legal and political forces. It follows that, in order to formulate policies that accommodate or address these multiple forces, those involved must appreciate the complexities of each discipline and their interactions in any given situation. The disciplines of psychology, economics, sociology and law are but some of the disciplines that can enhance our understanding of international marketing. The environmental sciences, political science and the behavioural sciences are essential to the formulation of a policy for national parks that defines the levels and types of tourism that are appropriate and desirable.

Defining the Focus of Tourism Policy: the Competitive/Sustainable Destination System

In a complex world of many jurisdictions, it is important to identify explicitly the geographical area to which a tourism policy applies. In this text, we refer to the generic entity in question as the 'tourism destination' or, more succinctly, as simply the 'destination'. A tourism destination, in its simplest terms, is a particular geographical region within which the visitor enjoys various types of travel experiences. There are, however, many types and levels of tourism destinations for which policy should be developed to suit the nature of the destination.

Types and levels of tourism destinations

Tourism destinations are most commonly defined in formal terms by recognized political jurisdictions such as:

- a nation or country;
- a macro-region, consisting of several countries (e.g. Europe), or other groupings that either transcend national borders (such as the European Riviera) or reflect economic trade zones (e.g. the North American Free Trade Agreement and the Americas);
- a province or state within a country;
- a localized region within a country, such as Western Canada, the US Northwest and the state of Bavaria in Germany;
- a city or town; or
- a very unique locale, such as a national park, a historic site or a memorial/monument that is in itself sufficiently significant to attract visitors. Other examples include substantive and readily identifiable institutions such as Disney World in Orlando, Florida, the Hermitage in St Petersburg and St Peter's in Rome. These may in themselves exert sufficient drawing power to be classified as a destination.

The major parameters of tourism policy and tourism destination management: competitiveness and sustainability

While the task of policy formulation and tourism destination management is a complex, multidimensional challenge, there are, when all the rhetoric is stripped away, two primary parameters that must be satisfied if the destination is to be successful. These are competitiveness and sustainability. As we stressed repeatedly in Chapter 2, neither is sufficient alone. They are both essential and mutually supportive.

The *competitiveness* of a destination refers to its ability to compete effectively and profitably in the tourism marketplace; that is, to attract visitors in a way that enhances the prosperity and overall well-being of a destination. *Sustainability* pertains to the ability of a destination to maintain the quality of its physical, social, cultural and environmental resources, while it competes in the marketplace. As discussed in Chapter 2, a major concern in this regard is to avoid the false appearance of economic profitability – a profitability that is derived from the subtle, often invisible (in the short run) depletion of the destination's natural capital. Conversely, sustainability may be viewed as encouraging 'natural capital investment', that is, programmes that attempt to enhance different aspects of the national environment while refraining from current consumption in order to restore capital stocks (those that are renewable), thus ensuring the availability of resources for future consumption (Prugh *et al.*, 1995).

Viewed in this light, we can see that successful tourism destination management involves traditional economic and business management skills balanced with environmental management capabilities (Fig. 8.3). The *economic and business skills* required are those related to effective resource development and deployment. They include strategic planning

for destination development, the marketing of the destination, the management of the human resources necessary to deliver quality visitor experiences, the management of the financial resources and investment required to support development, and the ability to develop the organizational capacity to coordinate and ensure the delivery of essential services.

The *environmental management* capabilities are those that are critical to effective destination stewardship. Traditionally, these have included the knowledge and skills for wildlife management, species protection, maintaining water quality, flows and levels, the securing and restoring of habitat quality, ensuring aquatic biodiversity, the reduction of human-caused mortality, maintaining the national diversity of vegetation communities, and the zoning of environmentally sensitive areas for effective human use management.

More recently, the concept of stewardship has been expanded to encompass management practices designed to both maintain and

COMPETITIVENESS (Resource deployment) Business/economic management skills	SUSTAINABILITY (Resource stewardship) Environmental management capabilities
• Marketing	• Water quality management
• Financial management	• Air quality management
• Operations management	• Wildlife management
• Human resources management	• Forest/plant management
• Information management	• Habitat management
• Organization management	• Visitor management
• Strategic planning	• Biodiversity management
	• Resident/community management
	• Commemorative integrity
Information management	
Destination monitoring	**Destination research**

Fig. 8.3. Some elements of successful 'total tourism destination management'.

enhance the commemorative, social and cultural integrity of the destination. It also involves the ability to effectively manage the human presence within the boundaries of the destination. This human presence has two main components: visitor management and resident/community management.

Finally, the tasks of resource deployment and resource stewardship are linked by the shared need for a *tourism destination management information system* (TDMIS) to support policy formulation, strategic planning, day-to-day decision making and overall performance evaluations (Ritchie and Ritchie, 2002). Information management has, in turn, two major components. The *monitoring* component provides stakeholders, particularly the DMO, with an ongoing auditing and assessment of destination assets and performance across a broad range of indicator variables. These indicator variables should be carefully chosen so as to be representative of the overall health of the destination in terms of both competitiveness and sustainability. Monitoring also includes an 'environmental scan' component, which seeks to identify unusual or emerging trends and forces that have the potential to significantly affect the competitiveness or sustainability of a destination, both currently and well into the future.

The *research* component of the TDMIS is normally structured to play several distinct roles. One of these is to provide research for policy formulation. Policy research is characterized by the analysis of the overall situation of the destination. It is undertaken with a view to providing information that assists in developing well-defined but broad guidelines that serve to establish priorities to direct the activities of the destination (Ritchie and Goeldner, 1994). More specifically, policy research seeks to gather and interpret macro-level data related to present well-being, and the evolution of trends of major economic, social, technological and political factors that bear on the success of the destination.

which policy is formulated, the overall structure of a policy, and the specific policy content found within that structure. In the same vein, it is necessary to distinguish among the static concepts of policy context, structure and content, and the dynamic concept of policy formulation. Context provides the setting within which policy is formulated. Structure and content define the 'what' of tourism policy; the process of policy formulation describes the 'how' of defining the structure of a destination's policy and determining the content of policy found within that structure. In tourism, the process, or the 'how', provides:

- an overview of the different stages or steps involved in the policy formulation process; and
- a review of the various possible methods that might be used within, or across, the stages of policy formulation.

The context of tourism policy

Macro-policy, or what some have referred to as 'total system mega-policy', involves determination of the postures, assumptions and main guidelines to be followed by specific policies. In brief, mega-policy represents a kind of holistic master policy that surrounds the tourism system of the destination and is clearly distinct from detailed discrete tourism policies (Dror, 1971). In this regard, tourism policy is viewed as being directly based upon and derived from the policies that direct the total socioeconomic system of the nation or region in which the tourism subsystem is located. In fact, it is the general content of these total system policies that provides much of the basis upon which to derive the tourism philosophy of the destination region in question.

Now that we have provided the definitional and contextual foundations for destination policy, we turn to an elaboration of its components.

Tourism Policy: Context, Structure, Content and Process

In discussing tourism policy, it is helpful to distinguish clearly among the context within

The components of tourism policy

As shown in our overall framework (Fig. 3.1), we view policy as encompassing some eight distinctive components, which, when combined, address not only intellectual policy formulation but also more pragmatic strategic planning, as well as the translation of both policy and planning into reality – a process commonly referred to as 'development'. The components of destination policy planning and development will now be discussed.

System definition

While conceptually simple, the first component of tourism policy (as shown in Fig. 3.1) is a formal definition of the destination in question and a determination of the identity and salience of each of its stakeholders. This component, while often neglected, is critical since all that follows relates directly back to the destination as it has been defined.

The first element of the system definition is a delineation of the geographical and/or political boundaries that physically and jurisdictionally define the destination. Examples of boundaries commonly used are those of countries, states, cities and regions. It must be emphasized here that destinations can be theoretically defined from both a demand and a supply perspective. While the tourism industry is usually more comfortable with the supply-side perspective, we must keep in mind that the tourist defines the destination not only in terms of geography and attractions but also in terms of the experiences it is likely to provide.

Tourism philosophy/values

An explicit tourism philosophy is an essential foundation on which to develop a coherent policy. In general, a philosophy may be defined as 'a system for guiding life, as a body of principles of conduct, beliefs or traditions; or the broad general principles of a particular subject or field of activity'. Adapting this general definition for present purposes, a tourism philosophy may be defined as a general principle or set of principles that indicates the beliefs and values of members of a society concerning how tourism shall serve the population of a country or region, and which acts as a guide for evaluating the utility of tourism-related activities.

It is important to stress the critical role that the values of destination residents exert in determining the context of tourism policy. In effect, the values of residents provide the foundation on which the policy and its various components rest. In the end, tourism policies that do not reflect the values of the destination stakeholders, or 'hosts', will inevitably fail to gain ongoing popular or political support. Policies that do not maintain long-term political support are doomed to failure.

The philosophical distinction sometimes made between value-driven and market-driven destinations, while conceptually appealing, is somewhat ambiguous in practice. No destination can be competitive unless it succeeds in appealing to profitable segments of the market over the long term. By the same token, no destination can be sustainable unless, while it generates economic rewards, it also succeeds in maintaining the value-driven legitimacy required by a democratic society.

The destination vision

Although a tourism philosophy sets out the overall nature of tourism in a destination, it is the destination vision that provides the more functional and more inspirational portrait of the ideal future that the destination hopes to bring about in some defined future (usually 5, 10, 20 or 50 years).

Visions can take many different forms. Some are very concise (the equivalent of a corporate mission statement); others are much more extensive and idealistic. Regardless of its specific form, the destination vision is the essence, and indeed the most critical component, of tourism policy. We will therefore devote a major part of the chapter to exploring the precise nature of a destination vision by providing two in-depth examples with which we are familiar regarding how the destination visioning process may be carried out. The first concerns a more pragmatic vision, while the second deals with a more idealistic one.

Crafting Versus Formulating a Vision

The preparation, formulation or crafting of a destination vision is a stimulating intellectual process that often attracts and involves the relevant stakeholders of a destination. However, the implementation or realization of the vision is always a demanding process that requires the acceptance of responsibility, the search for funding and the allocation of a considerable amount of energy and resources. It goes without saying that most of the effort in crafting a vision is wasted if a commitment to realizing the vision is not made. The first step in translating the vision into reality is to identify the specific destination development strategies that clearly define what must be done in terms of both supply development (destination facilities and services) and demand development (destination marketing).

Tourism development policy and the associated implementation strategies may be viewed as specific major actions or patterns of action over time designed to attain the objectives of the tourism system of a country or region. For both analytical and managerial purposes, these strategies can be divided into three broad categories: supply development strategies, demand development strategies, and organizational structure strategies.

Example 1: a pragmatic vision

This example of a more pragmatic vision relates to one prepared by the DMO for the city of Calgary, Canada. In this case a task force consisting of industry and citizen volunteers was given the general mandate to develop a strategic vision that would positively influence the development of the destination in directions that would strengthen the city in ways consistent with local values. More specifically, the task force was charged with the responsibility of attempting to establish Calgary as 'Host, Consultant and Educator to the World'. While grandiose in its terminology, the mandate of this task force was to determine how the city could best build upon its international reputation from the 1988 Winter Olympics, its legacy of sports facilities built for the Games, its proximity to the scenic Rocky Mountains, its world-class technical expertise in key sectors of the economy (notably oil and gas) and its situation as the most highly educated city in Canada, in order to develop itself as a major international travel destination.

Host to the world task force

Using this general mandate as a starting point, the task force developed a more detailed mission statement within its formal terms of reference (Table 8.2). As can be seen from this table, the critical initial component of the mandate of the task force was 'to develop a vision concerning the kind of tourism destination it believes Calgary should become as we move into the 21st century'.

The first step undertaken by the task force was to establish the principles that should underlie the vision for the destination. These principles are given in Table 8.3.

Elements of the vision

Once the mandate of the task force and the principles on which to base the process had been agreed upon, attention then focused on the primary goal of attempting to define a common vision of what Calgary could and should look like as a tourism destination some 15–20 years from now.

As might be expected, this process required several sessions and a considerable amount of iterative reflection, reaction and reformulation. As a result of this process, task force members agreed on a series of nine statements that, in their totality, provided a composite picture of how they envisage the Calgary of the future from a tourism perspective. These nine vision statements are given in Table 8.4.

An examination of this set of vision statements reveals that they fall into two general categories. The first category contains those that reflect some general values as to how the city should develop – almost without reference to tourism. The first two, in particular, fall into this category. It is important to keep in mind, however, that task force members insisted that such elements as the overall liveability of the city and environmental protection were indeed major tourism appeals. Furthermore, they insisted that if Calgary could not be maintained as a city that appealed to residents, it could not develop its attractiveness for others. The knowledgeable reader will immediately be able to provide examples of exceptions to the generality of this assertion. Nevertheless, it was judged to be important by Calgary residents.

Table 8.2.   Terms of reference for the Calgary Visioning Task Force (from Ritchie, 1993).

Terms of Reference Task Force No 6:
'Calgary . . . Host, Consultant and Educator to the World'
The formal terms of reference defined the overall mandate of the Task Force as being:
. . . to develop a vision concerning the kind of tourism destination it believes Calgary should become as
we move into the 21st century in order to truly establish the city as a major host, consultant, and
educator to the world. It should subsequently prioritize the major initiatives that will be essential to
achieving this vision. Finally, it should recommend and initiate specific actions/implementation steps that
will be required to translate the vision into reality.
In seeking to fulfill this mandate, the Task Force set itself seven (7) specific tasks. These were:
1. To formulate, in a reasonable amount of detail, a *vision* describing the Calgary of the 21st century as
    a tourism destination. This vision will define the kind of destination we want Calgary to be, and the
    kind of people we are likely to attract if such a vision is realized.
2. To identify and prioritize the *major facilities* that it will be necessary to put in place over the next 20
    years as Calgary moves to establish itself as the kind of host, consultant, and educator to the world
    defined by the above noted vision statement.
3. To identify and prioritize the development and/or enhancement of *major events* that are consistent
    with the vision statement and which will be necessary to realize it as we move into the 21st century.
4. To identify critical aspects of the *support and educational/training infrastructure* that it will be
    necessary to develop/enhance as we move towards realizing the vision.
5. To provide concrete specifications of the *image of Calgary* that will be portrayed nationally and
    internationally so as to accurately, yet competitively, position Calgary in the markets it seeks to serve.
6. To provide useful *estimates of the amount* of *funding* likely to be required to implement initiatives
    related to the facilities, events, infrastructure and other programmes identified by the Task Force. As
    well, the issue of possible sources of funding should be addressed. If it is felt necessary, the Task
    Force may authorize additional feasibility studies to be undertaken where financial support for such
    studies can be successfully solicited.
7. To identify *organizations/individuals* who can be encouraged to assume responsibility and/or
    leadership in implementation and/or development of the various facilities, events, infrastructures, and
    programmes deemed to be a priority by the Task Force.

Table 8.3.   Principles underlying the vision of Calgary (from Ritchie, 1993).

Principles underlying the vision of
'Calgary . . . Host, Consultant and Educator to the World'
- Developments related to the vision must always seek to ensure that Calgary and region residents are
  net beneficiaries (i.e. positive impacts must clearly outweigh any potential negative consequences)
- The vision should focus on initiatives which reflect our natural strengths, lifestyles and heritage
- The vision should incorporate and build upon the high quality of the natural, visual and built
  environment enjoyed by Calgary and the surrounding regions
- The vision should focus on significant themes and initiatives which will help position and develop
  Calgary as a major international destination and knowledge/education centre
- Although the concept of the 'host, consultant, and educator' is clearly applicable to all areas of
  excellence that Calgary enjoys, the vision proposes that we learn about the strategic combination of
  these areas through an initial focus on the oil and gas, agribusiness, and tourism sectors. In brief, we
  will first strive for excellence as hosts, consultants, and educators in these areas

The second category of vision statement described more explicitly the key dimensions of the city's character on which tourism should build as Calgary enters the 21st century. It is believed that each of these vision statements fully respects the principles presented in Table 8.3.

Realizing the vision

The definition of the nine vision statements and the subsequent elaboration of their specific meaning was viewed as fulfilling the first of the seven tasks contained in the overall mandate of the task force (Table 8.2). As the next step in

Table 8.4. The vision of Calgary (from Ritchie, 1993).

The vision of Calgary as
'Calgary . . . Host, Consultant and Educator to the World'
Calgary in the 21st century should be:
- A city which is safe, clean, attractive, and efficient, and whose priority is maintaining and enhancing its liveability
- A city which values and preserves the high quality and beauty of the natural environment, waterways, and setting with which it has been blessed
- A city which reflects its proud and dynamic western heritage and native cultures
- A city which values and supports knowledge and education, particularly in those spheres upon which it depends for its well-being and development
- A city which actively encourages and facilitates knowledge transfer between those who generate the knowledge and those who use it
- A city which genuinely welcomes visitors from all parts of the world in an environment that encourages the exchange of insight and understanding while striving to create new personal and professional friendships
- A city which values its cultural diversity and its artistic achievements
- A city which thrives in all seasons – and which is therefore attractive to visitors at all times
- A city which attracts attention and acclaim by providing first-class attractions and by hosting high-profile events which are of interest to its citizens

the total process outlined by the terms of reference, task force members subsequently focused their attention on efforts to both identify and prioritize the major *facilities, events* and *programmes* that they felt would be necessary to put in place over the next 20 years if Calgary was indeed to establish itself as the kind of 'Host, Consultant and Educator to the World' defined by the composite vision statement.

With this goal in mind, the task force first generated a large number of possible initiatives and then selected a more limited set of higher-priority items. The outcome of this process is shown visually in Figs 8.4–8.6. These figures identify the specific facilities (Fig. 8.4), events (Fig. 8.5) and programmes (Fig. 8.6) that members felt would contribute to the realization of each of the nine elements of the vision. It should be noted that each of the figures contains facilities, events or programmes that reflect:

- projects that are already in place and require additional support to encourage evolution towards recognized international excellence;
- projects that have been proposed by others and that are currently under review; and
- suggested new projects that flow logically from the vision defined by the task force.

While the individual facilities, events and programmes in Figs 8.4–8.6 are by nature very specific to the community in question, a number do have characteristics that could be generalized to other settings. The important point to be emphasized, however, is that each of the various facilities, events and programmes bears a direct relation to one or more of the vision statements developed by members of the community.

Developing an action plan

While space does not allow discussion here, the final steps in the process defined by the task force's terms of reference was to develop a relatively detailed action plan which specified, as far as possible, the organization(s) most appropriately responsible for undertaking each proposed initiative, the desired timing of various actions, and some preliminary estimate of the magnitude of the resources that would be likely to be required to develop a particular facility, event or programme.

Example 2: a more idealistic vision

The second case also concerns an example where the authors have direct experience. It

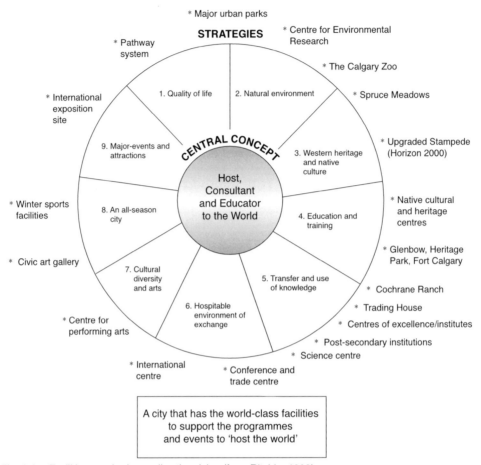

Fig. 8.4. Facilities required to realize the vision (from Ritchie, 1993).

involves a vision statement prepared for the Banff-Bow Valley Region, within which is located Banff National Park, Canada's oldest national park and the crown jewel of its national park system (Ritchie, 1999).

In this case, a professional task force was assembled by Canada's federal government to conduct what was formally known as the Banff-Bow Valley Study (BBVS). The task force was led by a prominent environmental studies academic and included a professional environmental consultant, a university biological scientist, a former executive from a large oil company and a tourism scholar.

The Banff-Bow Valley study's formal terms of reference described its purpose as follows:

The Bow Valley Study will be a comprehensive analysis of the state of the Bow Valley watershed in Banff National Park. The study will provide a baseline for understanding the implications of existing and future development and human use, and the impact of such on the heritage resources. The study will integrate environmental, social and economic considerations in order to develop management and land use strategies that are sustainable and meet the objectives of the National Parks Act.

(BBVS, 1996, p. 2)

Objectives

Within this overall purpose, the study had three major objectives:

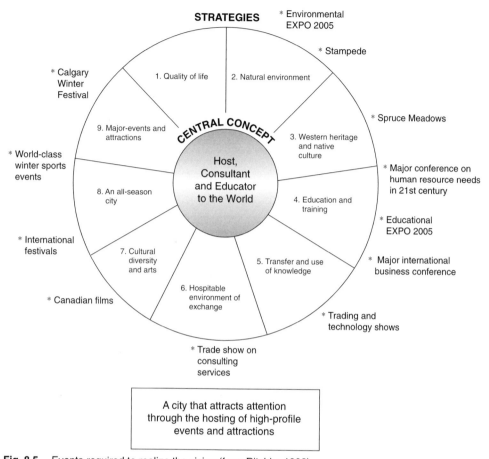

Fig. 8.5. Events required to realize the vision (from Ritchie, 1993).

- to develop a vision and goals for the Banff-Bow Valley that integrate ecological, social and economic values;
- to complete a comprehensive analysis of existing information and to provide direction for future collection and analysis of data to achieve ongoing goals; and
- to provide direction on the management of human use and development in a manner that will maintain ecological values and provide sustainable tourism.

The task force and study process

In assigning the task force this mandate, the then minister stressed the importance of consulting the Canadian public, in order to include them in the study process and to show respect for their views, when formulating final recommendations. As will be seen, this guideline heavily influenced the direction and work of the task force. At the outset, the task force identified six major initiatives it felt would allow it to fulfil its mandate:

- develop a programme to involve the public;
- collect and assess existing information about the Banff-Bow Valley;
- draft a vision, principles and values for the valley;
- identify and assess key issues;
- draft specific objectives and actions; and
- prepare recommendations for the Minister of Canadian Heritage.

The task force made an early decision that the study process should be explicitly driven by all stakeholder groups having an active and proven interest in ensuring the environmental, economic and social well-being of the park. In order to turn this philosophical commitment into hard reality, the task force established a formal round-table process. This round table served as the heart of the consultation, advisory and analysis activities that provided the task force with the information, ideas, insights and understanding used to formulate its final recommendations.

The round table: process, structure and composition

The round-table process, which served as the primary vehicle for soliciting public and community input, represented a shift from consulting the public. It asked them to share in the responsibility for making decisions about their national parks based on their interests rather than their positions (Fisher and Ury, 1991). This approach to consensus planning has been labelled 'interest-based negotiation' (IBN). In contrast to other approaches for obtaining public input and consensus, the IBN model not only sought consensus from participating stakeholders; it also transferred a meaningful percentage of actual decision-making power from the task force (representing the national government) to participating stakeholders (representing all Canadians). In specific terms, members of the task force agreed to the principle that if full consensus were reached by the round table on any recommendation of

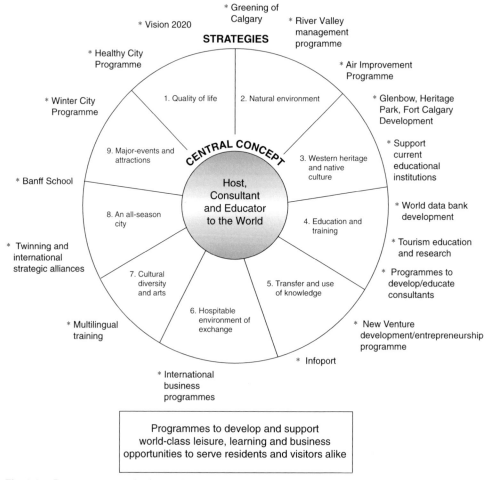

Fig. 8.6. Programmes required to realize the vision (from Ritchie, 1993).

substance, then that recommendation would, without further analysis or debate, be included in the task force's final report to the minister. In areas where full consensus was not achieved, responsibility for weighing the inputs received and the subsequent framing of final recommendations fell to the appointed task force.

The round table was composed of some 14 'interest sectors' (Fig. 8.7). Each of these sectors, as the name implies, was established to represent the interests of its constituents within the process designed to plan the future of the Banff-Bow Valley region. Each sector, in turn, comprised a chair, a working committee and a supporting constituency. The information-sharing and negotiation process was facilitated by a technical expert who worked with the round table members to develop procedural rules, to formulate a vision, principles and goals for the future of the region, to analyse the major issues involved, to reach consensus and to put forth final recommendations.

In imagining the future of the Banff-Bow Valley, the round table faced several unique challenges. These challenges stemmed largely from the valley's location in a national park. First, it had to consider that people in all parts of the country are concerned about what happens in Banff National Park. It is normal for the people who live in, work in and frequently visit the park to have a special interest in the Bow Valley. But national parks belong to all Canadians. Consequently, the vision had to reflect the ideas and aspirations of all citizens, regardless of their extent of visitation.

A second difficulty was the need to capture the essential purposes of a national park. While national parks make a useful and often sizeable contribution to the economy, their broader significance is not easy to quantify. The vision had to recognize the intrinsic value that dollars and cents have difficulty measuring (Prugh et al., 1995).

While crafting a vision is 'a license to dream', one must temper dreams with reality. In imagining the desired future for the Banff-Bow Valley, it was important to remember that achieving qualitative richness has a cost, one that all Canadians must be willing to pay. The

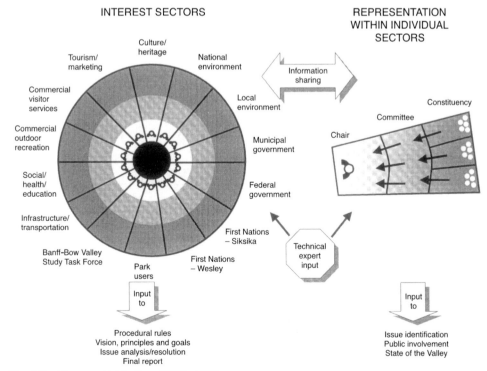

Fig. 8.7. The round table (from BBVS, 1996).

framework for the vision had to capture all these complexities.

Destination vision: a conceptual framework

As noted earlier, a vision can take many forms. In the present case, the members of the round table agreed upon the conceptual framework shown in Fig. 8.8. The framework had five distinct components. The first was a *preamble*, an introduction that sought to put the purpose, structure and content of the vision into context. The second component was a set of *anchor values* that defined the main values on which the development of the vision should be based. As Fig. 8.8 attempts to emphasize, the total vision rests firmly on the values from which it was derived. The set of values agreed to by members of the round table is summarized in Table 8.5.

The core vision

The third vision component, the *core vision*, consisted of a brief statement that consolidated all key dimensions of the desired future for the region. It was, in effect, the heart of the visioning document – a portrait describing how the task force hoped the region would evolve as it moved into the next century. The core vision reads as follows:

> The Bow Valley in Banff National Park reveals the majesty and wildness of the Rocky Mountains. It is a symbol of Canada, a place of great beauty, where nature is able to flourish and evolve. People from around the world participate in the life of the valley, finding inspiration, enjoyment, livelihoods and understanding. Through their wisdom and

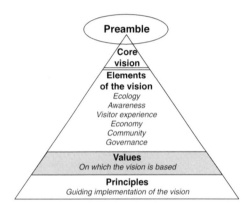

Fig. 8.8.   Destination vision: a conceptual framework (from BBVS, 1996).

Table 8.5.   A statement of the values on which the vision for the Banff-Bow Valley is based (from BBVS, 1996).

As Canadians concerned about the future of the Banff-Bow Valley, we are guided by these fundamental values:
- The value of exercising restraint and self-discipline today, for the sake of future generations
- The value of nature in and of itself
- The value of nature to human experience
- The value of national parks as protected areas
- The value of Banff National Park for all the people of the world as a World Heritage Site
- The value of the Banff-Bow Valley for its essential ecological role in the context of the park and the larger ecosystem
- The value of the Banff-Bow Valley, including the national transportation corridor, to the national, regional and local economy
- The value of safe, healthy, and hospitable communities
- The value of culture and history
- The value of open, participatory decision making
- The value of equal opportunity for a sense of wildness and a range of quality park experiences
- The value of predictable, consistent, and fair regulation
- The value of competent, accountable management
- The value of national parks to Canadians' sense of identity
- The value of wilderness preservation to Canada's image around the world
- The value of respect for others
- The value of freedom of access
- The value of education, enjoyment, and other park related benefits of the Bow Valley to visitors

foresight in protecting this small part of the planet, Canadians demonstrate leadership in forging healthy relationships between people and nature. The Banff-Bow Valley is, above all else, a place of wonder, where the richness of life is respected and celebrated.

(BBVS, 1996, p. 21)

Key themes

Following acceptance of the core vision, the working group felt it important, particularly from an operational standpoint, to identify a fourth component that consisted of a limited number of *supporting elements* that expanded on the core vision by developing various key messages in some detail. The intent was to ensure that the core theme will be translated into more specific statements that, while still inspirational in nature, provided more concrete yardsticks against which to measure success in translating the vision into reality. In the case of the Banff-Bow Valley, a total of six key themes were defined (BBVS, p. 21).

- *An ecological theme.* 'The Bow Valley in Banff National Park is a living example of the way in which ecological values are protected while appropriate kinds and levels of human activity are welcomed. Within the valley, natural systems and all their component native species are free to function and evolve. The Bow Valley supports and is supported by the natural systems of the region around it.'
- *A visitor experience theme.* 'The Bow Valley in Banff National Park is available to all Canadians and international guests who wish to participate in a diverse range of appropriate activities. They treat the park with respect. The quality of the natural environment is fundamental to the visitor experience, which is enriched by the quality of services provided.'
- *An awareness/education theme.* 'Understanding the value of our National Parks is a part of being Canadian. Education and awareness about National Park values, ethics, natural and cultural heritage, and services are provided both within and beyond the boundaries of the Park. Introduction to this knowledge is a fundamental part of each visitor's experiences.'

- *An economic theme.* 'A healthy economic climate, based on the heritage values of the Park, contributes to national, provincial and local economies. Businesses evolve and operate along aesthetically pleasing and environmentally responsible lines. Innovative ideas, designs and technology are emphasized when providing services including education, transportation, waste management, and other infrastructure.'
- *A community theme.* 'Communities in the Bow Valley are healthy and viable and are leaders in the quest for environmental and cultural sustainability. Residents are hospitable and pride themselves in accepting their responsibility for protecting and sharing this natural and cultural heritage for the benefit of present and future generations.'
- *A governance theme.* 'Federal, provincial and municipal authorities cooperate in protecting and managing the National Park and regional ecosystem. To achieve this, they nurture cooperation with businesses, organizations, and individuals. Public participation processes contribute to open, accountable, and responsible decision-making. Principles of precaution are exercised when the effects on the ecosystem are uncertain. Laws and regulations affecting the economy and the environment are consistent and predictable. Enforcement of regulations is consistent for all.'

Realizing the vision

The vision statement for the Banff-Bow Valley is admittedly rather idealistic and somewhat lengthy. Nevertheless, it has already served as the basis for the development of a heritage tourism strategy for the region (Sanford, 1997). This strategy, which stresses visitor education facilitated by both public and private sector programmes, is being guided in its realization by a series of guiding principles, which in themselves form the final component of the vision statement. The principles are given in Table 8.6.

In addition, the vision provided a considerable amount of direction for the preparation of

Table 8.6.   Principles guiding implementation of the vision (from BBVS, 1996).

The following principles guide all actions by government, business, communities, and the public.
- All actions, initiatives and programs undertaken to realize the Vision are implemented in full accordance with the spirit and requirements of the National Parks Act, Parks Canada's Guiding Principles and Operational Policies, and the Town of Banff Incorporation Agreement
- Standards are defined, enforced, and reviewed so as to ensure the maintenance of Ecological and Commemorative Integrity
- Regulation and decision-making are responsive, open, participatory, consistent, and equitable
- There is individual and shared responsibility to provide for protection and preservation of heritage resources, including buildings, within the Park
- Proactive, adaptive, and precautionary management take into account cumulative effects and limits to growth in recognition of the finite nature of the Valley
- Service and opportunities that provide high quality, affordable park experiences from front country to wilderness and that enhance understanding of national park values are stressed
- Stewardship, based on sound science, is practiced through environmentally sensitive management, mitigation, and restoration
- Education and experiences foster knowledge and understanding of the Banff-Bow Valley, its role in the larger ecosystem, and as part of a National Park and a World Heritage Site
- Educational opportunities are provided to foster understanding, appreciation, and respect for local culture
- Integrity and common sense underlie all decision making
- Economic analyses include consideration of natural, social, and cultural assets
- Only the kinds and levels of activities, facilities, and services that are appropriate to Banff National Park are permitted
- Marketing and communication programs are designed to develop a knowledge and understanding of Banff National Park, including expectations and limitations and reach out to all
- There is recognition that people enjoy and learn about nature in a variety of ways
- Residents within Banff National Park act in accordance with Park values, have a need to reside, and understand their ethical responsibilities to the rest of Canada
- The geographic area of the Town of Banff will not change, although the boundaries may be adjusted to achieve the goals of ecological integrity
- New communities are not developed within Banff National Park; the only communities that exist are the Town of Banff and the Lake Louise Visitor Centre
- The unique culture and history of the Bow Valley is preserved and presented
- Planning and decision making are coordinated on a regional basis
- The national transportation corridor is maintained and improved
- Partnerships are encouraged, subject to appropriate checks and balances
- There is a shared responsibility to achieve ecological, social, cultural, and economic sustainability

a revised Banff National Park Management Plan (Parks Canada, 1997). This plan is the primary document that prescribes the actions for all development decisions and for the ongoing operations of the Park.

Destination Positioning/Branding

Once consensus has been reached by stakeholders regarding the value-based philosophy and the vision that will drive the future of tourism in the destination, it then becomes possible to define the fourth major policy component:

the strategic positioning of the destination in the marketplace. In brief, positioning seeks to define how the destination is viewed both by the tourism market as a whole and by specific market segments in terms of the benefits and experiences it is likely to provide *vis-à-vis* the many competitive destinations from which travellers may choose. In effect, positioning involves strategic policy-level decisions by a destination regarding how it will seek to both differentiate itself from certain destinations while attempting to compete directly with others. In doing so, the destination will position itself so as to appeal strongly to certain market segments while accepting that it must forgo visitation from other market segments. On the basis of the positioning chosen, the destination then seeks to project this position to the marketplace through the development of a distinctive and strong destination brand. More formally, based on an adaptation of work by Aaker (1991), we define a destination brand as

> a name, symbol, logo, work mark or other graphic that both identifies and differentiates the destination; furthermore, it conveys the promise of a memorable travel experience that is uniquely associated with the destination; it also serves to consolidate and reinforce the recollection of pleasurable memories of the destination experience.
>
> (Ritchie and Ritchie, 1998, p. 103)

The first part of this definition addresses the traditional *identification* and *differentiation* functions of a brand. The second part, in contrast to traditional product branding, emphasizes that it is especially important that a destination brand convey, either explicitly or implicitly, the *promise* of the essence of leisure travel – *a memorable experience*: one that, if at all possible, is uniquely available at the destination in question. While product brands are also intended to convey a promise associated with satisfactory product use, the promise is usually of a more functional nature, being expressed in terms of either product performance or the quality of a particular service transaction. Exceptions might be for more pleasure-oriented products (such as perfume) or services (such as massage). In tourism, for a destination to compete and succeed, it must offer a high-quality stream of product/service transactions – or what is referred to as a 'quality experience' (Otto and Ritchie, 1995). At the same time, since anticipation and memory are significant components of a quality experience, any attempt at destination branding must attempt to reassure the individual concerning the promise or expectation of future pleasure and/or excitement. After travel, the brand can also play an important role in consolidating and reinforcing the post-travel recollections of a memorable destination experience.

Based on the foregoing discussions, we assert that in summary the primary roles of a destination brand are to provide:

Pre-experience: selection
- Identification ⎫
- Differentiation ⎪ the destination
- Anticipation ⎬ experience
- Expectation ⎪
- Reassurance ⎭

Post-experience: recollection
- Consolidation ⎫ of destination
- Reinforcement ⎬ memories

Some less important, or secondary, roles that a brand may play are listed below.

- To serve as a coordinating symbol for a broad range of community development and promotion efforts, many of which fall outside of the normal responsibility of a tourism DMO. Used in this fashion, a destination brand having tourism origins can greatly enhance the status of tourism within a community. The counter-risk, of course, is that the other agencies, whose efforts are being coordinated under the destination brand umbrella, may view destination branding as an attempt by the DMO to covertly assume some of their responsibilities and to co-opt associated resources.
- To generate revenue from the sales of clothing and memorabilia bearing the destination name or logo, etc.
- To serve as a security/theft identifier for materials and equipment belonging to the destination.

Destination Development

Once a destination has determined where it wishes to position itself in the marketplace and has developed a unique brand identity to differentiate itself from competitors (Morgan et al., 2002), the senior policy makers and managers of a destination must ensure that they have in place a rigorous programme of development that will translate the destination vision into reality. Since this is a complex topic, we deal with it more extensively in a later section. As will be seen, the strategic project management required to oversee development must constantly assess the degree to which the destination vision is being respected while maintaining a concern for both competitiveness and sustainability.

Competitive/Collaborative Analysis

Although this book is based on an ongoing concern for competitiveness, there is a growing recognition of the need for destinations to develop alliances (WTO, 2002) with a broad range of organizations, even to the point of collaboration with potential competitors. As an example, while New Zealand and Australia are competitive destinations in many ways, they recognize their interdependence and the benefits of strategic collaboration in selected major markets. Similarly, Canada and the USA, while also competitive in many markets, have also recognized the value of collaboration in the undertaking of research in markets of common interest (such as Europe).

At a more fundamental level, selected DMOs may seek to collaborate with other DMOs having a product that is competitive while having an element of mutual reinforcement. For example, Fort Worth, Texas, and Calgary, Canada, both of which position themselves as western/cowboy/rodeo experiences, may at times collaborate when attempting to enhance the mutual appeal of this visitation experience to Asian markets.

Yet other types of collaboration have a much stronger commercial flavour. Mega-events such as the Olympic Games and the World Cup are increasingly dependent on commercial alliances to help ensure financial viability. Credit card companies, automobile manufacturers and international fast-food retailers, such as McDonald's, are gaining a stronger visible presence both on-site and via television. Destinations such as Disneyland have for many years heavily involved a broad range of commercial partners, even though they risk siphoning off the benefits of their reputation and profits by doing so. Even competitive ski areas and resorts have found it beneficial to share some of their most strategic promotional programmes with competitors. Somehow, when chosen strategically, 'coopetition' (see Chapter 3) seems to work better than going it alone, at least in certain cases.

Clearly, the choice of collaborating partners must be made with care, and must be assessed from a policy as well as an operational perspective. The bottom line, however, is that the number of destinations, DMOs and firms that collaborate seems to be in the ascendancy.

Monitoring and evaluation

Another integral component of the process of destination policy, planning and development is the ongoing monitoring and evaluation of destination performance and the degree to which this performance is contributing to destination success. While destination success is a multidimensional concept, it is essentially related to the extent to which short to medium-term goals are being achieved, while in the longer term progress is being made towards realizing the vision that has been agreed upon by destination stakeholders.

One powerful means of carrying out the monitoring and evaluation process is by developing an 'index of success' for a destination. Such an index represents a combined set of carefully integrated multiple indicators that, over time, provides a longitudinal insight into the degree to which the destination is achieving success in relation to the goals it originally set for itself. We emphasize that the intent of such an index of success is not to be critical. Quite the contrary – the monitoring of destination performance is intended to provide an understanding of the kinds of actions and initiatives that work best in achieving success, so that they can be given even greater emphasis in future policies. Conversely, should certain policies and programmes be found less effective, then ongoing monitoring provides plenty of lead time for change and adaptation, where it seems appropriate.

Destination audit

The destination audit is the final policy component and represents a logical extension of the monitoring and evaluation process. In effect, the audit seizes upon the opportunity to take all we have learned about the competitiveness and sustainability of a destination from past performance, from ongoing research and from the managerial intuition of senior policy makers and managers, in order to make the destination work even better in the future. In brief, the audit represents the culmination of the policy/management cycle of learning, with a view to improved action in the future.

Because of the importance of the audit in helping to make the destination work better as we move into the future, we have devoted an entire chapter (Chapter 11) to this topic.

Relating Policy to Strategy and the Development Process

As we have stressed, the role of tourism policy is to establish a socioeconomic environment that will enable tourism to develop and prosper in a sustainable manner. It must constantly be kept in mind, however, that this sustainable development must in itself take place within a broader surrounding social, economic, environmental, cultural, legal and political system which provides the larger mega-policy framework that tourism must acknowledge and function within.

As tourism strives to develop, it must adopt specific strategies in order to implement the policies defined by the destination vision. As a first step in the adaptation, it is useful to specify a range of tourism objectives that operationalize the steps required to realize the destination vision.

The objectives of the tourism system should possess a number of important characteristics. First, since the objectives are formulated in the light of the tourism vision, their achievement should clearly contribute to the fulfilment of this vision. Second, in order for the objectives to be qualified as operational, it is essential that managers are able to measure the extent to which desired results have or have not been attained. This implies that we must have some explicit means of quantifying appropriate performance standards. Third, we must ensure that the measures selected with respect to each objective are indeed valid indicators of the desired results; that is, they measure what we truly want to achieve. Fourth, in the common situation where the tourism system has multiple objectives, it is advisable to indicate an order or priority among

objectives. This indication of relative importance provides a basis for decision making should different strategies or programmes for achieving the objective be in conflict. Fifth, the objectives must be related to a given time period, as is stated directly in the above definition. Finally, the objectives that are stated must be reasonable. They should serve to offer a real challenge, but as the destination seeks to realize its vision the goals that are virtually impossible to attain will quickly become a negative rather than a positive source of motivation.

One further remark concerning the formal statement of objectives is in order. Objectives identify those events or results that we wish to bring about. While not universally so, the word 'objective' implies that the result is a positive entity, such as a certain number of visitors. In fact, the managers of a tourism system may be seeking goals with respect to what they do not want to happen as a consequence of their activities. Examples include the avoidance of environmental and cultural pollution. These types of results could be stated as specific objectives of the tourism system. Although they are very important, their essentially negative nature provides little incentive for management action. An alternative and more satisfactory manner of dealing with effects that one wishes to avoid is to express them in the form of constraints. A common approach to formally stating constraints on system activities is to specify, where possible, the maximum level of each undesirable outcome (e.g. pollution) that can be tolerated as a result of tourism activity. Even where it is difficult to quantify the tolerable levels of undesirable outcomes, constraints can be formulated so as to at least provide explicit indications as to the type of outcomes to be minimized or avoided.

Tourism development strategies may be viewed as falling into three broad categories: supply development strategies, demand development strategies and organizational structure strategies.

Supply development strategies

Strategies in this category are concerned with major actions related to five main groupings of resources (Fig. 8.9), each of which is required to provide an attractive, viable tourism destination. These are physical resources, human resources, financial resources, information resources and programme/activity resources. Together, these five fundamental resource categories cover all of the many determinants of destination competitiveness/sustainability as defined by our basic model (Fig. 3.1).

When formulating tourism resource development strategies, it is essential that attention be paid to identifying the relative strengths and weaknesses of each of the above resource categories and their component elements in determining the principle actions necessary to upgrade the quality of each component/element of attractiveness. In so doing, it should be remembered that different destinations can (and normally do) arrive at satisfactory levels of attractiveness for each of the elements in different ways. Strategy formulation involves careful selection and development of those elements in each category that offer the greatest potential for the destination in question.

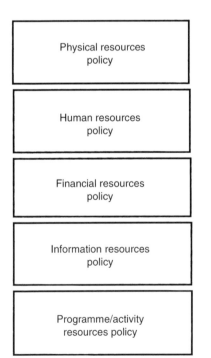

Fig. 8.9. Major components of tourism supply policy.

Physical resources policy

The *physical resources* of a tourism destination represent perhaps the most fundamental determinant of its attractiveness. For strategic planning purposes, these determinants of attractiveness can be viewed as falling into three major categories. These categories and the elements they contain are given in Box 8.1a. The first category of elements in value are those that reflect the *fundamental nature* of the destination and its people. These include the destination's *natural physiography*, its *climate* and its *social characteristics*, including its cultural and historic elements. These fundamental elements offer limited possibility of modification for tourism purposes, although the protection of historic sites can be critical. A modest amount of physical modification of

---

Box 8.1a.   Physical resources policy: dimensions of policy

Policies addressing the fundamental nature of the destination
- Enhancement of the appeal of the location
- Minimization of climatic factors on visitor enjoyment and satisfaction
- Historic and cultural site protection and maintenance

Policies to strengthen general and basic services infrastructure
- General services infrastructure
- Visitor access and transportation facilities
- Telecommunications infrastructure

Policies to maintain and enhance environmental integrity
- Improvement of carrying capacity without environmental degradation
- Comprehensive resource stewardship
- Monitoring of visitor impacts

Policies concerning the tourism superstructure
- Upgrading of cultural, historical and natural attractions/parks
- Ensuring excellence in tourism receptive plant (accommodation, food services)
- Innovation and quality in tourism attractions
- Convenience and efficiency in immigration facilities
- Enhancement of range and quality of visitor service facilities

the destination may also be done to minimize the impacts of unpleasant climatic conditions. They might include the irrigation of the land in dry, hot climates, or the provision of protective shelters in colder climates. The second type consists of policies to maintain and improve the *general infrastructure* and the *basic services infrastructure*. The third type includes those components of destination attractiveness that are directly related to and largely controlled by the tourism system, and that we refer to as the *tourism superstructure*. They include visitor access and transport facilities, residential and receptive tourism plant, tourism attractions and, to a lesser degree, attitudes or hospitality towards visitors.

Finally, an increasingly significant physical resource is *the environment*, where concern for determining the appropriate carrying capacity of a destination is critical, and largely determined by visitor impacts, which need to be carefully monitored. The end goal is a comprehensive programme of resource stewardship, of which the environment is only one part. Clearly, the ability of the tourism manager to directly influence the desirability of a destination differs for the different types of physical resources.

Human resources policy

Human resources represents a second major category of supply resources that must be considered when formulating supply development strategies in tourism (Box 8.1b). Concern here must focus on the quantity, the quality and the mix of personnel available to meet the tourism needs of the country or region in question. *Quantity* measures the number of persons wishing to work in tourism-related activities and is to a large extent determined by the attractiveness of working conditions in the tourism field relative to those provided by other opportunities. Strategic actions in this regard must therefore be directed at improving the desirability of tourism careers in terms of both their monetary and non-monetary dimensions. *Quality*, as it refers to human resources in tourism, is a more complex issue. It refers to the technical, professional and managerial competence of personnel as reflected in their ability to perform the tasks essential to the

provision of a broad range of necessary skills. These skills are difficult to define and even more difficult to measure. In essence, these human resources skills are those that deliver the functionality required, that give the tourist the feeling that their presence is both welcome and appreciated, and that service is being provided willingly and with enthusiasm. From a strategic management standpoint, the question of the quality of tourism personnel must be addressed through education and training programmes designed to improve both professional and human relations skills. Finally, the *mix* of human resources refers to the distribution of available tourism personnel throughout the tourism system, both in terms of quantity and quality. An imbalance in the mix exists when the number of personnel having particular skills is either insufficient or exceeds the requirements of particular sectors of the

---

Box 8.1b.   Human resources policy: dimensions of policy

Quantity dimension
- Level/number of personnel required by the tourism system of the destination

Quality dimension
- Technical, professional and managerial competence of personnel required by the destination

Human resource mix dimension
- Achieving the proper balance in terms of personnel types
- Achieving the proper balance in terms of seasonality of demand
- Flexibility, adaptability of personnel

Institutional capability
- Ensuring the availability of institutions capable of providing education/training to human resource needs

Enterprise development
- Initiatives to strengthen and maintain the entrepreneurial capability and spirit of individuals and firms in the destination
- Development and support of career paths for members of the local tourism industry

Hospitality development
- Encouragement and facilitation of resident willingness and ability to welcome visitors

tourism system. The strategic management of human resources must therefore be focused in two main directions. First, it must concentrate on forecasting human resource needs in order that educational and training activities can be appropriately adjusted. Second, in a field as diverse and seasonal as tourism, strategic human resource planning must be also concerned with developing flexibility among personnel in order to offer individuals greater opportunity while at the same time improving the performance of the total system.

Once the quantity, quality and mix dimensions of human resource policy have been formulated, it then becomes essential to determine how these needs will be met – either through the education and training of destination residents or by importing foreign labour. Given a policy of self-determination, it becomes necessary to define and develop the *institutional capabilities* that will be needed to deliver the education and training that are required to support the human resource policy needs of the destination.

As an underlying element of human resources policy, efforts should also be made to foster the entrepreneurial or *enterprise spirit* of individuals and firms within the destination. And finally, while the resident population may be viewed as a physical resource, efforts must be made from a training perspective to encourage and facilitate their willingness and ability to *host visitors in a hospitable manner* that will make them feel welcome.

Financial resources policy

Financial resources (Box 8.1c) is another component of tourism supply development strategies. Once the strategic development requirements have been identified with respect to physical and human resources, it becomes necessary to find the capital to implement the chosen strategy. In making this statement, it is recognized that the formulation of physical and human resource development strategies could not originally have been carried out without some reference to the possibilities of funding. The process thus tends to be an iterative one that necessarily recognizes the interdependence of physical, human and financial resources. Given this situation, financial

resource planning involves decisions concerning amounts of capital, sources of capital and the conditions under which it is obtained. The *amounts of capital* required depend on the size and scope of the actions planned for physical and human resource development. These capital needs will also depend on the amount required for *investment* (or destination facility development) and the amount required for *operating* purposes.

Identifying and selecting *sources of capital* is a complex issue and one that takes heavily into account the tourism philosophy and objectives of the country or region, as well as its available economic resources. Consequently, strategic decisions concerning sources of capital must consider the extent to which private or public funding is desired, whether foreign capital is to be sought or permitted, and whether funding is available from special sources, such as international development agencies. Finally, decisions must also be made concerning the conditions under which funding will be provided to projects in both the public and the private sectors. Examples of strategic decisions in this area are those regarding the desired mix of debt and equity capital, the optimal length of borrowing periods and the desirability or necessity of incentives, or public subsidization, for specific forms of development.

Information resources policy

Another critical support area of supply policy is that of *information resources* (Box 8.1d). While information may have been regarded as somewhat of a luxury in the past, DMOs are now fully aware of the vital role of relevant

---

Box 8.1c. Financial resources policy: dimensions of policy

Financial needs policy
- Supply of venture capital
- Long-term capital investment needs
- Operational capital needs
- Source of capital policy
  - Public versus private capital
  - Domestic versus foreign capital
  - Debt versus equity capital
- Special incentives policy

Box 8.1d. Information resources policy: dimensions of policy

Monitoring
- Market indicators, behaviour
- Destination performance
- Environmental scanning
- Visitor enquiry data

Research
- Market research
- Competitive analysis
- Destination effectiveness

Dissemination
- Membership support
- Resident awareness development
- Key stakeholder relations

Box 8.1e. Programme/activity resources policy: dimensions of policy

Facility development programmes
- Key success facilities

Event/activity development programmes
- Critical/new event development

Activity consolidation programmes
- Strengthening of safety and security
- Building of stakeholder support
- Political will development

and timely information. The ability to respond to shifting market demands and the growing social pressure on tourism is totally dependent on an awareness and understanding of these factors.

The *awareness* factor of information policy is typically fulfilled by the ongoing *monitoring* of market conditions and public opinion. This monitoring is commonly referred to as 'environmental scanning' – a process by which exceptions to managerial expectations serve as a trigger for DMO actions. In contrast to monitoring, the *understanding* factor of information policy is met by more focused and more in-depth *research* on critical topics identified by the environmental scanning process – or by issues that emerge on a crisis basis.

The factors discussed above represent *inflows* of information, but destinations must also concern themselves with the strategic outward *dissemination* of information. Efforts are directed primarily to the support of membership, building resident awareness of the significance of tourism and the need to welcome visitors, and particularly to information designed for building relationships with key stakeholder groups.

Programme/activity resources policy

The final component of supply policy represents to some extent a consolidation of all the dimensions (Box 8.1e). *Programme or activity resources* are the various focused activities

of a DMO that ensure that policies, ideas and concepts get translated into reality on a very practical basis. From a policy perspective, these efforts tend to be developed around three themes. The first of these is the planning and development of the *facilities* needed for the destination to compete successfully. Second is the planning and establishment of *events* of the kind of that will enhance destination appeal, with a constant effort being made to identify and support innovative ideas for new types of events that may be emerging – particularly those that will help build the destination vision. Third, there is a need for determining how best to categorize the broad range of activities that go on within a destination into *programmes*, so that they can be managed effectively and efficiently. Examples include membership development programmes that seek to expand and strengthen the membership of a DMO, and membership support programmes (training, access to financing). Other programmes that might be envisaged are collaborative promotions, consolidated purchasing programmes and community relations programmes.

To conclude, it must be emphasized that, once overall supply development strategies have been enunciated and appropriate implementation structures put in place, these strategies must be translated into specific programmes of an operational nature. At this level, the management process becomes one of detailed planning and execution of the many tasks necessary to provide the individual tourist with the satisfying yet challenging experience that he or she is seeking. A more detailed discussion of tourism management is given in Chapter 9.

The need to effectively translate strategic ideas into real-world actions cannot be stressed too strongly. Without effective execution, even the most brilliant policies will prove of little value.

Demand development (marketing) strategies

Demand development strategies in tourism involve decisions with respect to three primary components and three secondary components (Box 8.2).

Primary components

These are:

- the overall *level* of marketing support that should be provided;
- the selection of strategic *target* markets; and
- strategic destination *positioning* in strategic markets.

OVERALL LEVEL OF MARKETING SUPPORT. The total *level* of expenditures for demand development should ideally be derived from an analysis of the effort needed to meet the demand objectives in each target market. Commonly however, this ideal amount will exceed the maximum total of funds that are available to support such efforts. In these instances, the actual level of funds available may be defined by some arbitrary figure, possibly some percentage of total tourism receipts. In any event, the

amount that is finally available is especially critical in that it limits the extent to which the destination can compete against its many rivals.

SELECTION OF STRATEGIC TARGET MARKETS. The selection decision concerning appropriate *targets* of demand development activities is also critical since it determines which markets are excluded from future consideration. Given the importance of this decision, it is essential that it be based on the best possible information concerning the potential of alternative markets and the feasibility of tapping each market. Once the most desirable target markets have been identified, one then proceeds to define demand objectives that should be met for each market segment. These objectives form the basis for the ultimate evaluation of demand management efforts.

The determination of the appropriate *mix* of demand management efforts within each target market requires an in-depth understanding of the information needs and decision-making processes of the members of each target market segment. For certain types of markets, such as the corporate travel market, a highly selective personal selling approach may prove most effective. In the case of special interest groups, careful selection of print media may offer the greatest returns. In yet other markets, where awareness of a destination is low, traditional mass media advertising, accompanied by public relations press articles, may prove to be an essential first step in demand development. Most target markets can be most effectively attacked through a judiciously chosen combination of all available techniques.

DESTINATION POSITIONING IN THE MARKETPLACE. As mentioned previously, the positioning of a destination in the minds of potential visitors from strategic market segments is a particularly challenging task that demands considerable creativity. As such, it requires accurate and current information concerning market perceptions of each destination – and its competitors. Since the perceptions of any destination are not infrequently determined by factors largely outside the control of destination managers (such as schooling, press reports, television programming and previous experiences), we should not overestimate the ability of a

---

Box 8.2. Major components of tourism demand policy

Primary components
- Level of marketing expenditures
- Strategic target market selection
- Destination positioning in the marketplace

Secondary components
- Advertising/promotion policy
  - Level
  - Theming
  - Timing
- Pricing policy
- Packaging and distribution policy

destination to define its image in the market-place. Nevertheless, DMOs can have some meaningful influence on how potential visitors view their destination. Creative advertising, carefully orchestrated press stories, the hosting of major events and the judicious choice of symbols and icons can raise the profile and modestly modify the image of a city, state or country. Finally, uncontrollable world events can sometimes prove to be highly fortuitous and at other times highly negative.

Secondary components

While decisions regarding promotion policy, pricing policy and packaging and distribution policy may be termed 'secondary' from a strategic perspective, they are nevertheless not to be dismissed lightly. Although the decisions tend to be somewhat more operational in nature, they very directly affect the nature and structure of demand development. If not executed properly, they can negate the value of a brilliant overall policy.

ADVERTISING/PROMOTION POLICY.   Decisions concerning the allocation of available funds for destination advertising and promotion across target markets is directly related to the mix of efforts selected. Certain types of promotional activities may be more expensive relative to others. In addition, they may require some minimum or threshold level of expenditure to achieve any impact at all. Despite these complexities, decisions must be made concerning how to divide total available funds across target markets that offer different potential returns and which may be at different stages of development in terms of their current propensity to visit a given country or region. These different stages may require advertising and promotion designed to simply increase *awareness* of the destination as a potential vacation site. Somewhat better known destinations will place a greater stress on enhancing knowledge and understanding of the destination. In cases where the destination is very well known in a specific target market, advertising and promotion expenditures are more likely to focus on influencing more immediate decisions regarding destination choice for specific travel experiences.

Finally, decisions must be made concerning the most appropriate *timing* for the implementation of demand development efforts and the most appropriate *theming* within each target market. Given the variations in demand across different time periods that are commonly found in tourism and the highly variable mentalities of target markets, it is essential that strategies be developed to ensure that demand development efforts are instituted at the time when they are likely to have the greatest impact. Similarly, the message conveyed must be relevant and meaningful for each potential visitor.

PRICING POLICY.   One look at the advertisements in the travel section of any newspaper will highlight the importance that the travel industry places on 'visible prices' in the marketplace. One should not, however, be misled. The travel market is becoming increasingly sophisticated. With every passing year, the well-travelled elements of the market are increasingly able to discern true value in travel, and they cannot be duped in most circumstances. Accordingly, destinations that are seeking to be competitive on a sustainable basis must offer value for money. It follows that the pricing of travel experiences, to the extent that they are controllable by a destination, must be kept realistic in relation to alternative offerings. This requires high-quality information concerning visitor needs and competitive pricing and the ability to deliver travel experiences in an efficient manner.

PACKAGING AND DISTRIBUTION.   As discussed very early in this book, the nature of distribution of the travel product is evolving at an alarming speed. The traditional distribution channels (through travel wholesalers and retailers) are constantly being challenged by technologically driven alternatives. While all this is happening, however, destination managers and travel industry operators need to keep clearly in mind that they are selling unique travel experiences to many different individuals, who realize these experiences one at a time. Because of this, the need for simplification and for human concern in the delivering of tourism services is an underlying force that will never be totally replaced by high-tech solutions.

Organizational and development policy

Organizational policy (Box 8.3) is yet another area that, until recently, has received little formal attention. In effect, the organizational capability for developing and implementing tourism policy has often been essentially left to chance.

Today, however, the importance of the critical roles played by the DMO are well established (Getz *et al.*, 1998). Without the effective leadership and coordination of a committed Convention and Visitor Bureau, a destination is ill-equipped to be either competitive or sustainable. The entity to which this responsibility falls is the DMO. The exact nature and name of this DMO depends on the level and type of destination in question.

- At the country level, the organization is normally referred to as the National Tourism Organization (NTO). Examples are the British Tourism Authority (BTA) and the Australian Tourism Commission (ATC).
- At the state or provincial level, the organization is most commonly referred to as the State Tourism Office or the Provincial Department of Tourism.
- At the city or municipal level, the organizational structure that dominates is most frequently identified as a Convention and Visitor Bureau (CVB).

Box 8.3.   Major components of organizational development and policy

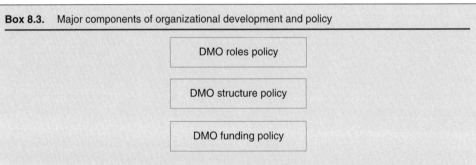

- Serve as the body responsible for coordinating the marketing and promotional efforts of the destination
- Provide leadership concerning the overall nature and direction of tourism planning and development for the destination
- Act as a catalyst to initiate and facilitate the realization of destination development priorities
- Serve as an effective voice of the tourism sector in efforts to enhance the awareness and understanding of both governments and the general public concerning the economic and social importance of tourism
- Act as a representative of the tourism sector in all public and private forums where the views and position of the tourism sector need to be presented and explained
- Provide an easily recognizable and easily accessible interface between tourism and other sectors of the economy
- Coordinate the identification and delivery of commercial visitor services (such as information/ service centres)
- Coordinate the identification and meeting of the information/research needs of the tourism sector with the destination
- Attempt to ensure that the education and training needs of the tourism sector are adequately met
- In certain cases, act as an investor/owner/operator of tourism facilities considered essential to the development and well-being of the destination
- Identify and coordinate the establishment of partnerships and alliances which strengthen the competitiveness of the destination
- Where possible and appropriate, assist in the search for sources of financial assistance for members of the tourism sector of the destination

Roles, tasks and responsibilities of the destination management organization

A DMO may be either a public sector agency or a private sector-driven organization. Whatever its nature, it must be constituted in a manner that provides it with certain key characteristics.

- It must be clearly identifiable as the organization responsible for coordinating and directing the efforts of the many parts of the diverse and complex tourism system.
- It must command the support of all important sectors and all major actors in the tourism system.
- It must be capable of influencing the decisions and actions of the many public sector agencies/departments and private firms that directly determine the nature and quality of the tourism experience provided to visitors.
- It must possess the tools necessary to stimulate and encourage the type and amount of supply development that is required by the overall tourism megapolicy.
- It must be sufficiently independent and flexible to develop innovative strategies that can be implemented in a timely manner in response to rapidly evolving market and environmental conditions.

Following a review of the above requirements, it becomes more evident why it is generally felt that the most effective organizational form is an independent organization, be it a ministry of tourism or a CVB. In cases where such a ministry or bureau does not exist, the explanation usually derives from two main sources. It may be that tourism is a relatively unimportant economic factor in the country, region or city in question and as such does not merit the expenditure of the funds necessary to support an independent ministry or bureau. In these cases, tourism policy and development responsibilities are commonly subsumed within some larger ministry or city department, such as those concerned with economic development, parks and recreation, or even cultural affairs. A second major reason why a ministry or bureau does not exist may reflect the political philosophy of the country, region or city. In certain

countries, notably the USA, the diversity of the country and the existence of relatively strong private sector associations in tourism have led to a low level of public sector leadership with respect to tourism development. In addition, this situation appears to be exacerbated by a lower level of government regulation of both supply and demand development activities than is found in many other countries.

Organizational structure of the destination management organization

In addition to defining the roles of the DMO (Box 8.3), organizational policy should also provide guidance concerning the appropriate internal structure for it. Several alternatives are possible. Some DMOs are primarily based on individual membership and others tend to be structured as a federation of supporting organizations (such as chambers of commerce, hotel associations, restaurant associations and other city 'booster groups'). The internal structure of others reflects the fact that they are, in reality, a department of the municipal government.

It is interesting to note that few, if any, countries/regions have experimented with more novel forms of organization lying somewhere between the public and the private models. For example, a public sector model has been used in a number of countries/regions to direct and coordinate national/provincial efforts in such diverse fields as air service, petroleum development, postal services, rural services, medical services and hydroelectric power. These fields have some common characteristics. Importantly, most of them are primarily involved in the provision of services (often public utilities) rather than the manufacture of products. Also, most depend heavily on the use of public or natural resources and all must satisfy some minimum standards of performance. Currently, the Korean Tourism Corporation is one example of a public sector corporation in tourism.

Alternatively, increasing pressure for privatization of the tourism system in some destinations has led to the creation of some hybrid organizational forms. In Canada, the Canadian Tourism Commission (CTC), while driven by the private sector, depends very heavily on public sector funding. In addition, it has incorporated into itself many of the resources and personnel of the former federal government department known as Tourism Canada. The province of Alberta, Canada, briefly experimented with a public/private sector model known as the Alberta Tourism Partnership. It was not particularly successful.

Funding policy for the destination management organization

The organizational structure that is adopted has a major impact on DMO funding policy. Membership-based DMOs rely heavily on membership fees; federation-based structures are usually financed by constituents of the federation. Municipal department DMOs, as might be expected, are highly dependent on local taxation for funding. These tax funds may come directly from city coffers or indirectly by means of a local hotel tax, which may be either voluntary or compulsory (the norm).

A problem of major concern in relation to DMO funding is the 'free-rider'. Many firms, organizations and individuals who benefit substantially from the leadership, coordination and promotional activities of the DMO refuse to become members of the DMO, or at least avoid becoming members or contributing to its financial needs. A large number may claim that they are not in the tourism business even though they may benefit significantly from visitor expenditures.

Given the above problems, which should be a policy issue addressed by the DMO's board of directors, they are often passed on to the DMO's manager, with the result that he or she will be forced to expend an enormous amount of time and energy raising funds – and consequently be diverted from managerial responsibilities. The practical problems of addressing DMO funding are dealt with at greater length in the chapter on destination management.

The process of tourism policy formulation

Discussion to this point in the chapter has focused on the structure and content of tourism policy. In this section, attention is directed towards understanding the process by which tourism policy, as presented in Fig. 3.1, may be developed. This process is conceptualized as containing 11 distinct stages grouped into four main phases (Fig. 8.10). These phases are identified as the definitional phase, the analytical phase, the operational phase and the implementation phase.

Definitional phase	Analytical phase	Operational phase	Implementation phase
Definition of tourism destination system	Internal analysis • Review of existing policies and programmes	Identification of strategic conclusions	Implementation of strategy for destination development, promotion and stewardship
Explication of a tourism philosophy	• Destination audit	Implications of conclusions for supply and demand development	
Crafting of a destination vision	• Strategic impact analysis		Allocation of responsibilities for recommendation implementation
	External analysis	Policy/programme recommendations	
Specification of destination objectives and constraints	• Macro-level analysis of current and future demand		Identification of sources of funding to support competitive initiatives and stewardship programmes
	• Micro-level analysis of current and future demand and behaviours		
	• Review of competitive and supportive tourism development and promotion policies		Specification of timing for recommendation implementation

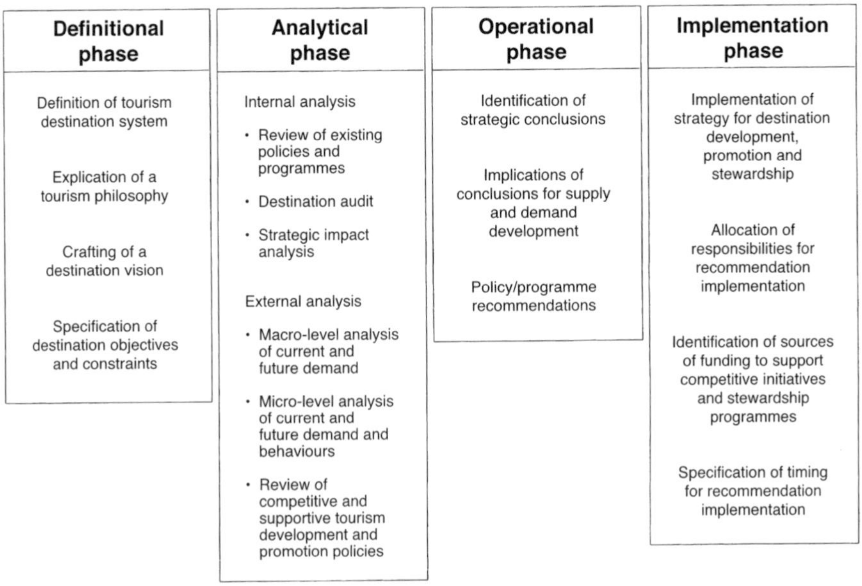

Fig. 8.10. The process of tourism policy and strategy formulation and implementation.

Definitional phase

The definitional phase of tourism policy formulation is concerned with the development of explicit statements that define the content and direction of the overall tourism system in question. As shown in Fig. 8.10, these statements deal with four different topics.

DEFINING THE TOURISM SYSTEM. The definition of the destination tourism system is the critical first step in the process of policy formulation. Despite its importance, this phase is frequently overlooked or implicitly assumed. As a result, it is common to find widely varying perceptions among policy makers and tourism officials concerning the nature and structure of the entity that they propose to manage. The consequence of this lack of perceptional congruence is that the subsequent thought processes of policy makers are frequently focused on divergent components of the tourism system. The most serious aspect of this phenomenon is that the individuals involved may not recognize these perceptual differences and assume that other policy makers view the tourism system in a manner consistent with their own perception.

The above statements are not meant to imply that a tourism system cannot be conceptualized and defined in different ways, since such is clearly not the case. Indeed, the fact that this is possible reinforces the need for a particular region to adapt a specific definition of its tourism system so that a common frame of reference is acknowledged by those involved in the policy-making process.

Figure 8.11 (from Goeldner and Ritchie, 2003) provides one model that might be useful as the basic conceptual framework to help define a tourism system. It views the tourism system as being constructed of two major components, the operating sectors and the planning/catalyst organizations. These in turn contain various sub-components which form the basis for identifying and classifying the individual organizations and actors (stakeholders) that make up a given tourism system. The detailed identification of destination stakeholders has been addressed earlier in this chapter. In any case, it is essential that each region develop a model of its structure and that it should identify its stakeholders in a way that

is generally accepted by the policy makers concerned. Once agreed to, these definitions should become a constant frame of reference for discussion and decision making.

The importance of the need to explicitly define the stakeholders in the tourism system has led certain countries to set up a separate framework and an associated system of accounts that clearly identifies the supply-side components of the tourism industry and their individual contributions to the gross domestic product. This special system of accounts is commonly referred to as a 'satellite account' (Smith, 1995; WTO, 2001).

The remaining three components of the definitional phase (Fig. 8.10) involve the explication of a tourism philosophy, the formulation of a destination vision, and the determination of tourism objectives and constraints for the destination. Previous discussion has described the content of these policy components; attention here focuses on issues concerning the process involved in specifying this content. In this regard, three comments are particularly relevant. First, since the specification of these components has implications that go beyond the tourism system itself, the process employed must ensure that inputs are obtained from the total environment, many parts of which are not normally associated with tourism. This environment may include a range of entities but particular importance must be attached to the overall views of the government of the day and those of the general public. Second, while a broad range of inputs must be sought, and listened to, the goal of the process is not necessarily consensus, since a high level of agreement from such a wide range of inputs is rarely achieved. Rather, what is required is a series of clear statements that reflect the desires of destination stakeholders while at the same time being realistic and capable of implementation. Finally, once agreed to by the majority of policy makers, there must be a clear commitment to these statements as the basis for policy making by all concerned for an extended period of time. While these statements should be reviewed periodically to assess their continued relevance, such a review should not occur too frequently. Constant questioning of the fundamental directions of a tourism system only serves to divert energies from the important implementation tasks that must follow.

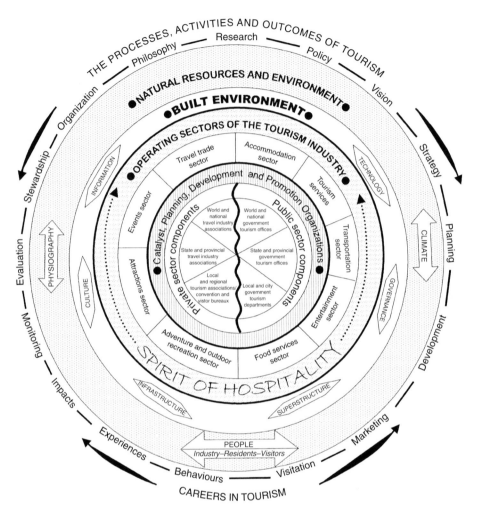

Fig. 8.11. The tourism phenomenon: components of tourism and tourism management (from Goeldner and Ritchie, 2003).

EXPLICATING A DESTINATION PHILOSOPHY. The explication of a tourism philosophy for the destination is a phase in which all destination stakeholders are forced to carefully assess their personal values with a view to reaching consensus on the fundamental role that tourism should play in the life of the region. Traditionally, tourism has been viewed primarily as a generator of economic well-being (income, employment). While an economic philosophy still tends to underlie the rationale for most tourism-related development, some destinations now incorporate social, cultural and environmental concerns, and even concerns for world peace, into

their destination philosophy. It may well be that pragmatic factors have stimulated the explication of these multidimensional philosophies. Whatever the reasons, we have seen a broadening of the philosophical justification for tourism development in recent years.

CRAFTING A DESTINATION VISION.   Perhaps the single most important and most challenging component of this phase of policy formulation is the crafting of a tourism destination vision. The use of the term 'crafting' is deliberate (Mintzberg, 1987). Whereas strategic planning has in the past been viewed as a highly deliberate and structured process, current thinking emphasizes the intuitive and interactive nature of effective strategy planning and policy formulation. Nowhere in the policy process is this truer than in the preparation of a destination vision statement. Given the fundamental importance of this phase of policy formulation, it has been addressed in detail earlier in this chapter (see *Crafting versus formulating a vision*, pp. 154–164).

SPECIFYING DESTINATION OBJECTIVES.   As noted earlier, a destination vision paints an inspirational portrait of an ideal future at some relatively distant point in the future. The visioning process is therefore a creative and value-laden one. In contrast, the process of specifying destination objectives requires a less idealistic process that is closer in touch with immediate realities. While still consensus-oriented, the process of setting objectives seeks to define measurable goals, which are most frequently tied to visitation and revenue levels and to organizational performance (effectiveness and efficiency). In addition, the time frames involved are much shorter and more tightly defined.

SPECIFYING DESTINATION CONSTRAINTS.   The process of specifying policy constraints must also be considerably more hard-nosed than the process of visioning. Here it is necessary to have common agreement on the negative possibilities that simply cannot be tolerated. While environmental groups often play a dominant role in this area, the realities of the marketplace and human nature are also major determinants of the constraints that are placed on tourism development within a destination.

Analytical phase

The analytical phase of tourism policy development, while perhaps less stressful than the previous one from a managerial standpoint, involves considerably greater amounts of effort. The definitional phase requires fundamental, value-based decisions concerning the nature and direction of tourism development in a region. The analytical phase accepts these decisions as a given and proceeds to carry out the extensive collection and assessment of information needed to identify and assess the desirability of alternative means of attaining the destination vision and to achieve the goals defined by the vision.

The overall process of analysis is best viewed as being composed of two major subprocesses: an *internal* or supply-oriented analysis, and an *external* or demand-oriented analysis.

The *internal/supply analysis* consists of a thorough review and analysis (frequently termed an audit) of two major elements. The first element relates to existing policies and programmes for the development of the various components of tourism supply. These policies/programmes must be reviewed critically to determine the extent to which they are both consistent with and effective in developing the type of tourism facilities and services that are likely to achieve the goals of the region, given the nature of demand facing that region. As can be quickly seen, this statement implies a direct interaction between the supply analysis and the demand analysis. In effect, the analytical phase involves parallel, iterative forms of analysis that must constantly relate one to the other.

A second element of the supply analysis is termed a resource audit. A resource audit should be conducted with two goals in mind. First, it should provide a comprehensive catalogue of the quantity and distribution of tourism facilities and services within the tourism system. Such information is basic to an understanding of the current state of affairs of supply development. Second, the resource audit should provide some assessment of the quality of existing facilities and services. Again, the execution of the audit to assess the adequacy of the quantity, distribution and quality of supply can only be meaningful if it is eventually related to the analysis of demand. There are no absolute measures of desirability in terms of supply – only those that relate to a given demand at a given point in time for a given market segment are relevant.

The third form of internal analysis is a strategic impact analysis. This analysis seeks to provide policy makers with well-defined benchmarks of the extent to which tourism is currently impacting the destination in economic, ecological, social and cultural terms. Economic benchmarks have traditionally been the most requested forms of impact analysis as both managers and politicians seek to measure and understand the level of tourism receipts as well as the incomes and employment they create. Virtually any proposal for investing in tourism development is required to provide at least a global estimate of the economic benefits and taxes to be generated. More comprehensive economic impact analyses will also estimate the possible negative impacts, such as exorbitant land prices resulting from increased tourism and the additional taxes that may be required to build a facility such as a municipal convention centre.

In addition to economic reviews, ecological (or environmental) impact analysis is increasingly becoming another standard requirement for meaningful policy formulation. Typically a 'state of the ecology' report is a starting point for tourism policy formulation in any region that is in any way environmentally sensitive. In such cases, these 'state of' reports are normally complemented by an Environmental Impact Assessment (EIA) for all proposed tourism developments.

In certain instances, social and cultural impact benchmarks and analyses may also be requested. These are typically, but not always, restricted to situations where a culture is threatened or where a community feels that increased tourism will adversely affect its way of life.

The external/demand analysis is composed of three distinct types of analytical activity. The first involves macro-level analysis of data that describe and define the overall nature and structure of current tourism demand and those markets having a potential for future demand. This form of analysis relies heavily on aggregate statistics measuring the flows of tourists and travel-related expenditures within a region; it must not limit itself to such historical data. In addition, macro-level analysis must be future-oriented and attempt to monitor the environment constantly in order to identify shifts or trends in social, political or technological factors that might significantly affect the region's success in its field of tourism.

The second type of external/demand analysis is micro-level analysis. Here, rather than focusing on aggregate trends in tourism demand, attention is directed towards gaining an understanding of the motivations and behaviour of the different segments of the total tourism market. The purpose of gaining this understanding is to provide those responsible for supply development with the information needed to design facilities and services which will appeal most to each of the various demand segments. In addition, such data facilitate the task of those responsible for the promotion of existing facilities and services.

The final component of external/demand analysis involves a review and evaluation of competitive and supportive tourism development and promotion policies and programmes. Competitive analysis is a common form of managerial investigation. In this case, it is designed to produce a clear picture of the identity, strength and strategies of those tourism destinations most likely to be appealing to the same segments of demand as those of interest to the tourism region in question. Such information is essential if a region is to effectively counter the efforts of such competitors from the standpoint of both supply development and demand modification.

The analysis of supportive policies and programmes is an activity that is frequently neglected in the highly competitive world of tourism. As a result, policy makers may overlook potential sources of synergy that may be developed by cooperating or forming alliances with either other tourism regions or other public/private sector organizations within the region, but in non-tourism fields. While care must be exercised in deciding what forms of cooperation are most likely to be attractive, failure to explore such avenues may deprive a region of the possibility of appealing to new or distant markets.

Operational phase

Once the various types of analysis have been carried out, policy makers must move to develop specific strategies and action plans that can be implemented. As shown in Box 8.3, this operational phase is envisaged to contain three conceptually different types of activity; in reality these different activities are executed almost simultaneously.

The *identification of strategic conclusions* flows directly out of the analytical phase and has as its goal the synthesis of the large amounts of information obtained into a limited number of major conclusions. In addition to specifying the major findings from each type of internal and external analysis, this process must also attempt to provide conclusions that assess the impact of the trade-offs that are inevitable when attempting to match supply and demand.

The strategic conclusions themselves may be viewed as reasonably factual information; that is, they are the result of a logical process of analysis that would give rise to generally similar findings irrespective of the investigator. In contrast, determining the *implications of the conclusions for supply and demand development strategies* involves a high degree of judgement on the part of the individuals involved. The goal of this process is to attempt to assess the significance of each conclusion for tourism in the region. While the actual conclusions may be clear, determining their implications for the kind of policies and programmes needed to deal with them involves a considerable level of interpretive skill, derived from both experience and a creative mind.

The subsequent stage of the policy formulation process is the identification of specific *policy/programme recommendations for supply and demand development*. For the present purposes, this rather complex activity has been over-simplified in reality; a range of policy options would normally be developed which attempt to respond to alternative implications or alternative scenarios. Some judgement would then be exercised as to which implications or scenarios are most likely to occur. Policy/programme recommendations most appropriate to the most likely events would probably, although not necessarily, be adopted.

Implementation phase

Finally, for a destination tourism policy to truly succeed, it is essential to include an *implementation phase*. At a minimum, such a strategy must: (i) identify the individual groups or organizations that will assume responsibility for each major dimension of the policy realization; (ii) establish initial estimates of the financial requirements; and (iii) provide preliminary timelines for the launching of all major facilities, events and programmes that support the destination vision.

POLICY FORMULATION METHODS.   While a detailed examination of policy, planning and research methods is beyond the scope of this book, it is important to be aware of some of the most popular and most effective approaches currently in use:

- Delphi technique;
- brainstorming;
- focus groups;
- nominal group technique;
- household surveys;
- industry expert interviews;
- evaluation research;
- impact analysis (economic, environmental, social, cultural);
- panel research;
- interest-based negotiation; and
- destination visioning.

Summary

This chapter points out that tourism policy is needed for destinations at all levels and for all types of political jurisdictions. It also stresses that although destination policy and destination management may address overlapping topics, a clear distinction must be made regarding the intellectual nature of policy concerns as opposed to the more pragmatic, day-to-day manner in which they are addressed by management efforts.

The chapter also emphasizes throughout that, in all cases, competitiveness and sustainability must be the primary goal of policy – and that the effective pursuit of each of these goals requires a different set of skills and capabilities. With this background firmly in place, the chapter then fulfils two major roles.

The first of these roles is to provide a *framework describing the structure* and composition of a formal tourism policy. The primary components discussed are the philosophy for tourism and the formulation of a long-term vision for the destination. This vision provides important guidance for the definition of specific objectives for a tourism destination and for the identification of any constraints that must be observed as tourism is developed. These objectives, in turn, provide a basis for formulating long-term development strategies for the region. The detailed components of supply and demand development strategies are then discussed.

Finally, the chapter focuses on the *process of policy formulation*, the processes by which all of the foregoing components of policy are defined. The chapter identifies the major components of tourism policy and strategy formulation and implementation and discusses the activities involved in each.

References

Aaker, D.A. (1991) *Managing Brand Equity: Capitalizing on the Value of a Brand Name.* Free Press, New York.

BBVS (Banff-Bow Valley Study Group: Page, R., Bayler, S., Cook, J.D., Green, J.E. and Ritchie, J.R.B.) (1996) *Banff-Bow Valley: at the Crossroads.* Technical Report, Banff-Bow Valley Task Force. Prepared for the Honourable Sheila Copps, Minister of Canadian Heritage, Ottawa, Ontario, Canada.

Bedbury, S. and Fenichell, S. (2002) *A New Brand World: Eight Principles for Achieving Brand Leadership in the 21st Century.* Viking/Penguin Group, New York.

Dror, Y. (1971) *Design for Policy Sciences.* American Elsevier, New York.

Fisher, R. and Ury, W. (1991) *Getting to Yes: Negotiating Agreement Without Giving In.* Penguin Books, New York.

Getz, D., Anderson, D. and Sheehan, L. (1998) Roles, issues, and strategies for convention and visitors' bureaux in destination planning and product development: a survey of Canadian bureaux. *Tourism Management* 19, 331–340.

Goeldner, C.R. and Ritchie, J.R.B. (2003) *Tourism: Principles, Practices, Philosophies,* 9th edn. John Wiley & Sons, New York.

Mintzberg, H. (1987) Crafting strategy. *Harvard Business Review* 65(4) 66–75.

Morgan, N., Pritchard, A. and Pride, R. (eds) (2002) *Destination Branding: Creating the Unique Destination Proposition.* Butterworth-Heinemann, Oxford.

Otto, J.E. and Ritchie, J.R.B. (1995) Exploring the quality of the service experience: a theoretical

and empirical analysis. *Advances in Services Marketing and Management* 4, 37–61.

Parks Canada (1997) *Banff National Park Management Plan.* Minister of Public Works and Government Services, Ottawa, Ontario, Canada.

Prugh, T., Costanza, R., Cumberland, J.H., Daly, H., Goodland, R. and Norgaard, R.B. (1995) *Natural Capital and Human Economic Survival.* ISEE Press (International Society of Ecological Economics), Solomons, Maryland.

Ritchie, J.R.B. (1993) Crafting a destination vision: putting the concept of resident-responsive tourism into practice. *Tourism Management* 14, 379–389.

Ritchie, J.R.B. (1999) Crafting a value-driven vision for a national tourism treasure. *Tourism Management* 20, 273–282.

Ritchie, J.R.B. and Goeldner, C.R. (1994) *Travel Tourism and Hospitality Research: a Handbook for Managers and Researchers.* John Wiley, New York.

Ritchie, J.R.B. and Ritchie, R.J.B. (1998) The branding of tourism destinations: past achievements and future challenges. *Conference Proceedings of the Annual Congress of the International Association of Scientific Experts in Tourism (AIEST), Marrakesh, Morocco, 1 September,* pp. 89–116.

Ritchie, R.J.B. and Ritchie, J.R.B. (2002) A framework for an industry supported destination marketing information system. *Tourism Management* 23, 439–454.

Sandford, R.W. (1997) *The Banff Bow Valley Heritage Tourism Strategy.* Heritage Tourism Working Group, Banff, Alberta, Canada.

Sheehan, L.R. and Ritchie, J.R.B. (2002) A theory based exploration of destination stakeholder identity and salience. Working Paper, University of Calgary, Alberta, Canada.

Smith, S.L.J. (1995) The tourism satellite account: perspectives of Canadian tourism associations and organizations. *Tourism Economics* 1, 225–244.

WTO (2001) *Tourism Satellite Account (TSA): Implementation Project – The Tourism Satellite Account as an Ongoing Process: Past, Present and Future Developments.* World Tourism Organization, Madrid, Spain.

WTO (2002) *Tourism in the Age of Alliances, Mergers and Acquisitions.* World Tourism Organization, Madrid, Spain.

9

Destination Management: the Key to Maintaining a Sustainable Competitive Advantage

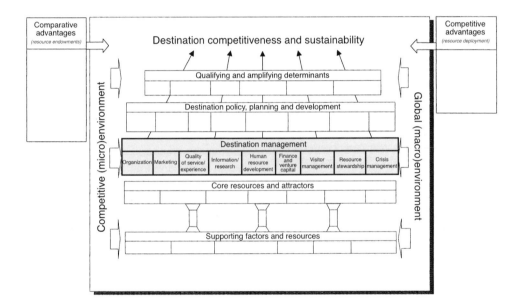

In the previous chapter we examined how tourism policy provides a framework within which a competitive tourism destination can be developed on a long-term, sustainable basis. Tourism policy is seen as critical for creating the conditions within which tourism can succeed and for providing visionary guidance as to how tourism development most appropriate for the destination can take shape and grow successfully. This policy formulation seeks to take maximum advantage of the degree to which a destination's core resources and attractors are first capable of attracting visitors and then providing them with a memorable visitation experience. In doing so, the policy attempts to minimize the degree to which the destination's qualifying determinants eliminate it from consideration by potential visitors or maximize the degree to which amplifying determinants can enhance its appeal in the highly competitive marketplace.

In this chapter, we assume that the policy, planning and development process has succeeded in creating the framework for a competitive/sustainable destination. The challenge now faced by the destination is to manage its various components in a way that ensures its economic profitability while avoiding degradation of the factors that have created its competitive position.

The Process of Destination Management

As seen from our model of destination competitiveness and sustainability, given in figure on the previous page, the destination management module consists of a total of nine components, presented in a linear fashion within the module. Each component contains individual destination managerial tasks that must be carefully attended to by the destination manager. While presented linearly, the process of destination management is, in practice, much more circular or iterative. That is, it is not always obvious which component comes first, and in addition, all components are highly interdependent. Thus, while resource steward-ship is addressed towards the end of the discussion in this chapter, it is in reality an ongoing management activity that must continually be considered along with all of the other eight components of the destination management process. Readers should keep this conceptual reality clearly in mind as they review the total-ity of the chapter. This said, if there is any management activity that must be performed before the others, it is probably organization, and it is with this topic that we start the chapter.

Organization

In Chapter 8, we saw that tourism policy provided the guidelines for the framework within which to establish and operate the organization that will provide the leadership and coordination necessary to make a desti-nation function competitively on an ongoing basis. Chapter 8 also pointed out that the actual structure of the destination management organization (DMO) that any given destination puts in place depends on many factors, most notably the nature of the destination and the level of funding that is required or that can be

made available. In any case, it is essential that a destination's DMO be functional from both the strategic and the operational perspective. As noted, the leadership and coordination roles that a DMO must perform are the essence of ongoing, long-term success. However, as the chief executive officers of many DMOs have found out, the DMO must also effectively perform the many tactical roles that demand close daily attention if it is to maintain the competitiveness of the destination for which it is responsible.

As Chapter 8 also pointed out, tourism policy broadly defines the *roles* of the DMO, the nature of the *structure* that is appropriate in the circumstances, and the general means by which *funding* to support operations will be generated. In this chapter, we now examine, from a managerial perspective, how these policy directives can be implemented. Before doing so, however, it is important to make clear how circumstances can modify the implementation of basic policy guidelines.

Level of the destination management organization

While Chapter 8 discussed some six levels of destination, there are essentially three funda-mental levels at which a DMO most commonly functions. They are the national level the regional/state/provincial level, and the urban/municipal/city-state level. While there are many commonalities across these levels, it is wise to keep these distinctions in mind when discussing managerial responsibilities and the means of meeting them. While the basic roles of a DMO are generally similar at all destina-tion levels, the type of structure which is used and the approaches to funding tend to vary substantially. These latter two areas will be examined first.

DMO structures

Table 9.1 shows the range of alternative DMO structures that are commonly found at different destination levels. It is important to understand the structure that exists at any particular desti-nation since it can have profound implications

Table 9.1. Some alternative DMO structures at different destination levels.

Level	Alternative structures
National (country)	• Government tourism department • Government tourism and economic development/recreation/parks/culture department • National tourism commission • National tourism authority • Crown/government corporation
State/ provincial	• Government tourism department • Joint public/private agency

Urban/ municipal/ city-state	• City tourism department
	• Convention and visitors bureau
	  • Member-based
	  • Non member-based
	• City Inc. (joint Economic Development and Promotional Agency)

for the nature of the challenges that destination management faces. One of the most significant of these implications concerns whether DMO management reports to a publicly elected official, to a board of directors elected by industry members, to a corporate/agency board of directors (who may often be appointed by government) or, in certain cases, to a partnership involving a joint public/private sector board of directors. Regardless, the organizational structure can modify both the tone and the specific DMO managerial practices that tend to dominate. What is particularly critical is whether the board to which management reports has a public or private sector orientation. In the first case, the organizational philosophy to which managers must respond will tend to have an emphasis on public service and community development. In the latter, the private sector philosophy will tend to view the DMO as a business in which cost controls and accountability will normally dominate the environment within which the DMO management functions. It is not that either the public or the private philosophy is better or worse than the other; as is normally the case, each has its merits and each its shortcomings.

Since national and state/provincial governments often seem to mirror one another in

their structure and mode of functioning, it is primarily at the urban/municipal/city-state level where different types of organizational structures begin to appear. At present, there are commonly two main alternative organizational structures that set the tone for city-oriented tourism development and promotion. The city tourism department is the public service equivalent of the national/provincial tourism department, while the City Convention and Visitor Bureau generally claims to be a private sector organization (despite the fact that it often draws heavily on public funds). Consequently, this type of DMO management varies in its public/private emphasis in decision making – and must be constantly looking over both shoulders.

Tasks of the DMO

If we assume that the policy-level issues surrounding the basic structure of the DMO and the nature of its funding base have been determined (admittedly, these are major assumptions), then we must address the daily managerial tasks that are essential to an effective, smoothly operating DMO. Table 9.2 summarizes these managerial tasks. In general, they tend to fall into two major categories: internal and external programmes. While these two categories are not entirely separate, internal programmes have, in general, an inward-looking nature, whereas external programmes are outward-looking and as such tend to communicate what the outside world (including DMO stakeholders) sees as the functioning of the DMO.

Internal programmes

Even within this category, there are programmes (or activities) that are very much internal in nature, while others, although internal to the destination, are primarily concerned with destination members rather than DMO members. Indeed, many are truly more administrative than managerial. Just the same, they are critical to the success of the DMO. As shown in Table 9.2, the internal tasks are primarily those required to enable the DMO to function

Table 9.2. Managerial tasks to ensure an effective, smoothly operating DMO.

Internal
- Definition of organizational by-laws
- Determination of committee structures
- Determination of budget/budgeting process
- Organizational administrative procedures
- Membership management
- Community relations
- Publications

External
- Marketing
- Visitor services/quality of service/visitor management
- Visitor management
- Information/research
- Finance and venture capital management
- Resource stewardship
- Human resource management

administratively. The external tasks are, with one exception, the major managerial challenges facing the DMO. That one exception is constant concern for financing and the DMO budget.

DMO funding

Most of the organizational funding issues that must be addressed by DMO management flow directly from – and are answered by – the kind of DMO organizational structure that has been put in place, as discussed above. In the distant, traditional past, it was generally much easier to be a government department and to simply ask the question 'how much do we need this year?' of political masters. But somewhere in the 1980s (or so), governments at all levels started to face programme funding demands that exceeded revenues. As a consequence, DMO management at all levels was forced to start looking for alternative sources of funding, and most of this had a private sector origin. Some typical sources that have emerged are discussed below.

- *Increased membership fees* for industry members. While this approach seems to make sense to many, it has generally not been successful and has frequently weakened the DMO that seeks to implement it. In effect, membership can decline as the

original members of the tourism industry feel the added cost cannot be justified. The consequence is often the emergence of the free-rider problem, a situation in which many who benefit from tourism refuse to join the DMO or to support its efforts. Consequently, this funding alternative is not particularly popular or well-accepted.

- *A local hotel tax*. Such a tax may be legislated or voluntary. In either instance, while it may provide a substantial, relatively stable source of DMO funding, it is often viewed by the hotel sector as one-sided, and thus unfair. The argument is that hotels represent only part of the tourism industry and its associated revenues. The counter-argument is that visitors do not come to a destination just to stay in hotels – and so the hotel sector benefits enormously from the investments in facilities and promotion that must be made by all other components of the tourism sector. It is also usually pointed out that a hotel tax is much simpler to administer than many other ways of raising funds, since it can be incorporated into existing sales tax collection procedures.

- In an attempt to retain both equity and integration of collection, certain jurisdictions have attempted to legislate a *tourism/recreation tax*. Because it is much more widely spread than a hotel tax, it can be much lower as a percentage of sales. But while conceptually logical it is not so simple in practice, since it becomes difficult (if not impossible) to define which firms are in the tourism/recreation industry and which are not. While many retail shops benefit from visitor expenditures, many do not. Similarly, while many recreation facilities also benefit from visitor expenditures, a large percentage do not. As a consequence, this seemingly logical approach has tended to fail because of its complexity of administration.

Other approaches to DMO funding have sought to go completely outside of government grants and various forms of taxation. One of the most popular has been the private sector sponsorship alliance.

- The *private sector sponsorship alliance* is an arrangement in which firms that benefit substantially from visitor travel agree to donate a certain amount or given percentage of their revenues within a destination to the DMO in return for prominent advertising visibility throughout the destination and in the destination's promotional programmes. Companies in the credit card business, the alcoholic beverage industry and gasoline retailing are typical candidates for such sponsorship alliances. However, despite their short-term potential, such alliances have not always provided the levels of long-term, stable revenue that a DMO requires if it is to be effective on a sustainable basis.

Internal managerial tasks

First, for the DMO to run in a way understood by all, it requires a set of *by-laws* that define the rules of governance of the organization. While responsibility for maintaining a current set of by-laws is usually regarded as a fairly boring task, it is only when the DMO faces an organizational or political crisis that their value is appreciated. Since by-laws determine such things as officer responsibilities, voting rights, election procedures, terms of office and the distinction between volunteer and full-time paid positions, they are important, but they tend to go unnoticed in times of normal operation.

Another managerial task that is often viewed as rather mundane is the determination of *committee structures and membership*. If structures are defined by organizational by-laws, then membership decisions may be made by either volunteers or full-time staff, depending upon the organizational nature of the DMO. The purpose of DMO committees is to allocate responsibilities for specific managerial and administrative tasks to small subgroupings of the total managerial team.

One committee of traditional significance is the budget committee, which, as the name indicates, is responsible for managing the *budgeting process* for the DMO. While final decisions or budget allocations are normally the responsibility of the DMO board of directors, it is the management and staff of the DMO who, in

most cases, are charged with preparing detailed budget proposals for review and approval.

Budget preparation is just one of the many *administrative procedures* that go on within a DMO. A large number pertain to the financial management of the budget resources, once these have been approved. Procedures for the preparation of an operating statement, describing the financial status of the DMO, the monitoring of cash flows, the maintenance of industry and government funding programmes, and the achievement of all budgeted revenue are all procedures that are triggered by the budget.

In addition, other *control procedures* may be part of a DMO's internal management tasks. For example, the monitoring of merchandizing programmes, fixed asset performance, the accommodation reservation system and all information systems in general are important managerial responsibilities that must not be neglected.

Managing DMO membership

The first task facing DMO management is to comprehensively identify those stakeholders of the destination region who are legitimate potential members. This task is not as trivial as it may sound. As discussed above (see *DMO funding*) the free-rider issue makes this task a challenging one. When identified, an active and ongoing campaign of membership recruitment must be put in place – and when an individual or organization is formally signed up, the task of dues collection truly confirms membership. Throughout the processes of recruitment and dues collection, a functional database of members needs to be established and maintained for accuracy.

Once membership has been confirmed and recorded, the DMO must then make sure that members perceive membership as worthwhile. To get things off on the right foot, an orientation programme that helps the new member fully understand how the DMO can help the organization or individual benefit from membership is essential for maintaining the enthusiasm of new members. It also helps new members feel that they are truly part of the DMO family.

In order not to lose enthusiasm once it has developed, the internal task of membership management is to put in place a comprehensive membership programme that delivers value for the members. Such a programme commonly includes three elements. The first consists of routine, ongoing programmes that primarily include regular meetings and networking sessions. The second element, special area programming, may involve guest speakers, strategic planning sessions and visits to member facilities. Third, membership development programmes are for many a major reason for loyal DMO membership. They consist of education and training that can be either periodic or systematic, and workshops and seminars on timely topics – the latter are often appreciated but may not provide as much substance as a more systematic, long-term training and certification programme.

Regardless of the membership development programme that is adopted, these three elements are all essential for membership maintenance and renewal. If members do not renew, the DMO is faced with the difficult question of why they have not done so.

The next two areas of DMO managerial responsibility may be viewed as either internal or external.

Community relations

The task of community relations is primarily intended to maintain the DMO's visibility and reputation in the community that it serves. The community relations programme can be focused on those who make the decisions on DMO funding or can be more broadly directed towards the entire DMO membership, or even the entire community. In any event, the message to be conveyed is 'your DMO cares about your support and is attempting to serve your needs'.

Publications programme

Again, a DMO publications programme must serve both internal and external audiences. Many publications are produced for the DMO membership and for the entire community the DMO serves. Traditionally, a paper-based publications programme has been very costly. With the advent of the Internet, much of the paper has been replaced by an effective DMO home page. Despite this change, management must pay close attention to the content and effectiveness of the information it makes available to the members, all stakeholders, the community at large and potential visitors.

External programmes

The external managerial tasks of the DMO, listed in Table 9.2, are generally so important that they merit detailed discussion. For this reason they have been identified in our model as distinct components of destination management. So, rather than considering them simply as sub-components of the organization function, we present them at the same level of importance. Before doing so, however, we feel the need to address an as-yet unresolved debate.

The DMO debate: destination marketing or destination management organization?

Marketing, or perhaps more correctly, promotion and selling, has for many years been the primary task that destination managers felt was their job. In the past, the importance of the marketing and promotion roles of the DMO were of such a high priority that the DMO label was understood to mean 'destination *marketing* organization'. It is only in recent years that DMOs have acknowledged how significant their non-marketing roles are in developing, enhancing and maintaining destination competitiveness. Nearly all progressive and effective DMOs in today's world now appreciate the importance of their more broadly based mandate and use DMO to mean 'destination *management* organization'. We strongly agree with this position.

Marketing (Promotion?)

Regardless of one's position in the foregoing debate, marketing remains an important function of the DMO. Because of this, the development of demand strategies (the essence of marketing) is viewed as a major component of destination policy. In this chapter we attempt to provide more operational insights into how the elements of marketing (Fig. 9.1) are implemented. Nevertheless, there are limits on the level of detail that can be provided in this book, and readers wishing a greater level of detail about the total marketing process are referred to the books by Morrison (1989) and Kotler and Bowen (1998).

Another debate that lies below the surface in the tourism marketing world is the distinction between tourism marketing and tourism promotion. In discussions with practitioners, one often gains the clear impression that these two terms are considered to be equivalent. In particular, there seems to be considerable neglect of the product innovation and development dimension of the traditional 'four Ps' (product, promotion, price, place) and particular emphasis on the promotion dimension of the total marketing 'onion', although admittedly there is also great concern for pricing and for the distribution of the tourism product.

This seeming lack of concern for product is, however, somewhat deceptive. It is simply that in the traditional tourism world the

destination planning and development function is often not viewed as an integral part of the marketing function.

Our framework clearly places a high priority on the destination product by recognizing it as a critical component of the overall competitiveness and sustainability model. We will not repeat here our discussion on destination (product) development. However, we stress that, from an effective marketing perspective, the product being delivered to the customer (in this case the destination visitation experience) needs to be viewed as an integral part of the marketing function.

Identification of strategic markets for the destination

The first operational marketing challenge facing the destination manager is to determine explicitly which specific visitor markets the destination should actively pursue. The initial

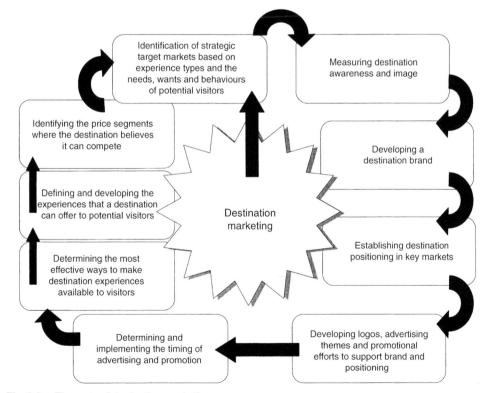

Fig. 9.1. Elements of destination marketing.

questions destination managers must ask about their destinations are: who have we attracted in the past? and who can we best serve now, given our strengths? As part of this process, destinations need to review visitor history data to understand visitation trends among various market segments. In this process, destination managers should realistically delineate the strengths of the destination in terms of the experiential benefits it can provide to the potential visitor. This analysis will very quickly define whether the destination will appeal to the leisure market or the business/convention/ meeting market, or to both markets.

More explicitly, destination managers should seek to identify the experiences for which they feel they have a possible competitive advantage. Examples of the types of experiences they might consider for the leisure and business/convention/meeting markets are outlined in Tables 9.3 and 9.4, respectively.

Once the range of experience types is understood by a destination, management is then in a position to undertake a process of experience market matching based on a comparison of the experiences the destination is capable of offering and the needs, wants and behaviours of markets where it is deemed that the destination is potentially competitive.

In carrying out this matching process, destinations must keep in mind behavioural, locational and cost constraints that may negate an ideal match because the client is, in practice, unable to pursue the satisfaction of his or her needs and desires at the destination. Distances may be impossible to overcome because of timing or cost. Certain locations may be unacceptable for legal or cultural reasons. While a destination may be able to provide the desired experience for some markets, it may be unable to so for others because of religious factors, or simply because of functional reasons that involve specific or unusual facility requirements.

Measuring destination awareness and image

Once feasible ideal target markets have been identified by a destination for both the leisure and the business markets, the marketing challenge becomes one of attempting to determine which market will be most cost-effective to address on a sustainable basis. This requires measurement of the current level of awareness and the image of the destination in each potential market. A low level of awareness and/or a poor or misunderstood image implies much higher costs for efforts to enhance the destination's competitive appeal in a given target market. Clearly, a balance must be sought between the apparent profitability of a feasible ideal target market and the costs associated with efforts to obtain these profits.

The *measurement of a destination's awareness* can be undertaken in two main ways. 'Top-of-mind' awareness measures attempt to determine whether prospective clients in the destination are simply aware of the existence of a destination for a given type of experience. Conversely, 'prompted recall' measures of awareness indicate whether or not the respondent can recognize the destination when its identity is given in one of several forms.

The *measurement of destination image* has been a major focus of much tourism research for many years. Echtner and Ritchie (1991) have identified three major dimensions along which image should be measured (Fig. 9.6). They are:

- a dimension that distinguishes between the *functional* characteristics (specific benefits provided) and the *psychological* characteristics (the more abstract feelings experienced) of a destination;
- a dimension that measures the specific *attributes* of a destination versus the measurement of a more *holistic impression* of the destination (Table 9.5); and
- a dimension that distinguishes between the measurement of aspects that are *common* to virtually all destinations versus those that are *unique* to a particular destination.

While it is important that a destination be perceived positively with respect to those functional and psychological attributes that are common to most destinations, and that a favourable holistic impression is created, what is especially desirable is the development of a positive unique image that distinguishes one destination from the many competitors that

Table 9.3.   Examples of leisure market benefits and experiences.

- **The get-away-from-it-all relaxation experience**
  The typical 'sun, sand and sea' or other type of holiday experience vacation in which visitors are seeking a period of rest and renewal
- **The exploration experience**
  The experience in which the visitor is seeking to expand his/her visitation horizons. The newness of the experience depends on the individual. For novice travellers, virtually any different locale may be new. For the experienced traveller, it may be difficult to find new travel horizons
- **The adventure experience**
  In these experiences, the visitor is seeking the 'adrenalin high' that may come from whitewater rafting, heli-skiing, jungle exploration, mountaineering, Antarctic expeditions or even visitation to insecure, war-torn areas
- **The social experience**
  These experiences provide an opportunity for the visitor to share the travel experience with old friends, or to make new ones. To some extent, the actual destination may be unimportant
- **The family travel experience**
  A special subset of the social travel experience in which the social network involved is very special to the visitor – especially in relation to the stage of the family cycle for the visitors. Clearly, young families are seeking quite different experiences from more mature families. Nevertheless, underlying the motivation to visit a destination is the desire to create and retain a very special experience for the given stage of the family life cycle
- **The educational or learning experience**
  This type of travel experience has grown in significance lately, and often reflects the desire of more mature, more sophisticated travellers to enhance their depth of understanding of a destination, its culture, or some special characteristic it may possess
- **The quick get-away experience**
  This is again a subset of a broader type of experience, the get-away-from-it-all relaxation experience. In this case, however, the emphasis is more on the get-away-from-it-all than on total relaxation and renewal. These experiences are often as short as a weekend and may not be all that distant from the individual's place of residence
- **The VFR (visit friends and relatives) experience**
  For many, the VFR experience is by far the most valued, and may be the only type of experience they seek for most of their lifetime. For a destination manager, the challenge is to discuss how the destination in question can benefit most from this popular form of travel
- **The return to a single destination experience**
  As Plog pointed out many years ago, there is a certain segment of the travel market that eschews all the glamour of international travel and simply wishes to return to a comfortable destination repeatedly. While this comfortable destination may be a privately owned recreation facility, it may just as well be a public destination site to which the visitor has become attached for a whole range of reasons
- **The special event experience**
  Many destinations have come to appreciate the appeal that a special event may have in attracting visitors who might otherwise have little or no interest in visiting the destination. Destinations that host such one-time mega-events as the Olympic Games or World Cup events can increase visitation both during and after the event as a result of enhanced awareness, reputation and image. Alternatively, the successful repeat events, such as the Boston Marathon, Oberammergau, the Master's Golf Tournament, the New Orleans Mardi Gras and the Calgary Stampede, attract what are often one-time visitors. This market is large, and it can be a major source of reputation and of visitation as part of total destination marketing strategy
- **The participation event experience**
  In contrast to events that draw visitors to observe the event, other events can draw visitors who are seeking to actively participate in the event, or who wish to watch a close friend or family member perform in the event. Examples include amateur sporting events (softball, hockey, soccer, American football, races, etc.), music festivals, beauty festivals and children's festivals

continued

Table 9.3. *Continued.*

- **The nature-based experience**
  As concern for and interest in the environment has grown, the appeal of destinations that provide the opportunity for visitors to commune with nature are also growing in significance. Destinations that contain areas such as national parks are often viewed as the epitome of the nature-based experience. Here the opportunity to explore environmentally sensitive, yet protected regions and to view wildlife in close proximity is becoming increasingly valued

- **The spiritual experience**
  Destinations that, for historical reasons, have a particular spiritual attraction to individuals around the world have a special advantage in their ability to provide a spiritual experience. Cities such as Mecca and Rome that are the seats of major religions, and those that are the homes of recognized religious structures, can focus on their ability to provide spirituality-related experiences. But not all spiritual experiences are related to traditional religions. Other destinations, such as Nepal, have over time gained a special spiritual reputation in many areas

- **The entertainment experience**
  While broad in concept, a destination may focus on the provision of various types of entertainment on the basis of its primary market appeal. While the previously cited examples of London, New York, Las Vegas, Nashville, and Branson, Missouri have become classic examples of the providers of entertainment experiences, they are certainly not alone. The essence of this experience is the opportunity for the destination visitor to observe performances that are either well known in themselves or presented by well-known stars. To the extent that a destination can develop a critical mass of these entertainment experiences, it can position itself as an entertainment-based destination

- **The attractions experience**
  Certain attractions can become so well known that they can provide the basis of the appeal of an entire destination – and indeed may almost become the totality of the destination. Disney World in Florida is undoubtedly the classic example of an attraction that many families feel they must experience at least once in the lifetime of the family. Indeed, this attraction experience has become so pervasive that it forms the foundation for most of the tourism industry in the city of Orlando, Florida

- **The take-a-chance experience**
  More commonly referred to as gaming or gambling, the take-a-chance experience is designed to appeal to those whose adrenalin is stimulated by the risk-taking associated with a broad range of games of chance. Many well-known destinations owe their origin, and often their continuing existence, to the legalization of activities that 50 years ago were considered both illegal and immoral. Times have changed – so much that just about every destination wants to add a gaming component to its array of attractions. In the meantime, Las Vegas, Atlantic City and Monte Carlo continue to maintain their pinnacle position as providers of this type of experience. The first two, located in North America, combine gaming with entertainment. In contrast, Monte Carlo's European location emphasizes class and eliteness in appealing to a select market segment

- **The no-holds-barred experience**
  This experience often has names that are much less socially acceptable. Sex tourism was, in the past, a popular but disguised travel experience that the World Tourism Organization and some governments have now explicitly declared undesirable, and even illegal. The Club Med for many years implied that visitors to certain of its many resorts around the globe could expect a vacation free of normal social constraints. The piles of broken glass around night spots in Spanish seaside resorts following all-night festivities give evidence of behaviours not normally engaged in by many of their UK (and other) guests. And since what seems to be the beginning of time, the Carnival of Rio de Janeiro and the Mardi Gras of New Orleans have attracted both residents and visitors seeking experiences that attract very specific segments of the market

- **The get-to-know-your-global-friends experience**
  This type of experience represents what many feel tourism should be all about – visitation experiences that encourage the visitor to get to know members of the host destination. There are many ways to attempt to achieve this goal, but Ireland has been offering an approach that many consider to be *par excellence*. For years, the Irish Tourist Board has worked with residents to develop a comprehensive network of homes that are willing to welcome visitors from around the world to visit not only the house,

Table 9.3.   *Continued.*

but also to a certain degree, household members. While admittedly (and necessarily) having multiple dimensions that can be difficult to manage in terms of quality control, it is a risk that many visitors consider very worthwhile (see www.irishfarmholidays.com)
- **The understand-the-real-world experience**
While some may interpret this kind of experience as a version of the adventure experience, it depends on the traveller. What this experience implies is visitation to a destination in which the traveller is not artificially protected from some of the realities of living that many of the world's residents experience every day. Visits to many regions of Africa, India, China and Asia in which the visitor does not stay in high-quality hotels, eats the food of the common people and travels using the local modes of transportation are not for everyone, but they can provide memorable lifetime experiences for those in good physical condition and in the right mindset

are actively courting the same potential visitors. Such symbols as the Eiffel Tower in Paris, the Taj Mahal in India and the Great Wall of China are invaluable icons that help to reinforce the uniqueness of the destinations they symbolize. The creation of such a globally recognized icon is the dream of every destination manager.

While the attributes in Table 9.5 provide a foundation for measuring destination attributes, the parallel measurement of holistic impressions is more difficult to standardize. One common approach is to ask potential visitors open questions, such as:

- What images or characteristics come to mind when you think of XXX as a vacation destination? (functional holistic component)
- How would you describe the atmosphere or mood that you would expect to experience while visiting XXX? (psychological holistic component)
- Please list any distinctive or unique tourist attractions that you can think of in XXX. (unique component)

After obtaining answers to these questions from a number of respondents, it becomes possible to identify the main themes or images that are common for a destination. As an example, Table 9.6 provides the most frequent responses to the above open-ended image questions for the island of Jamaica (Echtner and Ritchie, 1993). Although attribute measures and holistic measures are frequently used by themselves, it is recommended that they be used in combination in order to gain the richness of understanding of a destination's image that is necessary for reliable planning and decision making.

Monitoring destination awareness and image

While the measurement of destination awareness and image at a given point in time is useful in itself, it is much more useful from a managerial standpoint to monitor both levels and changes in levels of destination awareness over time and in the image that the market has of the destination.

Monitoring also enables the destination manager to assess the effectiveness of a specific advertising/promotional campaign in a specific target market, or to determine the impact that the hosting of a particular mega-event has had on market awareness of the host destination. Figure 9.2 (p. 197) summarizes a now classic study on the impact that the hosting of the 1988 Olympic Winter Games had on the levels of awareness of the host city, Calgary, in ten cities in North America and ten cities in Europe over the 4-year period from 1986 to 1989. As one basis of comparison, the levels of awareness of Calgary's sister city, Edmonton, were also tracked. In addition, the images and the evolution in the images of the two cities were also monitored to permit a similar comparison (Ritchie and Smith, 1991).

Destination branding

Given the prevalence and impact of branding in a broad range of travel/tourism-related activities, it is perhaps not surprising that the travel destinations in which these travel/tourism brands are located have awakened to the need to brand themselves. This was initially

Table 9.4.   Examples of business and organizational market benefits and experiences.

- **The organizational convention experience**
  This form of experience is the main foundation of the convention centre phenomenon; that is, the steady growth in convention centre facilities around the world over the past three decades. Indeed, we are now at the point where any major destination that does not possess such a facility feels (and probably is) non-competitive in the regional, national or global marketplace, depending on the scope of its potential market.
  The convention experience reflects the perceived need of organizations and their members to assemble together periodically to build both the social and political fabric of the organization on a face-to-face basis. It also furnishes an opportunity for members and external contacts to develop commercial relationships and highlight recent new product development through trade fairs
- **The association conference experience**
  While similar in nature to the convention experience, the conference experience tends to have more of an intellectual component. In general, it reflects the desire of an organization and its members to participate in a forum within which all members can come together both to enhance the social networking of the members and to develop professional capabilities through the sharing of existing and emerging knowledge
- **The corporate energizer experience**
  Akin to the organizational convention experience is the corporate energizer experience. This experience draws together members of an organization that generally have a common purpose within the corporation. The gathering of sales and marketing personnel to review past progress and to convey new corporate strategies is probably the most popular energizing experience. It may bring together either employees or a vast array of individuals who are retained on a commission basis
- **The legal requirement experience**
  Corporations are often required by legislation or their own internal rules to gather together annually, or according to some other timeframe. While such meetings are commonly held at corporate headquarters, such facilities may not be large enough to accommodate all attendees, thus opening the door for convention facilities at destinations
- **The corporate meetings experience**
  Usually smaller and more focused on strategic planning issues, the corporate meetings experience nevertheless represents a significant opportunity in cases where the corporation wishes to combine business with relaxation. Where the opportunity for relaxation is not included in the meeting agenda, destination managers can seize on such experiences to subsequently lure corporate attendees for follow-up holiday experiences
- **The high-profile presentation experience**
  Many types of organizations periodically seek to either educate and inform their members, or to heighten the profile of their organization through the sponsoring of a special presentation involving a high-profile speaker. These events can often require facilities that are much larger than those to which either a corporation or an association normally has access, thus providing an opportunity for the destination manager
- **The seminar/workshop experience**
  While sometimes contained within some of the above experiences, the seminar/workshop experience is of growing importance in today's knowledge society, in which the desire of individuals to raise their knowledge and skill levels in very focused areas of expertise often seems insatiable. In this area, the destination manager can assume either a reactive or a proactive stance, or both. The reactive approach involves seeking out those seminar/workshop experiences that corporations or associations are planning to put on. Conversely, the proactive stance involves identifying opportunities to sponsor seminars and workshops that appear to possess broad market appeal to a variety of corporations, associations, and individuals
- **The political gathering experience**
  The global democratization that is occurring has meant that there is an increasing need for facilities that can host both large and small gatherings of political groups involved in political planning and decision-making processes. Again, it is the astute destination manager that can anticipate these needs and position the destination as the most appropriate site for these gatherings

Table 9.5. Examples of attributes used by researchers to measure destination image (from Echtner and Ritchie, 1991).

	Number of studies measuring the attribute*
Functional (physical, measurable)	
Scenery/natural attractions	13
Costs/price levels	9
Climate	8
Tourist sites/activities	8
Nightlife and entertainment	8
Sports facilities/activities	8
National parks/wilderness activities	7
Local infrastructure/transportation	7
Architecture/buildings	7
Historic sites/museums	6
Beaches	6
Shopping facilities	5
Accommodation facilities	5
Cities	4
Fairs, exhibits, festivals	2
Facilities for information and tours	1
Crowdedness	4
Cleanliness	4
Personal safety	4
Economic development/affluence	3
Accessibility	2
Degree of urbanization	1
Extent of commercialization	1
Political stability	1
Hospitality/friendliness/receptiveness	11
Different customs/culture	7
Different cuisine/food and drink	7
Restful/relaxing	5
Atmosphere (familiar versus exotic)	4
Opportunity for adventure	3
Opportunity to increase knowledge	2
Family or adult-oriented	1
Quality of service	1
Fame/reputation	1
Psychological (abstract)	

*Total number of studies referenced is 14.

more of a defensive measure designed to protect the good name that many destinations had built up over the years. However, branding has now become a much more proactive and positive dimension of a destination's overall marketing strategy (Morgan et al., 2002). Despite this shift to a more positive approach, the concept of destination branding is often being applied without a clear understanding of the true nature and the fundamental functions of a destination brand.

When US states such as Florida and Utah claim that 'FLA/USA' and 'Utah!' are brands, what do they really have in mind concerning the roles or functions that the brand will play? While it may not have been a conscious strategy, a select number of resort destinations and ski centres have built up over the years what effectively amounts to a brand identity. Spas such as Baden-Baden in Germany and resorts such as Palm Springs in California, USA, evoke strong images in the minds of travellers. Ski centres

Table 9.6. Most frequent responses to open-ended image questions for Jamaica (from Echtner and Ritchie, 1993).

Images or characteristics evoked when thinking of Jamaica as a vacation destination
- Beaches (80.5%)
- Tropical climate (61.1%)
- Sun (44.3%)
- Ocean (30.2%)
- Negroid peoples (25.5%)
- Music/reggae (25.5%)
- Rum and tropical drinks (18.1%)
- Poverty (17.4%)
- Friendly, hospitable (16.1%)
- Palm trees (16.1%)
- Water sports (16.1%)
- Scenery (13.4%)
- Culture (11.4%)
- Fun, parties (11.4%)
- Tropical vegetation (11.4%)
- Food, fruits (10.7%)

Descriptions of the atmosphere or mood expected while visiting Jamaica
- Relaxing (55.0%)
- Friendly, hospitable (41.6%)
- Fun, parties (38.9%)
- Slow pace (38.3%)
- Happy (21.5%)
- Exciting (17.4%)
- Tropical (11.4%)
- Romantic (10.1%)

Distinctive or unique tourist attractions in Jamaica
- Beaches (57.3%)
- Water sports (17.9%)
- Ocean (16.2%)
- Music/reggae (14.5%)
- Culture (13.7%)
- Tropical climate (12.0%)
- Montego Bay (11.1%)

such as St Moritz, Kitzbühel, Chamonix and Cortina d'Ampezzo in Europe, and Aspen, Vail, Lake Tahoe and Whistler (BC) in North America all have names that are immediately recognized world-wide. Whether or not such name recognition alone constitutes branding is questionable. However, there is little doubt that these centres are greatly concerned with maintaining and protecting the reputation that their names are associated with.

While the importance of reputation protection should not be minimized, branding has

many other functions that are equally important, if not more important, from an overall marketing perspective. Before examining these, it is essential to have a basic understanding of fundamental brand theory and brand management. As a first step in gaining this understanding, it is useful to review a summary of the terminology of branding (Upshaw, 1995) (Table 9.7). With these definitions as a foundation, we now turn to the development of a definition of destination branding.

A simple transference of Aaker's well-known definition of branding would infer that a destination brand is a 'distinguishing name and/or symbol (such as a logo or trademark) intended to identify the destination and to differentiate it from competitive destinations' (Aaker, 1991, p. 7).

Because of the importance that we attach to the concept of experience in tourism theory and management, we propose the following definition:

> A destination brand is a name, symbol, logo, trademark or other graphic that both identifies and differentiates the destination; furthermore, it conveys the promise of a memorable travel experience that is uniquely associated with the destination. It also serves to consolidate and reinforce the post-travel recollection of pleasurable memories of the destination experience.

The branding of experience

Since our definition heavily involves the concept of experience, some further background will be useful. The branding of experience is one of the most powerful contributions that tourism and leisure research has made to the marketing field (Pine and Gilmore, 1999). In effect, this paradigm asserts that consumers are not really concerned with the quality of a particular product or the quality of a particular service transaction. What is truly important is their overall satisfaction with the product use experience. While part of this satisfaction certainly involves the product, it also involves many other factors that surround and influence the use of a product.

From a tourism perspective, we similarly must recognize that the overall travel

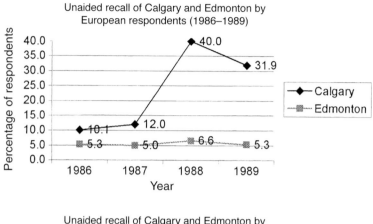

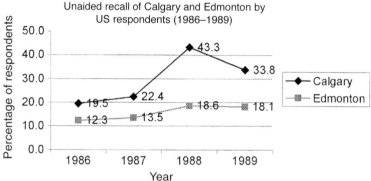

Fig. 9.2. Measuring the extent to which the 1988 Olympic Winter Games in Calgary, Canada increased levels of awareness of the host city over the period 1986–1989: a comparison with the neighbouring city of Edmonton, Canada (from Ritchie and Smith, 1991).

Table 9.7. The basic terminology of branding (from Upshaw, 1995).

- Brand equity: the total accumulated value or worth of a brand; the tangible and intangible assets that the brand contributes to its corporate parent, both financially and in terms of selling leverage
- Brand identity: part of the brand's overall equity; the total perception of a brand in the marketplace, driven mostly by its positioning and personality
- Brand positioning: what a brand stands for in the minds of customers and prospects, relative to its competition, in terms of benefits and promises
- Brand personality: the outward face of a brand; its tonal characteristics most closely associated with human traits
- Brand essence: the core or distillation of the brand identity
- Brand character: having to do with the internal constitution of the brand, how it is seen in terms of its integrity, honesty and trustworthiness
- Brand soul: related to the brand character, defined as the values and emotional core of the brand
- Brand culture: the system of values that surrounds a brand, much like the cultural aspects of a people or a country
- Brand image: generally synonymous with either the brand's strategic personality or its reputation as a whole

experience consists of a chain of transactions and behaviours that together define the travel experience (Otto and Ritchie, 1995). Taking this concept one step further, we can argue that the marketing focus should be on the experiential benefits provided by a company or a brand as a whole. From another perspective, Schmitt and Simonson (1997) argue that 'The consumer of today makes choices based on whether or not a product fits into her or his lifestyle; whether it represents an exciting new concept – a desirable experience'.

Viewed in this context, a destination can usefully view itself as a provider of destination experiences. If this approach is accepted, the issue then becomes one of determining: (i) the overall nature of the experience that the destination wishes to provide; and (ii) the set of benefits or sub-experiences that, taken together, will provide the satisfactory destination experience that the visitor is seeking.

Distinguishing among elements of the destination experience for branding purposes

A challenge facing destination managers is to decide which aspect of the destination experience should provide the basis for a brand. As Fig. 9.3 demonstrates, it is important to distinguish between the core elements of the destination experience and its secondary and peripheral dimensions. While it seems obvious that the brand should focus on the core experience provided by a destination, there is a risk that the necessary singular focus be diverted by the attributes or activities

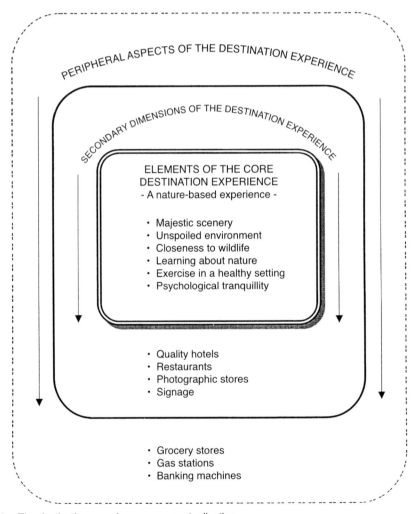

Fig. 9.3. The destination experience: a conceptualization.

related to the secondary or even the peripheral dimensions of the destination in an attempt to make sure that everything and everyone receives attention – particularly for political reasons.

The first part of the definition of branding given above (see *Destination branding*) addresses the traditional *identification* and *differentiation* functions of a brand. The second part, somewhat in contrast to traditional product branding, emphasizes that it is especially important that a destination brand should convey, either explicitly or implicitly, the *promise* of the essence of leisure travel – a *memorable experience* – and one that, if at all possible, is uniquely available at the destination in question. While product brands are also intended to convey a promise associated with satisfactory product use, the promise is usually of a more functional nature in terms of either product performance or the quality of a particular service transaction. Exceptions might be for more pleasure-oriented products (such as perfume) and services (such as massage). In tourism, for a destination to compete and succeed, it must offer a high-quality stream of product/service transactions – or what is referred to as a 'quality experience' (Otto and Ritchie, 1995). At the same time, since anticipation and memory are significant components of a quality experience, any attempt at destination branding must attempt to reassure the individual concerning the promise or expectations of future pleasure and/or excitement. Following travel, the brand can also play an important role in consolidating and reinforcing the post-travel recollections of a memorable destination experience.

Measures of brand effectiveness

Based on the foregoing discussions, we assert that the primary roles of a destination brand are to provide:

Pre-experience: selection
- Identification ⎫
- Differentiation ⎪ of the destination
- Anticipation ⎬ re: the destination
- Expectation ⎪ experience
- Reassurance ⎭

Post-experience: recollection
- Consolidation ⎫ of the destination
- Reinforcement ⎭

It follows that the effectiveness of a brand is dependent on how well it performs each of these roles. Measures of these preferences are summarized in Table 9.8 (Ritchie and Ritchie, 1998).

Assessing destination brand effectiveness

Once we have defined the measures of brand performance, they become a useful basis for assessing brand effectiveness. Figure 9.4 shows a worksheet designed for this purpose. In this particular worksheet the destinations are states of the USA and international city-states.

In summary, the task of the destination manager is to ensure that a destination brand performs all of the foregoing functions and that it does so as effectively as possible. Table 9.8 summarizes the roles that a destination brand should perform and provides indicators that may be used to measure this performance. Going one step further, Fig. 9.4 provides a basic worksheet for analysing and comparing the effectiveness of destination brands.

Obviously, the same framework can be used to assess brand effectiveness for any comparable set of destination attributes.

Achieving success in branding

Len Berry, an internationally recognized expert in service marketing has argued that a successful service brand will be one based on a distinctive and consistent message that reaches consumers emotionally, is associated with trust, and is supported by an organization that performs its core services well (Berry, 2000). In order to attain a successful brand, Berry urges the service organization (in this case, the DMO) to:

- dare to be different;
- determine its own area of fame (something that is important to customers);

Table 9.8. Measures of destination brand performance (from Ritchie and Ritchie, 1998).

Roles	Measure
Selection *Sub-components*	• The extent to which the destination is chosen over others
Identification	• Degree of recognition/association
Differentiation	• Lack of confusion with other destinations • Lack of confusion with other products/services
Anticipation	• The extent to which brand generates a desire to visit the destination • The intensity of the desire to visit that the brand generates
Expectation	• The nature and importance of the specific benefits the visitor expects to realize from the destination experience
Reassurance	• The extent to which the brand provides a 'cloud of comfort' for the visitor – a feeling that all is well or will go well during the destination visit
Recollection *Sub-components*	• The ease, frequency and strength of recall of the destination experience • The extent to which the brand helps create memories of the destination and the visitor's experiences • The intensity or warmth of memories elicited • The degree of comfort provided that the future/current choice is/was a sound one
Consolidation	• The ability of the brand to serve as a catalyst to tie together the many memories of the destination experience
Reinforcement	• The ability of the brand to cement a consolidated and coherent memory of the destination experience

• make an emotional connection with consumers (by communicating values that consumers relate to); and
• ensure internalization of the brand by front-line employees, who represent the destination and directly influence the visitor experience.

While destination policy (Chapter 8) provides the framework for defining key target markets and the kind of image and brand that the destination wishes to establish for itself within each of these markets, it is the daily marketing and promotion activities that determine whether or not these policy objectives are attained. One important reason for measuring the image of one's own destination in key strategic markets is to provide some critical basic information for the development of a destination brand.

As indicated previously, the first management task is to establish the existing level of *awareness and image* of the destination in key target markets, a task that should be built into the ongoing information-gathering and research programme of a destination. It is only once this fundamental understanding of the perception of the destination by primary potential visitors has been gained that the necessary and appropriate advertising/promotional programme can be developed and initiated.

Perhaps the first stage of this development is to estimate the level of expenditure that will be required in order to have the desired impact in each key target market. To make these estimates, destination managers should at least have insight into the level of competitive advertising/promotion, the rest of the various advertising/promotion alternatives that are available in each target market area, and the travel and decision-making behaviours of residents of target market areas.

Destination positioning

An important underlying reason for a destination to measure and understand its image and to develop a destination brand is so that it can effectively position itself against competitors in the marketplace.

In brief, a destination's 'position' in the market is how a destination is perceived by potential and actual visitors in terms of the experiences (and associated benefits) that it provides relative to competing destinations. The perceptions that establish a destination's

Destination (examples)	Brand effectiveness dimension								
	SELECTION	Identification	Differentiation	Anticipation	Expectation	Reassurance	RECOLLECTION	Consolidation	Reinforcement
States of the United States									
Florida									
Texas									
New York									
California									
Vermont									
Oregon									
Illinois									
Kansas									
National city-states									
Paris									
Munich									
Rome									
New York									
London									
Beijing									
Sydney									
Toronto									
Rio de Janeiro									
Tokyo									
Seoul									

Fig. 9.4. A worksheet for assessing the effectiveness of destination brand.

position can be based on how the consumer perceives the attributes of a destination's image, or on its holistic image. Some very basic examples of how the same destination may be positioned differently depending on the importance of the primary positioning criteria are given in Fig. 9.5. As shown (depending on the market segment), Las Vegas may be positioned as either a family or an adult experience destination. In fact, this has been a positioning issue that the management of Las Vegas has had to address as the destination has evolved from primarily a gaming destination to a more multidimensional one providing an array of different experiences. As a gaming experience destination, Las Vegas' competition is a destination such as Atlantic City. As a family fun vacation experience, it must compete with destinations such as Disney World.

While Disney World may compete with Las Vegas for family vacations as a fun experience, when it comes to family vacation experiences that emphasize education, even Disney's Epcot Center must take a back seat to destinations such as Washington, DC.

In the same vein, while Paris, France, and Vancouver, Canada, compete as attractive, liveable cities, Paris competes with Rome, Italy, as a historical city while Vancouver competes more with a city such as Oslo, Norway, as a city that emphasizes environmental quality.

Figure 9.6a–c provides some basic examples of how the positioning of destinations is sometimes represented, and how a destination (Jamaica) may be positioned differently depending on the positioning criteria employed.

Fig. 9.5. An example of how one particular destination (Las Vegas) may be positioned differently, depending on the importance of positioning criteria to the market.

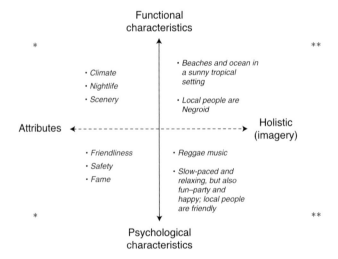

*Information in quadrant supplied by scale items.
**Information in quadrant supplied by open-ended questions.

Fig. 9.6a. The attribute/holistic and functional/psychological components of destination image for Jamaica (from Echtner and Ritchie, 1993).

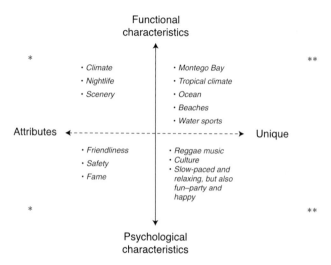

*Information in quadrant supplied by scale items.
**Information in quadrant supplied by open-ended questions.

Fig. 9.6b. The common/unique and functional/psychological components of destination image for Jamaica (from Echtner and Ritchie, 1993).

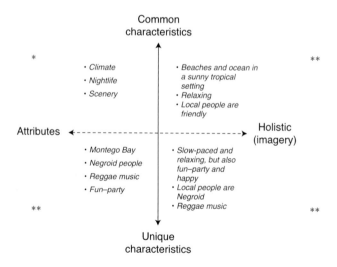

*Information in quadrant supplied by scale items.
**Information in quadrant supplied by open-ended questions.

Fig. 9.6c. The attribute/holistic and common/unique components of destination image for Jamaica (from Echtner and Ritchie, 1993).

In summary, a destination's competitive position depends upon the market segment of relevance. Each segment will seek different experiences – while a destination may be competitive primarily with a particular destination regarding one type of experience, this same destination may be an irrelevant competitor for other types of experiences. Given this reality, a destination must fully understand the concept of market segmentation when establishing its market position and not attempt to over-simplify the use of positioning.

Market segmentation

As Kotler and Bowen (1998) point out, there are many ways to segment a market. But in making this statement they also assert that, to be useful, market segments must have certain characteristics, and these are summarized in Table 9.9. The challenge facing destination marketing is to use the right combination of segmentation criteria that identify enough markets where the destination is truly competitive in the experiences it provides.

Once the above insights have been gained, destination managers are then in a more realistic position to formulate the specifics of the advertising/promotion types and themes that will be necessary to build the desired destination brand and to support the intended competitive position in the minds of the consumer.

Developing logos, themes and advertising support

While the development of a destination logo is an integral part of the process of destination branding, the entire effort must be actively supported by thematic advertising that communicates the brand message to all major target markets. This requires the involvement of a creative advertising agency. Once the message is created, management must oversee the timing of the actual advertising by market segments. Timing decisions must consider the behavioural patterns of individuals and/or groups in key target markets, the cost of alternative media during different time periods, the nature of competitive timing of advertising and promotion, and the lead time required to ensure that desired time periods can be captured. In the case of certain promotional activities, such as the hosting of familiarization visits by tour operators and travel writers, the schedules of others often determine the timing of these activities.

As for destination logos themselves, Blain and Ritchie (2002) have studied the process of developing them in some detail. While it is clear that destination managers attach great importance to the development of a destination logo – and, indeed, equate it heavily with the branding process – it is surprising that few carry out a significant amount of research to understand how their logos are perceived and interpreted by the travelling public and by the industry itself.

Examples of the logos of several of the major urban areas included in the Blain and Ritchie study are given in Fig. 9.7.

Table 9.9. Requirements for effective segmentation (from Kotler and Brown, 1998).

- Measurability. The degree to which the segment's size and purchasing power can be measured. Certain segmentation variables are difficult to measure, such as the size of the segment of teenagers who drink primarily to rebel against their parents
- Accessibility. The degree to which segments can be accessed and served. One of the authors found that 20% of a college restaurant's customers were frequent patrons. However, frequent patrons lacked any common characteristics. They included faculty, staff and students. There was no usage difference among part-time, full-time and class-year of the students. Although the market segment had been identified, there was no way to access the heavy-user segment
- Substantiality. The degree to which segments are large or profitable enough to serve as markets. A segment should be the largest possible homogeneous group economically viable enough to support a tailored marketing programme. For example, large metropolitan areas can support many different ethnic restaurants, but in a smaller town, Thai, Vietnamese and Moroccan food restaurants would not survive
- Actionability. The degree to which effective programmes can be designed for attracting and serving segments. A small airline, for example, identified seven market segments, but its staff and budget were too small to develop separate marketing programmes for each segment

Fig. 9.7. Some examples of destination logos.

Managing the Quality of Visitor Service and the Visitor Experience

Next to marketing, the provision of visitor services (particularly information) has traditionally accounted for most of the external efforts of DMOs. While this is still probably true, the conceptual nature of this component of destination management has evolved considerably in recent years. In brief, the DMO must now be concerned with efforts to ensure that the destination provides a total high-quality visitor experience. Despite this evolution in thinking, perhaps the most straightforward manner in which to apply a services marketing perspective to tourism is to borrow general marketing measurement instruments directly from the field and apply them to tourism. Most research of this nature has focused on the evaluation of

service quality and on the more functional and technical aspects of service delivery. In fact, traditional measures of service quality have been shown to apply in the evaluation of services in the leisure and tourism industries. For example, the dimensions that LeBlanc (1992) found that travellers used in evaluating service quality in travel agencies were not materially different either from those captured by the SERVQUAL instrument (Parasuraman et al., 1985) (e.g. timeliness, competence, physical evidence) or from those used to evaluate service quality in organized tours, as noted by Luk et al. (1993). Similarly, Fick and Ritchie (1991, p. 9) showed SERVQUAL to be adequate for monitoring and comparative purposes in service industries such as ski resorts. However, Fick and Ritchie also advocated the use of supplementary qualitative measures to capture key dimensions, noting that a strictly quantitative scale does not adequately address those affective and holistic factors 'which contribute to the overall quality of the *service experience*'.

However, focusing only on the objective, technical aspects of tourism services leaves untapped a crucial aspect of total visitor satisfaction. This is the ability to understand and manage the true nature of consumer satisfaction as it occurs in the context of service delivery. Research has shown that affective or emotion-based elements form the basis of much of the quality of the service experience. In brief, they contribute a significant, but often ignored, portion of visitor satisfaction (Oliver, 1993). We conclude, then, that a more complete measure of the quality of the service experience might be a useful complement – if not an alternative – to traditional quality of service measures.

Table 9.10 demonstrates, from both a conceptual and a measurement standpoint, the difference between the quality of service and the quality of experience (Otto and Ritchie, 1995).

Perhaps more than any other service industry, tourism holds the potential to elicit strong emotional and experiential reactions in consumers. Accordingly, at least two other researchers in the field have noted that utilitarian and rational information processing schemes, which focus on functional or purely attribute-based elements, are not commensurate with leisure and tourism. Dimanche and Samdahl (1994) refer to tourism as unique, owing to its symbolic expressive dimensions, while Arnould and Price (1993) focus on the extraordinary experience offered by extended leisure pursuits (in their case, white-water rafting trips), both of which render the experience incompatible with traditional evaluative paradigms. These authors advocate a focus on the self to truly understand satisfaction with such phenomena.

We further argue here that even when tourism sectors have a clear functional component, as do accommodation and transportation services, experiential benefits will remain a critical part of the process evaluation. The intimate, hands-on nature of the service encounter itself affords many opportunities for affective responses. Elements of the physical environment – what Bitner (1992) calls the 'servicescape' – also have strong potential to elicit emotional and subjective reactions (Wakefield and Blodgett, 1994). For example, the tranquil beauty of a mountain resort's setting affords psychological benefits that clearly transcend the physical need to sleep somewhere. In addition, it has long been acknowledged that human interaction itself is an emotionally charged process. The extended interaction with a tour guide or other service provider can also lead to experiential reactions (Arnould and Price, 1993). In other cases, as in purely recreational activities, the experiential benefits will be ends in themselves (Holbrook and Hirschman, 1982).

Structure of the service experience

Our research has found that the service experience in tourism can be envisaged to contain four main dimensions (Table 9.11). The *hedonics* dimension reflects the desire/ need of tourists to be doing what they love or like, to have their imaginations stirred, and to be thrilled by the service/experience activities. Further, they want to be able to have

Table 9.10. Comparison of QOS and QOE frameworks (from Otto and Ritchie, 1995).

Framework	QOS (*quality of service*)	QOE (*quality of experience*)
Measurement	Objective	Subjective
Evaluative model	Attribute-based	Holistic/Gestalt
Focus of evaluation	Company/service provider/ service environment (external)	Self (internal)
Scope	Specific	General
Nature of benefits	Functional/utilitarian	Experiential/hedonic/symbolic
Psychological representation	Cognitive/attitudinal	Affective

Table 9.11. Dimensions of the service experience in tourism (from Otto and Ritchie, 1995).

Dimension one: hedonics
- Doing something I really like to do
- Doing something memorable
- Doing something thrilling
- Having a once-in-a-lifetime experience
- Sharing my experience with others later on
- A feeling of escape
- Being challenged in some way
- My imagination is being stirred
- On an adventure
- Having fun
- Doing something new and different

Dimension two: peace of mind
- Physically comfortable
- Property is safe
- Relaxed
- Personal security
- Privacy is assured

Dimension three: involvement
- Involved in the process
- Element of choice in the process
- Have control over the outcome
- Being educated and informed
- Cooperation

Dimension four: recognition
- Taken seriously
- Important

memories to keep to themselves and/or to share with others later on. Second, visitors seek *peace of mind*, the desire for both physical and psychological safety and comfort. Third, tourists seek *involvement* in the process of service delivery, a distinct willingness to be active participants in certain service systems, as indicated by the desire to have choice and control in the service offering. On the other hand, tourists seem to also demand that they be educated, informed and imbued with a sense of mutual cooperation within the service experience. Finally, tourists want to derive a sense of *personal recognition* from their individual service encounters and the service experience as a whole, such that they feel important and are confident they are being taken seriously.

In managerial terms, it appears critical that practitioners in the tourism industry should not lose sight of the true nature of consumer benefits, motivations and subjective responses.

Our research has shown that service experience factors are not soft, elusive abstracts, but rather are specific dimensions that can readily be measured so that satisfaction can be better understood. Indeed, if industry managers use only service quality or attribute-based measures in their satisfaction evaluations, they may be forcing people to evaluate tourism services on more functional and utilitarian dimensions than is appropriate or even relevant.

From the perspective of marketing strategy, advertising experiential benefits is not new to either product or services marketing. A clearer understanding of the customer-specific experience as it relates to a service or company can contribute to a more effective strategy for positioning, promotion and communication, a point that has been supported in previous research. Vogt *et al.* (1993) found that travellers demonstrated the need for aesthetic information as well as for functional information. In other words, consumers will, consciously or otherwise, seek out information on what type of experience to expect at the level of both the destination and, by extension, the company. In practical terms, this means that the need for information on such aspects as pricing and operating hours may be supplemented (if not supplanted) by the need to promote psychological factors. While this may be obvious and commonplace in advertising for tours and attractions, incorporating experiential dimensions into more functional services may offer a unique competitive edge. As noted by Arnould and Price (1993), 'although it may seem a stretch to promise a renewed sense of self from stopping at McDonald's for breakfast, several award-winning advertisements do just that'. Effectively accomplishing this objective is tied into the type of medium used to convey product information. While glossy brochures are an advantage over newspapers, the current trend to video-based advertising in tourism will provide even more opportunity to convey the richness of the customer experience in service encounters.

The multifaceted nature of the service experience also implies that it could be a useful means by which to classify services. Our data have provided evidence that both the nature and the degree of the service experience differ significantly across the sectors of tourism.

Clearly, the primary message emerging for tours and attractions is 'entertain me', while that for airlines and hotels is 'keep me feeling safe'. Of secondary importance to both airlines and hotels is the tourist's need for recognition as a customer, while for tourism and attractions both involvement and peace of mind are primary considerations. Looking closely at these differences indicates a means by which one can categorize services based on their respective experiences. That is, certain services will offer experiential benefits as they relate to the way the business is run (i.e. they are process variables) while others will offer experiential benefits as they relate to the overall purpose of your business (i.e. they are outcome variables). An example of the former would be airlines, whose primary purpose is functional (transporting passengers from A to B), while the delivery of the service can be enhanced by the incorporation of experiential benefits. An example of the latter would be a theme park, whose purpose is experiential but whose service environment would be enhanced by the incorporation of service quality or functional variables. In other words, the functional and the experiential are two ends of a continuum along which both service processes and outcomes might be evaluated and classified.

Of course, the challenge will lie in translating the service experience into specifics concerned with service encounter, service delivery and service environment. As noted above, the coexistence of these ostensibly opposing dimensions (thrills versus safety, functional versus experiential) underscores the need for service providers in tourism to understand their customers fully so that they can provide an environment which offers that critical balance. From a measurement standpoint, a related difficulty arises in the need to get more involved in measuring and understanding one's customers and their feelings rather than simply focusing on the more readily assessed and more easily controllable internal measures, such as waiting time and uniform style. In the short term, implementation of service experience standards will potentially increase marketing costs, as the administration of customer surveys is naturally more expensive than internal audits and reviews. According to Ozment and Morash (1994), however, the payoff from an investment in this kind of consumer understanding is high. They further argue that it is more efficient and economical to design all service standards based on proper consumer understanding in the first place than to have to retrace one's steps and redesign systems that were built according to inaccurate or even insufficient information.

While it is conceptually satisfying to understand the nature of the challenge facing the destination manager who is seeking to provide a rewarding visitation experience within the total destination experience, it must be recognized that there are many links in the total 'experience chain'. The greater challenge facing the destination manager is to attempt to ensure, as far as possible, that all the 'experience links' within his or her destination are all satisfactory and mutually reinforcing. Unfortunately, it is also a reality that overall visitor satisfaction with a total travel experience will relate to links in the experience chain that are beyond the control of the DMO. An exasperating experience with an airline used to reach the destination may disproportionately colour the memories of the destination visit. This reality must be communicated to all destination stakeholders.

An indirect way of enhancing the quality of visitor services and the visitor experience is to take a leadership role in the design and development of service standards within a destination. Those operators meeting these standards are then allowed to display decals or some other form of recognition that conveys to the visitor their commitment to the delivery of quality services.

Management implications of adapting a quality-of-experience framework

The foregoing discussion strongly implies that the DMO needs to examine the total visitor experience from the moment they start searching for a destination to visit until after they arrive back home after the trip. Admittedly, much of the travel experience is outside the destination's control, or even its influence. Nevertheless, the truly competitive DMO should be constantly searching for ways in which it can effectively and profitably (from the destination's standpoint) enhance the quality of the total visitation experience. This may be done by efforts to help ensure high-quality service from all firms and organizations that provide services to the visitor, be they functional or pleasure-oriented. The provision of quality service can be promoted through the training and education of service providers (discussed later in this chapter) and workshops on the design and development of attractions and facilities. The enhancement of the overall quality of the visitor experience can be maintained and improved through the DMO's leadership and coordination roles. The DMO first seeks to create a critical mass of core attractions. It then seeks to coordinate the efforts of these attractors and functional service providers in such a way that they realize how interdependent they all are in the delivery of a high-quality total visitation experience. The visitor is normally oblivious of all this behind-the-scenes activity to provide what (hopefully) appears to be an effortless, natural visitation experience designed and developed specifically for each individual visitor. By means that are imperceptible to the

visitor, a well-designed, integrated backroom system provides the foundation that enables well-chosen, well-trained front-line staff to deliver the personalized understanding and attention that creates destination experiences and memories that may be treasured for a lifetime. As Bedbury and Fenichell (2002, p. 19) have so aptly put it, 'We are defined by the experiences and actions of our lifetime. So are brands.' In the present context, for 'brands' read 'destination brands'.

Managing Information/Research (I/R)

A management task which has grown in significance over the past two decades – and which will undoubtedly continue to soar in importance – is that of managing the information and research (I/R) needs of the destination. As Fig. 9.8 indicates, there are essentially two different flows of I/R that must be generated and managed. Inward flows are those that provide information to the DMO management so that

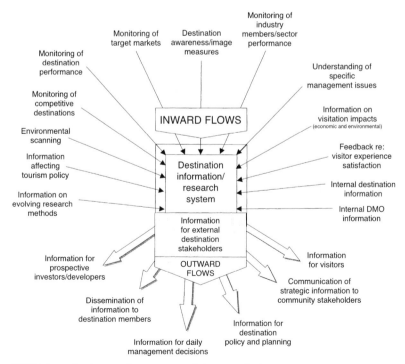

Fig. 9.8. DMO information/research management: types and roles.

it can function more competitively and more sustainably. The inward flows are of two main types: monitoring flows, which involve information collected on a continuous basis, and research flows, which involve information obtained periodically as the need arises. Outward flows of information pertain to information that should be provided to a broad range of both close and distant destination stakeholders. Wise and prudent management of outward information flow is often neglected.

Managing inward I/R flows

As Fig. 9.8 demonstrates, there are many different types of I/R that a competitive/ sustainable destination must gather, interpret, understand and utilize as it seeks to establish an effective destination management information system (Ritchie and Ritchie, 2002).

The *monitoring of target markets* perhaps provides the most fundamental information that a DMO must have available as guidance for the development of its 'experience products' and for the design and delivery of its advertising and promotional programmes. One specific sub-component of target market monitoring is the gathering of *destination awareness and image measures*.

While target market monitoring focuses on the attractiveness and behaviours of current markets, the process of *environmental scanning* is designed to identify new trends that are likely to create the markets of tomorrow.

Both of the these flows of information concern visitors before they arrive at the destination. It is also important to monitor *visitor satisfaction* regarding their experience at the destination. Ryan (1995) provides an excellent technical source of guidance to DMOs for the design, collection and use of visitor satisfaction data. In parallel with understanding the level of visitor satisfaction is the monitoring of the *visitation impacts* brought about by these visitors. All dimensions of these impacts – economic, environmental, social and cultural – should be considered.

An equally fundamental form of internal DMO information is that which captures the *performance of the destination*. This information can take several forms. The most basic information is that provided by *the DMO's own internal accounting system*, which informs management about its control over cost and expenditures, with emphasis on identifying deviations from the budget that has been approved by the DMO's board of directors. A second set of destination performance measures is external to the DMO, but internal with respect to the destination as a whole. These measures seek, in effect, to monitor the extent to which the destination is meeting its overall performance goals. Thus, they first measure collective factors, such as total visitation, total revenues and total employment in the tourism sector. In addition, they also seek to monitor the distribution of visitation among all destination attractions and to measure the profitability of individual attractions/stakeholders. These measures not only allow individual firms to compare their performance with colleague firms within the destination, but they may also permit a critical comparison of major destination components with those of competing and collaborating destinations.

In addition to the above incoming flows of information, which are largely under the control of the DMO and its stakeholders, destinations must also attempt to systematically gather information on *competitive activities* and *competitive performance*. Some of this information may be obvious and easy to collect, but much of it may be difficult to access, and then only on a quid pro quo basis. It is here that industry associations may play an important role.

A final form of inward flowing information is defined as *formal management research*. This involves the undertaking of structured research enquiries that seek to provide understanding and insight into the resolution of specific management problems or concerns. For example, sudden increases in employee turnover, unexplained drops in visitation from certain strategic target markets and the need to determine areas of resident support/non-support for future development all lend themselves to in-depth research that may assist DMO management in both daily decision making and long-term policy formulation. Other research, such as a review of the evolving impact of government regulations and fiscal and taxation policy on the competitiveness and sustainability of tourism, may focus much more specifically on the formulation of strategic tourism policy.

The foregoing discussion of information pertains to the important flow of information from outside the DMO, so as to allow more effective marketing and improved visitor experiences. It is also important to note that, in tourism management, there is also heavy flow of information from the destination to the marketplace. Travel is one area of consumer expenditure where the buyer often does a lot of research into the choice/purchase decision. It is not uncommon for prospective travellers to accumulate and access information on alternative destinations for many months. This reality has increased with the advent of the Internet. Consequently, from a competitive perspective it is essential that consumers have access to the amount and variety of information that they desire, and that this information should be of the highest quality. But, as destinations provide this information, they will have to continuously assess the cost-effectiveness of each information channel and each information type.

Managing outward I/R flows

While the management of I/R is viewed by many as the management and use of inward flows, an effective DMO must also acknowledge a certain need to manage outward flows of information to different categories of stakeholders. Most obvious is the responsibility to disseminate to DMO members the information they require in an organized and useful form, so that they can plan and perform effectively. This is seen by many as the primary tasks of a DMO's research manager.

A second, highly sensitive stakeholder group for whom the need for effective information has been increasingly recognized by DMO leaders consists of those in the political environment who affect the destination's growth and development. Most obviously, these may be *local, regional and national politicians* who may influence the DMO's level of funding. Less obviously, but perhaps more significantly in the long run, there are those who determine the policy framework within which destinations must operate and compete.

Since politicians' views are democratically determined by the population at large, a DMO must attempt to develop processes that keep *destination residents* aware and informed regarding the value of tourism to the community, and how future development can enhance community well-being. While this is not an easy task, it cannot be neglected.

Yet another outward flow of information that virtually all DMOs recognize – and that most handle well – is that provided to both *potential and actual visitors*. The flow to potential visitors is defined as promotion and advertising, while the flow to current visitors is usually subsumed under visitor services.

A final and often demanding request for destination information comes from *potential investors*. While these requests are frequently made indirectly by consultants who serve many masters and not all have the destination's interests at heart, they nevertheless are difficult to ignore.

Human Resource Development

We now enter an area of critical importance to the success of the destination but over which the DMO has relatively little control, or even influence. As Table 9.12 demonstrates, it is not until well along the life learning curve of its members that the DMO is in a position to play a directly significant role in the training and education of its members. Despite this, it should be kept in mind that a progressive DMO can play a very important role in supporting the establishment of tourism-related training and education programmes at local and national institutions that are willing to give priority to these programmes. Indeed, this type of DMO backing is absolutely essential in obtaining government support and fund-raising for tourism training and education purposes. This support can make the difference between international-level excellence and mediocrity, or even no programming at all.

To summarize, although DMOs have traditionally played an active role in training and certification programmes aimed at front-line staff, their support for both junior and senior management development programmes (degree

Table 9.12. Levels and types of human resource training and education relative to tourism.

- Basic family learning
  Much of what all members of the workforce know, especially their attitudes towards work and acceptance of responsibility, is learned in the home/family setting. Its relevance to the well-being of society goes well beyond the needs of the tourist sector
- Basic societal/education system learning
  Again, the learning and human formation which occurs in primary and secondary schooling is of a general, fundamental nature, intended to meet the broadest needs of society. While tourism benefits from the emergence of an educated, responsible individual, much of the system has not traditionally recognized the merits of many tourism-related opportunities and careers
- Post-secondary technical training
  It is here where tourism has traditionally felt that it receives the greatest benefits from the formal education/training system. Many technical school graduates possess the technical and industry-oriented skills that make them highly desirable as entry-level employees
- Post-secondary academic training
  More recently, the tourism industry has recognized the benefits that a broader education can provide, especially when combined with a certain degree of technical training. So-called hybrid programmes which combine and integrate technical training and general and/or management education, are currently producing graduates that the industry has found to be highly appealing, and who are starting to achieve levels of success unknown in the past
- Career-based learning
  In today's world, 'lifelong learning' has become a reality. In tourism, this has meant the establishment of ongoing programmes to maintain and update technical skills, as well as executive development programmes to provide a level of access to learning that has been previously denied to managers in the industry, and to enhance the effectiveness of those with a basic post-secondary education. The Certified Destination Management Executive (CDME) programme offered by the International Association of Convention and Visitor Bureaus (IACVB) is one such example
- Localized workshops and seminars on special topics
  In addition to extended programmes such as CDME, many DMOs take the opportunity to provide their members with local workshops and seminars on special topics that reflect the needs of the day. A few topics that are typically covered include Destination Management Information Systems (DMIS), Destination Marketing and Financial Management and Supervisor Training

and non-degree) is growing in significance as the industry becomes increasingly complex and sophisticated from a management perspective. It is not necessary for DMOs to be directly responsible for the design and delivery of these management programmes. However, they should exert their moral leadership role in this area by encouraging and supporting those institutions that are in a position to assist them. The leverage to be gained through this approach can be substantial.

Finance and Venture Capital Management

The discussion to this point in the chapter has laid out an admittedly aggressive management agenda for the DMO if it is to ensure the ongoing success of the destination. It should be emphasized that the DMO cannot and should not try to carry out all these management functions by itself. Rather, the challenge facing the DMO is to oversee all of these management processes and ensure that, where possible, they are done largely by someone else. Overcoming this challenge is not an easy task, since the DMO has relatively few levers it can pull to force anyone to fulfil a great many of the management roles. Its structure and skill in coordination and the use of moral persuasion will be severely and consistently tested – but succeed it must in these areas if the destination itself is to succeed. There is, however, one factor that the DMO can bring to bear, and that is the provision of destination stakeholders and operators with *financial assistance* and access to *venture capital.*

While true success in this area is probably more a policy than a management issue, an effective DMO should do all it can to assist its members in gaining ready access to funding and to assist them in determining how best to access and manage venture funds. While this latter role falls into the category of member services, anything the DMO can do within the external financial environment to improve the financial community's understanding of the nature of tourism and the opportunities it provides for both firms and the community as a whole will be a service that will be valued highly and greatly appreciated. In addition, this ambassador/educator role within the financial community is one that the DMO is best positioned to play on behalf of tourism. Only the DMO has the necessary understanding of tourism, and the mutual moral ground it shares with the financial community renders it credible in this role.

In some cases, DMOs have been known to take equity positions in certain key developments within their destination. However, in most cases, their financial assistance takes the form of promotional expenditures, frequently in collaboration with private operators. As for access to venture capital, the DMO's role is largely one of providing information to both sides: to the private sector operators regarding sources of capital, and to venture capitalists regarding potential investments in the local tourism industry.

Visitor Services and Visitor Management

Services and the experience economy

While leisure travellers who visit a destination are looking for high-quality service, in a more meaningful sense they are seeking quality total experiences that are memorable. As Pine and Gilmore (1999) have pointed out, the Walt Disney Company is continually 'imagineering' new offerings by which to apply the experiential expertise it has developed through Disneyland and Disney World over several decades in an effort to continually create new visitor experiences. As a result, Disney has, for example, created the Disney Institute and the Disney Cruise line.

The implication of the search for experiences is that each and every destination manager must attempt to view his or her destination not simply as a place to visit and a place to do things, but, more importantly, as the provider of visitor experiences – preferably enjoyable, memorable experiences – that will generate high levels of visitor satisfaction and the subsequent favourable word-of-mouth advertising that is essential to both competitiveness and sustainability.

It is also important for the entire tourism industry within a destination to realize that an individual or a family's degree of satisfaction with a business trip or family vacation is dependent upon the entire series of events and/or service transactions that occur from the time the individual/group leaves home until they return (Otto and Ritchie, 1996). In fact, satisfaction with the total travel experience is dependent on all the links in the experience chain (Fig. 9.9). A bad experience with respect to only a few links – or even one important link – in the experience chain can leave the traveller with a feeling of dissatisfaction regarding the entire travel experience.

The challenge facing destination managers would be difficult even if they controlled the quality of the experience for all links of the experience chain. However, as we all know, they do not. Many of the links are not even located within one destination, and are thus beyond the control or even the influence of a

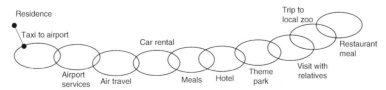

Fig. 9.9. The links in the travel experience chain.

single destination manager. Indeed, this is the case more often than not. All that a given destination manager can realistically do on a daily basis is to focus on ensuring that as many as possible of the experience links within his/her destination deliver what they promise. From a longer-term, broader perspective it is thus clearly important that all destination managers work together in an attempt to deliver an industry-wide quality travel experience.

The foregoing emphasis on the need for quality links, both within a destination and across the industry, underscores the importance of the DMO and regional, national and international tourism industry associations. It is only through the cooperation and coordination that is provided by these leadership organizations that the tourism sector can hope to strengthen the highly interdependent links of the travel experience. While the degree of perfection required for total traveller satisfaction is clearly unattainable, either within or across destinations, this ideal must constantly be our goal.

Systems for visitor management

While we must keep in mind the need for a quality total experience for the visitor, the traditional approach to visitor services is an external DMO activity that has always been viewed as one of the cornerstones of the DMO's being and of its success – to the point where one of the first locations sought out by the visitor is the DMO visitor information centre. Despite this importance, the visitor information centre is still but an element in a DMO's total efforts to help ensure a high-quality visitor experience. Another major component of the total information services provided to visitors is often the one responsible for their visit. Destination visitor call centres, using a toll-free telephone number, have traditionally been the nerve centre through which potential visitors have gathered screening information to help them make their destination choice. The Internet has now substantially replaced the visitor call centre, although many people still appreciate the assistance provided by a human being.

As the size of tourism grows, and as the number of visitors to each individual destination, site or monument grows, it has become more important to develop visitor management systems that are fair, efficient and cost-effective, while at the same time allowing a satisfactory visitor experience. Although the advent of computers has made the task of visitor management somewhat easier, great care must be taken to avoid the impression that visitors are being herded like animals for the convenience of an attraction operator. Visitors realize that some degree of mechanization or depersonalization is necessary in order to deal with large crowds at popular venues. At the same time, the ability to maintain the personal touch wherever possible remains extremely important.

Table 9.13 provides some examples of the types of approaches that have been developed to minimize the negative impacts on the visitation site and to provide fair and equitable access to locales that have a limited capacity to provide a high-quality experience to visitors.

An examination of the approaches to visitor management in Table 9.13 reveals that they are essentially of eight main types:

- those that seek to attract only visitors who are likely to have a minimal negative impact while still providing benefits to the destination;
- those that admit visitors only to those parts of the destination that are least sensitive from a physical, environmental or cultural perspective;
- those that seek to restrict the number of visitors to sensitive areas through pricing policies that attempt to redirect those visitors likely to negatively impact that destination or, failing that, to ensure that the costs of negative impacts are covered;
- those that actually limit the number of visitors to sensitive areas;
- those that allow only certain types of transportation modes within the destination;
- those that carefully control the flow and parking of traffic;
- those that limit the amount of time that visitors may spend in sensitive areas/sites within a destination; and
- those that seek to alter visitor behaviour before or during the visit.

Table 9.13.   Some approaches to visitor management.

- Advertise/promote only to appropriate types of visitors
- Greeting of visitors at points of entry
- Visitor service centres supplying information on local 'threats' and appropriate types of behaviour in specific locations
- Visitor interpretation centres explaining the history, special nature and sensitivity of the surrounding point of interest
- Allowing access only by public transportation
- Limiting amount of parking at locales with limited capacity
- Allowing rotating access by day of week, origin of visitor
- Differential pricing by day of week, time of day, origin of visitor
- No universal access pricing; pricing only by type of activity
- Randomized right of access
- Defined time of visitation to a given locale or site
- Previsitation reservation systems
- Controlling availability of amount and types of information

Examples of destinations that have had to address the visitor management issue in a major way include:

- the city of Venice, Italy, whose sensitive canal system simply could not handle the hordes of visitors generated by its popularity;
- the Acropolis in Athens, which found that the volume of visitors climbing over the site was physically degrading historic treasures that were already being threatened by air pollution;
- the town of Byron Bay in Australia, which has considered charging visitors a fee just to enter the town;
- the Alhambra Palace in Spain, which uses a computer system to issue tickets that specify the time of entry and the required time of exit;
- Banff National Park in Canada, which provides a very limited amount of parking space near some of the most popular isolated sites, in effect restricting levels of visitation; and
- the island of Bermuda, which, because of limited water supply, restricts water use by visitor facilities.

The above are but a very few of the many examples of situations where the management of visitor behaviour is an integral part of the process of destination management. In all cases, the underlying challenge for destinations fortunate enough to have excessive demand is to ensure that all visitors who are allowed to visit the destination have a high-quality experience but leave the destination unimpaired for future visitors.

While responsibility for visitor management is normally the responsibility of the individual owner/operator, the DMO can enhance the overall reputation of the destination by encouraging its members to adopt effective visitor management and to advertise the nature of its visitor management processes. It may also encourage the sponsoring of local seminars and workshops on how to design and implement visitor management systems. Again, as in most instances, leadership and coordination are the key principles that the DMO must observe as it seeks to ensure high-quality, memorable visitor experiences.

Stewardship: Taking Care of the Tourism Resource Base

From the beginning, this book has stressed the competitive dimensions of destination management, but always with sustainability in mind. Despite our emphasis on competition, the reader needs to be fully cognizant of the fact that, in order to be effective as a competitor, it is essential to constantly care for the most fundamental of all the resources on which tourism ultimately depends: the physical resource base and the human resource base. The management of these two primary resource bases, because of its special emphasis on caring for the long-term well-being of the resources in question, is referred to as 'stewardship'.

In our view, the concept of stewardship is essential to sustainable destination management. In the case of the physical resources, the concept implies a special effort to ensure that the physical and ecological integrity of the destination is maintained. The motivation for this special effort, while pragmatic in the sense that the industry does not want to destroy the goose that lays the golden egg, reflects a genuine moral concern for the ecological health of the destination region. In a similar vein, the concept of stewardship applies equally well to the management of the human resource base. Also, since destination stewardship requires a high degree of cooperation among those who are often competitors, we often characterize destination stewardship as competing by caring and cooperating.

Once it is accepted that stewardship of all components of the destination is a major component of destination management, the task facing managers is how to ensure stewardship. Since this concept is fairly new, its implementation has not yet received widespread attention. However, one approach that has been proposed is the creation of a Tourism Stewardship Council (Woolford, 1998). According to the Woolford framework, the primary purpose of a Tourism Stewardship Council is to turn the idea of sustainable tourism within a destination into reality. In effect, this means that a programme must be put in place to ensure that the broad range of potential impacts of tourism is controlled so as to ensure the sustainability of tourism in the region. The particular impacts identified by Woolford are shown in Table 9.14.

What Table 9.14 points out is that stewardship is a very multidimensional concept – and that caring for the destination, depending upon the complexity and diversity of its resources, can represent a very major challenge if it is to be done thoroughly. To simplify the task, Table 9.14 demonstrates that stewardship needs to be tackled along at least three major dimensions.

Stewardship of the *natural environment* is the area most commonly of concern. As shown in the table, it has at least five distinct aspects. Each of these aspects in turn requires its own type of scientific expertise simply to determine if the impacts of tourism are serious enough to be of concern. And once it has been confirmed that the threat from tourism is real, each consequence requires its own particular form of stewardship in order to address the impacts that have been identified.

Stewardship of the *built environment* may not require the same level of monitoring or scientific expertise to find out whether a problem exists. While this would appear to be an advantage from a stewardship perspective, it only masks a difficulty of another form – the fact that measurement of the impacts is heavily 'value-laden'. Whereas the measurement of environmental impacts tends to be relatively scientific and objective, measures that relate to change in character through development and beautification or 'uglification' can be highly subjective. Thus, it is often more difficult to reach consensus on whether the impacts of tourism are real or imagined, or negative or positive.

While the impacts of tourism on the *cultural and social environment* may be slightly easier to measure in objective terms, they can also be highly influenced by the values of those defining the measures and gathering the impact data. Although the leakage of foreign exchange and the exclusion of local produce and materials can be measured in reasonably objective terms, the adoption of servile attitudes towards visitors, for example, may be hard to distinguish from improved quality of service. Whether the impact is categorized as positive or negative may well depend on the values and perceptions of the researcher examining the impact.

Must stewardship be formalized?

The managerial function of stewardship can readily be viewed as a generic responsibility that belongs to everyone and should therefore pervade the entire tourism destination. Woolford (1998) has argued, however, that to ensure effective stewardship this function must be formalized – and not just from a top-down policy perspective. Furthermore, he asserts that the traditional Environmental Impact Assessment (EIA) approach, while valuable, tends to be very subjective, and that 'the elements it addresses vary enormously dependent

Table 9.14. Some potential impacts of tourism (from Woolford, 1998).

Aspect	Potential consequence
Impacts on the natural environment	
Species composition	Disruption of breeding sites Killing of animals through hunting or as souvenirs Vegetation damage by feet and vehicles Deforestation through firewood gathering
Pollution	Water pollution through sewage or discharge Air pollution from vehicle emissions Noise pollution from tourist activities
Erosion	Soil compaction causing increasing run-off Increased risk of landslides Damage to topography through development
Natural resources	Depletion of water supplies for golf courses or swimming pools Depletion of non-renewable fuel supplies Depletion of mineral resources for building Overexploitation of biological resources Change in land use for farming
Visual impact	Facilities: hotels, airports, car parks, litter, sewage
Impacts on the built environment	
Urban environment	Change in character through development Contrast between tourist and traditional structures
Infrastructure	Overloading or upgrading of infrastructure
Visual impact	Increased numbers of people Beautification or uglification
Historic sites	Restoration or increased damage and erosion through visitor numbers and pollution
Impacts on the cultural and social environment	
History	Selling off artefacts, heritage exportation 'Museumization' or protection
Traditional arts	Disruption of traditional practices, 'aestheticization' Renaissance of traditional culture, music, literature
Religion	Increased importance of festivals Increased pressure on shrines
People	Displacement and dislocation through development Move from self-sufficiency to dependency Disruption by dominance of Western TV and clothing
Values and norms	Changes in family structures and values Increases in prostitution, criminality, alcohol consumption Adoption of servile attitudes towards tourists
Economy	'Leakage' of foreign exchange Exclusion of local produce and materials Economic polarization through inequitable distribution of tourist incomes

upon by when, and for whom the assessment is made' (p. 26). He further argues that since host governments that conduct EIAs are often keen to pursue the promise of jobs and foreign exchange over and above planning controls restricting free market development, that there is a need for the industry itself to adopt a responsible attitude. Woolford is concerned

that the industry may not adopt such a responsible attitude on its own, despite the need to
protect the assets and which its future rests;
he argues for establishing a formal Tourism
Stewardship Council to persuade industry of
the benefits of long-term planning and to
enable destinations to adopt systematic, effective EIAs and planning measures to oversee
the stewardship of destination resources.

While Woolford acknowledges that support for broadly based local participation in
exercising the stewardship function may be
theoretically and democratically desirable, he
believes that practical limitations make the
industry a better choice.

While the concept of the Tourism Stewardship Council may not yet be sufficiently developed to obtain widespread acceptance and
implementation, it is felt that certain destinations may wish to consider the possibility in
order to facilitate consideration of its adoption.
Some of the key concepts put forth by Woolford
are summarized in Box 9.1.

Crisis Management: the Emergency Side of Stewardship

In the previous section we emphasized the
importance of taking care of the destination
and its many diverse and complex resources on
an ongoing basis. In recent years, in particular,
we have also learned that it is also essential
for a destination to develop the capability to
anticipate and address the broad range of
crises that have the potential to undo many
years of careful stewardship. Indeed, this
concern has been so serious that it has been
the topic of a special issue of the *Journal of
Travel Research*. In this issue, Pizam (1999),
based on a review of 300 acts of crime and
violence that occurred at tourism destinations
around the world, reports the comprehensive
typology that he has created. The typology,
which is given in Table 9.15, identifies:

- five attributes of the criminal/violent act,
  namely motive, victim, location, severity
  and frequency;

Box 9.1. Some key concepts of a tourism stewardship council (from Woolford, 1998)

Concept definition

The tourism stewardship council (TSC) would be an international, independent, charitable,
not-for-profit and non-governmental organization representing all interests within the tourism industry,
from tour operators and tourists, to host governments, local communities and NGOs. It would offer a
collaborative forum within which mutually shared objectives could be identified as the basis on which
to promote responsible, environmentally appropriate, socially beneficial and economically viable
tourism activity, while maintaining the natural and social capital of the host environment. This would
be guided by developing:

- a set of principles to guide sustainable tourism development
- a set of criteria by which holidays and/or destinations would be independently certified as
  sustainable
- A TSC certification logo as a market incentive to promote a 'quality' product

The TSC would thus require that sustainable holidays or destinations be based upon:

- the maintenance of natural and social capital in host environments
- the development and maintenance of effective tourist management systems
- compliance with relevant local/national laws and standards
- the full cooperation and participation of all concerned stakeholders

The organizational structure of a TSC would comprise:

- an international coordinating body, the TSC, with representatives from all stakeholder groups
- a series of TSC-accredited independent certifying bodies, either national or international, and
- a series of national alliances between tour operators that commit to servicing certified destinations
  and/or providing certified holidays

continued

Box 9.1. *Continued.*

Principles and criteria are at the heart of the TSC concept and are designed to guide sustainable tourism. Validity would be achieved through their development in an international consultation process involving all relevant tourism stakeholders. They would then be used as the standard in a third-party, independent, voluntary certification programme administered by TSC-accredited certifiers. Only holidays and/or destinations that conform to these principles and criteria would be eligible for certification and a TSC logo.

The recognition that market incentives have the potential to improve tourism development underpins the concept of the TSC. The central aim is to go beyond NGO-funded project work and regulation, and link sustainable tourism development to consumer power.

In summary, stewardship and certification would provide incentives to work towards sustainable tourism development by achieving the following goals:

- a guaranteed sustainable holiday and/or destination product;
- a commitment by all stakeholders to the creation of this product;
- competitive advantage and associated financial benefits for holiday suppliers and retailers through the provision of a differentiated quality product; and
- independence and credibility that other certification initiatives lack.

Two alternative models for certification, 'holiday' and 'destination', are proposed. These are mapped out diagrammatically below. Both aim to harness the power of the market to drive the pursuance of sustainable tourism. The basic difference lies in the choice of unit of certification – either the holiday or the destination is targeted. Consequently, each model has differing implications for the functionality and roles of the participating actors. Both, however, rely upon the existence of an overarching multistakeholder body, the 'TSC Partnership', that draws up principles and criteria and accredits independent certifying bodies. The TSC partnership is supported by voluntarily committed national groups, and the output in either case is a certified 'product' that is promoted through the TSC logo and associated marketing. Thus, a direct output of TSC certification is the creation of consumer demand. A useful way of drawing together the ideas behind a TSC is to consider the potential roles of such an organization. They are:

- to provide a neutral multistakeholder forum for debate
  - establish principles and criteria for Sustainable Tourism Development and Practice, and broker partnerships between companies, 'host' governments and local communities
  - maintain continuing consultation between actors and act as a mechanism to reach consensus on specific development
- to educate
  - educate the industry, host governments and communities, and the consumer about sustainable tourism development
  - educate consumers about destination community needs
  - inform destination communities about consumer needs and requirements
- to campaign
  - encourage market-leaders to raise standards voluntarily and so preempt restrictive legislation
  - lobby destination governments for appropriate planning and EIA for tourism development that incorporated all stakeholders in the process
  - promote the acceptance of joint responsibility
- to monitor and accredit
  - accredit independent destination/holiday certifiers, and monitor the tourism 'chain of custody' and 'circle of responsibility'
- to market
  - market the TSC logo to create demand for quality products and encourage differentiation and diversification, resulting in competitiveness on more than price
  - create a framework in which companies can plan for long-term development at destinations without the fear of being uncompetitive

- three attributes of the effect, namely magnitude, expanse and duration;
- methods for prevention;
- parties responsible for prevention;
- methods for recovery; and
- parties responsible for recovery.

In addition, as part of this special issue of the *Journal of Travel Research*, Mansfeld (1999) presents information on a study that examined the management of tourism crises in Israel in the wake of security breakdowns in this high-profile Middle Eastern country. More specifically, he reviews the determinants and the

Table 9.15. Pizam's typology of acts of crime and violence related to tourism (from Pizam, 1999).

1. Nature of criminal/violent act		3. Prevention methods	
Motive	● Economic ● Social ● Political ● Personal		● Legislation ● Enforcement ● Safety and security training for employees ● Installation of security devices ● Tourist education ● Citizens' awareness ● CPTED (Crime Prevention Through Environmental Design) ● Social change ● Political solutions ● International agreements
Victim	● Residents ● Political figures ● Famous personalities ● Tourists ● Businesses (all types)		
Location	● Off tourism-business premises ● On tourism-business premises		
Severity	● Loss of property ● Bodily harm ● Loss of life ● Mass destruction of life and property	**4. Parties responsible for prevention**	● Law enforcement agencies ● Community ● Tourism industry ● Tourists ● Businesses ● Government ● International community
Frequency	● Rare (once a year or less) ● Occasional (2–3 times a year) ● Rapid succession (every month) ● Constant (several times a month)		
Type	● Crime ● Civil or political unrest ● Riots ● Terrorism ● War	**5. Recovery methods** Information dissemination	● Tourists ● Citizens ● Employees
2. Effects on tourism demand		Publicity and public relations	
Intensity	● No effect ● Slight decrease ● Significant decrease ● Drastic decrease ● Cessation	Marketing	● Pricing ● Packaging ● Positioning ● Promotion
Expanse (geographical area affected)	● Local ● Regional ● National ● International	**6. Parties responsible for recovery** Governments Tourism industry Businesses Community	
Duration	● Short (a few weeks) ● Medium (2–4 months) ● Long (more than one tourism season) ● Indefinite		

management of these crises and the subsequent recovery of the Israeli tourism industry. In doing so, he identifies principles and guidelines on how destinations should cope with cycles of violence in tourism. A second, more recent examination of the impact of political crises on tourism in Israel and the Middle East has been reported by Beirman (2002).

Sonmez *et al.* (1999) present a second study in this special issue in which they discuss terrorism as a tourism crisis and offer suggestions for managing the effects of terrorism. In other examples in the special issue, Leslie (1999) examines the effects of terrorism on tourism in Northern Ireland, while Ioannides and Apostolopoulos (1999) examine tourism on the divided island of Cyprus and discuss the prospects for crisis management and recovery. Also, Dimanche and Lepetic (1999) present a case study that examines crime and tourism situations in New Orleans and show how various stakeholders have responded to the problem.

Finally, the special issue contains two articles examining the role of tourism after the violence in the destination has ceased. The first of these, by Anson (1999), uses a second example involving Northern Ireland. The second, by Richter (1999), explores the nature of political unrest in the Philippines, Sri Lanka and Pakistan, and makes suggestions as to what steps need to be taken to provide a better foundation for future tourism. Another, more recent work examining the management of a tourism crisis in South-east Asia in the late 1990s, with emphasis on the important role of national tourism organizations, has been reported by Henderson (2002).

A particularly useful paper, in that it seeks to provide a general framework for addressing and managing the impacts of tourism-related disasters (Table 9.16), is due to Faulkner (2001). In another highly relevant paper, Young and Montgomery (1998), based on their research on crisis management and its impact on destination marketing, provide a detailed guide for Convention and Visitor Bureaux. They assert that the standardized crisis management procedures they recommend will contribute to faster and more efficient recovery for any destination. The details of these procedures are summarized in Table 9.17.

As the foregoing examples and the events of 11 September 2001 in New York City appear to demonstrate, terrorism has generally become the most common and most widespread generator of crises in tourism. Despite this, terrorism is not the only generator of tourism crises, or necessarily the most serious. As Miami, Florida and Washington, DC, came to realize in the 1990s, ordinary street crime can create its own crises; these can cause fear among visitors and eventually destroy the appeal of the environment that attracts them. As a further example, the floods in Europe in 2002 had a major impact on tourism. Similarly, a fire in the Uffizi Gallery in Florence, Italy, in 1993, which was caused by terrorists, damaged many valuable paintings and sculptures, some of which could not be saved, thus effectively detracting from the gallery's cultural appeal to tourists forever. These are only a few examples of the broad range of crises that can seriously affect tourism in a destination.

As executives in all areas of business have come to realize, crises can hit even good companies and, by extension, good destinations (Marconi, 1997). Every effort must be made to manage crises before they happen. This point has been made very forcefully in an excellent book on crisis management by Mitroff and Anagnos (2001). Their arguments are most eloquently based on a five-component best-practice model for crisis management, which is summarized graphically in Fig. 9.10.

As shown in the figure, their best-practice model identifies five factors that companies must understand and manage before, during and after a major crisis. These five factors are: (i) the types and risk categories of crises they face; (ii) mechanisms to deal with these crises; (iii) the organizational systems that assist in detecting, interpreting and acting upon the crises; (iv) the stakeholders who can assist in addressing a crisis; and (v) scenarios for crisis resolution.

Types of risk/crisis

While it is extremely difficult, if not impossible, to give a precise and general definition of a crisis, Mitroff and Anagnos (2001) provide a guiding definition of a major crisis. First, a

Table 9.16.   Faulkner's tourism disaster management framework (from Faulkner, 2001).

Phase in disaster process	Elements of the disaster management responses	Principal ingredients of the disaster management strategies
1. Pre-event When action can be taken to prevent or mitigate the effects of potential disasters	**Precursors** • Appoint a disaster management team (DMT) leader and establish DMT • Identify relevant public/private sector agencies/organizations • Establish coordination/consultative framework and communication systems • Develop, document and communicate disaster management strategy • Education of industry stakeholders, employees, customers and community • Agreement on, and commitment to, activation protocols	**Risk assessment** • Assessment of potential disasters and their probability of occurrence • Development of scenarios on the genesis and impacts of potential disasters • Develop disaster contingency plans

2. Prodromal
When it is apparent that a disaster is imminent
	Mobilization
	• Warning systems (including general mass media)
	• Establish disaster management command centre
	• Secure facilities
		Disaster contingency plans
		• Identify likely impacts and groups at risk
		• Assess community and visitor capabilities to cope with impacts
		• Articulate the objectives of individual (disaster-specific) contingency plans
		• Identify actions necessary to avoid or minimize impacts at each stage
		• Devise strategic priority (action) profiles for each phase
		  • Prodromal
		  • Emergency
		  • Intermediate
		  • Long-term recovery
		• On-going review and revision in the light of
		  • Experience
		  • Changes in organizational structures and personnel
		  • Changes in the environment

3. Emergency The effect of the disaster is felt and action is necessary to protect people and property	**Action** • Rescue/evacuation procedures • Emergency accommodation and food supplies • Medical/health services • Monitoring and communication systems	
4. Intermediate A point where the short-term needs of people have been addressed and the main focus of activity is to restore services and the community to normal	**Recovery** • Damage audit/monitoring system • Clean-up and restoration • Media communication strategy	
5. Long-term (recovery) Continuation of previous phase, but items that could not be attended to quickly are attended to at this stage. Post-mortem, self-analysis, healing	**Reconstruction and reassessment** • Repair of damaged infrastructure • Rehabilitation of environmentally damaged areas • Counselling victims • Restoration of business/consumer confidence and development of investment plans • Debriefing to promote input to revisions of disaster strategies	
6. Resolution Routine restored or new improved state establishment	**Review**	

Table 9.17.   Overview of a comprehensive crisis plan for Convention and Visitor Bureaux (CVBs) (from Young and Montgomery, 1998).

I.   Physical emergency procedures for the CVB

a) *Corporate continuity of management* – An outline of the chain of command to be followed in a crisis for the CVB's CEO, President and Board of Directors should be developed, including information on who maintains authority in emergencies in day-to-day activities.

b) *Formation of CVB's safety team* – A safety team should be established, consisting of key members of the Bureau. The team serves to divide and coordinate responsibilities, to maintain order, and to ensure that all emergency procedures are carried out efficiently.

c) *Formation of communication trees* – Communication trees should be developed among CVB employees to disseminate any special information. Trees may be divided according to different departments, or may include one tree for the entire organization. In a communication tree, for example, a department manager might be assigned to call or personally notify two specific employees, and so on. When the last person in the tree receives the information, then he/she would call the first person in the tree (the department manager, for example) to confirm that the information had been received by everyone.

d) *Profile of potential crises* – The safety team or a professional crisis management consultant should assess the internal and external environments of the CVB and the local community, in order to determine its susceptibility to certain crises. Those crises that are most likely to have an impact on the destination and the CVB should then be profiled in detail. An example of a crisis profile might include, but is not limited to: (1) a list of common characteristics for the crisis and common damages resulting from it; (2) a description of any potential warning signs; (3) a list of precautions that can be taken in advance to help alleviate any damages from the crisis; and (4) a list of local officials to contact first should that particular crisis occur.

e) *Division of duties* – The specific duties to be performed by the CVB's safety team should be divided and outlined for each of the specific crises. Duties might include turning off gas and power, closing and securing CVB facilities, or initiating a communications tree among CVB employees.

f) *Evacuation and emergency procedures* – Bureau employees should be provided with detailed emergency instructions for each of the crises. This includes evacuation procedures, procedures to be followed if evacuation is impossible, and actions to be taken after a crisis.

g) *Safety of CVB facilities* –

1. Prior to the occurrence of any crisis:
   a. Annual inspections and inventory of contents of the CVB building and exterior should be made to avoid underinsured penalties.
   b. Computer systems and other important databases should be backed up daily and stored weekly in a secure area.
2. During the crisis, to the extent that time and conditions allow:
   a. The safety team should ensure that all electrical equipment inside CVB facilities, such as computers, fax machines, and telephones, are unplugged and tightly wrapped in plastic.
   b. Gas, water, and power should be shut off completely.
   c. All doorways and windows should be tightly locked and, if necessary, sealed with sandbags.
3. After the crisis:
   a. Move all electrical equipment to safe locations.
   b. Call necessary repair professionals to assess damages to equipment, and schedule any repairs and reinstallations.
   c. All damages to both the CVB's interior and exterior should immediately be reported to the insurance carrier.
   d. Photos should be taken of all visible damages.
   e. Careful records should be kept of all expenditures related to recovery, including labour costs.
   f. Retrieve all back-up data from safe-deposit box, reinstall data, and recover any lost data for computer systems.
   g. Ensure that any necessary bids requesting FEMA (Federal Emergency Management Association) funds are processed, and keep accurate records of communications and expenses for FEMA.

continued

Table 9.17. *Continued.*

II. Internal communications for the CVB

  a) *Communication and employees*

    1. Safety teams should meet to discuss the essential information that needs to be disseminated to CVB employees. Each safety team member should then contact the department managers, or those responsible for initializing the communication trees, and relay the information to them.

    2. Continuous information updates should be provided by means of a telephone information line, communication tree, or a bulletin board.

  b) *Communication with key public officials*

    1. The safety team should determine which public officials are essential for immediate crisis recovery in each of the crises profiled in the crisis management plan (i.e. firefighters or electricians).

    2. The safety team member designated as the external communications spokesperson for the CVB should continuously provide public officials with updated information and any internal information that may assist them.

III. External communications for the CVB

  a) *Media communications*

    1. The external communications spokesperson must train all volunteers and CVB employees of the proper procedures for responding to media inquiries.

    2. An updated list of media sources and contacts should be maintained, along with a list of local associations, organizations, and community leaders.

    3. A meeting should be held with local public relations directors in the travel industry in order to coordinate public messages concerning the conditions of tourism facilities, attractions and services, and recovery efforts in the destination.

    4. Designated CVB staff members should be assigned to call certain public relations directors, media sources, local associations, organizations and community leaders mentioned above, in order to ensure that each and every one of the individual people and/or organizations is contacted and informed. A communication tree designed specifically for these sources may be an efficient way to ensure that all of the calls are made.

    5. Up-to-date press releases should be distributed frequently to local, regional, and national news media. Information should include updates on the destination's condition, the operating status of tourist resources, and recovery steps being taken by the CVB.

    6. In addition to press releases, travel advisories should be disseminated to media sources, providing up-to-date information on travel conditions in the destination.

    7. Feature stories should be submitted to travel publications and newspapers, containing updates on local conditions, operating status of tourist resources, any recent recovery efforts, and any other pertinent information.

    8. News conferences should be held with key authorities in the area and, if possible, aired on major networks.

    9. Key journals should be brought to the destination for press trips, allowing them to experience recovery efforts firsthand.

    10. Press in major travel markets, particularly those generating significant group and convention business, should be brought to client/press briefings in each city. In addition, roundtable discussions and interview sessions should be held with journalists, answering any questions.

    11. The CVB should solicit and respond to any personal interviews with local, national, international and travel media to offer an industry analysis of the state of the destination and the recovery of tourism in the destination.

    12. A documentary/promotional video should be produced and distributed to media sources, outlining the destination's recovery efforts and re-emphasizing the destination's positive aspects.

    13. A telephone hotline should be established, with up-to-date daily recordings in a variety of languages.

  b) *Travel trade communications*

    1. Frequent tourism advisories should be compiled and sent to travel agents, tour operators, meeting planners, and travel and trade organizations on a regular basis.

Table 9.17. *Continued.*

2. The telephone hotline providing up-to-date information and conditions should be well communicated and publicized to travel agents, tour operators, meeting planners, and travel organizations and associations.
3. A promotional video should be sent to all travel trade resources, in addition to the media.
4. A promotional piece profiling the destination's strengths should be designed and mailed to travel agents, tour operators, meeting planners, and travel and trade organizations, both nationally and internationally.
5. CVB employees should personally call every meeting planner with conventions business booked in the destination for the next year, reassuring them and reconfirming their bookings.
6. CVB employees should call all members of relevant trade associations, as well as managers of major travel agencies, updating them with accurate information and urging them to reinstate tours and group bookings and continue scheduling new ones.
7. Informational updates on the destinations should be placed in computer reservation systems regularly assessed by travel agents (for example Sabre, Apollo and PARS).
8. Travel trade should be brought to the destination for familiarization tours, in order to allow them to experience recovery efforts firsthand and get a personal perspective on the condition of tourist resources in the destination.
9. A schedule of international and domestic sales trips and travel trade shows should be developed, in order to encourage confidence in the destination and support from travel trade.
10. Print advertisements should be published in major convention and travel publications, focusing on recovery efforts and the destination's strengths and positive aspects.

c) *Member communications*

1. A newsletter and/or travel advisory should be sent to members on a regular basis, keeping them updated with any new information.
2. The CVB should ensure that all Bureau members are informed of the telephone information hotline.
3. The documentary video should be made available to members.
4. CVB staff should personally contact each of its members in order to keep them fully briefed on the status of tourism resources and CVB services – perhaps with a communication tree.
5. CVB staff should hold a roundtable meeting with representatives from each of their member organizations in order to answer questions and reassure them of recovery efforts and continuing service from the CVB.
6. The CVB should hold a seminar with member organizations to assist them in developing and implementing crisis management plans on an individual basis, and to inform them of the CVB's crisis recovery and post-crisis recovery strategies.
7. CVB employees should donate all time possible in order to assist Bureau members with any individual assistance that may be warranted.
8. If time and resources permit, the Bureau should sponsor fundraising activities to help the hardest hit tourism organizations in the area, particularly Bureau members.
9. A permanent emergency information network should be formalized among the CVB, Bureau members, and state Travel Information Centers, by the use of fax and telephone communications.

d) *Consumer communications*

1. The telephone hotline should be highly publicized to consumers.
2. Travel Information Centers should provide travelers with emergency travel and lodging information, and local residents with evacuation and temporary lodging information.
3. Special news releases and other publications should be issued to inform tourists of the status of local tourist resources and the recovery effort.
4. Special advertising campaigns should be implemented in travel publications, newspapers, etc., placing emphasis on the destination's strengths, as well as the destination's recovery efforts.
5. The CVB should conduct consumer surveys in order to track changing public perceptions of the destination and its viability in comparison with the actual condition of tourism in the destination.

continued

Table 9.17. *Continued.*

6. Special letters or memos should be mailed to potential visitors and those consumers requesting information about the destination, addressing the condition of tourism in the area, the recovery efforts, and any other important information or commonly asked questions.

IV. Local assistance from the CVB

a) *Focus on recovery*

The Bureau should play a visible role in the community during the recovery process. By taking actions such as helping local businesses clean up debris, replacing signage and any other visible structures, etc., the CVB is sending a positive message that things will soon be back to normal.

b) *Local communications and public relations*

1. The CVB should meet regularly with area organizations and businesses, such as local associations, municipal offices, tourism organizations, and so on, to ensure an adequate flow of information and a consistent message is being sent to the public, and to coordinate local recovery programs.

2. Furthermore, CVB staff should regularly send memos or newsletters to all local hotel sales and operations staff, airlines, tour operators, travel agents, local consular corps, etc., informing them of the availability of local tourist resources and any other important travel information.

c) *Update inventory of local tourism organizations*

The CVB needs to maintain a continuous inventory of which tourist attractions, facilities, and services are open and available to the public. This information then needs to be available to the public. This information then needs to be communicated to Bureau employees, the media, travel trade, and consumers by means of press releases, the hotline, travel advisories, advertisements, etc.

d) *Continuation of CVB programs*

The CVB should assess the possibility of continuing with all scheduled activities in the area, and continue with programming as soon as possible. The media, CVB employees, and any booked groups should be informed of the continuation or cancellation of any CVB programs. Such information should also be made available by means of visitor information centers and the telephone hotline.

---

major crisis affects or has the potential to affect the whole of an organization. If it is an event that will affect only a small, isolated part of the organization, it may not be a major crisis.

A major crisis will also exact a substantial toll on human lives, property, financial earnings and the reputation and/or general health and well-being of a destination. Often these effects occur simultaneously. As a result, a major crisis cannot be completely contained within the destination's boundaries. And some major crises, such as the financial one suffered by Barron's Bank several years ago, can virtually destroy an organization (or destination). Similarly, in the travel and tourism field, both TWA and Eastern Airlines in the USA were brought down by financial crises.

Mitroff and Anagnos divide major crises into seven general types and/or categories of risk:

- *economic crises*, such as labour strikes, labour shortage, market crashes, major

declines in stock prices, and fluctuations or declines in major earnings;

- *informational crises*, such as a loss of proprietary and confidential information, tampering with computer records or the loss of key computer information with regard to customers and suppliers;

- *physical crises*, such as loss of key equipment, plants and material suppliers, breakdowns of key equipment and industrial plant, loss of key facilities and major plan disruptions;

- *human resource crises*, such as loss of key executives, loss of key personnel, increased absenteeism, increased vandalism, an increased number of accidents and a rise in workplace violence;

- *reputation crises*, such as slander, gossip, rumours, damage to corporate reputation and tampering with corporate logos;

- *crises resulting from psychopathic acts*, such as product tampering, kidnapping,

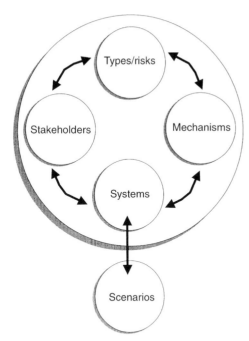

Fig. 9.10. The components of a best-practice model for crisis management (from Mitroff and Anagnos, 2001).

hostage-taking, terrorism and workplace violence; and
- *natural disasters*, such as earthquakes, fires, floods, explosions, typhoons and hurricanes.

They further stress that, although the major categories of crises share many similarities, there can be substantial differences in the impact they have on an organization. More specifically, a crisis brought about by a natural disaster will probably affect a destination very differently from one caused by the loss of a key executive. Given this reality, Mitroff and Anagnos suggest that the best management approach is to try to prepare for at least one crisis in each of the categories. Unfortunately, they note that the majority of organizations do much less, in that they tend to consider at most one or two categories. For example, most companies prepare for natural disasters. Organizations that do broaden their preparations for crises other than natural disasters often do so only for 'core' or 'normal' disasters that are specific to their particular industry. The chemical industry, for example, prepares for explosions and fires, since these crises are part of the industry's day-to-day operating experience. Similarly, fast-food companies prepare for food contamination and poisoning.

While companies have a legitimate reason to be concerned about crises that they know will occur in their particular industry, they must not assume that the crisis they anticipate will be the crisis they will face. The fast-food industry, for example, can be hit with a crisis that has nothing to do with food contamination.

In other words, every organization can be hit with a crisis of any of the types listed above. Take product tampering. One naturally thinks of the food and pharmaceutical industries as being particularly vulnerable. But what about tourism destinations? Because they are complex and multidimensional, they risk being affected by virtually all or any of the seven types of crisis, none of which at first glance might seem to have much relevance to tourism. For example, the late 1990s concern about bovine spongiform encephalopathy (mad cow disease) appeared to be primarily a health-related problem. However, the widespread and deep-seated nature of human concerns for the problem (Pennings *et al.*, 2002) brought into force travel restrictions that affected the tourism industry. These effects involved both reduced visitor volumes, the need for visitation controls, and related procedures designed to restrict visitation from countries that were particularly affected by the disease.

Mitroff and Anagnos argue that an organization need not prepare for every specific type of crisis within each of the categories. As noted earlier, all of the specific types of crisis, within a particular category or type, share strong similarities. Consequently, the broader the range of crises for which a destination is prepared, the stronger its crisis management capabilities. But in the beginning, it may be sufficient to prepare for one particular crisis in each category.

One final and important note. In today's world, any crisis is capable of setting off any other crisis. Consequently, destinations should prepare not only for each individual crisis they have selected as part of their 'crisis portfolio', but also for the simultaneous occurrence of multiple crises. In other words, crisis management is strongly systemic. Like total quality management or environmentalism, if it is not done systemically, then it is not being done well.

Mechanisms to deal with crises

The second component of the Mitroff and Anagnos model involves mechanisms to prepare for and respond to crises. Not surprisingly, they assert that the best form of crisis management is preparation before a crisis occurs. The first mechanism involves signal detection; that is, the ability to detect the early warning signals that all crises send out. It follows that if a destination wants to detect these signals, it must have signal detectors in place. Mitroff and Anagnos have observed that very often the signals of an impending crisis may be clearly visible but no one is paying attention. They also assert that the intensity and nature of the signal play a role. The signal detection employed by a destination must, therefore, reach a level that indicates that it is a genuine threat to the destination. Also, since different types of crises send out different signals, each destination must ask what might count as a signal of the impending occurrence of a particular type of crisis. All of this information needs to be built into the destination's monitoring system, which, as discussed in Chapter 8, is an integral part of the policy formulation process. In summary, it is critical when designing the destination monitoring system to put in place crisis-signalling mechanisms that:

- have signal detectors that can pick up the signals;
- have intensity thresholds established so that people know when a signal indicates a dangerous situation for the destination; and
- clearly communicate what people should do when a signal is detected.

Organizational systems

The third component of the Mitroff and Anagnos crisis management framework involves different destination organization

systems that assist in detecting, interpreting and acting upon impending crises. The outermost layer of these systems normally consists of various technologies. These, in turn, are imbedded in and run by humans within the framework of complex organizational structures, of which DMOs are the primary example in tourism. Because of their diversity and heterogeneity, these structures often lead to errors as messages and communications travel across different and multiple layers of the DMO. A particularly important dimension of a DMO that can influence DMO reaction to a crises is its organizational culture. A culture that encourages and rewards open and swift lines of communication to the right people is capable of better reacting to crises than one that possesses a defensive culture, that is, one which commonly includes defence mechanisms involving what Mitroff and Anagnos identify as denial, disavowedness, grandiosity and compartmentalization. These mechanisms act to prevent effective crisis management.

Destination stakeholders

The fourth element of the Mitroff and Anagnos model that must be involved in crisis management is the destination's stakeholders. As discussed in Chapters 5 and 8, a destination has many stakeholders. Crisis management must include developing the right relationships with these stakeholders well in advance in order to ensure the smooth functioning of the destination in the heat of a major crisis.

Crisis management scenarios

Once the first four elements of the crisis framework are understood and are in place, a destination is then in a position to develop scenarios for what will happen if a certain crisis occurs. How will the DMO and its employees and members react? What steps will have to be taken? These are the kinds of questions that must be answered in building scenarios. A common approach in this regard is to create a best-case/worst-case scenario.

Summary

To summarize the framework presented by Mitroff and Anagnos (2001), effective crisis management means:

- understanding and preparing for the different types of crises that may arise;
- implementing the important mechanisms that will help the destination prepare for these crises;
- understanding the impact of your destination's systems – from organizational structure and culture to human factors and the psychology of crisis management;
- developing the right relationships with stakeholders in advance of a crisis; and
- establishing best-case/worst-case scenarios and identifying the most appropriate reaction to each.

These five components identified by Mitroff and Anagnos are suggested as a framework for an audit of a destination's crisis management programme. A crisis audit will reveal any weaknesses in one or more of these areas that might hinder crisis management capabilities.

Another useful reference manual for crisis management, *The PR Crisis Bible*, has been authored by Robin Cohn (2001), an expert with 20 years' experience in the management of public relations crises. He provides insights that could help save a destination from the horrors of public suicide in the face of a potential public relations catastrophe. Cohn's views are summarized (Table 9.18) in the 'seven deadly sins' that he believes no person or organization (destination) should commit when facing bad news on a major scale.

Some final observations on crisis management

- *Telling the truth is vital to crisis management.* The question is not whether the truth will be revealed, but rather when that truth will become public and under what circumstances. Crises only become worse when a cover-up is attempted.
- *Distinguish between crises of different turbulence in terms of their duration and intensity.* This distinction provides an appropriate framework (Fig. 9.11) for selecting a management response (Ketelhohn, 1989).
- *Assume responsibility or pay the price.* If you don't assume responsibility immediately, a chain reaction of crises is guaranteed.
- *Crisis management is not the same as risk management.* Risk analysis involves crises with which an organization is familiar and examines the probability of future occurrences of similar crises. Such analysis assigns low probabilities to crises that are least likely to occur. However, much of crisis management involves anticipating and preparing for those crises that have never occurred before.
- *Crisis management is an exercise in creative thinking.* Do not go for the obvious response based on probabilities of past occurrences.
- *Identify a destination champion to lead the way in crisis management.* Someone in the DMO who has experience and capability in crisis management and to whom stakeholders can look with confidence for guidance in difficult times. This might well be the chief executive officer, but it may be someone with more specialized skills.

In Fig. 9.11, Duration reflects management's view on how long the turbulence has gone on and how much longer it will last. Intensity refers to the impact and disruption it is having on business, as perceived by management. Duration and intensity are inversely correlated. Managers learn to cope with sustained turbulence. Thus, the perceived intensity of a continuing disruption tends to decline over time.

Table 9.18. Cohn's Seven Deadly Sins of crisis management (from Cohn, 2001).

1. The belief that it will never happen here
   'A full-blown crisis can arise out of a simple comment, or lack of a comment', Cohn writes. Remember the media is faster now than ever. 'Reporters can be on a company's front steps before the CEO knows there's a problem', she writes. 'A CEO has to be ready, fast.' Get prepared for a crisis now, she continues, because 'organizations prepared for a crisis recover two to three times faster with significantly less financial and human cost than unprepared ones'.

2. The feeling that I don't care how it looks
   'Attempting to stay insulated and disengaged during a crisis will undoubtedly exacerbate the crisis', Cohn writes. Perception controls public opinion more than reality, so organizations must focus on what the public sees and hears to bring a crisis under control. 'People assume a company is uncaring if its leaders aren't out-front and center when crises hit', she explains, adding that 'it's far more important to utilize images while fixing the problem, not hiding it'.

3. Conveying the impression of 'Let them eat cake'
   Ignoring the damage caused by your organization is a great way to lose the public's favour. 'Never underestimate the way emotion controls public opinion', Cohn writes. Corporate executives need to come across as caring individuals to get public support. 'Sensitivity is the key', she writes. Tell the public you are in charge, you care about what happened and you are going to find out what went wrong, and fix it. 'People who are hurt or scared need to be reassured, not ignored', Cohn explains.

4. Taking the position that it's not our fault
   This response to a problem is the reason companies and CEOs lose their reputations. 'When a company is facing a problem, taking responsibility is not only the right thing to do, it's the easiest and produces the best results', Cohn writes. Mismanaged problems can bring an extended duration of negative press, angry customers and shareholders, lawsuits, government investigations, public interest groups, low employee morale and productivity, and a drop in stock price and earnings.

5. Just saying 'No comment'
   When a company doesn't talk to the press, it is giving up control of the story', Cohn explains. When a company spokesperson replies to a reporter's question with 'no comment', research shows that more than half of the public believes this means 'guilty'. Don't burn reporters, because their grudges can mean bad press. 'It's best to help reporters do their jobs', writes Cohn. She provides a list of several perfectly rational examples that will satisfy the media's need for quotes without sinking an organization deeper into disaster.

6. The belief that they're just numbers on a balance sheet
   'Maintaining internal stability also requires serious attention', Cohn writes. Although the workers in a company tend to get overlooked while a crisis is in full swing, they could easily become the source of large problems. According to Cohn, many external crises begin internally. Communication can help to manage this. 'Employees who feel valued and are treated with dignity are not going to turn on a company in bad times', she writes.

7. Reacting first, thinking later
   'This happens when executives make decisions without thinking of possible consequences', Cohn writes. Don't become your worst enemy by getting cornered into a snappy statement you might regret. 'There is no problem too small to be blown out of proportion', she warns. Turn your sins into blessings by thinking your problems through before facing the media.

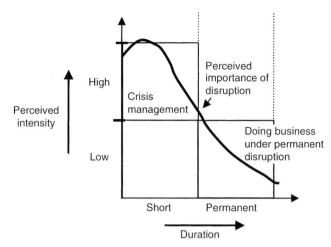

Fig. 9.11. Duration and intensity of crises: a useful distinction for defining management response (from Ketelhohn, 1989).

References

Aaker, D.A. (1991) *Managing Brand Equity: Capitalizing on the Value of a Brand Name.* Free Press, New York.

Anson, C. (1999) Planning for peace: the role of tourism in the aftermath of violence. *Journal of Travel Research* 38, 57–61.

Arnould, E.J. and Price, L.L. (1993) River magic: extraordinary experience and the extended services encounter. *Journal of Consumer Research* 20, 24–45.

Bedbury, S. and Fenichell, S. (2002) *A New Brand World: Eight Principles for Achieving Brand Leadership in the 21st Century.* Viking/Penguin Group, New York.

Beirman, D. (2002) Marketing of tourism destinations during a prolonged crisis: Israel and the Middle East. *Journal of Vacation Marketing* 8, 167–176.

Berry, L.L. (2000) Cultivating service brand equity. *Journal of the Academy of Marketing Science* 28, 128–137.

Bitner, M.J. (1992) Servicescapes: the impact of physical surroundings on customers and employees. *Journal of Marketing* 56, 57–71.

Blain, C. and Ritchie, J.R.B. (2002) Destination branding in practice: the practioner's perspective. Working Paper, University of Calgary, Calgary, Alberta, Canada.

Cohn, R. (2001) *The PR Crisis Bible.* Truman Talley Books, St Martin's Press, New York.

Dimanche, F. and Lepetic, A. (1999) New Orleans tourism and crime: a case study. *Journal of Travel Research* 38 (Special Issue), 19–23.

Dimanche, F. and Samdahl, D. (1994) Leisure as symbolic consumption: a conceptualization and prospectus for future research. *Leisure Sciences* 16, 119–129.

Echtner, C.M. and Ritchie, J.R.B. (1991) The meaning and measurement of destination image. *Journal of Tourism Studies* 2, 2–12.

Echtner, C.M. and Ritchie, J.R.B. (1993) The measurement of destination image: an empirical assessment. *Journal of Travel Research* 31, 3–13.

Faulkner, B. (2001) Towards a framework for tourism disaster management. *Tourism Management* 22, 135–147.

Fick, G.R. and Ritchie, J.R.B. (1991) Measuring service quality in the travel and tourism industry. *Journal of Travel Research* 30, 2–9.

Henderson, J. (2002) Managing a tourism crisis in Southeast Asia: the role of national tourism organisations. *International Journal of Hospitality and Tourism Administration* 3, 85–105.

Holbrook, M.B. and Hirschman, E.C. (1982) The experiential aspects of consumption: consumer fantasies, feelings, and fun. *Journal of Consumer Research* 9, 132–140.

Ioannides, D. and Apostolopoulos, Y. (1999) Political instability, war, and tourism in Cyprus: effect, management, and prospects for recovery. *Journal of Travel Research* 38 (Special Issue), 51–56.

Ketelhohn, W. (1989) *Doing Business in Turbulent Environments.* IMD Perspectives, Vol. 4. International Institute for Management Development (IMD), Lausanne, Switzerland.

Kotler, P. and Bowen, J. (1998) *Marketing for Hospitality and Tourism*, 2nd edn. Prentice-Hall, Upper Saddle River, New Jersey.

LeBlanc, G. (1992) Factors affecting customer evaluation of service quality in travel agencies: an investigation of customer perceptions. *Journal of Travel Research* 30, 10–16.

Leslie, D. (1999) Terrorism and tourism: the Northern Ireland situation – a look behind the veil of certainty. *Journal of Travel Research* 38 (Special Issue), 37–40.

Luk, S.T.K., de Leon, C.T., Leong, F.-W. and Li, E.L.Y. (1993) Value segmentation of tourists' expectations of service quality. *Journal of Travel and Tourism Marketing* 2, 23–38.

Mansfeld, Y. (1999) Cycles of war, terror, and peace: determinants and management of crisis and recovery of the Israeli tourism industry. *Journal of Travel Research* 38 (Special Issue), 30–36.

Marconi, J. (1997) *Crisis Marketing: When Bad Things Happen to Good Companies*. NTC Publishing Group, Chicago, Illinois.

Mitroff, I.I. and Anagnos, G. (2001) *Managing Crises Before They Happen: What Every Executive and Manager Needs to Know About Crisis Management*. Amacom, New York.

Morgan, N., Pritchard, A. and Pride, R. (eds) (2002) *Destination Branding: Creating the Unique Destination Proposition*. Butterworth-Heinemann, Oxford.

Morrison, A.M. (1989) *Hospitality and Travel Marketing*. Delmar Publishers, New York.

Oliver, R.L. (1993) Cognitive, affective, and attribute bases of the satisfaction response. *Journal of Consumer Research* 20, 1–13.

Otto, J.E. and Ritchie, J.R.B. (1995) Exploring the quality of the service experience: a theoretical and empirical analysis. *Advances in Services Marketing and Management* 4, 37–61.

Otto, J.E. and Ritchie, J.R.B. (1996) The service experience in tourism. *Tourism Management* 17, 165–174.

Ozment, J. and Morash, E.A. (1994) The augmented service offering for perceived and actual service quality. *Journal of Marketing Science* 22, 352–363.

Parasuraman, A., Ziethaml, V.A. and Berry, L.L. (1985) A model of service quality and its implications for future research. *Journal of Marketing* 49, 41–50.

Penning, J.M.E., Wansink, B. and Meulenberg, M.T.G. (2002) A note on modeling consumer reactions to a crisis: the case of the mad cow disease. *International Journal of Research in Marketing* 19, 91–100.

Pine, B.J. II and Gilmore, J.H. (1999) *The Experience Economy: Work is Theatre and Every Business a Stage*. Harvard Business School Press, Boston, Massachusetts.

Pizam, A. (1999) A comprehensive approach to classifying acts of crime and violence at tourism destinations. *Journal of Travel Research* 38 (Special Issue), 5–12.

Richter, L.K. (1999) After political turmoil: the lessons of rebuilding tourism in three Asian countries. *Journal of Travel Research* 38, 41–45.

Ritchie, J.R.B. and Ritchie, R.J.B. (1998) The branding of tourism destinations. Keynote address, *Annual Congress of the International Association of Scientific Experts in Tourism (AIEST), September 1998, Marrakesh, Morocco*, pp. 89–116.

Ritchie, J.R.B. and Smith, B. (1991) The impact of a mega-event on host region awareness: a longitudinal study. *Journal of Travel Research* 30, 3–10.

Ritchie, R.J.B. and Ritchie, J.R.B. (2002) A framework for an industry supported destination marketing information system. *Tourism Management* 23, 439–454.

Ryan, C. (1995) *Researching Tourist Satisfaction: Issues, Concepts, Problems*. Routledge, London.

Schmitt, B. and Simonson, A. (1997) *Marketing Aesthetics: the Strategic Management of Brands, Identity, and Image*. Free Press, New York.

Sonmez, S.F., Apostolopoulos, Y. and Tarlow, P. (1999) Tourism in crisis: managing the effects of terrorism. *Journal of Travel Research* 38, 13–18.

Upshaw, L.B. (1995) *Building Brand Identity: a Strategy for Success in a Hostile Marketplace*. John Wiley, New York.

Vogt, C.A., Fesenmeier, D.R. and MacKay, K. (1993) Functional and aesthetic information needs underlying the pleasure travel experience. *Journal of Travel and Tourism Marketing* 2, 133–146.

Wakefield, K.L. and Blodgett, J.G. (1994) The importance of servicescapes in leisure service settings. *Journal of Services Marketing* 8, 66–76.

Woolford, J. (1998) *Stewardship Council: Applicability of the Model and Stakeholder Attitudes*. TSC Research, University of London, London.

Young, W.B. and Montgomery, R.J. (1998) Crisis management and its impact on destination marketing: a guide for convention and visitors bureaus. *Journal of Convention and Exhibition Management* 1, 3–18.

10

Qualifying and Amplifying Determinants: Parameters that Define Destination Potential

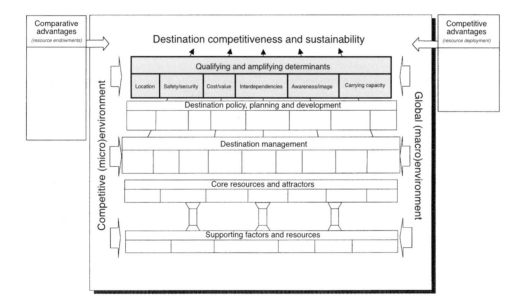

We now turn our attention to the last main component of the conceptual model of destination competitiveness. In this chapter we examine what we have labelled as *qualifying and amplifying determinants*, which, as we briefly introduced them in Chapter 3, represent factors whose effect on the competitiveness of a tourist destination is to define its scale, limit or potential.

Qualifying and amplifying determinants or *conditioners* are factors of competitiveness that either moderate, modify, mitigate and filter, or magnify, strengthen, enhance and augment the impact of all other determinants. A destination may, for example, be inherently competitive because it is innately attractive, is well managed and possesses strong supporting resources, but still be uncompetitive because the situation it finds itself in qualifies this potential in one or more significant ways. Conversely, a destination which is intrinsically weak may have its tourism potential boosted by some amplifying factor which enables the destination to attract a larger market share than its traditional touristic qualities would suggest *vis-à-vis* its competitors.

These conditioners may affect competitiveness by subtle and incremental amounts. But their effect can also be so fundamental, dramatic and dominant that they might completely overpower other categories of determinants, turning an otherwise strong or weak destination into a respectively minor or major competitor. One recent dramatic example of such a qualifying determinant is the impact of the terrorism events of 11 September 2001 in the USA, which overwhelmed other competitiveness factors in varying degrees for many tourism destinations.

These conditioning factors are not static – they are circumstantial and can therefore change over time, either gradually or abruptly. Situational changes are subject to some very broad and complex phenomena, and might depend on a variety of social, economic, political and cultural events or trends. Consequently, they are not subject to micromanagement by destinations or the tourism industry alone. While qualifying and amplifying determinants may exert powerful influences on a destination, they are in turn not affected by tourism phenomena other than in quite minor ways. Consequently, this category of determinants of destination competitiveness lies beyond the ability of destination managers to control. The tourism sector may exert *some* influence, but this is likely to be superficial. For this reason, this group of determinants is shown in Fig. 3.1 as being separate from the more manipulable factors constituting the destination management category. Qualifying and amplifying determinants are also shown cutting across the pathways to destination competitiveness in order to depict the intervening nature of their impact.

Although it may be beyond a destination's ability to do much about changing its situational conditioners, it is vital that it should have an understanding of their impact so that it is in a position to exploit favourable circumstances and defend itself against unfavourable developments or trends. Such an understanding also enables a destination to articulate its concerns and wishes to policy makers and stakeholders in general, so that the industry's voice is heard in wider spheres of influence. In addition, knowledge of such factors is likely to sensitize a destination's managers to trends, events, evolving conditions and potential discontinuities that may change the fortunes of the destination. Destinations with an eye on qualifying and amplifying determinants will be more likely to act proactively because they are in a better position to predict opportunities and threats, or at least judge the probability of them. For example, the competitiveness of a destination will be enhanced by anticipating the emergence of new markets and the decline of traditional markets, and by positioning itself to lead rather than lag behind these changes as a function of changing circumstances.

There is also another important reason why this group of intervening determinants is important. A destination with its eyes closed to the reality of these conditions is more likely to make poor judgements when it comes to priorities for tourism development. For example, there is little point in expanding hotel capacity, building new airports, enlarging a convention centre or budgeting more on promotion if a qualifying determinant imposes a ceiling on any growth in tourism demand that these improvements are expected to produce. Conversely, certain amplifying factors may act to leverage other alternatives that might otherwise be judged to be of little value.

The conceptual model of destination competitiveness identifies six qualifying and amplifying determinants. We now discuss each of these individually to illustrate their roles in shaping destination competitiveness. We begin by examining the significance of destination location. Destination safety, cost, image, carrying capacity and the interdependent nature of relationships with other destinations are then covered in turn.

Destination Location: Blessing or Curse?

A destination's physical location can have a huge impact on its ability to compete for and attract tourist markets. All other things being equal, a more (less) favourable location amplifies (qualifies) tourism potential. And usually a more favourable location can be equated with a location that is closer to the most important origin markets.

Of course, rarely are all other things approximately equal because differences in proximity to origin markets usually also affect other determinants in the model of destination competitiveness. In particular, *accessibility* is closely correlated with location. Normally, although not necessarily, accessibility improves the closer the destination is to its markets. In addition, *market ties* (i.e. various forms of association between a destination and its tourist markets related to religion, trade, culture, etc.), the extent of *marketing* activity and the availability and dissemination of general *information* between a destination and its markets are also to some extent a function of the destination's relative location. For this reason it is perhaps difficult to assess how significant location *per se* is in determining destination competitiveness when it is confounded with these other variables, which are addressed separately elsewhere in the model.

We do believe, however, that the effects of location are not fully explained by differences in accessibility, market ties, marketing and information, and that location introduces certain overarching effects that would be missed in our model if it were omitted as a qualifying and amplifying determinant.

What are the additional or incremental effects of location *per se* and how do they influence the competitiveness of tourist destinations? In Chapter 3 we noted that, although the absolute physical location of a destination cannot change, its location relative to important origin markets can change over several years. Market segments are not static. They grow, mature and decline, or perhaps largely disappear. New markets emerge as travel tastes change. Old markets might fade as changing economic, demographic or social circumstances alter abilities and desires to travel. A destination's present markets are probably different from what they were in the 1970s or 1980s, and future markets are just as likely to be different again. These market shifts have locational implications that can improve or harm the competitiveness of a destination.

On a global scale, the greatest of these market changes since the 1950s has been the emergence of new markets around the Asia-Pacific Rim arising largely from economic progress in a number of countries in this region, including Japan, South Korea, Taiwan, Singapore and Hong Kong. The prospects for economic change in other neighbouring nations, such as China, Malaysia, Thailand and possibly Indonesia, are likely to continue this trend. It is no coincidence that destinations in the Asia-Pacific region have experienced the highest rates of growth in tourism demand over this period. Destinations that were once a world away from the traditional tourism hub in Western Europe, North America and the North Atlantic now find that their distant location from these traditional markets is no longer a competitive disadvantage, as new markets have arisen on their doorstep. Australia and New Zealand, for example, once received the majority of their international visitors from the UK, but now find their most important markets in Asia.

Market changes such as these can occur on any scale from local through to the sorts of global changes evident in the above examples. For example, a destination in a developing country, relying initially on foreign markets, may find that as its economy improves and diversifies over time an increasing proportion of its customers comes from among its own residents.

Population changes, too, can alter the distribution of origin markets. Globally, birth rates are typically lowest among developed nations. Migration also shifts the spatial location of people and wealth. In the USA, relative population growth has occurred in the south and west. In Canada, the western provinces, particularly British Columbia and Alberta, account for an increasing proportion of Canada's residents. In Australia, there has also been a shift in population from southern to northern states, particularly to Queensland. The density and redistribution of people often also have significant economic consequences. Areas growing in population require housing and other services, and this spurs demand in numerous industries. Populations move in search of jobs, a better climate or a better quality of life. What motivates young married couples to move is often quite different from the motives stimulating retirees.

Sociocultural and political developments and trends present similar gradual or sudden changes in tourist markets and behaviour. Relatively sudden changes, such as the dismantling of the Iron Curtain, the worsening crisis in the Middle East, the transition from British to Chinese rule in Hong Kong and the signing of free trade agreements can produce major and abrupt shifts in the locational fortunes of destinations. More gradual social changes can be equally profound and are potentially even more profound. For example, attitudes towards and interest in other cultures have changed dramatically. Although racism and racial stereotypes still exist in abundance, people throughout the world are today more tolerant of and curious about other cultures than ever before. Migration and global communication has had much to do with this. Take, for example, attitudes to food: the diet of Western consumers today is much more diverse as a consequence of increased exposure to foods from other cultures.

Political and sociocultural changes such as these have altered the mobility of people and stimulated changes in attitudes, interests and opinions towards other cultures. In turn, these latter changes have reconfigured the nature and spatial pattern of relationships between races, cultures and nations.

The geographical distribution of tourist markets and market segments therefore ebbs and flows as a function of economic, demographic, social, cultural and political forces, and the fortunes of destinations wax and wane accordingly.

When these changes occur, destinations are likely to respond reactively. That is, one would expect to observe a lag or delay between a change in a destination's locational situation and its response to a new realization that proximate and distant markets are either disappearing or growing. For example, the belated recognition that a nearby origin market of potential tourists is emerging is likely to result in efforts to improve accessibility. Airlines rarely lead demand in air traffic. Demand must be proven before airlines are willing to commit resources to serving new markets. Increased trading ties are likely to follow, and destination marketing programmes typically appear to be tied more to market share than future prospects for developing the market.

In other words, it normally takes a period of time for the tourism industry in a destination to adjust to new market opportunities, so that the destination's competitiveness increases as a result of improved locational fortunes before

some of the other determinants of destination competitiveness begin to explain improved performance. This is most obvious when changes in relative location occur suddenly, as occurred in East European countries following the breakdown of communism, for example. Admittedly, much of this sudden change had to do with improved accessibility, but it was at least as much the abrupt psychological shift that opened up new opportunities for East European destinations.

To the extent that a destination responds early to locational changes in markets, or perhaps even anticipates these changes by redirecting some resources towards them, a destination can amplify its competitive position. To do this successfully, the destination needs to have one eye on the future. It will naturally be paying close attention to its existing important origin markets, but if it hopes to remain competitive, efforts to track market trends and to sense particularly the economic, political and sociocultural changes in potential new markets are very important.

Two further points need to be made regarding location as a qualifying and amplifying determinant. First, we should consider the attributes of location as a geographical construct. Perceptions of distances and spatial relationships can greatly distort reality. You may have seen the wall poster that depicts a New Yorker's view of the world. It shows the various boroughs of New York spreading away from Manhattan. Beyond the Hudson River lies the rest of the USA and the insignificant area representing the rest of the world rests on the horizon. The point is that our mental map of the world bears only a limited resemblance to reality. The world seemed a much larger place to the likes of Columbus, Vasco de Gama and Magellan. To these explorers, the phrases 'it's a small world' and 'it's a shrinking world' would have seemed quite incomprehensible. Our distorted mental map of the world and the implied spatial relationships between destinations and tourist origin markets evolve under influences of the sorts discussed above.

The second point is that proximate locations, although normally advantageous, are not universally so. Distant destinations somehow seem more exotic and may beckon the tourist powerfully. Nearby destinations may appear too familiar. Location can therefore act as a double-edged sword. Canada, for example, which receives around 13 million American tourists per year, seems to suffer somewhat from this affliction.

Thus, destination location in itself governs competitiveness in a number of important and complex ways. Destinations seeking to enhance their competitive position need to recognize and understand this group of influences if important pieces of the puzzle are not to be overlooked.

Destination Safety: Security or Threat?

The degree to which tourists feel safe in a destination is a further qualifying and amplifying determinant that can affect the competitiveness of a destination in dramatic, and possibly catastrophic and sudden, ways. Tourists expect to feel safe but will display a level of tolerance for low levels of risk. A destination with a reputation and image for exceptionally high levels of security may therefore find that its competitiveness is amplified to some modest extent. Above a certain threshold representing the limits of general tolerance, however, the incremental impact of an increased level of safety is likely to be marginal. The upside for a destination is therefore probably not particularly significant, but the downside consequences can be powerful to the extent that they can overwhelm most other positive tourist attributes. No matter how attractive a destination, if it is inherently unsafe many potential visitors will choose to stay away. Reputation rather than reality governs choices by tourists, so even a 'bad rap', as the Papua New Guinea Tourism Promotion Authority understands,[1] can significantly harm a destination's image.

Having recognized the normal situation, it is important to acknowledge that some tourists are not averse to all risks. Indeed, risk seems to be a vital part of many forms of travel when tourists choose to visit a destination precisely because it is different and somewhat unfamiliar. It is this sense of *exploration* that spices up a journey. If there were no form of risk whatsoever, the intrigue and excitement would

largely disappear. Some travellers are clearly not merely non-risk-averse but actually seek risky experiences; they are risk-seekers or risk-takers. These tourists seek thrilling, challenging and conquering experiences. Examples are not hard to find: mountain climbers, lone sailors, polar explorers, bungee jumpers, around-the-world bicycle riders, white-water rafters, and the list goes on. There are even examples of people travelling to war-torn areas or the sites of natural disasters. Clearly, there is a side of human nature that values risk and insecurity. The thrill, adrenalin rush and euphoria that come from confronting and conquering fear can represent pleasure to many people. Destinations need to know what forms and levels of risk tourists seek and what they would prefer to avoid.

Issues of safety for tourists appear to fall into three principal categories: physical, psychological and financial safety. Many situations that arise for the tourist, however, involve more than one of these forms. Crime, for example, jeopardizes all three forms of safety. Levels of crime are often well publicized and certain nations, states and cities have strong reputations for being either particularly dangerous or safe in terms of the threat from criminal activity. Japan, for example, has enjoyed a reputation for low rates of crime, although the poison-gas terrorism incidents a few years ago and the increased media coverage of Japanese gangs (particularly in movies) has tarnished this image.

American crime statistics (particularly for crimes involving the use of guns), the international influence of the American media, and the dramatization and the popularization of crime in American movies and on television have raised a great deal of concern in the minds of tourists. Some cities, such as New York and Chicago, have had a long-standing reputation for high rates of criminal activity. However, the image of New York has improved considerably now that former mayor Rudy Giuliani has achieved a degree of real and perceived success in lowering crime statistics. Other reputations have been acquired more recently. Perhaps the best example is the state of Florida, where several events involving criminal acts against Canadian and European tourists have been well publicized internationally. In September 1993 it was reported, following the shooting death of a

German tourist, that eight visitors to Florida had died violently as a result of crime in the past year. After a 'bump-and-rob' tactic, which is used by some robbers on Florida roads, the German tourist kept driving, as advised in a safety pamphlet provided by car rental firms, but was killed by a shot fired through the window of the car.[2] A British tourist, the ninth victim, was murdered a week later. Two of the nine victims were Canadian. Canada is the most important source of foreign tourists for Florida. After the incident involving the British tourist, Canadian Holidays started offering full refunds to tourists who had booked a trip to Florida.[3] The tourism industry in Florida reacted with great concern, developing a strategy to address both the crime problem itself, insofar as it posed a threat against tourists, and to handle the public relations dimension of the threat (personal interview with W.C. Peeper, Executive Director and CEO of the Orlando/Orange County Convention and Visitor Bureau, 23 September 1993). One result was to introduce a fleet of rental cars equipped with electronic maps advising visitors of appropriate routes to take when navigating the streets of Miami. The system also provided a 'panic button' that signalled the nearest police department via satellite whenever a tourist needed help.[4] But the bad press for Florida continued. In March 1997 a Florida sheriff made international news by warning that the state was too dangerous to visit after the release of 300 violent felons as a result of overcrowding in prisons. The same news item reported that a further 2400 prisoners would go free early 'in the coming months and years'.[5] Other destinations with growing crime problems affecting the tourism industry include Russia and South Africa. In 1995, an armed Russian seized 25 South Korean tourists in a tourist bus parked in Red Square, Moscow, initially demanding a ransom of US$10 million. The gunman was shot to death by about 20 commandos who stormed the bus, freeing all hostages.[6] Strong growth in South African tourism following the end of apartheid took a turn for the worse after 'gruesome tales of crime and violence splashed across newspapers and television screens around the world [which] have spooked potential tourists and given an edge to other countries' (Cheary, 1996). South African crime statistics are among the worst in the world, with 18,983 murders reported in 1995. Crime in Cape Town and Johannesburg has particularly hurt the industry.[7] Australia's reputation in the UK as a safe destination was significantly tarnished by recent separate events, including the murder of two backpackers in 2001 and 2002 and the death of six British backpackers in a deliberately lit fire at a backpacker hostel in the state of Queensland in 2000. More recently, two British tourists in outback Northern Territory were forced off the road. The female tourist was bound but managed to escape and the male tourist is presumed murdered. Two German tourists were also bound and tied to a tree in the same area of the country. Both events received a considerable amount of coverage in the Australian and foreign media, raising concern about the image of Australia as a safe destination for tourists.

Related activities involving terrorism, wars, social and political unrest, overzealous police and security forces and authoritarian governments create similar problems. Before 11 September 2001, terrorism had its worst years in the mid-1980s, centred on the Mediterranean and Middle East. Several incidents involving tourists at airports, on a cruise ship and elsewhere severely affected tourism in this region. Religious fundamentalists have focused on tourists in Egypt as an easy economic target in their struggle to gain political power. The first Gulf War in 1991 made tourists nervous about travel all around the world. The second Gulf War in 2003 has again depressed international tourism, and the resulting concerns that this war may worsen the threat of terrorism in the future are likely to dampen the prospects for a recovery in international tourism for some considerable time. Continuing social and political unrest and atrocities in Algeria, Central Africa, the Balkans, the Middle East, southern Russia and elsewhere have drastically curbed tourism in these regions, whereas peace in other areas (e.g. Central America, and the peace accord between Israel and Jordan, until the dramatic increase in suicide bombing by Palestinians and the retaliatory action by the Israelis in 2002) has substantially improved prospects for the growth of tourism. Race riots in Los Angeles in the early 1990s were shown on news telecasts around the world. The occasional poor treatment of visitors and tourists by security forces, legal authorities and authoritarian governments is a further concern. China and Singapore have unfavourable reputations in this regard. Some years ago, the film *Midnight Express* portrayed the legal system in Turkey in most unflattering terms. The threat of physical, psychological and financial harm from incidents such as these can decimate a destination's tourism industry for months or even years.

But the impact of terrorism in the USA on 11 September 2001 surpassed that of all previous violent events that had significantly altered the competitive position of tourism destinations. The effect was such that many people felt that the world had changed for ever on that day. There was also a strong sense that further similar acts of terrorism were likely in the USA, Britain and indeed other parts of the world. The demand for travel and tourism around the world changed in an instant. The effect was most dramatic in the USA but the ramifications were felt globally. The US airline industry closed down for several days. Even a year later there still appeared to be a long way to go before travel and tourism in the USA would fully recover. On the other side of the world in Australia, the immediate aftermath of 11 September also produced a decline in tourism, but the industry there has recovered much more quickly. The bombing of a Bali night club on 12 October 2002, targeting Western tourists, and the 2003 war against Iraq are the most recent dramatic examples of conflict affecting tourism.

The safety and security of tourists is further threatened by the risk of accident and misadventure. Tourists are typically exposed to higher levels of such risk compared with local residents, who are more familiar with risks in their own environment and how to minimize them. For example, in northern tropical Australia it is usually the tourist, not the local resident, who is taken by a crocodile swimming in waters that locals know to avoid. Something as simple as crossing the street in a foreign country, where cars travel on the opposite side of the road, or driving with unfamiliar traffic regulations, exposes the visitor to additional dangers. Some tourism activities themselves, as discussed above, are inherently more dangerous than the usual daily mix of activities at home.

There is also the threat, real or perceived, contained in a destination's natural environment. These threats can range from wildlife, through natural disasters to severe weather conditions. Reports occur annually of bear and occasional cougar attacks on campers and hikers in western Canada. Visitors to Australia fear spiders, snakes, sharks, crocodiles and sea wasps. Tornadoes, hurricanes and earthquakes regularly afflict regions of North America. Aircraft, bus and passenger ferry accidents have made headlines at times over the years. For example, in 2000 a large group of tourists drowned while canyoning in Switzerland, when a heavy rainstorm produced a flood surge that swept many members of the group to their deaths.

The actual risk posed by many of these events is usually very small and is often less than the risk people take in their daily lives driving to and from work. But the dramatic, shocking and often explicit coverage of these events heightens their horror and magnifies the perception of risk.

Destinations that lack safe drinking water, well-behaved motorists, well-maintained and safe infrastructure, proper building and fire regulations, reliable emergency services, qualified medical practitioners, modern and sterile hospital facilities, safe sanitary conditions, appropriate regulations and controls for food safety and hygiene, etc., or that expose visitors to high risk of diseases, such as malaria, AIDS and infection with exotic and dangerous viruses, present additional risks. These health risks demand a significant amount of predeparture preparation (medicine and knowledge) and they also involve costs that are often not covered by insurance. Airline flights out of India stalled for a few days some years ago when there was an outbreak of a dangerous disease. For a while, baggage handlers at Toronto airport refused to unload aircraft arriving from India. In Britain, the tourist industry was affected dramatically when it was reported that Creutzfeld–Jakob disease may have been been transferred to humans from cattle with bovine spongiform encephalopathy (mad cow disease) and when this was followed by an outbreak of foot and mouth disease in cattle. The most recent impact of disease affecting tourism occurred when a number of travellers from Asia contracted severe acute respiratory syndrome (SARS), resulting in a number of deaths. The impact in the affected countries was substantial and the fallout for tourism has been severe. Mature or elderly travellers, particularly those who require medication or who are at some health risk during their trip, are likely to pay particular attention to such concerns. Disabled travellers, too, will be most concerned to ensure that a destination will be able to meet their needs. The presence of embassies and consulates may alleviate the fears of some tourists in countries where risks are perceived to be high. One Australian entrepreneur developed a business helping ill and injured Australian travellers overseas into a $5.5 million-a-year enterprise, handling 7000 cases involving Australians, and arranged over 100 evacuations in 1991 alone. The company, Worldcare, works in conjunction with insurance underwriters. Many customers involve companies with executives travelling and working in places like China (Thomas, 1991).

A further group of risks faced by tourists concerns their vulnerability as consumers. In foreign destinations, particularly those encumbered with an unreliable legal system, tourists can be easy prey for unscrupulous operators. Tourists in such a situation are often reluctant to seek redress or take legal action when they are not clear about their rights, are unsure where to turn for help, and have limited time and resources available. To deal with these occurrences, destinations may introduce a code of practice or take action against companies that violate consumer laws. Government regulation may be required in certain sectors. Some industries establish compensation funds to protect tourists in cases in which fraud or bankruptcy occurs. Where consumer protection is insufficient, a destination can gain an unfavourable reputation that spreads throughout markets and the travel trade. Increasingly, however, tourists are beginning to assert their legal rights more forcefully. A number of cases have been reported in the media in which tourists have sued travel agencies or tour operators for failing to meet their obligations. One Michigan tourist sought US$4 million in actual damages and US$10 million in punitive damages from a travel agency and its parent company, claiming that he was misled into believing he could engage in water sports safely. He spent 51 hours in shark-infested water in the Caribbean after a rented jet-ski broke down (*Calgary Herald*, 1994). In another case, 45 Canadian tourists planned to initiate a class-action lawsuit against a Montreal travel agency after they were robbed in Venezuela when their bus was hijacked by three bandits at an apparently deserted Caracas airport at 3 a.m. (Hustak, 1994).

Finally, there is the psychological risk involved when tourists confront unsettling or disturbing situations, particularly when travelling in Third World destinations and foreign cultures. Poverty, squalor, starvation, begging and even brutality are unfortunately a part of life in many parts of the world. Although tourists usually have some understanding of the conditions they can expect, they are rarely prepared for the reality. For example, some tourists to India find their experience witnessing poverty and squalor quite disturbing.

As noted earlier, conditions in a destination that pose a threat to the physical, psychological or financial safety of tourists can be so significant as to overwhelm any capacity a destination might have to compete effectively in tourism markets. Although many of these problems might be beyond the power of the tourism industry alone to rectify, if they are left unattended other competitive actions by a destination might be quite ineffectual.

When tourist safety is threatened, the consequences for a destination can be immediate and might be quite out of proportion to the real risk. The resulting drop in competitiveness can be rapid, but it may take a great deal of time to overcome the problem and the lingering unfavourable market perceptions.

Destination Cost Levels: Reality or Perception?

Cost is a fundamentally critical element of competitiveness, so much so that one frequently finds, when reading an article on competitiveness (particularly when it has been written by an economist rather than a marketer), that the author is really talking about cost-competitiveness and not competitiveness in its broader sense. In very simple terms, competitiveness in a market can be broken down into two dimensions. These are: (i) what you get (i.e. the product); and (ii) what you pay for what you get (i.e. the price). Taken together, these two dimensions determine the value gained in purchasing a product.

Porter (1980) recognized that, fundamentally, a competitive advantage can only be sustained in one of three possible ways that relate to the two dimensions identified above. A firm has a competitive advantage either because it is the *lowest cost producer* or because it offers a better product. The product may be better either because it is *differentiated* from other competing products in ways which offer added value to the customer, or because the firm, by *focusing* on the needs of a particular segment of the market and providing superior service to that segment, serves the total needs of its customers more effectively. Differentiation and focus enable a firm to develop a competitive advantage and charge a price premium that reflects the added value in their product compared with that of the lowest-cost producer.

For the purpose of this discussion we draw a distinction between *cost* and *price*. Price is the amount charged to a customer. Cost is the expenditure that a producer incurs in providing the product to the customer. The difference represents the profit to the producer from the transaction. Costs are therefore a major (but not the only) determinant of price. As price is a significant factor in customer choice, costs of production are critical. The prices charged by a tourism destination depend both on the cost structure of the tourism and hospitality industry and on the nature of competition among rival firms, which affects rates of profitability. The cost of factor inputs and the productivity of an industry in converting inputs into products are therefore significant determinants of the industry's cost-competitiveness.

For a product like tourism, price has numerous components. The costs of goods and services purchased in a destination would normally account for the major portion of the total price. The cost of transportation to a destination may also be quite significant, particularly in the case of long-haul air travel. Other costs and factors, such as travel insurance, the opportunity cost of travel time and changes in exchange rates, may be important and can affect costs.

A further aspect includes the price of other substitute or complementary products. A potential visitor to a particular destination has the option of spending their vacation in any number of alternative destinations. Alternatively, the potential traveller may decide to forgo a trip altogether in order to purchase another product (e.g. a new car or home furnishings). Hence, the price of these other products may well influence the demand for travel to a particular destination.

Price is therefore a complex construct in the case of tourism destinations. Price may be measured in either absolute or relative terms. If the price is measured in relative terms, should it be related to the cost of tourism services in the traveller's country of residence, the cost of tourism in alternative destinations (and if so, which destinations), or the cost of other goods and services? How should changes in exchange rates be taken into account? Are travellers more or less sensitive to changes in exchange rates than they are to changes in foreign or domestic prices? Should the cost of transportation to a destination be regarded as part of the price of the destination?

A further complication concerns the complexity of price information. Tourism is an amalgam of goods and services. Therefore, it is extremely difficult to define the tourism price, as it is a function of the total mix of goods and services consumed by each tourist. Although some attempts have been made to develop a tourist price index (World Tourism Organization, 1985; Martin and Witt, 1987), such information is limited. Frequently, tourism prices in destinations have been represented by published consumer price indexes (CPIs). The choice of CPIs has been largely expedient, but it has been argued both that the mix of goods and services consumed by tourists is not too different from the mix constituting the CPI and that the changes in the CPI fairly reflect changes in the prices of goods and services consumed by tourists. One can also gauge the cost of living in a destination based on per diem allowances paid by governments to Foreign Service personnel, or by the United Nations to its staff in foreign postings. Runzheimer International has measured the per diem costs (based on a night's lodging and the price of three meals) for business travellers in various cities worldwide and found the five most expensive cities to be Hong Kong, Tokyo, Moscow, Buenos Aires and Paris. Hong Kong, the world's most expensive city, came in at US$474 for a first-class hotel room and three meals (*Business Week*, 1997).

Much of the research evidence suggests that tourists' response to changes in exchange rates is not the same as their response to changes in the cost of living within national destinations. Tourists are generally much better informed about exchange rates but have imperfect knowledge of local price levels (Little, 1980, p. 42; Lin and Sun, 1983, p. 52; Truett and Truett, 1987, p. 183; Tremblay, 1989, p. 480). Hence, tourists may base their decisions prior to departure on a knowledge of exchange rates but might alter their intended length of stay and level of spending upon arrival as they adjust to local currency prices. Little (1980, p. 47), quoting from an article in *The Economist*, suggested that 'nominal exchange-rate movements have predictable effects on tourist spending' but 'tourists could often be kidding themselves that things are cheaper over the fence, until they find out what that weak currency has done to retail prices in their holiday haven'.

A study by one of us (Crouch, 1992), which reviewed the empirical results of a large number of studies into the determinants of international tourism demand, found that although results have been quite mixed, in general the cost of transportation to a destination, exchange rates and the local currency price of tourism services each have a significant impact on the demand for travel to a destination.

What can a destination do to improve and manage its cost-competitiveness? The answer is probably not a great deal, and it is for this reason that our model of destination competitiveness places *cost* among the *qualifying and amplifying determinants* rather than among elements of *destination management*. We do not suggest that a destination has no responsibility for its costs. Indeed, there are a number of things destinations can do to improve their cost-competitiveness. However, because costs are driven by a broad range of economic, technological, sociocultural, political and environmental factors at the regional, national and global levels, it is more appropriate to recognize that the impact which a tourist destination is able to exert on costs is rather limited.

We noted above the importance of productivity improvements in an industry with respect to the maintenance of competitive advantage. For a long time it was felt that there was little scope for productivity improvements in the service sector. Whereas technological innovation has been the basis of enormous advances in productivity in other areas, such as manufacturing, agriculture, mining and construction, the service sector was regarded as offering minimal opportunities for productivity improvement. The labour-intensity of many services, it was felt, severely limited alternatives for substituting technology for labour, and therefore the service sector was a drag on productivity and prosperity. These attitudes, however, have begun to change in the light of new evidence on service productivity.[8]

With respect to a tourist destination, potential improvements in efficiency exist in many areas. Global distribution systems have enormously enhanced the ability of the travel trade to distribute information efficiently and effectively and to handle reservations. The preference of airlines for reducing reliance on travel agents and marketing directly to consumers has lowered airline costs. The Internet and other online tourism marketing systems are also revolutionizing the way in which other tourism and hospitality enterprises are reaching customers. The focal, coordinating role played by industry associations and destination management organizations and the increased number of marketing and operational alliances, partnerships, consortia, networks and joint ventures have had a positive impact on destination productivity. At the same time, as noted in Chapter 5, tourism industries have become more sophisticated and competitive in general. Increased rivalry between firms places emphasis on innovation, cost control and process improvement. Although many small, independent operators still characterize the tourism industry, management contracts and franchising are bringing specialization and greater skills to the industry.

Productivity improvements are not necessarily reflected in lower costs. In the service sector, many efforts at productivity improvement have been aimed at improving service quality rather than reducing or containing costs. And the link between price, quality, value and the destination's reputation, image and overall competitiveness is critical. Keane (1996) examines this link through the economics of reputation and quality decisions for a tourism destination, and identifies the implications of these decisions for destination competitiveness. A study by Tourism Canada (Stevens, 1992) concluded that measures 'of travellers' price/ quality perceptions are key to determining a country's or industry's competitiveness, because competitive advantage grows out of a value that a country is able to create for its buyers'.

Tourism markets hold various *perceptions* of the price and value offered by different destinations. A further way in which a destination can improve its competitiveness is by influencing these perceptions. Murphy and Pritchard (1997) found price–value perceptions to vary seasonally and according to the origin of the visitor. Lawson *et al.* (1995) investigated the awareness of prices for attractions and activities in destinations and concluded that the level of knowledge about actual prices charged was low. Destinations should track levels of awareness and perceptions of both price and value over time to monitor competitiveness in this respect.

Although, as noted earlier, many aspects of the cost structure and price of a destination lie beyond the capacity of the tourism industry to change, players in the industry certainly have it within their capacity to voice their concerns and wishes to policy makers on matters relating to taxation, regulation, industrial policy, promotional programmes, infrastructure and the many other areas which can govern the overall cost of a destination.

Destination Interdependencies: Synergy or Substitute?

Another qualifying and amplifying determinant that can significantly shape the competitive fortunes of destinations is the nature of any interdependent relationships among destinations. In simple terms, this relationship can either be synergistic or adversarial. In a synergistic relationship, competitive strengths in one destination convey advantages on other destinations with which it shares the relationship. In an adversarial relationship the opposite is true; that is, a strong destination weakens the competitiveness of the destinations that constitute its adversaries. In the former case,

destinations are complementary while in the latter they are competitive substitutes.

The relationship between two or more destinations is much more complex than this, however, as noted in Chapter 5. Two destinations may, for example, be adversaries fighting for a share of one market segment, but might work synergistically to attract a different segment. This is often the case where market segments are defined geographically and is apparent when the most extreme cases are considered. For example, the provinces of Ontario and British Columbia in Canada are clearly adversaries in their attempt to attract domestic tourists from within Canada. One of these two provinces is likely to attract domestic tourists at the other's expense because a domestic tourist is less likely than an international tourist to visit both provinces in a single trip. A foreign tourist, however, particularly if residing in a very distant market, such as New Zealand or South Africa, is more likely to choose Canada as a destination, including a visit to both provinces, if each province builds on the other's competitive advantages. For this reason, it makes no sense to make a blanket statement that destination A is destination B's substitute or complement unless the specific market segment connected with the adversarial or synergistic relationship, respectively, is specified.

The relationship between two destinations is also not necessarily reciprocal. There is nothing in theory that would indicate that an interdependent relationship is perfectly symmetrical, although it is difficult to imagine a case where a synergistic or adversarial relationship would not exist in both directions, even though the significance of the dependency might vary. Take, for example, the case of destinations that rely on stopover traffic for a significant share of their visitors. While Fiji, Hawaii and Tahiti are attractive destinations in their own right, they do attract a substantial portion of visitors for a few days as a stopover in their travel across the Pacific. Were Australia and New Zealand, for example, to decline in competitiveness, there would be some significant impact on visitation of these island destinations around the Pacific Rim. Countries like Australia, New Zealand, Hong Kong and Thailand also benefit from the fact that travellers from North America are able to break their long journey across the Pacific in these islands, so that the overall relationship between the island destinations in mid-Pacific and continental countries is complementary. The advantage, however, is probably greatest for the islands as they are more likely to serve as secondary destinations.

The categorization of destinations as primary versus secondary is not confined to those where stopover traffic is involved. Many international tourists visit more than one country in a single trip, as national borders often represent rather artificial barriers. Americans visiting Europe frequently enter a number of countries but often one or two (e.g. the UK and France) serve as the primary destination(s), other peripheral countries acting as secondary attractions.

If one considers the interdependencies between destinations in the light of the enormous growth in global travel since the 1950s, it seems reasonable to conclude that, by and large, alternative destinations have profited from the increased competitiveness of destinations worldwide. As more companies enter an emerging industry, the effect is often to expand the size of the total market such that all competitors are better off for the added competition. Increased competition can have the effect of justifying or legitimizing the industry. The combined marketing efforts of competitors can attract much greater attention and develop overall demand more effectively. Although competitors may be fighting over a share of the market pie, the result of competition may be to increase the size of both the pie and of each individual share, more than compensating for the effect of dividing the pie among a greater number of players.

We can also think of the interdependent relationships between destinations in either a horizontal or a vertical sense. Vertically, there exists a hierarchy of destinations, each higher-order destination encompassing two or more lower-order destinations. At the lowest levels are the smallest meaningful units of analysis, such as local resort areas. Bordas (1994) referred to these as 'clusters'. In some cases this might include a single, all-inclusive operation, such as a Club Med. More often, however, it will include a town or city, or some defined natural region surrounding a valley, lake, mountain, beach or forest. For example, Surfers Paradise is a resort city on the coast of Queensland,

Australia, and has been one of that country's principal vacation destinations for many years. In combination with Broadbeach, Burleigh Heads, Coolangatta and other communities, it forms part of the larger destination region along this area of the southeast Queensland coast known as The Gold Coast. Several other coastal resort areas exist along the 1600 km of populated Queensland coast, including The Sunshine Coast, The Whitsunday Island region and Far North Queensland, centred on Cairns. As a state, Queensland is Australia's most rapidly developing tourist destination. At the national level, Queensland and the other states and territories combine to offer international tourists a broad range of attractions and activities, including beaches, rainforests, deserts and the outback, country towns and cosmopolitan cities. At the next highest level, the region known as Oceania, covering Australia, New Zealand and the South Pacific, forms a further destination identity. Finally, the entire Asia-Pacific Rim region encompasses perhaps the highest meaningful destination unit in this part of the world.

Vertical interdependencies occur between destinations at different levels in this hierarchy, whereas horizontal interdependencies concern destinations at the same level. The competitiveness of any one destination at any level is inextricably dependent upon its network of horizontal and vertical relationships with other destinations in this hierarchy. A change in the competitiveness of any destination will reverberate through the network, the impact being a function of the synergistic and adversarial relationships tying the fate of the destinations together.

To a large extent, interdependent relationships between destinations are governed by geopolitical circumstances that cannot be readily actuated and manipulated at will. However, the actions of a destination might affect relationships at the margin. For example, the marketing strategy of a destination might choose to emphasize any complementary relationships with other destinations (or destination levels) to communicate the added value that such a relationship offers the potential tourist, or it might explicitly aim to position the destination against its competitive substitutes.

Any decision to ignore or exploit such interdependencies carries with it certain risks. A decision to link the destination with another works well as long as that other destination remains competitive. But should the other destination suffer some problem, such as publicity over crime or a devastating hurricane, the drop in competitiveness of that destination will carry over to affect other destinations with which it is associated.

There are therefore advantages and disadvantages in trying to manage interdependent relationships. A go-it-alone strategy, however, also faces risks. Linkages developed with other complementary destinations may help to buffer the destination from the vicissitudes of its own fluctuating and uncertain fortunes.

Destination Image: Perceptions of People and Place

The awareness and image of a destination in the mind of potential visitors is, not surprisingly, one of the most important of the factors that affect destination competitiveness. Indeed, as the role of most destination management organizations centres around the promotion of the destination, a considerable amount of attention, effort and activity is devoted to the task of developing a strong awareness of the destination in key markets, and shaping the formation of a favourable, attractive and enticing image of the destination in order to attract tourists.

Despite the efforts that most destinations these days go to in order to establish awareness and shape an image, awareness and image are usually a function of such a wide variety of sources and forms of information about a place and its people that explicit efforts by a destination management organization in this regard normally play only a minor role – often perhaps only a very minor role. Consider, for example, the awareness and image of China as a tourism destination. How much of your awareness and image of China stems from promotional activity carried out by organizations engaged in the Chinese tourism industry? Initially, probably very little. But if you start to contemplate a trip to China and get to the point of actually gathering touristic information on China, then you might begin to be influenced by more of the tourism-targeted information, which attempts to develop a favourable image.

Our model addresses destination marketing, positioning and branding elsewhere, under the categories of both destination management and destination policy dimensions. We have situated destination awareness and image under qualifying and amplifying determinants in order to recognize the fact that these elements are largely driven by a diverse range of influences that often extend well beyond the design or control of destinations themselves.

Hence, a very favourable image of a destination combined with high levels of awareness in an important target market can serve to amplify the competitiveness and success of the destination in that market. On the other hand, a very poor image of a destination or low awareness will constrain or qualify the destination's ability to attract visitors.

Research on the way in which tourists consider, compare and evaluate alternative tourism destinations suggests that the choice process is cognitively structured in terms of *choice sets* of destinations (Woodside and Lysonski, 1989). Those destinations of which tourists are either unaware or insufficiently aware constitute the *unawareness set*. The *aware* destinations may be mentally assigned by the intending tourist to one of three sets. The *inept set* comprises destinations that the tourist regards as being unable to satisfy their particular travel needs and desired experiences because their image of such destinations is, in some way, negative with respect to these needs and experiences. Destinations that have rather neutral images in the mind of the intending traveller (i.e. the image of the destination does not contain strong positive or negative content *vis-à-vis* the traveller need) may be grouped together as the *inert set*. Those destinations that come to mind most readily when the tourist first starts to consider which alternatives are most likely to satisfy their needs or desires are known as the *evoked set*. Rarely do more than just a few (typically three to five) destinations make the evoked set, and those that do are the ones of which the tourist is usually most aware and which present the strongest or most unique image as related to the particular needs of the intending tourist.

Of course, images may not be accurate or correct. But if such images represent how tourists perceive reality, their travel decisions and therefore the competitiveness of the destination will be affected accordingly. For example, many first-time visitors to China today are surprised by the modern and clean character of its large cities compared with their image of a mostly poor country.

Strong images are hard to develop and even harder to change, once formed. They have an inertia such that individual pieces of information will do little to change them unless they are reinforced by other consistent messages and information. This builds up over time until a point is reached when the weight of evidence is such that an individual begins to question the accuracy and validity of the previous held perceptions. It may therefore be possible, over time, to correct false or out-of-date impressions and images, but it is doubtful that tourism promotion can alter mostly accurate but unfavourable images unless other sources of information about a destination, the place and its people can be suppressed in some significant way.

In seeking to enhance a destination's competitiveness through the target market's awareness of the destination and through its image, several steps can be identified:

- assess the destination's present image and level of awareness in those target markets of interest, recognizing that different markets may well have different images;
- understand why or how these images have formed and what sources of information or influences have, over the years, led to this image;
- determine what image is desired or ought to be developed, recognizing reality and the challenges involved in changing an image; and
- develop a plan for bringing this about – while such a plan may include an important role for destination promotion and communication, success will depend on the degree to which the plan formulates an integrated strategy involving and incorporating all image-formation influences, organizations and entities.

Studies of destination image point the way in terms of how the first step in this task can be accomplished (e.g. Echtner and Ritchie, 1993).

While destination promotion and marketing can clearly play an important role in creating awareness and shaping image, an approach which involves the tourism industry going it alone would seem unlikely to be successful. For this reason, in recent years some countries or destinations have adopted a comprehensive branding approach which integrates tourism, economic development, international or inter-regional trade, social development and other place-marketing goals into an integrated place-branding strategy (see Kotler et al., 1993, for examples and an approach to place marketing).

Carrying Capacity: Hard and Soft Constraints to Growth

The last qualifying and amplifying determinant in our model of destination competitiveness is the destination's carrying capacity. Carrying capacity concerns a destination's ability to host demand and therefore represents some form of upper limit to the volume of demand it can handle. Yosemite National Park in the USA is an example of a destination operating under capacity conditions during peak tourism periods. Limited accommodation and camping facilities act as a constraint on overnight visitor numbers. While Yosemite is a breathtakingly beautiful area and draws large numbers of visitors, its attractiveness is adversely affected by the size of crowds in summer. Additional accommodation facilities could be provided, but the visitor experience would diminish.

The notion of a maximum desirable destination carrying capacity has received increased attention as the concept of sustainability has permeated modern approaches to tourism development. Carrying capacity has received most interest and attention with respect to the potential negative impact of tourism development in ecologically sensitive areas. But the concept of carrying capacity can also be applied in connection with adverse sociocultural impacts, or in terms of capacity constrained more objectively by limited infrastructure or tourism superstructure. For example, limited accessibility to a site in terms of travel mode, limited accommodation facilities and other constraints on tourists and tourism activity can equally present a barrier to tourism growth and potential.

Although there are some similarities across these different sources of limited carrying capacity in that they each imply some notional maximum level of tourism demand that can or should be accommodated, there are also important differences. For example, where the destination is underdeveloped and demand is currently constrained by the limited availability of accommodation or transportation facilities, expanding these facilities may address the problem or constraint and therefore improve the destination's competitiveness. However, where capacity is constrained by social or environmental factors, the alternative of increasing capacity may be quite nonsensical. Instead, a destination might seek to alter the form of tourism to lessen environmental or social impacts, so that possibly larger numbers of tourists might be accommodated without adding to the negative impacts. For example, in a national park where tourists have previously ventured unconstrained, making their own trail, specific trails might be built and tourists constrained to these trails so that larger numbers of visitors present fewer problems than the previously smaller number of visitors presented. Similarly, when social problems arise in connection with excessive numbers of tourists interacting with indigenous populations, it might be possible to build some sort of visitor centre in order to present cultural experiences to visitors without the attendant social problems.

It is comparatively easy to measure a destination's carrying capacity objectively with respect to man-made facilities and services and to know when it has been reached. For example, one can analyse hotel occupancy rates, port arrivals, convention centre usage, the length of lift queues at ski resorts, the size of audiences at entertainment venues, the volume of water in storages, etc. The capacity of such infrastructure or superstructure is normally quite definite. In contrast, determining carrying capacity in terms of ecological and social impacts is much more subjective and is therefore controversial. While certain objective indicators might be used, such as the number of resident complaints, the count of endangered species, crime statistics in tourism resorts, and satellite maps of vegetation and habitat loss, it is often difficult to find agreement among the different interested parties as to what level constitutes a problem.

Hard capacity constraints, such as the number of hotel rooms, act as a definite ceiling to the level of demand that can be satisfied. Provided demand is less than capacity, all such demand can be serviced. Soft constraints occur when there is no definite ceiling to capacity, but demand is self-regulating. For example, the growth in demand may begin to soften as the increasing number of visitors begins to have an adverse effect on the quality of the visitor experience. When this threshold is first crossed, the decline in the visitor experience is only marginal, so that demand continues to grow. As the visitor experience further deteriorates with increased visitor numbers, demand plateaux as every additional visitor is offset by the loss of one other discouraged visitor. If these strained circumstances persist, it is possible that word-of-mouth or deteriorating physical conditions might lead to an overall decline in visitor interest.

Destinations can address these types of problems by explicitly incorporating the question of carrying capacity into a strategic plan for destination development. This way, carrying capacity issues become planned for rather than default outcomes. Forecasts of demand need to be made for this purpose. The destination's target market strategy might be influenced, as a result, by consideration of which types of tourists (and their impacts) best fit the destination.

As the tourism industry continues to grow worldwide and more destinations find that their ability to satisfactorily serve demand begins to come under strain, or environmental or social problems arise, those destinations that take the time to understand and anticipate their carrying capacity and plan accordingly will outperform those that do not.

Notes

[1]   In an article titled 'Falling off the map: Papua New Guinea's bad rap is keeping tourists away - and locals poor', the author observes that 'The headlines aren't wrong: the fractious young nation faces huge

problems. Crime is one of them, and tourists are occasionally attacked, robbed or raped. But headlines aren't the whole story. Most of the country is tranquil and its people friendly' (Feizkhah, 2002).

[2]   'Tourism trouble: latest Florida killing has officials scrambling' (*Calgary Herald*, 14 September 1993).

[3]   'So far, tourists take slayings in stride' (*Calgary Herald*, 22 September 1993).

[4]   'Florida tourists hit panic button' (*Calgary Herald*, 14 September 1994).

[5]   'Florida "very dangerous" for tourists, sheriff warns after 300 prisoners freed' (*Calgary Herald*, 15 March 1997).

[6]   'Tourists get the jitters: Russia's image hurt by bloody incident' (*Calgary Herald*, 16 October 1995).

[7]   'Crime puts the choke on South African tourism' (*Calgary Herald*, 24 November 1996).

[8]   There is a 'tendency of existing data to understate service productivity growth – to fail to capture important classes of productivity advances' (Magnet, 1993, p. 48). 'Services are the unsung heroes in keeping overall rates [of inflation] down' (Mandel, 1997, p. 36).

References

Bordas, E. (1994) Competitiveness of tourist destinations in long distance markets. *Tourist Review* 3 (94), 3–9.

Business Week (1997) The daily tab for travellers. 7 April, p. 30.

Calgary Herald (1994) Florida tourists hit panic button. 14 September, p. C1.

Cheary, M. (1996) Crime puts the choke on South African tourism. *Calgary Herald*, 24 November, p. A8.

Crouch, G.I. (1992) Effect of income and price on international tourism demand. *Annals of Tourism Research* 19, 643–664.

Echtner, C.M. and Ritchie, J.R.B. (1993) The measurement of destination image: an empirical assessment. *Journal of Travel Research* 31, 3–13.

Feizkhah, E. (2002) Falling off the map: Papua New Guinea's bad rap is keeping tourists away – and locals poor. *Time*, 18 March, p. 12.

Hustak, A. (1994) Holiday horror: travellers sue after heist in Venezuela. *Calgary Herald*, 20 March, p. A2.

Keane, M.J. (1996) Quality and pricing in tourism destinations. *Annals of Tourism Research* 24, 117–130.

Kotler, P., Haider, D.H. and Rein, I. (1993) *Marketing Places: Attracting Investment, Industry, and Tourism to Cities, States, and Nations*. Free Press, New York.

Lawson, R., Gnoth, J. and Paulin, K. (1995) Tourists' awareness of prices for attractions and activities. *Journal of Travel Research* 34, 3–10.

Lin, T.-B. and Sun, Y.-W. (1983) Hong Kong. In: Pye, E.A. and Lin, T.-B. (eds) *Tourism in Asia: the Economic Impact*. Singapore University Press, Singapore, pp. 1–100.

Little, J.S. (1980) International travel in the US balance of payments. *New England Economic Review* (May/June), 42–55.

Magnet, M. (1993) Good news for the service economy. *Fortune*, 3 May, p. 46–52.

Mandel, M.J. (1997) Whodunnit to inflation. *Business Week*, 12 May, p. 36–38.

Martin, C.A. and Witt, S.F. (1987) Tourism demand forecasting models: choice of appropriate variable to represent tourists' cost of living. *Tourism Management* 8, 223–245.

Murphy, P.E. and Pritchard, M. (1997) Destination price–value perceptions: an examination of origin and seasonal influences. *Journal of Travel Research* 35, 16–22.

Porter, M.E. (1980) *Competitive Strategy: Techniques for Analysing Industry and Competitors*. Free Press, New York.

Stevens, B.F. (1992) Price value perceptions of travelers. *Journal of Travel Research* 31, 44–48.

Thomas, T. (1991) Saving lives with a fast getaway. *Business Review Weekly*, 8 November, pp. 56–57.

Tremblay, P. (1989) Pooling international tourism in Western Europe. *Annals of Tourism Research* 16, 477–491.

Truett, D.B. and Truett, L.J. (1987) The response of tourism to international economic conditions: Greece, Mexico and Spain. *Journal of Developing Areas* 21, 177–190.

Woodside, A.G. and Lysonski, S. (1989) A general model of traveler destination choice. *Journal of Travel Research* 27, 8–14.

World Tourism Organization (1985) *Guidelines for Constructing a Tourist Price Index*. World Tourism Organization, Madrid, Spain.

11

The Destination Audit: Putting the Model to Work

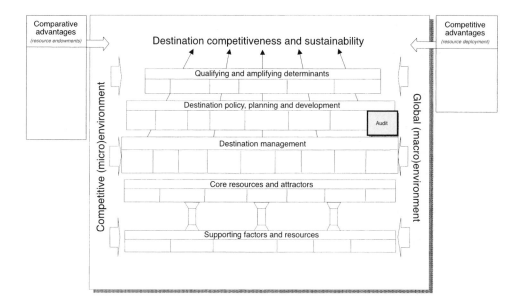

In this book we have endeavoured to develop a general understanding of the concept of competitiveness, explore how the concept might relate to the management of tourist destinations, and construct a conceptual model that identifies the elements and structure of destination competitiveness and sustainability. The aim of this work has been to create a tool that can be used by any destination wishing to enhance and maintain its competitiveness in a sustainable way. As almost every nation, state, province, region, city and town around the world today identifies tourism as an important

component of its economic development, and perhaps also of its sociocultural fabric and ecological environment, such a tool could play a very useful role.

How might this model be put to use? There are three main uses we envisage for the model. The first of these is as a *communication tool*. The model establishes a lexicon for understanding, studying, diagnosing, discussing and sharing ideas and thoughts about a destination's competitiveness. An important part of the challenge of dealing with any problem involving multiple parties is to establish a language with which each party can discuss and understand points of view and thereby educate others. This may be the most important of the three uses because of the very large number of organizations, enterprises, groups and individuals participating in, or associated with, a destination's tourism industry. Without some shared sense of the problem and means of communicating 'what' and 'how', efforts to address competitive problems are likely to stall.

The second use of the model is as a *framework for management*. In our executive development work, many of the participants have remarked that they find the model provides a useful vehicle for comprehending the magnitude and complexity of the challenges they face daily as they seek to fulfil their responsibilities. It is easy to overlook potentially important factors or to focus effort on the management of just a subset of factors when faced with complex tasks. So the model can be a managerially useful mechanism for explicitly acknowledging all important factors and for ensuring that destination managers do not lose sight of the forest for the trees.

The third use, which is the subject of this remaining chapter, concerns the application of the model in order to undertake what we call a *destination audit*. The idea of an audit is familiar to most – it is some sort of an official examination to make sure that everything is in order, and where things are not in order the audit makes recommendations and seeks to provide answers to questions which might arise. In the context of a tourism destination, such questions may include: where is the destination headed? which are the destination's most significant competitors? what is the destination's image in key market segments? in what areas is the destination competitively strong (weak)? does the destination's current strategy meet present and future challenges? and does the present development of the destination meet the needs and aspirations of the residents of the destination?

While the principal tourism-related organizations in a destination may conduct their own periodic, organizational review, rarely is this carried out for the destination as a whole. Destination or tourism development plans themselves rarely consider all the potentially important elements of destination competitiveness and often focus on marketing or, more

narrowly, promotional issues alone. Even when some attempt is made to conduct such a review, it is rarely objective or methodical.

In this chapter, therefore, we suggest a means by which the model can be used to perform the function of a destination audit. We begin by examining the concept of the audit in other fields, such as management, the environment, finance and marketing. We then adapt these philosophies and approaches to describe a systematic procedure for carrying out a destination audit.

The Philosophy of the Audit Concept

Audits play a vital role in civilized society. Flint (1988) emphasizes the social role of auditing and its importance to, and concern for, the well-being of society. The purpose of an audit is to ensure that those organizations and individuals that have an interest or stake in the performance of some organization or entity know how well that entity is performing and whether the claims and assertions made about its performance can be relied upon. The audit concept, therefore, finds particular application in business and government. An annual audit is required of all public and large proprietary companies. Government departments, statutory authorities, municipalities, government companies and business undertakings, and not-for-profit organizations are also subject to audit.

The basic concept and approach to conducting an audit derives principally from the practices of the accounting profession and focuses on financial performance and accountability. The American Accounting Association (1973, p. 2) defines auditing as:

> a systematic process of objectively obtaining and evaluating evidence regarding assertions about economic actions and events to ascertain the degree of correspondence between those assertions and established criteria and communicating the results to interested parties.

Statutory audits are audits required by law and have their scope determined by legislation. Private audits, on the other hand, involve no legal obligation and are undertaken, as desired, by an interested party and have their scope determined as narrowly or broadly as desired for the purpose (Woolf, 1997, p. 8).

Three general types or categories of audit can be identified (Gill and Cosserat, 1996). The financial report audit, which is the most common, involves 'obtaining and evaluating evidence about an entity's financial report for the purpose of expressing an opinion on whether the financial report is prepared . . . in accordance with an identified financial reporting framework' (p. 4). A compliance audit gathers similar information but seeks to determine if the entity conforms to any special conditions, rules, regulations or policies laid down by management, creditors or government. A performance audit, in contrast, is aimed at evaluating and improving the efficiency and effectiveness of an entity's operating activities as they relate to that entity's mission and goals.

It is this last type of audit, the *performance audit*, which is of principal interest here because competitiveness results directly in a certain level of performance. Whereas performance relates to what was achieved, competitiveness implies a focus on why it was achieved.

These different types of audit illustrate that the general philosophy of the audit can be applied to a variety of fields, such as communications (Downs, 1988), management (Alexander Hamilton Institute, 1984), marketing (Berry *et al.*, 1991; McDonald, 1993), operations (Lindberg, 1972), the environment (Glover and Flagg, 1994; Young, 1994; Nelson, 1998) and social concerns (Crowther, 2000).

Marketing is that area of management most closely concerned with an entity's competitiveness. Hence, the marketing audit approach is particularly relevant here. Kotler (1988, p. 747) defines the marketing audit as:

> a comprehensive, systematic, independent, and periodic examination of a company's – or business unit's – marketing environment, objectives, strategies, and activities with a view to determining problem areas and opportunities and recommending a plan of action to improve the company's marketing performance.

The four principal characteristics of the marketing audit identified above are consistent with the philosophy of the audit concept and are worth examining in detail. The marketing audit needs to be *comprehensive* to ensure that the source of problems or weaknesses is properly identified. Too often, symptoms of problems, rather than their underlying causes, can easily lead one astray to focus effort in the wrong places or just a few trouble spots. A comprehensive approach is a more effective means of identifying the real source of problems. Our efforts to develop a model of destination competitiveness have endeavoured to identify such a comprehensive set of the important dimensions and elements for this purpose.

The audit should also be *systematic*. Just as the financial audit follows a set of procedures and processes to perform the task, the marketing audit also requires a planned and orderly sequence of diagnostic steps. Information needs to be gathered and analysed, and various parties need to be consulted and included in the audit process, particularly where the entity extends beyond the bounds of a single organization, as is the case with a tourism destination.

Ideally, the audit should also be in some way *independent*, consistent with the notions that the entity's stakeholders need to be sure that it is unbiased and objective and that any problems identified and solutions proposed are likely to result in improved performance. The purpose of an audit is not to make certain organizations look good. Kotler (1988) notes that the marketing audit can be conducted in six ways: (i) self-audit; (ii) audit from across; (iii) audit from above; (iv) by the company auditing office; (v) company task-force audit; and (vi) outsider audit. This characteristic may be less problematic in the context of the destination audit since the elements of our model of destination competitiveness range across a broad number of issues, factors and jurisdictions, so that the reputation of no one organization is at stake in the process.

The last characteristic is for the audit to be conducted on a *periodic* basis. Markets change, environments alter and competitors come and go. The environment following the acts of terrorism in New York and Washington, DC, in 2001 showed how quickly events can change, affecting the fortunes and competitive positions of tourism destinations. Periodic audits would benefit destinations in both good health as well as bad. A destination should not wait to fall into competitive decline before acting, and a destination audit will sound the alert before problems become painfully obvious.

The Nature of a Destination Audit

The application of this philosophy and these principles to a destination is straightforward. While relevant government tourism departments, national tourism offices, Convention and Visitor Bureaux and other similar organizations might assert that they constantly evaluate their performance and operations, these do not constitute an audit of the destination. They are too limited in scope to be an audit and, while focusing on the performance of an organization, do not take a perspective of the destination as a whole.

When destinations do look at themselves as destinations rather than in terms of certain key tourism organizations, the catalyst is often a particular problem that has arisen, needing urgent attention. Naturally, when this occurs, the focus of attention is the problem itself, and solutions tend therefore to be narrow. An audit of the destination, in contrast, is concerned more with preventing problems than with fixing them once they have been discovered.

A destination audit is much like an annual check-up with your doctor. Instead of waiting until one becomes ill, a check-up is designed to be preventative. If medical problems are discovered and attended to early, the prognosis for treatment is usually much brighter. A thorough medical check-up has all the characteristics of an audit. It comprehensively evaluates the wide range of physical and biological factors characterizing one's state of health. It is undertaken systematically, relying on the use of various standard tests, activities and indicators. As an independent expert, the doctor is skilled and able to assess the patient's state of health objectively. Doctors themselves seek the assistance of other doctors when evaluating their own medical condition because of the need for a diagnosis free of emotion. Finally, check-ups are advised on a periodic basis, with the period dependent on the potential pace of change (usually quicker in the case of older patients).

It is a fallacy, therefore, to use destination audits at times of crisis. Indeed, successful,

competitive destinations that use the destination audit concept regularly can conceivably reap the greatest rewards from this approach. Destinations can always find room to improve their competitive position and condition. It has been said that the one thing harder than getting to the top is staying on top. Complacency is often the undoing of many competitors that reach the top. Even the most competitive destinations need to seek continuous improvement since few destinations can expect to be successful in the long term by maintaining the status quo. Experience has shown that destinations occasionally need to reinvent themselves in order to avoid the fate of the so-called destination life-cycle. Butler (1980) used the notion of the product life-cycle from the marketing literature to develop the concept of a tourist area cycle of evolution. The concept of the destination audit is therefore as applicable to healthy and successful destinations as to sick destinations.

Hence, in addition to the above characteristics, the distinguishing features and most important purposes of the destination audit are as follows:

- it should not be a crisis-motivated activity, but should be part of a regular routine of good management and on-going success;
- it is a carefully structured programme of appraisal in which the destination, rather than any single organization, serves as the subject of the audit;
- it is primarily preventative and only secondarily curative;
- although involving an evaluation of the past and present (diagnosis), a destination audit is ultimately concerned with the future (prognosis);
- although it is particularly interested in identifying competitive weaknesses, it is also concerned with more effectively deploying strengths and revealing hidden opportunities; and
- it requires the participation of, and input from, many varied organizations and stakeholders, many of which may not be regarded primarily as a player in the tourism industry.

The model of destination competitiveness (Fig. 3.1) identifies the components of the destination audit. Chapters 4–10 of this book provide a detailed discussion and framework for analysing and assessing the competitive state of health of the destination within each of these components. The section on destination diagnostics later in this chapter suggests some of the sorts of variables or indicators of competitiveness that might be used in the audit process. Before we look at these diagnostics, however, we consider the issues involved in preparing for and implementing a destination audit.

Preparing for a Destination Audit

The information and work needed to carry out an audit comprises both desk and field research. The desk research will mainly entail a review, analysis and assessment of existing information concerning the destination. Such information may cover:

- domestic and international visitor statistics;
- destination-specific studies established to provide for the assembly of a destination management database;
- tourism development strategies and plans;
- economic development studies and assessments;
- annual reports, documents and publications by tourism organizations;
- reports on competitor destinations; and
- a wide variety of available information covering various elements of the destination competitiveness model.

This information may be sourced from relevant destination management organizations, government departments, tourism research bureaux, university research centres, economic development agencies, industry associations, tourism enterprises, etc.

The field research required involves:

- meeting with representatives and assessing the relevant roles of all major organizations with responsibilities and programmes affecting the development of the destination in significant ways;
- identifying the mechanisms in place that govern these different responsibilities and facilitate coordination and cooperation;

- inspection of the state of tourism resources; and
- carrying out destination audit-specific research activities and instituting an ongoing research programme to provide improved timely information for future audits.

For an audit to be systematic, a structured process for conducting the audit needs to be developed. While various alternative processes might serve this purpose, they ought to have certain basic features in common if they are to achieve the goal of an audit. These are illustrated in Fig. 11.1.

The first task of the audit is to *determine the destination vision, goals and objectives*, because competitiveness needs to be judged and evaluated against these desired outcomes. This was emphasized in Chapter 2. Clearly, it is impossible to determine the competitiveness of anything without knowing what it is competing for. Knowledge of these desired outcomes also clarifies which segments of the tourism market are being targeted by the destination.

It is quite possible that no such destination vision has ever been expressed formally. If this is the case, then clearly one of the most important outcomes of the destination audit will be to recommend that a programme for achieving such a destination vision be prepared and carried out as a high priority. As the tourism industry professionalizes, more destinations are engaging in strategic planning exercises. At the national and state or provincial levels, a good number of destinations have gone to the trouble these days of formulating a vision for the destination. Many major cities have also done the same. At the regional or small-town level, however, it is common to find no formalized destination vision. Nevertheless, it is usually possible to gain some sense of the informal, implied vision for the destination by speaking with the key players in the industry.

With this information at hand, the next step in the process is to *establish the principal competitors and the market structure*. The determination of the destination vision reveals the destination's various target markets. This, in turn, helps to identify the other destinations that become the main competitors against which the destination needs to be compared and benchmarked. Where target markets have not been

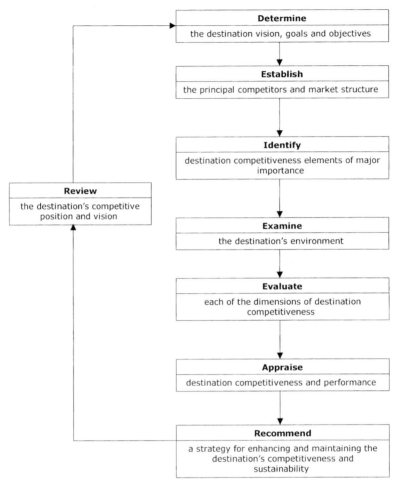

Fig. 11.1. The destination audit process.

identified explicitly, one can again develop a sense of these markets by examining the marketing programmes of key tourism enterprises and destination management organizations. Information on the main origins and characteristics of existing visitors will also indicate the combined outcome of these marketing programmes.

The comprehensive character of an audit requires all elements of the conceptual model of destination competitiveness and sustainability to be evaluated, but, depending on the destination vision, key competitors and target markets, certain elements of the model may be much more important than others. For example, a city destination targeting the conventions and meetings market segment will need to pay particular attention to elements such as

accessibility, infrastructure, tourism superstructure and entertainment. In contrast, an ecotourism destination will be more concerned with physiography and carrying capacity. The next step, therefore, is to *identify destination competitiveness elements of major importance*. The audit should then pay particular attention to these critical areas.

Before doing so, however, it is necessary to *examine the destination's environment*. Chapters 4 and 5 can be used as a guide to undertaking this examination of the destination's global (macro)environment and the competitive (micro)environment respectively. This examination will reveal important environmental trends, changes and developments that could have a significant impact on the destination, either currently or at some point in the future. It will help to place the evaluation of the elements of the destination's competitiveness into the proper context.

The central and probably most detailed and time-consuming part of the audit process then follows – to *evaluate each of the dimensions of destination competitiveness* as specified in the conceptual model. Chapters 6–10 serve as a guide to this critical part of the audit process, and the final section of the present chapter (*Destination Diagnostics*) suggests many of the measures that might be used depending on the particular circumstances defining the audit's domain.

Up to this point, the audit has determined 'what is'. Now attention turns to 'what should be'. The auditor therefore needs to *appraise destination competitiveness and performance*. The standard for making this appraisal was established in the first step, when the destination vision, goals and objectives were determined. To the extent possible, the auditor should document the appraisal by linking each element of destination competitiveness to the degree to which each has contributed to or hindered the pursuit of the destination vision. Where problems are noted, the appraisal might suggest some action to improve the destination's competitiveness with respect to that element. Alternatively, it may be that the destination vision is in need of either change or fine tuning.

Hence, the final two stages in the audit process are to *recommend a strategy for enhancing and maintaining the destination's competitiveness and sustainability* and to *review the destination's competitive position and vision*. Although some recommendations might be broad and others quite specific, all recommendations should be actionable. That is, there should be a clear indication of the type of corrective action or improvement needed. To facilitate the implementation of the corrective action, recommendations should state what is needed, who or what should assume responsibility, and what time frame for completion is desirable and appropriate.

When a review of the destination's competitive position and vision is required, although the auditor needs to be clear about the reasons for a review and may make some suggestions, it is not the role of the auditor to decide on a change of vision. As discussed in Chapter 2, the destination vision should be a function of the views and preferences of all stakeholders – with respect both to the tourism industry itself and to residents and the broader community.

Implementing the Audit

The overall objective of a destination audit is to improve its performance, competitiveness and sustainability as governed by a vision for the destination. To achieve this objective, a number of specific audit sub-objectives are relevant. These sub-objectives concern the information upon which the auditor bases the evaluation and recommendations. Organizations have a vested interest in their continued existence and support. As the auditor will be relying on market research reports, economic impact studies, advertising conversion studies, etc., part of the job of the auditor is to assess the reliability and validity of the information for the purpose of making the audit.

An example of how these concerns have become significant relates to studies of advertising effectiveness. Governments have substantially increased the destination advertising budgets of many destination management organizations in recent years to cope with an increasingly competitive tourism industry. As this funding has increased, there has been an increase in the scrutiny of these programmes in order to verify whether they provide an adequate return on the expenditure. The validity of some of the claims made in such studies, however, is sometimes questionable. The reason for this lies more in the difficulty of measuring the incremental impact of advertising expenditure than in any attempt deliberately to produce favourably biased results. In any event, it is the responsibility of the auditor not to take the information provided at face value, but to also assess the accuracy of the conclusions drawn and claims made.

The auditor must therefore evaluate the evidence used (following Gill and Cosserat, 1996, pp. 158–160) in terms of:

- assertions about the *existence or occurrence* of various tourism resources, assets or events;

- assertions about the *completeness* of all measures used to assess the competitive position of the destination;
- assertions about the *roles and responsibilities* of the various key tourism organizations and destination stakeholders;
- assertions about the *valuation or measurement* of visitor numbers, visitor expenditure, economic impacts, advertising effectiveness, environmental quality or condition, etc.; and
- assertions about the *presentation or disclosure* of the potential adverse consequences of tourism development on the ecological environment, culture and society, aboriginal communities, etc., including conflicts of interest involving stakeholders.

As noted earlier, the destination audit needs to be undertaken by an independent party that can exercise objectivity in their appraisal and can be free to criticize and praise as appropriate. Although some significant degree of impartiality and independence is therefore important, the auditor must also be very experienced, knowledgeable, competent and creative in order to adequately evaluate destination competitiveness and identify courses of action that will improve the destination's prospects.

The self-audit approach requires the principal destination management organization to conduct the audit. The main advantage is that the audit is carried out by someone already very knowledgeable about the destination, and it is also the least expensive approach. The main disadvantage is that the organization is unlikely to be very critical of its own performance, and it may not have sufficient time to do the audit.

Recommendations are likely to involve only minor change. However, for small destinations, this may be the only viable option.

An improvement in the level of independence occurs with the 'audit from across' approach, in which destination managers assess not their own but someone else's organization or area of responsibility. This benefits from a familiarity with activities and an understanding of inter-organizational relationships, but the auditing destination managers' views may be biased either to be highly critical or not critical enough.

The 'audit from above' approach relies on higher-level managers or organizations assessing subordinate organizations or managers. Similar problems with independence apply and no one is left to review the most important player in the destination – the organization or manager at the top.

A further option would be for the government to establish or use an auditing office. Independence would be increased but the auditor may have limited experience of only the one destination or, if responsible for other audit needs in government, may have insufficient knowledge of the tourism industry and issues.

An approach that could work quite well for a destination audit, given that a destination is a collection of organizations rather than a single organization, would be to establish a task force. The members of the task force could be drawn from a range of destination organizations and stakeholders, such as representatives of the local community and various important interest groups. This is likely to lead to a more balanced appraisal and benefits from the fact that no one organization can dominate the task force. A task force's recommendations also tend to carry more weight and authority. A potential disadvantage concerns the time it may take to complete an audit undertaken in this way, unless the task force is adequately resourced with research assistance and a strong chairperson.

Employing a specialized consultant as an outside auditor is likely to ensure the most independent and objective appraisal. Unfortunately, with regard to the audit of destinations, few such experienced consultants are available. They are likely to be costly and must spend a great deal of time becoming familiar with the destination to begin with. However, an experienced consultant may also bring a broader knowledge of the issues facing other destinations and the strategies and solutions that have worked in other contexts.

Destination Diagnostics

As a systematic approach is one of the characteristics of a good audit, some type of systematic measurement method is desirable. For example, in the literature on marketing audits,

Kotler presents a 'Marketing-Effectiveness Rating Instrument' that includes five major attributes of marketing orientation, each one including a number of items to be scored for the company (Kotler, 1988, p. 745). A similar indexing method was developed by Berry *et al.* (1991) for use in a marketing audit of services. Their 'Index of Services Marketing Excellence' (ISME) consists of six dimensions, each covering various facets of service measurement.

To facilitate the conduct of a destination audit and to enable the construction of an 'Index of Destination Competitiveness and Sustainability' (IDCS), we have constructed a set of operational measures of destination competitiveness and sustainability for each of the elements of our model, following a similar approach to the marketing audit measures. Our operational measures, which we refer to as 'destination diagnostics', although comprehensive, are not exhaustive of the possible measures that might be employed to facilitate the audit process. Different destinations will find some measures much more applicable, available and meaningful than others and may identify additional diagnostics that can play a useful role in the assessment.

Our destination diagnostics have been developed from two different, yet highly complementary perspectives: objective industry measures and subjective consumer measures. We end this book, therefore, with a listing of these destination diagnostics in Tables 11.1–11.5 (adapted from Ritchie *et al.*, 2001). Regardless of the emphasis (industrial or consumer), we should consistently keep in mind that measurement is truly the key to strategic success (Schiemann and Lingle, 1999).

Table 11.1. Consumer versus industry measures of competitiveness: a comparison of core resources and attractors.

Subjective consumer measures	Objective industry measures
Component: physiography and climate	
• Perceived comfort	• Amount of sunshine
• Aesthetics/eye appeal	• Average temperature
• Variability of terrain	• Amount of precipitation (snow, rain)
• Perceived majesty of scenery	• Existence of mountains, sea
• Perception of appropriate levels of development	• Existence of wildlife
	• Existence of unspoiled nature
• Perception of cleanliness and unspoiled nature	• Existence of facilities complementary to physiography and climate
• How values of different types of destinations change over time	• Lack of garbage/human spoils
Component: culture and history	
• Perceived richness of the culture	• Age of culture
• Perceived contributions to human development	• Number of museums
• Extent to which culture has been studied	• Number of historical sites
• Perceived exoticness	• Literary citations regarding culture
• Consumer familiarity with culture	• Level of investment in cultural facilities
• Perceived uniqueness of the culture	• Extent of historical documentation
• Perceived sophistication of the culture	• State of repair of cultural facilities
• Consumer liking of different dishes	• Number of identifiable historical stars
• Consumer liking of local music	• Extent of international duplication of art/sculptures
• Perceived eye appeal of distinctive architecture	• Level of media attention
• Consumer acceptance/fear of different religions	• Different language
• Consumer acceptance/fear of different races	• Number of different foods
• Degree to which distinctive dress creates cultural identity of people	• Distinctive music
	• Distinctive architecture
• Interest created by traditions	• Distinctive religion
• Interest created by work habits/practices	• Dominant race within culture
• Interest created by leisure activities/behaviours	• Distinctive mode of dress (everyday/special occasion)

continued

Table 11.1. *Continued.*

Subjective consumer measures	Objective industry measures
• Interest created by unique social/family structures • Interest generated by educational system/practices • Different perceptions of 'old world' and a new world	• Number of distinctive traditions • Distinctive work habits/practices • Number of distinctive leisure activities/behaviours • Unique social/family structures • Distinctive educational system/practices

Component: market ties

• Importance that destination residents attach to maintaining family/ethnic ties • Degree to which employees in key industry sectors attach to maintaining personal/business ties with colleagues in sister cities • Difference between past (historical) and future (emerging) ties	• Percentage of population having strong ethnic/personal ties to key markets • Extent of business travel in specific industries of importance to destinations (e.g. petroleum, computers, fashion, banking) • Extent of sports ties

Component: mix of activities

• Special appeal to the individual of available activities • Individual preference for certain form of activity • Perceived quality facilities for activities • Liking for a mix of activities vs. individual activities • Price sensitivity of individuals	• Unique/distinctive activities available within the destination • Particular way certain activities are performed at destination (e.g. swimming in a pool vs. an ocean) • Number of different activities available • Range of activities available • Cost of activities

Component: special events

• Desire/ability to participate in multiple events during visit • Importance visitor attaches to uniqueness • Strength of desire to see mega-event • Importance attached to having seen an event of international renown • Desire to see an event that reflects nature of destination • Extent to which visitor identifies event with destination (e.g. Boston Marathon)	• Number of events per year • Timing of events over the year • Uniqueness of event(s) • Annually recurring mega-event(s) • International reputation of mega-event(s) • Local support for event • Expenditures on site/facilities to host event(s)

Component: entertainment

• Consumer preference for passive vs. active experiences • Visitor desire to expand range of life experiences • Values of visitor and resulting acceptance/liking of different forms of entertainment • Desire to experience entertainment first-hand vs. indirectly • Importance of seeing personalities live	• Amount of entertainment available • Diversity of entertainment available • Size and scope of entertainment • Uniqueness of entertainment • Appropriateness of entertainment for destination • Media coverage of destination entertainment • Personality/reputation of entertainers

Component: superstructure

• Consumer liking for built attractions • Consumer preference for different types of accommodation • Preference for professional vs. personal travel • Perceived degree of maintenance of superstructures	• Number of attractions at destination • Investment in attractions • Range of different attractions • Number and quality of lodging units • Number of independent vs. chain units • Existence and quality of convention centre

Table 11.2. Consumer versus industry measure: a comparison of qualifying and amplifying determinants.

Subjective consumer measures	Objective industry measures
Component: location	
• Consumer perception of closeness/remoteness of destination • Consumer perception of remoteness may differ for different individuals and markets • Consumer acceptance of/tolerance for distances to destination via land/air/sea • Consumer perceptions of severity of barriers to reaching a given location/destination • Consumer perceptions of ease of access/level of 'hassle' to reach destination	• Absolute distances from key target markets • Relative distances from key target markets compared with major competitor • Possibility of land access by major target market groups • Possibility of sea access by major target market groups • Frequency/capacity of air access by major target market groups
Component: interdependencies	
• Likelihood of traveller diversion en route • Consumer acceptance/ability to function using a foreign language/currency/reservation system • Visitor acceptance of or desire for local gastronomy • Event (e.g. riots) in substitute or complementary destinations can effect visitation	• Need to pass through/stop-over in another destination en route • Domestic use of a foreign currency • Use of an international reservation system (airlines/hotels) • Use of outside travel statistics/research • Need to use English (other foreign) language • Need to import foreign foodstuffs
Component: safety/security	
• Level of resident concern/discomfort re: personal safety • Visitor perceptions regarding concerns for personal safety • Perceived trust that visitors place with destination police/security forces	• Crime statistics on local robberies, assaults, homicides, etc. • Statistics re: attacks on visitors and foreigners • Incidents of terrorism, hostage-taking at a near destination • Expenditures on anti-burglary equipment for local homes/businesses • Number of guns in destinations • Number of media stories on crime • Existence of a state of war/insurrection • Number of prison cells serving destination • Number of police personnel in destination • Number of inquiries received from potential visitors regarding safety of destination
Component: awareness/image	
• Awareness levels re: destination • Nature of perceived image of destination • Strength of consumer image of destination • Consumer attitudes towards destination	• Relative level of awareness compared to competitors • Accuracy of potential visitor image • Relative level of knowledge of destination compared with competitors • Relative liking of destination compared with competitors • Positioning of destination relative to competitors

continued

Table 11.2. *Continued.*

Subjective consumer measures	Objective industry measures
Component: cost/value	
• Consumer perceptions of value received for a range of travel products and services • Consumer reactions to advertising messages on value for money spent	• Price levels at destination as per Travel Price Index • Price levels at destination as compared with other destinations • Exchange rates at a given point in time and over periods of time • Advertising expenditures to convey message of value for money spent
Component: carrying capacity	
• Perception of overcrowding • Perception of environmental impacts • Perception of social impacts • Perceived conflicts between different market segments • Difficulties making reservations or achieving access to the destination	• Occupancy rates • Yield on transportation modes • Visitor number capacities at specific attractions • Results from scientific studies of the environment with respect to the impacts of visitor numbers • Results from resident surveys indicating tolerances to visitor levels and attitudes towards tourism

Table 11.3. Consumer versus industry measure: a comparison of supporting factors and resources.

Subjective consumer measures	Objective industry measures
Component: infrastructure	

• Consumer perceptions of the adequacy of each component of the infrastructure in relation to:
  • Their functional needs
  • Infrastructure at their place of residence
	• Extent and quality of road system at/in destination
	• Extent and quality of airports at destination
	• Extent and quality of cruise boat harbours
	• Extent and quality of modernity of telecommunications/media system
	• Quality and safety of electricity, water, and waste disposal systems

Component: accessibility	

• Consumer perceptions as to how easy it is to gain access to the destination	• Number of ports of entry to destination:
	  • Number of road entrances
	  • Number of airports
	• Number of airlines, flights serving a destination

Component: facilitating resources	
• Consumer perceptions regarding the extent to which visitor's entry is made easy or difficult	• Visa requirements • Ease/cost of obtaining visas • Customs procedures • Attitude of customs agents • Red tape re: entry/exit

Table 11.3. *Continued.*

Subjective consumer measures	Objective industry measures
Component: hospitality	
• Visitor perceptions as to friendliness of destination residents • Visitor sentiment that the region wants them to visit • Visitor perception that destination is providing information services that reflect an appreciation of their visit	• Resident acceptance of/support for tourism industry • Extent to which residents welcome visitors, in general • Existence of resident hospitality development programmes (e.g. B.C. Superhost and the Calgary Way) • IRRIDEX Index • Resident reaction to requests for information/assistance • Visitor usage of information/service centres
Component: enterprise	
• Perception of an industry that truly wishes to satisfy the visitor • Perception that facilities, services and experiences have been adapted to individual preferences	• Programmes to monitor/ensure high levels of visitor satisfaction • Research to understand visitor likes and dislikes regarding destination • Responsiveness to visitor needs/wants in the design and development of tourism facilities and experiences
Component: political will	

• Perceptions of government and institutional support for tourism such as:
  • Level of accessibility by tourists to public resources
  • Perceived level of various tourism taxes
  • Perceived extent of destination marketing activity initiated by government
	• Level of government funding for destination promotion
	• Seniority of the relevant government department and respective minister or secretary in the hierarchy of government
	• Level of financial support provided by government for basic industry research
	• Degree of government participation in destination development plans
	• Level of cooperation between relevant government departments

Table 11.4. Consumer versus industry measure: a comparison of destination policy, planning and development.

Subjective consumer measures	Objective industry measures
Component: system definition	
• Visitor perception that destination signage clearly identifies destination boundaries and membership	• System structure, boundaries and membership are well defined
Component: philosophy/values	
• Visitor perception that destination has a clear idea of the kind of destination it wants to be and the kinds of experiences it wants to offer	• Existence of a formal vision for the long-term development of tourism in the destination

continued

Table 11.4. *Continued.*

Subjective consumer measures	Objective industry measures
Component: vision	
• Global consumer perception of the degree of congruency across all facets of destination development and direction	• Existence of a strategic plan for the destination • Existence of a well-articulated vision of destination development • Degree to which stakeholders in the destination contributed to the development of the vision and support its goals • Progress towards the actual implementation of the vision
Component: destination audit	
• Consumer perceptions of the adequacy and desirability of current destination offerings • Consumer appreciation for the efforts being made to assess and respond to their preferences	• Existence of a formal destination audit that inventories and assesses the availability and quality of tourism-oriented resources and experiences • Inventory of most significant attractors, facilities, services and experiences offered by a destination • Quantitative and qualitative assessment of most significant attractors, facilities, services and experiences offered by a destination • Identification of most significant shortcomings (gap) in present offerings
Component: positioning/branding	
• Consumer perceptions as to the 'evoked set' of destinations they view as primary alternatives when choosing a travel destination in a given set of circumstances • Consumer definition of the ideal destination for a given type of travel	• Industry has a clear understanding of its position in the market (e.g. its strengths and weaknesses *vis-à-vis* its competitors) • Existence of a formal destination vision • Identification of major competitors and the experiences, attractors they offer
Component: development	
• Consumer perceptions of the ongoing emergence of an exciting, high-quality destination • Consumer views as to type of development most needed to enhance the appeal of the destination • Favourable consumer reaction to specific new facilities, services and programmes	• Existence of a coherent, long-term destination development plan flowing from destination vision • Consistent, systematic translation of development plans into reality (e.g. on-the-ground facilities, services and programmes for visitors)
Component: competitive/collaborative analysis	
• Consumer perceptions regarding the desirability of visiting several complementary destinations during a single trip • Consumer preferences for the larger critical mass of facilities, services and experiences available in a collaborating superdestination	• Competitive; similar to positioning • Collaboration; identification of other destinations whose attributes might justify/require a cooperative or 'coopetition' strategy
Component: monitoring and evaluation	
• Consumer desire/willingness to provide feedback via surveys and/or focus groups • Consumer reactions to developments that have been undertaken and completed based on their input	• Existence of a systematic, rigorous and ongoing monitoring/evaluation system to assess product performance and visitor satisfaction • Concrete examples of how monitoring evaluation information is used to improve the quality of facilities, services, programmes and experiences

Table 11.5. Consumer versus industry measure: a comparison of destination management.

Subjective consumer measures	Objective industry measures
Component: marketing	
• Favourable consumer reaction to destination brand and supporting visual icons • Consumer understanding and liking of the type of experience they can expect at the destination	• Level of total marketing expenditures • Clear definition of target markets • Understanding of experiences desired by each target market • Destination brand that conveys the essence of desired vision • High levels of brand recognition • Effective packaging of destination experiences • Strong relationships between destination and travel trade
Component: service experience	
• Measures of consumer satisfaction regarding a range of major services • Consumer perceptions as to major shortcomings in different types of services • Consumer views on how best to overcome major shortcoming in service/experience delivery • Consumer views on how best to deliver a quality 'experience chain'	• Agreed-upon, well-defined measures of appropriate/expected standards for major types of services delivered to visitor • Well-defined quantitative and qualitative measures of how well services are actually performed • Measures of productivity regarding the delivery of services
Component: visitor management	
• Views of visitor regarding the adequacy of visitor management programmes • Views of visitors concerning the extent to which visitor management affected (+ or −) on their enjoyment of destination	• Well-defined processes for ensuring fair and efficient allocation of access to destination facilities, services, programmes and experiences
Component: resource stewardship	
• Visitor acceptance of/liking for programmes to support destination stewardship • Views of visitors regarding which approaches they prefer, and why	• Measure of extent to which visitor behaviours affects environmental integrity at the destination • Effectiveness of visitor management in minimizing negative environmental impacts, while enhancing visitor enjoyment • Ability of tourism/visitation to enhance quality of environment
Component: human resource development	
• Employee perceptions as to the adequacy of their education/training • Consumer perceptions regarding the extent to which front-line staff and industry managers are well/appropriately trained	• Number and quality of education and training programmes in support of tourism/hospitality • Measure of employment, employment opportunities, front-line/managerial shortages/oversupply • Measure re: match between education/training capabilities and needs at destination • Information on career paths in industry

continued

Table 11.5. *Continued.*

Subjective consumer measures	Objective industry measures
Component: finances and venture capital	
• N/A	• Measures regarding adequacy of/access to venture capital for destination development
	• Actual amounts of venture capital absorbed by tourism/hospitality industry at the destination
Component: information/research	
• Consumer willingness to serve as respondents in destination research projects	• Amounts spent on research/monitoring
	• Number of research projects
	• Extent to which research findings are integrated into planning and decision making
	• Number of different types of methodologies employed
Component: organization	
• Consumer and community perceptions regarding the roles, visibility and contributions of the DMO	• Measures of community support for the DMO
	• Similarity of DMO structure and roles to those in other destinations
Component: crisis management	
• Impressions of the nature of crises affecting the destination	• The track record of the destination in dealing with crises
• Perceptions of the risk involved for the visitor	• The extent to which the destination has a disaster plan in place
• Sense of the destination's ability to cope with a crisis and to protect the interests of the visitors	

References

Alexander Hamilton Institute (1984) *Management Audit: Maximizing Your Company's Efficiency and Effectiveness.* Modern Business Reports, New York.

American Accounting Association (1973) *Committee on Basic Auditing Concepts.* American Accounting Association, Sarasota, Florida, p. 2.

Berry, L.L., Conant, J.S. and Parasuraman, A. (1991) A framework for conducting a services marketing audit. *Journal of the Academy of Marketing Science* 19, 255–268.

Butler, R.W. (1980) The concept of a tourist area cycle of evolution: implications for management of resources. *Canadian Geographer* 24, 5–12.

Crowther, D. (2000) *Social and Environmental Accounting.* Financial Times/Prentice Hall, London.

Downs, C.W. (1988) *Communication Audits.* Scott, Foresman, Glenview, Illinois.

Flint, D. (1988) *Philosophy and Principles of Auditing.* Macmillan Education, Basingstoke, UK.

Gill, G.S. and Cosserat, G.W. (1996) *Modern Auditing in Australia,* 4th edn. John Wiley, Milton, Queensland, Australia.

Glover, H.D. and Flagg, J.C. (1994) *Environmental Auditing: Risk Assessment Guidelines.* Institute of Internal Auditors, Altamonte Springs, Florida.

Kotler, P. (1988) *Marketing Management: Analysis, Planning, Implementation, and Control,* 6th edn. Prentice-Hall International, Englewood Cliffs, New Jersey.

Lindberg, R.A. (1972) *Operations Auditing.* Amacom, New York.

McDonald, M. (1993) *The Marketing Audit: Translating Marketing Theory into Practice.* Butterworth-Heinemann, Oxford.

Nelson, D.D. (1998) *International Environmental Auditing.* Government Institutes, Rockville, Maryland.

Ritchie, J.R.B., Crouch, G.I. and Hudson, S. (2001) Developing operational measures for the components of a destination competitiveness/sustainability model: consumer versus managerial perspectives. In: Mazanec, J.A., Crouch, G.I., Ritchie, J.R.B. and Woodside, A.G. (eds) *Consumer Psychology of Tourism, Hospitality and Leisure,* Volume 2. CAB International, Wallingford, UK, pp. 1–18.

Schiemann, W.A. and Lingle, J.H. (1999) *Bullseye! Hitting Your Strategic Targets Through High Impact Measurement*. Free Press, New York.

Woolf, E. (1997) *Auditing Today*, 6th edn. Prentice Hall, Hemel Hempstead, UK.

Young, S.S. (1994) *Environmental Auditing*. Cahners Publishing, Des Plaines, Illinois.

Index

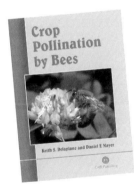
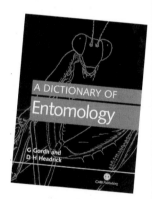
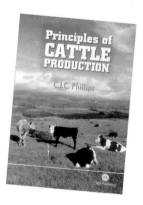